O State St.
ugusta, ME 04355

36845

rdest I've cried since March. I wanted a
so long, through so much sorrow and
. For a decade this has been a dream
I thought I couldn't have due to
asthma. Several doctors told
us it would probably never
work. And then we got this guy
and I was so scared! It was
really good to get some of that
out. It will probably take a few
more times, too.

Thanks and be well,
Ashirah Knapp

ast
fo

"This is a remarkable book. The story of how Maine governor Janet Mills and constituent Ashirah Knapp, a homesteader with young children, supported each other from a distance through the storms of the coronavirus pandemic, it is far more than just a record of those unsettled years. It captures both history and humanity as it tells the life stories of the two women who faced an unprecedented crisis and how they set a course through it. It is a story of work, worry, art, faith, community, life, and hope. An instant classic."

— **Heather Cox Richardson, author of**
How the South Won the Civil War

"Shannon Mullen's *In Other Words, Leadership* is a heartfelt and moving story of a young mother's correspondence with Governor Janet Mills during the recent pandemic. Just as important, it's also a well-timed lesson in civics."

— **Richard Russo, author of** *Empire Falls*

"This delightful book tells the compelling, intertwined stories of Governor Janet Mills and a young idealistic Mainer trying to do the right thing — one for her state and the other for her family — during a most difficult time, and it is a dramatic reminder that politicians need to do more than win elections and score points for their team; they need to lead."

— **Howard Dean, former governor of Vermont**

In Other Words,
Leadership

How a Young Mother's Weekly
Letters to Her Governor
Helped Both Women Brave
the First Pandemic Year

SHANNON A. MULLEN

LEBANON, NEW HAMPSHIRE

Copyright © 2023 by Shannon A. Mullen

ALL RIGHTS RESERVED

For information about permission to reproduce
selections from this book, write to:
Steerforth Press L.L.C., 31 Hanover Street, Suite 1
Lebanon, New Hampshire 03766

Cataloging-in-Publication Data is available from the Library of Congress

ISBN 978-1-58642-368-1

Printed in the United States of America

1 3 5 7 9 10 8 6 4 2

For my sister Kelly Mullen Wieser, with profound gratitude — her unconditional devotion to the welfare of others, especially those in her community and, critically, in our family, has fostered my understanding of a true leader's role, burden, and unifying reach.

Contents

CHAPTER ONE

"... a leg to stand on ..."

The first month of spring in Maine can feel more like winter, with a monochromatic landscape of stubbornly leafless trees, impassive pine forests, and bleached coastline. Dirt-covered dregs of snowbanks refuse to melt, and raw weather stokes resentment of the perpetual need for wool sweaters. For weeks the only things that will grow outside are daffodils and dandelions, with a blinding yellowness that is somehow too much and not enough. That time of year can make even pleasant little villages with cheerful main streets seem disheartened. Maine's capital city of Augusta had been struggling to muster much cheer for decades before the COVID-19 pandemic arrived in the state. Some downtown areas had been revived with new retail chains, but Water Street, which ran through the historic business district, was lined with dilapidated mill buildings and too many empty storefronts. Against that backdrop, the regal Blaine House, official residence of the governor of Maine, looked almost cartoonishly out of place. The twenty-eight-room Federalist mansion, with its porticos and belvederes and black-tipped chimneys, was built in 1833. It stood in especially striking contrast with the atmosphere of the city in the early weeks of Maine's pandemic response, when a thick crowd of protesters staged a rally outside the building on April 20, 2020, to demand that the state's first woman governor, Janet Mills, a seventy-two-year-old Democrat, "reopen Maine's economy."[1]

Police estimated that there were three to four hundred people on foot, and several dozen in cars circling the area, despite the governor's order that all Mainers stay home "at all times unless for an essential job or an essential personal reason."[2] Her order had also directed schools and nonessential businesses to close, banned gatherings of more than ten people, and imposed capacity limits on establishments deemed essential. Violators faced jail time and a

$1,000 fine. The Augusta protest, like others around the country, followed complaints by President Donald Trump that some governors were "being unreasonable" and had put "crazy" restrictions in place in response to the coronavirus.[3] An anonymous press release announcing the Maine rally accused Governor Mills of "tyranny."[4] In a more measured stance, Republican state representative Chris Johansen, who helped organize the event, said on his Facebook page that Maine businesses were "slowly suffocating."[5] He encouraged protesters to wear masks and maintain "social distance," a practice the US Centers for Disease Control defined as avoiding gatherings and keeping six feet away from others. Most of the protesters took none of those precautions. They carried signs with slogans ranging from ALL BUSINESSES ARE ESSENTIAL to DON'T TREAD ON ME and GIVE ME LIBERTY OR GIVE ME COVID-19.[6] One man told a reporter that he went to the rally to exercise his constitutional right to free speech so he would not have to use his right to bear arms.[7] The event remained peaceful, and police made no arrests despite protesters' outright violations of the governor's orders.

By then 35 Mainers had died of the virus and 875 had tested positive, out of a population of 1.34 million.[8] Nearly five weeks had passed since Maine had confirmed its first case of COVID-19 — a naval reservist in her fifties had tested positive after returning from duty in Italy — and, three days later, on March 15, Governor Mills had declared a civil state of emergency. That designation had brought the state "to highest alert" and allowed the governor "to deploy all available state resources" and "take every action she reasonably deems necessary" to protect her constituents.[9] She had since drawn both scorn and praise for her use of dozens of executive orders to manage the crisis, including the "Stay at Home" order that barred most public interaction. She had used other orders to deal quickly with issues that arose because of the restrictions, ranging from expiring driver's licenses and contact lens prescriptions to unlawful evictions.[10]

The owners of two gun stores were among the first to object to business closures, as the governor noted in her journal on the last weekend in March. They had "complained that I'd shut them down so people can't buy guns," she wrote on Saturday. At 9:45 PM that night, some state lawmakers joined the outcry. "The senate Republican leaders . . . send me a letter demanding that I stop 'closing gun stores.' Jesus. Of course, it's an election year. How could I possibly forget that." Earlier in the day the Trump administration had added gun sellers to its "Guidance on the Essential Critical Infrastructure Workforce," allowing their stores to open after pressure from gun-rights advocates.[11] The Mills administration was compelled to do the same in Maine. Pawnshops and auto dealers were next to criticize the governor's orders. "Sheesh, who knew all these folks were so essential," she wrote. "In Italy, meanwhile, 10,000 people have died. Surreal."

Governor Mills kept her journal on a laptop and added to it almost daily, a habit instilled by her father when she was a child. "He prioritized integrity and character building," she explained. "When I was five years old, I had a [news]paper route . . . and at night I kept a journal, even though I couldn't write very well."[12] As governor she still made her entries at night, after dinner and several more hours of work — she rarely went to sleep before midnight, especially during the pandemic. Shortly after the gun store controversy she wrote that she had spent "pretty much all day on drafting a new executive order about travel." She was "trying so hard in each of these actions to find that careful balance between certain constitutional rights and the exigent need to keep people apart and in virtual solitude, isolation." She compared the crisis to "a hurricane with no wind, a flood with no water," lamenting that there was "no playbook for a pandemic . . . no 'Virus Crisis For Dummies' instruction manual." Her administration was "working this, day by day, hour by hour, in the very best way we know how, and with the best scientific, medical information and wise counsel available."

A former state senator reinforced that dynamic publicly and eloquently in a Maine newspaper opinion column later that month.[13] Jill Goldthwait, who was also a retired nurse, noted that the governor's resources for managing the pandemic were "not insignificant," including her cabinet, the nation's other governors, and federal authorities. There were also experts in Maine's academic and healthcare communities who were "quick to answer the call." Ultimately, though, it was the governor's "unenviable job to sift through the mountain of information and opinion and choose a course for her own state. On top of all that, she is expected to offer human warmth, solace, encouragement and hope." By comparison, Jill admonished readers, it was "easy to second-guess the decisions being made that have separated us from friends, family and work and devastated the economy." In closing she invoked some lyrics from the song "Girl on Fire," by Alicia Keyes, noting that a rendition of it was part of the governor's inauguration ceremony in January 2019: "She got both feet on the ground and she's burning it down, she got her head in the clouds and she's not backing down." Jill added that Governor Mills was "every bit of that. At least we've got that going for us."

Janet Trafton Mills was sworn in as Maine's first woman governor four days after she turned seventy-one. She was openly exuberant that night when she gave her inauguration speech in a packed convention center in Augusta, wearing a royal-blue blazer and pencil skirt, her round, droll face framed by a blond pixie cut. When the COVID-19 pandemic started, Governor Mills had been in office for little more than a year, but had decades of experience in politics, state governance, and practicing law. Her family had a prominent legacy of public service, but her own track to the state's highest office was refreshingly unusual, not least because it included multiple derailments. She was born in Farmington, in the foothills of Maine's western mountains, and had lived in the state for most of her life. As a child she sometimes assisted her grandfather, a town clerk, with issuing marriage, fishing, and dog licenses.[14] She loved comic books, though they featured "mostly male superheroes" like Superman and Spider-Man, and she read them "every day after school (sometimes during school)."[15] At age fifteen she had two surgeries to correct spinal curvature from severe scoliosis and spent most of that year in a hospital bed in her family's living room, wearing a cast from her hips to her neck. "I think that kind of thing, when a kid goes through something like that, you learn some patience," she said. Tutors helped her keep up with school. She also developed her wry and slightly corny sense of humor. "I would lie around and write jokes," she remembered. "What else do you do when you can't do anything?"

After high school she enrolled at Colby College in Maine but "didn't take it terribly seriously" and dropped out after three semesters.[16] The school had been "too close to home . . . only thirty-eight miles from my house," she said. Both her parents had studied there, and they "kept showing up. You know, if I'd go to a fraternity party after the football game and try to have fun . . . my father and mother would walk in the door. You can't have fun as a college kid when your parents are right behind you." She had "no aims" other than not wanting to "go straight through school or have any big career goal," so she moved to San Francisco during the Summer of Love in 1967.[17] "So much was happening in the world and I just wanted to see a lot of things and a lot of places, like a lot of young people."[18] The next year, though, she resumed her undergraduate studies at the University of Massachusetts in Boston. "I think I got a 4.0 the first semester," she said. "I worked hard and I enjoyed it more."[19] She also studied in Paris at the Sorbonne and learned to speak French. During the Christmas holiday that year she went hitchhiking in southern Spain, where the poet Federico García Lorca grew up — she loved his work, which was "contraband" under then dictator Francisco Franco, and she would read it to the young people who gave her rides, if they weren't singing "the universal language" of Beatles songs.

After graduating with a bachelor's degree in French and a minor in English, she spent a couple of years in Washington, DC, working for a law firm that handled intellectual property.[20] "I was secretary . . . then I was their first paralegal," she recalled. She quickly realized that the men she worked for "were making a lot of money and . . . I can draft this, I can draft that, you know, feeding them stuff, maybe I should go to law school." Around that time she went through a traumatic breakup with the boyfriend she had been living with. She described him as "a lovable, intelligent, good-looking alcoholic, and when he was drinking he played with guns."[21] She added: "I was going to save him because, yeah, that always works!" One night when he was drunk, he held one of his guns, loaded, to her head. She escaped unharmed and never saw the man again, returning to their apartment with a friend only to take the guns apart and dispose of the ammunition. Then she moved back to her home state to earn a law degree from the University of Maine. During her studies she started working in a district attorney's office. Again she found herself thinking, "Hey I can do this, I know the rules of evidence, I can put on a case, and putting together the puzzles of a trial was fun — oral argument, closing argument, all those things."

After law school she worked as an assistant attorney general until there was an opening in a DA's office when its occupant left to become US attorney. "There were no women DAs . . . none, and I thought, well, I'll try it." She sought the interim appointment from Maine's governor, for whom she had worked when he was the state's attorney general, and won, beating out some male candidates who had "been there a while, felt they deserved it, merited it." Almost immediately she had to launch her formal campaign for the office. "I ran around three counties, I talked to Democrats everywhere and gave little stump speeches," she remembered, adding with a laugh that she had "never done that before, never." She won the election, becoming the first woman DA in New England, and was reelected three times.

DA Mills was the first member of her Republican family to enroll as a Democrat, doing so during law school, where hers was "the first class to have any substantial numbers of women . . . about a third."[22] She explained the decision as "a natural inclination after the experiences of the sixties" — she had "marched a few times" against the Vietnam War, and the causes she cared about, such as the country's voting age and "so-called 'women's issues,'" skewed more Democratic than Republican.[23] She also mentioned the influence of the Watergate scandal, which played out while she was working in Washington; she remembered standing outside the White House the night President Nixon resigned. "It was just an incredible evening, the vibrations in the air, the most bizarre groups of people gathering, they didn't know why, some of them."[24] Watergate then loomed over her law school studies. "We focused so much on 'what's this going to do [to] the legal profession,' because so many lawyers were involved in such evil ways. And the law schools I think, nation-

wide, felt that they had to start concentrating on ethics." Her
parents' response to her choice of party was no worse than when
she "dropped out of Colby College, their alma mater, and left town,
you know, for San Francisco . . . After that nothing could shock
them." She added: "I think they were glad I wasn't something else,
something lower than a Democrat."

The Mills clan was among a succession of prominent civic leaders
from Maine who had made outsized and enduring contributions to
American political affairs as representatives of one of the country's
least populous states. All four of the governor's grandparents held
elected public office. Her father, a World War II veteran, served as
US attorney under Presidents Eisenhower and Nixon, as well as in
both houses of the Maine legislature. Her younger sister, Dr. Dora
Anne Mills, was a physician who led the state's Center for Disease
Control and Prevention for nearly fifteen years, starting in the late
1990s, and went on to serve in other leadership roles in Maine's
healthcare system. The governor's older brother Peter served in
both chambers of the state legislature and as director of the Maine
Turnpike Authority. Another brother, Paul, was an energetic estate
lawyer with an encyclopedic knowledge of political history. He had
served as moderator at more than two hundred town meetings in
Maine and was a regular columnist for a regional newspaper.[25]

The Mills family had been called a political dynasty in the state, a
term that Paul dismissed as inaccurate hyperbole.[26] "It wasn't as if
we had a morning line," he explained, pointing to two unsuccessful
gubernatorial bids his brother Peter made. Another case in point
was a campaign for Congress that DA Mills ran briefly in 1994, when
she was routed during the primary election. Those losses illustrated
that "people evaluate her, and us, on our own merits," Paul said. The
governor's close friend Charlie Miller, who had lived in Maine for
most of his life, believed that not even the Mills family would have
predicted her election. "She wasn't the one who was . . . perceived as
going to be successful, or beautiful, or personable, or charming — a
winner," he said. "When she ran for governor, and she won, her
siblings could not have been more supportive and I don't think they
could have been more surprised."

Regardless of whether the Mills siblings were interested in seeking office, they "heard a lot about politics" when they were growing up. One major influence was their parents' close friend, Republican US senator Margaret Chase Smith, the first woman elected to both chambers of Congress.[27] A favorite family story recalled photographs of Senator Smith holding a newborn Janet Mills, who later memorized the senator's famous "Declaration of Conscience" speech.[28] The 1950 address to the Senate, during the rise of McCarthyism, denounced Wisconsin US senator Joseph McCarthy's conduct but never mentioned his name — Senator Smith instead rejected her party's embrace of "a philosophy that lacks political integrity or intellectual honesty."[29] The nation "sorely" needed GOP leadership, she told her colleagues. "But I do not want to see the Republican party ride to political victory on the Four Horsemen of Calumny — Fear, Ignorance, Bigotry, and Smear." A teenage Janet Mills delivered the fifteen-minute speech for a high school contest and won.

Decades later, her path from the DA's office to the Blaine House was fairly direct, if somewhat protracted, and she made history again along the way. First she served four terms as DA for three counties, then left public office to practice law with her brother Peter. During that time she ran for election to the Maine legislature and won a seat in the house. Representative Mills broadened her expertise while serving on several committees, including appropriations and public safety. After a seven-year stint in the legislature she was elected by her fellow Maine lawmakers as the state's first female attorney general. AG Mills held that office four times before becoming governor in 2019, the first in more than fifty years to win by a majority.[30] She also won more votes than any gubernatorial candidate in Maine's history.[31]

Governor Mills was a published poet, only the second of Maine's chief executives with that distinction; the first, Enoch Lincoln, a lawyer and US congressman, was said to have been a distant relative of President Abraham Lincoln. He was Maine's governor from 1827 until he died of a cold two years later, at age forty.[32] The poetry of Janet Mills was first published in 1975, when she was still in law school, in *Balancing Act: A Book of Poems by Ten Maine Women*. The collection's editor, who became a friend, described the future governor's two contributions to the book as "a relief" — her poems were "playful and witty" and "not bogged down with angst." Another longtime friend, former Maine poet laureate Wesley McNair, was struck by how easily the woman he first encountered as a DA could "shrug off her importance and become a human being," as he told *Down East*, a monthly general-interest magazine about life in Maine.[33] "From the moment you meet her, you can see that she's open to you . . . You immediately get the feeling that you are seeing the whole person — mind, heart, and soul. Poets tend to be like this." Apart from becoming a published poet, Governor Mills stood out among her predecessors as a leader who "genuinely loves poetry, literature and art," according to Maine's state historian, Earle Shettleworth. "I think that's a great thing. It's reminiscent to me of how sensitive to the arts John F. Kennedy was . . . that whole Kennedy-esque mystique of the role the arts can play in really improving the culture of the country. I think that's a wonderful vision and goal."

Governor Mills often quoted poets and other writers in her public remarks. She thought there was "always a place for literature and poetry" in one's life and work, to help "bring things together across the world. It helps you make the connections that you don't otherwise make."[34] She routinely shared poems she loved with close friends in group email threads but kept her own work mostly private. As for her poet's sensibility, some of the openness that Wesley McNair found remarkable was the governor's conscious practice; in her view civility was a "character trait" and she kept a sign in her office at the state house, printed with the phrase OPEN DOOR, OPEN MIND, OPEN HEART.[35] Longtime friends attested that she had the same persona in her public life as she did in private: warm and unpretentious, always game for adventure, and preternaturally calm when faced with adversity. The owner of an independent bookstore in the governor's hometown of Farmington, who had known her for decades, described her as an "old school" customer who often bought books as gifts for long lists of recipients and was "always game for participating in things," such as playing a witch in a promotional video he made for the Harry

Potter book series. He added that no level of influence she attained
had changed her character.

Her fashion sense, however, did evolve by the time she was
elected governor, from a lack thereof to classy-with-an-emphasis-on-
comfortable. "When she was starting to run . . . I remember telling
her she could not go downtown in her paint-covered sweatpants," said
Janice David, one of the governor's closest friends. "There were a lot
of us that, in one way or another, kind of indicated to her, in as kind a
way as possible . . . you need to get a decent haircut, you need to think
about makeup, you need to think about how you're going to look on
TV." Janice blamed "Yankee frugality" for much of her friend's reluctance to update her wardrobe. "It was pulling teeth because something was 'still good,' you know? No, Janet, it's been out of style for
fifteen years. You can't wear that!" Janice also mentioned that the
governor "doesn't have time to go to salons all that much to get her
hair done" and was "a great believer in Lady Clairol but she doesn't
like the conditioner that comes with it." Janice sometimes came home
to find "a tube of the conditioner on my bench sitting by the door-
way." She added: "Now if that isn't a regular person . . ."

Governor Mills might have come around to dressing more like a
career politician, but she often disregarded or playfully subverted
expectations for her conduct, such as arriving at an elegant garden
party with supplies for roasting marshmallows, having heard there
would be a fire. After moving into the Blaine House she had an
old-fashioned rope swing with a wooden seat installed in the garden,
where it hung from the branch of an enormous maple tree. She
called the swing her "sole contribution to the landscaping" and loved
to sit in it at sunset, watching the light glint off the copper dome of
the statehouse across the street. The governor preferred spontaneous gatherings to making formal or elaborate social plans. She
also had a tendency to turn small companies of friends into parties
by adding people to the guest list with negligible notice. She thrived
on the company of interesting people and especially loved contact
with her constituents.

When the pandemic began Governor Mills was deeply distressed
by the isolation, disruption, and other negative effects on people's

lives of the extreme measures that medical and other experts advised her to take — and which she felt she must — to protect the state from COVID-19. Maine had the country's oldest population, with more than 21 percent of its residents aged sixty-five or above. That range was most at risk of dying from infection with the coronavirus, according to early warnings from the US CDC.[36] Nearly a quarter of older Mainers were also living in poverty, among more than 11 percent of the total population.[37] By the end of April 2020 the state's unemployment rate had risen from around 3 percent to more than 10, and most businesses were shut down indefinitely.[38] Maine's vital summer tourism season was just over a month away. The ongoing business closures foretold an unprecedented crisis for the hospitality industry, which contributed $7 billion to the state's economy in 2019 and employed one in ten Mainers.[39]

In the midst of so much uncertainty, and just as spring was teasing the warmer weather New Englanders craved after another seemingly endless winter, a "bomb cyclone" storm brought more than a foot of heavy snow in some parts of Maine. A quarter of a million homes lost electricity, further complicating the lives of those in lockdown.[40] "A lousy week in the pandemic universe," Governor Mills wrote in her journal. "Not only were people under an order to stay home, but they were not able to watch TV or cook or have heat or, in some cases, access the Internet." In a radio address that week she acknowledged that her constituents were frustrated and tired of being "asked to meet new and never-ending challenges."[41] Regarding the surprise snowstorm, the governor added: "I mean, we really needed this, right?" A few days later there was an explosion at a paper mill in west-central Maine that employed five hundred people.[42] The governor "broke down" when the news reached her. She remembered exclaiming to her staff: "When are the locusts coming?" To her shock and relief no one at the mill was injured, in part because only a small fraction of its workforce had been on site at the time, but the facility suffered major damage that soon prompted layoffs.[43]

Governor Mills understood why her constituents were feeling impatient and scared, even as other states struggled or failed to manage much higher COVID-19 infection and hospitalization rates than Maine was experiencing. That disproportion only emboldened critics who felt that the governor's restrictions were excessive, especially a statewide mandate that adults wear face coverings in public when they could not maintain social distance. Governor Mills was among forty-three governors, including nineteen of her Republican counterparts and all two dozen Democrats, who issued stay-at-home orders and shut down most businesses in their states for weeks.[44] Despite that overwhelming consensus she had felt deeply conflicted in taking such extreme measures. The emergency declaration did not "feel like the right thing to do under almost any circumstances, but I had to do it," she recalled.

The evening after signing the March 15 proclamation of civil emergency, Governor Mills, alone in the Blaine House, called a friend — Independent US senator Angus King, who had served as governor of Maine from 1995 to 2003 — for advice. "I have this pit in my stomach," she remembered telling him over the phone. Senator King told her that he had declared a state of emergency in 1998, during his first term as governor, after an historic ice storm left nearly half of Maine's population without power, in some cases for more than two weeks. It caused unprecedented damage and was blamed for at least four deaths. Senator King remembered sharing two pieces of advice with Governor Mills regarding COVID-19. "One, in retrospect, was pretty funny," he said. "My best advice [was] to be straight with people, tell them the truth, you know, and they'll understand that. My other piece of advice, going back to the ice storm, was [to] be out and be visible, be around, and of course that didn't fit for the pandemic." Governor Mills added: "We didn't know . . . God almighty. You'd never have dreamed it was going to last more than a month."

During the early weeks and months of the pandemic she stayed in frequent contact with her sister, who had run Maine's CDC for more than a decade. Dora was now in a leadership role in the state's largest healthcare system and recalled that the country had been "hearing news out of New York about bodies in trucks. We didn't want that to happen in Maine."[45] She recommended that the governor stay at the Blaine House and that her security team remain isolated when they were off duty.[46] Dora was also in continuous communication with Maine's top health officials, including the current CDC director, Dr. Nirav Shah. "He'd call me up and say, 'Are you seeing this at Maine Health?' We have a number of hospitals, so if he wanted to get a quick pulse on what we were seeing, I could quickly get that for him. And I'd call him up and say we're seeing this or we're seeing that . . . sharing what we knew, and that was happening across the country." For the first few weeks she found herself sharing information with the governor when they saw each other, as well as with Dr. Shah and the state's health commissioner. Dora remembered that it "took a little while to get the formal channels of communication a little more ironed out" so that "everybody had the same information."

By April 20, when protesters rallied outside the Blaine House in forty-degree weather, Governor Mills may have seemed to them remote and imperious, holed up in lavish comfort while her constituents coped with oppressive mandates she had imposed, which were costing people their jobs, homes, and businesses.[47] Her reality, though, consisted of relentless workdays filled with the lonely weight of unfathomable choices and nights on end in a house full of empty rooms, with only her state police security detail for company. The governor was a widow at the time of her election in 2019 — her husband, Stan Kuklinski, had died four years earlier after suffering a stroke. Her five stepdaughters from the marriage had their own homes and families, so she lived by herself in the sprawling Blaine House. The pandemic only magnified her isolation. "I'd lived alone before," she explained, "but I wasn't governor."

Before COVID-19 the mansion had been open to the public for tours during daytime hours, and Governor Mills entertained routinely. "I'm so glad I had that under my belt, that first year," she said. Between her inauguration and the start of the pandemic, she hosted a run of joyful celebrations, including a refugee day with "seventy or eighty people who'd never been to the Blaine House, Iraqi refugees who were living in Augusta, it was really tearful." She also orchestrated a Passover seder and an Easter dinner, as well as the Muslim celebration of Eid, when "all these women came and took over the kitchen." The governor held a suffragette costume party to mark the centennial of the Nineteenth Amendment, and she arranged a Pride Picnic in the mansion's backyard. "We had so many nice events, and it was a welcoming place," she remembered, "and then boom, it's shut down."

Once the pandemic set in, most of her staff worked remotely. When Governor Mills was not using her office at the statehouse, she operated from a much smaller one on the second floor of the Blaine House. Sometimes she would take a break and sit in the garden, trying to identify birdcalls that she could hear more clearly "because it was all silent, no trucks going by, no planes overhead," she remembered. "You know, it's Augusta, Maine, and it was so silent, except for the birds and squirrels." For meals she "made peanut butter and jelly sandwiches every day." At night, after responding to an endless stream of emails, text messages, and voicemails, she would make entries in her journal or call close friends. "My lifelines were certain people that I would talk to almost every night," she said. One was Charlie Miller, who in turn described her as "the best friend I could imagine." He recalled that they had first met at a political fundraiser a few years before the pandemic. Charlie was a high school English teacher turned philanthropist, whose nonprofit work focused on child welfare and infrastructure improvement in the developing world. When his friend was running for governor he accompanied her to a "slew" of public events, despite his "very singular existence" and aversion to social occasions. "I think there was a need on her part to have a guy," he explained. "It's not just a matter of the photo op . . . it's no fun going to a dinner party by yourself." He character-ized their relationship as "two people who really, truly love each other and they're both seventy-four. You know what I mean? We've lived our lives, I've had my girlfriends, she had her marriage, and here we are washed up on the shore in the eighth decade, and happy for the gifts we can give each other." During some of their early pandemic conversations Charlie had seen her "break down and cry when it was too much." He felt that "most politicians become impervious to . . . the mortal ramifications of their decisions — she never did."

The late-April protest outside the Blaine House coincided with Patriots' Day, a public holiday that Maine and five other states observe to commemorate the first battles of the American Revolution. By coincidence Governor Mills was not in the residence — she had left Augusta that day for a ride through Farmington to check the mail at her house there and for a change in scenery between work calls. She noted in her journal that one of those calls, a weekly tele-conference between Vice President Mike Pence and the country's governors, "lasted for almost two hours." He urged state leaders to improve their COVID testing capacity, but the vice president stressed that decisions about when and how to ease pandemic restrictions would be theirs.[48] Governor Gretchen Whitmer of Michigan asked, in response to a protest in her state, if President Trump would publicly "reiterate the importance of staying home." The vice president assured her the administration would. Governor Mills described him in her journal as "polite and informative," but she added that within hours of the call President Trump "was blasting all of the governors for their 'whining' about testing . . . accusing us of playing politics with the disease." She felt that the president's behavior was "encouraging protesters, who are in turn inciting violence."

One week later Maine became the first New England state to announce that restaurants would be allowed to resume dine-in service in just over a month, on June 1, as part of the Mills adminis-tration's four-phase plan to reopen its economy. "Of course, no one is happy," the governor wrote in her journal that night. "Why am I angry. Why so ready to weep. Sad that people are willing to take reckless risks." Two days later, a restaurateur named Rick Savage, who owned a large brewpub in western Maine, appeared on the national prime-time Fox News show *Tucker Carlson Tonight* and accused Governor Mills of acting "rogue on her own" and "not consulting experts."[49] He added that he planned to defy state law and reopen his establishment the next day. The show's controversial host had strong personal ties to Maine, having spent summers in the state's western region since he was a child. He echoed his guest's frustration, calling Governor Mills "the most incompetent, self-involved, dictatorial governor I have seen in a long time." He then

wished the restaurateur "Godspeed, good luck" in his plans to break
the law, and smirked while his guest proceeded to announce the
governor's personal cellphone number. The live segment aired
during the show's highest-rated quarter — at that time it had become
the most watched program in the history of cable news.[50]

That night Governor Mills received "thousands of just vulgar,
nasty" text and voice messages and had to change her phone number.
President Trump seemed to acknowledge the incident in a Twitter
post, using it to criticize the governor's pandemic leadership.[51] "Many
complaints coming in about Maine," he wrote. "Don't make the
cure worse than the problem itself. That can happen, you know!"
Governor Mills would not disclose whether her security protocol
was heightened after the segment aired. She insisted that she was
never afraid for her safety. "I'm kind of thick skinned," she said,
adding that the stunt was a "dirtball thing to do, that's all." The
governor used her weekly radio address, broadcast the next day, to
acknowledge critics' concerns about her management of the
pandemic.[52] She also noted that some Mainers were against relaxing
restrictions — she assured both groups that her reopening plan was
based on "fact and science." The plan was also designed to be flexi-
ble in case the pandemic eased or worsened. She told listeners that
she had "thought long and hard" about the potential effects on
Maine people and businesses of every action she took and encouraged them to share constructive feedback. She also reminded her
constituents that tens of thousands of people had died from COVID
in states around the Northeast, including 252 in one day that week in
Massachusetts, just fifteen miles from Maine's southern border. "We
can't simply flip a switch," the governor said, and "do business as
usual," risking an outbreak that could "devastate our entire economy for years to come." In closing, she called on Maine people not
to give up on each other but to "keep talking."

Two days later another protest against pandemic restrictions
drew a bigger crowd in front of the Blaine House than the first, and
this time the governor was home.[53] She sat in a small room on the
opposite side of the building, studying a painting by Jamie Wyeth
that the artist had loaned her. Its subject was a lone seagull flying

fiercely behind an unseen boat. As demonstrators chanted outside, she wrote "a small poem" in her journal, giving it the same title as the painting: "Wake."

> *No one knows these waters better —*
> *the tide, the flow, the spray,*
> *the foam, the whites and purples,*
> *defiant golds and greys,*
> *the gull-spewn air,*
> *the deep green fullness*
> *and the awful emptiness —*
> *No one knows these*
> *weary, fearful waters*
> *Better than the bird, and you,*
> *navigating an angry wind.*

In that same entry she also wrote that her day was one of "relief and success" — she had been working to convince the US Food and Drug Administration to allow the Maine-based animal diagnostics company IDEXX Laboratories to produce and sell a COVID-19 test kit. "I get a call this evening from the FDA guy's assistant, a woman who is from Maine, telling me that the [emergency authorization] has been approved. I tell her she doesn't know how many lives she has just saved, including thousands right here in Maine." Later that week Governor Mills announced that the state planned to buy enough of the IDEXX test kits to more than triple its virus testing capacity. This would "soon allow anyone in Maine suspected of having COVID-19 to receive a test."[54]

By then a total of fifty-seven residents had died and more than 1,100 virus cases had been confirmed in Maine, including hundreds at long-term care facilities around the state and about two dozen at two urban homeless shelters.[55] Maine CDC director Dr. Shah also reported a growing outbreak at a poultry processing plant with a predominantly immigrant workforce of nearly four hundred people.[56] The plant in Portland, the state's largest city, was shut down to try to limit the spread of the virus. Dr. Shah, who had been holding media briefings almost daily since the pandemic started, was "becoming a bit of a meme, a hero," as Governor Mills mentioned in her journal. Mainers were "tuning in to his daily reports, delivered in his calm, compassionate and professional manner." Meanwhile, opposition to the governor's reopening plan intensified that month, after her administration opted not to allow bars to reopen or hotels to lodge visitors until July 1.[57] She also imposed a mandatory quarantine period of fourteen days for out-of-state visitors. More than two hundred businesses joined a videoconference call with Maine's economic development commissioner to question the quarantine requirement.[58] A group representing thousands of hospitality workers in the state sent the governor a letter calling her plan "a death march for restaurants."[59] Her predecessor, Republican Paul LePage, said of her reopening plan that Governor Mills "ought to resign," and he vowed to challenge her in 2022.[60] He had served two consecutive terms, from 2011 to 2019, the limit under the state's constitution, which allowed a third term after a four-year hiatus — since leaving office he had been working as a bartender at a seafood restaurant in Maine and spending winters in Florida with his wife.[61]

By early May the governor's office was inundated with mail from both supporters and opponents of the state's pandemic response. Hundreds of letters and cards arrived daily, and the job of managing them belonged to the director of constituent casework, Martha Currier, a Republican who had joined the administration after working for then attorney-general Mills. Martha would come to the office a few times each week to open and screen the mail. "Initially it was a lot because we were in unknown territory," she said. "People didn't know what to expect. The notion of having to stay home and not-do-what-I'm-allowed-to-do-in-America, that just sounds crazy, right?" She recalled that a lot of Mainers were "just shocked by the change in behaviors because none of us have been through that sort of situation before, save for a few people who were much older than all of us."

Before the pandemic, opening the mail had been a comparatively small part of Martha's role. She mostly served as a sort of go-between for people who asked the Mills administration for help. Martha would reroute them to the appropriate agency, through what could otherwise have seemed "like a huge maze" of government. She loved the work, which she felt she was "made to do," having grown up in Augusta and worked during high school as a constituent services intern under Governor King. "It's a great privilege to be able to help people solve their problems," Martha explained. Issues she dealt with ranged from some taxpayers wanting a culvert repaired in front of their house to "I'm having trouble getting child support payments for my children, that sort of thing." Then the pandemic arrived in Maine, and before long the governor's office was fielding requests from Mainers who needed dire assistance, such as help processing unemployment benefits so they could pay their heating bills. "Some of those things really would wear on me and I'd worry about the people who couldn't feed their kids," Martha remembered. "As a mother I can't imagine."

She struggled to keep the job from overwhelming her personal life, especially while working mostly from home, where her three adolescent children were trying to adapt to remote learning. She took solace in the number of positive messages of simple gratitude that people sent Governor Mills, often "just thank you cards or quick postcards from remote corners" of the state. Martha found herself stopping to read many of them because she "needed the boost." In the middle of May, she opened an envelope with a return address in Temple, Maine, about forty miles away, and took out a letter written by hand on two pages of lined, three-hole-notebook paper. The sender's penmanship was "small, tight" and so distinctive that Martha read the whole letter, which was now a week old according to its date. Its writer, Ashirah Knapp, explained that she and her husband, Chris, were in their early forties and had two adolescent children. She described their family as homesteaders who ran an outdoor education business teaching "resilience living skills." Ashirah also had a part-time job in a medical office, but, for now, the family's income was "at a 100% standstill for as far ahead as we can see."

The Knapps had no debt but were living on savings, she wrote, "through being very thoughtful . . . and because we provide for a great deal of our needs from our land," including grain, vegetables, eggs, meat, and milk—about 70 percent of the food they consumed. Nonetheless their business was among those that "cannot open right now." Ashirah added that she was sharing her family's situation because she felt they had "a leg to stand on when we say we support you." She wrote that she had "been so grateful throughout" to have Governor Mills in office during the pandemic. "We've felt strong and sensible leadership from you, which has been a great comfort and confidence-builder." The Knapps had been listening "with horror and disappointment" to news stories of protests and people and businesses defying laws. "We have had many good discussions with our kids . . . about freedom, choices, social responsibility and laws." Ashirah felt that there were "no easy answers with this one"—that no matter what decisions the governor made, "people will get sick, people will lose money and people will get angry." She added: "I'm sure your own hopes and dreams for your work have been upturned just like the rest of ours."

In closing her letter, Ashirah lamented both the unprecedented situation Governor Mills was "dealt" and the unfair criticism "being leveled at you right now." She believed that "no one in the world knows how to get through this and there's no way through that does not have anger, fear and death along it." In the Knapps' "small circle of friends and neighbors" there was "strong support" for the governor's choices, but Ashirah knew that "that knowledge can fade quickly in the face of vocal criticism." To counter all the negativity she promised to send a letter every week "until we get through this time, to keep reminding you of the many people who agree with the path you are choosing for our state." Lastly, she added: "Please share our thanks with your staff as well." Martha remembered thinking that Ashirah's letter "definitely had more detail and emotion" than most. She added it to a stack of mail with positive messages that she had decided to set aside for Governor Mills to read for a morale boost. These days were long, Martha had thought, and the governor was "a real person with real feelings" who was "always questioning" whether she was doing enough to protect people. "That is something I remember her being very emotional about, and who can blame her?" Martha said.

Governor Mills was surprised to learn that she was getting so much complimentary mail and started taking some of it home to read at night. There were notes from elderly Mainers confined to apartments or care homes. One woman wrote from an assisted living facility in central Maine and asked for magazines, so the governor wrote back and included some of her own issues of *The New Yorker* and *Down East*. Children sent handmade cards, including a ten-year-old girl named Savannah, who wrote that she hoped the pandemic would not "isolate our hearts from one another,'" the governor remembered. "If she's thinking that, a lot of ten-year-olds are thinking that. How do you fix that as governor?" A woman named Paulette wrote that Governor Mills had "the hardest job in Maine right now. You are between a rock and a hard place." A registered nurse named Patricia wrote: "I feel I can call you Janet, because I've seen you and heard you speak so many times that I can be familiar enough and caring enough to call you by your first name."

The governor found her constituents' support "very fortifying," adding that she "wasn't looking for it, but it was good to have. It saddens you, but it builds your morale to know there are people out there who are thinking of you, and who know you're thinking of them." When she found Ashirah's letter in the mix Governor Mills was taken aback: "I'm in the Blaine House in this aquarium bubble and she's there at the farm in Temple, Maine, trying to eke out a living and raise two kids and I know this is real." Another letter from Temple arrived two weeks after the first, dated May 15, 2020. Ashirah started it with an upbeat if obvious refrain: "I am writing my weekly letter of support for you and all your staff." She credited the measures the governor had taken, "in large part," for the fact that Maine seemed to be "succeeding in beating this thing." By then the country was "flattening the curve" she wrote, referring to the daily average number of new COVID-19 cases, which had plateaued nationwide.[62] In Maine a total of sixty-nine people had died.[63] The daily average of new cases in the state was less than 40, compared with 74 in neighboring New Hampshire, 1,155 per day in Massachusetts, and 2,164 in New York.[64]

Ashirah's children, Owen and Pamela, were attending school remotely. Their curriculum that week had included "looking at some of the graphs showing the number of cases and the number of deaths in different countries." They could see "how the US curve has flattened," but the family had discussed "how COVID is right there still" and now was "not the time to relax any of our vigilance." Ashirah and Chris had explained that their family was "part of that flattened curve" and that everything they were not allowed to do, or were choosing not to do out of caution, was "all part of that success and we can feel very good about that." One obstacle Ashirah foresaw to "opening things up again" was that "not everyone" was "using the same level of care." She pointed to the recent protests in Maine and, on the global stage, America's conspicuous absence from a recent virtual summit of world leaders aimed at pooling resources to develop COVID-19 vaccines.[65] "It just boggles our minds," she wrote.

From there Ashirah took the familiar tone of an old friend, as if she was simply adding another chapter to the sort of yearslong correspondence that needs little context, if any. Chris's unemployment benefits had come through, including a weekly Pandemic Unemployment Assistance of $600, for which the Knapps were grateful. She was "blessed with a good hourly wage" but had taken a pay cut at her part-time job running the office of a medical clinic about forty minutes from Temple, which administered treatment mostly for opioid addiction. She was "in no danger since the doctors have switched to telemedicine," but she was now making half what Chris received each week. Ashirah then abruptly changed the subject to the "more lighthearted news" that her family's two milk goats had just delivered two healthy kids. She was offering their milk for baby formula "to anyone low on money," along with some extra rolls of toilet paper, which had become scarce. The Knapps had also bought some "inexpensive" grain mills to sell at cost to "anyone willing to buy whole grain" in bulk and process it themselves during what was becoming a flour shortage. "There has been such an outpouring of care between people and among communities during this period," Ashirah wrote. "It is wonderful to see and be part of." She closed the letter by mentioning a relative who, she'd learned, was working for the Mills administration on the governor's newly formed economic recovery committee. "We are so glad you have him as a moderator," she told the governor. "I imagine feelings can run very hot in a situation like that and we know that David is very good at his job. He has eased many Thanksgiving and Christmas family discussions through the years!"

Governor Mills was charmed: apart from Ashirah's praise, her letters were handwritten, which meant that they were "even more genuine and sincere." They also stood out to the governor's staff as an exception among the occasional "repeat writers" who, Martha Currier explained, "just want to make sure the governor hears what their opinions are on a matter." She tried to help those she could while managing their expectations, but the pandemic made both goals more difficult. "There's an element of people, any person, if they get pushed enough they can't be nice anymore," she explained. Some were "just nasty" and would demand that "you people need to fix this right now." Martha felt that some were "coming from a place of being scared." The majority of constituents she dealt with were kind and appreciative, she said, especially those who sent handwritten letters. "I think that that written word, taking pen to paper, maybe forces a person to be a little more honest and a little more kind." She felt that this woman homesteader from Temple was both, but Martha knew firsthand how challenging the pandemic had been for families so far, especially working parents with young children. She questioned whether Ashirah would have enough time to keep writing so regularly, much less persistence. "Our habits peter off, whether it's a New Year's resolution, or that sort of commitment," Martha remembered thinking. "At some point she's going to say that's enough."

CHAPTER TWO

"... the train coming at us ..."

The only numbered public highway that entered the town of Temple, Maine — State Route 43 — also happened to end there. After winding west for just over a hundred miles from Old Town, home of the world's oldest and largest canoe manufacturer, the road ended suddenly in Temple's southeastern corner, where it branched into secondary roads. Those branched off too after a while and were designated for all-terrain vehicle use; there was at least one ATV in most driveways in town, if not a tractor or snowmobile. In Temple's annual report for 2020, its road commissioner celebrated the fact that his crews "were once again able to keep our back roads open through the spring." Ashirah Knapp and her family lived several miles past the END 43 sign, beyond the point where the patched and repatched pavement stopped, along with any mobile phone service.

From there the road started to look more like the Oregon Trail. The turn for the Knapps' rutted driveway was marked by a hand-carved wooden sign for their Maine Local Living School. The sign also stated: WELCOME ALL RELIGIONS, ALL COLORS, ALL NATIONALITIES, ALL GENDERS, ALL AGES, ALL PEOPLE. The road to their homestead was about three-tenths of a mile and wound through a dense forest. More handmade signs were posted along the way: BREATHE DEEP, SMELL THE EARTH, YOU ARE ON THE RIGHT PATH, followed by, THE TREES ARE SINGING, THE LAND WELCOMES YOU. As a bridge led across a stream, a final sign read: THE WATER IS TALKING, ENJOY A LISTEN. The drive ended abruptly at a small, packed-dirt yard and the doorstep of an octagonal, timber-frame structure with enormous curved eaves. From the outside its effect was delightfully unusual and inviting, like a dwelling from the pages of Grimm's Fairy Tales or J. R. R. Tolkien's The Hobbit. The building housed the school's classroom, a large and open central space under a semi-vaulted ceiling. Clockwise along its perimeter there was a kitchen, a small library, a music area with a piano and some string instruments, foraging equipment for processing acorns, and a workshop full of curious carving tools. The building had windows in nearly every wall, a small loft upstairs, and a roof supported by spokes of long timber thinned from the surrounding woods. The front door was pinned on both sides with quotes written on pieces of paper, their authors ranging from the thirteenth-century Persian poet Rumi (WEAR GRATITUDE LIKE A CLOAK AND IT WILL FEED EVERY CORNER OF YOUR LIFE) to the Argentinian guerrilla leader Che Guevara (AT THE RISK OF SEEMING RIDICULOUS, LET ME SAY THAT THE TRUE REVOLUTIONARY IS GUIDED BY A GREAT FEELING OF LOVE).

The classroom was the largest structure on the homestead. It faced the Knapps' root cellar, a building that, from the outside, could be mistaken for a Gold Rush–era miner's cabin — weathered but welcoming and just big enough to move around in. It was built into the side of a hill and stored, in a ten-foot circle, most of the food the family ate during the winter, keeping everything in darkness at an ideal temperature and humidity. "The vegetables just go to sleep for the winter but they're still alive," Ashirah explained. She revered the root cellar as vital to her family's ability to live mostly on food they grew themselves. The Knapps stored grain sacks full of carrots, parsnips, beets, rutabagas, turnips, potatoes, and twenty or so boxes of apples. The cellar also held fermented pickles, sauerkraut, and dilly beans and shelves heavy with cabbages, canned tomatoes, jam, whole berries, and maple syrup, as well as rendered lard and bone broth. "The fact that it can store food for eight to nine months of the year without me having to do anything other than build a building — I put my food in there, the food keeps — that is such a beautiful, perfectly working system," Ashirah said. "That's why I call it a magical building."

Outside the root cellar, a well-worn footpath led past an elaborate outhouse to the middle of the homestead, where a few more structures seemed like natural extensions of the land. A tiny greenhouse doubled as a solar-heated indoor shower. A conical "earth lodge" was built from peeled fir and spruce trees; there apprentices and students could opt to sleep on ground lined with intensely fragrant balsam boughs. The Knapps' two-story cabin was partly secluded behind its own grassy knoll, in a back nook of their land that felt protected and private. Their home resembled a life-sized gingerbread house, with a patchwork of additions they built as their family grew, for a combined footprint of about five hundred square feet. Each wing was made from a different type of wood, and the window frames were painted either yellow, blue, purple, or red. A curved eave swooping over the front door held up an old-fashioned rope swing with a wooden bench — one of several swings on the homestead and the same type that Governor Mills had added to the grounds of the Blaine House.

At the center of everything, a handful of goats grazed near the Knapps' half-acre garden. In the spring and summer months there were also ducks wandering, birds calling, brooks trickling, and leaves rustling, all surrounded by teeming bogs and lush forests. At that time of year the days were long and the earth was "pumping out life," including hordes of mosquitoes and biting deerflies so incessant that the Knapps did not offer classes for the month of June. Protective nets were essential for most outdoor activities, or if one valued one's sanity. "We also have no way to cool our house down," Ashirah said. "We really feel the heat of the summer, the good and the bad of it." The way of life that she and Chris had chosen for their family exposed all of them to Temple's elements to an extent that both enriched and ruled their existence year-round. Fall brought cooler days and nights and the thrill of watching the colors of their forest change from within, but the days were ever shorter, with less light for harvesting the garden and gathering the acorns they processed to make flour for the year. Their house had no electricity, except for a small solar power system and a generator for charging batteries. For Ashirah winter was "the best example of the beauty and the harshness" of life there, with mornings when temperatures dove well below zero. "It's very cold, and at the same time, being out in minus ten is invigorating and exhilarating in a way that nothing else is," she explained. Snow turned Temple into "a gigantic playground" for cross-country skiing and other forms of "walking on water" that the Knapps delighted in, but there were also long runs of days when the animals' water froze in the barn and the car refused to start or the driveway was dammed with ice or otherwise impassable until spring, when the length of it turned to mud.

Temple's inhospitality to humankind was among the factors that had suppressed its population since the town was incorporated in 1803 by eighty-three settlers from around New England, who must have been intrepid souls. "Many of their number" came from "a town of the same name and similar topography in New Hampshire," according to a copy of a 1946 study on Temple's "Rise and Decline."[1] Its author, Richard Pierce, had been a minister in Temple and submitted the work as his graduate school dissertation, at Boston University in Massachusetts. He believed "that a thorough investigation of this one typical back town" could be applied to "scores of similarly situated towns" throughout the region. He described Temple as part of "a belt of settlements" situated across northern Maine, New Hampshire, and Vermont on land that was "mountainous, rocky and ill-suited to agriculture."

Dr. Pierce found that Temple's population peaked by 1840 at around 950 "by means of a high birth rate and diligent application to farming." For the next century it "dwindled at the rate of ten persons a year" until it bottomed out around 250 in the 1940s. The town's numbers were drained, he wrote, by the rise of the American West and the country's burgeoning urban centers of industry, followed by the First and Second World Wars. Dr. Pierce held that from the start, Temple and its ilk had participated "so slightly in the general culture and economic life of New England" as to be considered the region's "frontier." It was "difficult to wrest a living from the barren hill-sides" and over time the town showed "a common pattern of decay and collapse of economic exhaustion, of cultural disintegration and social deterioration." To wit, he found that among the grievances brought before the members of one of Temple's churches as early as the 1820s were "threatening to knock a man's teeth down his throat," "appearance of intoxication," "refusing to make restitution for bad butter," and "extortion 'in a general sense.'"

Despite Dr. Pierce's dim view of the town's long-term prospects, its population slowly increased to 527 residents as of the 2020 US

Census, with a median age of about forty-three.[2] By then the town had reassuring pride of place, from its neatly mowed baseball field, home of the Temple Tigers, to a charming historical society with a fastidious array of unusually interesting artifacts. Dr. Pierce's report was kept there in a locked cabinet. The rest of the collection was housed in one room of the town office building and included an impressive display of baseball trophies won by the Tigers over the decades. There was also a rack of back issues of *The Good Old Days* magazine. In a poignant exhibit of American military uniforms, mostly from the Second World War, each was pinned with a photograph labeled by hand with the name and rank of the veteran who wore it, such as NORMAN T. FOSS, US NAVY, 1943–1946. Manifestly the town had stemmed its cultural and social disintegration.

When the Knapps visited Temple to consider buying land there, they were looking for a property big enough that it "could still feel like a wilderness living school no matter what was happening around it," with neighbors who would welcome that sort of business. They liked the town's location, including that it was far enough from the ocean to have snowy winters. It also bordered the historic Main Street town of Farmington, which had a population of about seventy-four hundred and, Ashirah thought, "a really nice feel." She appreciated that the community was home to one of the campuses in the University of Maine system, the first school in the state to offer public higher education circa 1863.[3]

She and Chris bought their one-hundred-acre property in 2004, only a few years into their marriage. Their dream was to start a school that would teach practical skills for sustainable "local living," such as carving and weaving, growing and foraging food, and composting waste. "Really what we're doing is creating a place of active hope," Chris said. He explained that to examine human history, especially justice issues or environmental stewardship, could feel like "studying the failure of human beings." In contrast he and Ashirah hoped their program would foster "the renewed sense that human beings are amazing and have a really integral place in the ecosystem" — that people also had "the ability to do good for the earth and for each other and be in relationship, and recognize that relationship, and work on it consciously." Ashirah added that the kind of outdoor education the Knapps offered had "always been some form of helping people connect and interact with their local land and their local resources." She and Chris made a point of "pretty strongly saying to people, this is what we've taken for our lifestyle, but you don't need to do all of this, or any of this." Nevertheless many of their students came to the homestead, she said, "because they want something, or some of this," even if they were not sure what, or how much.

Ashirah related to that sense of an unmet need, having spent the first part of her life feeling intensely drawn to nature and wildly out of place anywhere else. She grew up in Cleveland, Ohio, which she described as "just not a good match, me in the city." She was the oldest of four children and was happiest on weekends when her parents would take the family to state parks to go fishing or car camping. The rest of the time, Ashirah said, she was "selfish and lazy" and "very, very shy." When she was not taking horseback riding lessons or "out in the country somewhere" she read fantasy books. Her favorites included *The Earthsea Cycle* by Ursula K. Le Guin, *The Last Herald-Mage Trilogy* by Mercedes Lackey, Frank Herbert's *Dune*, and *The Last Unicorn* by Peter S. Beagle. She disliked school, and her parents were sympathetic — her mother, Pam, a nurse, and her father, Gabe, a Jewish educator, often excused Ashirah to travel with Gabe on his work trips. His specialty was incorporating nature into teaching the traditions of Judaism.

When Ashirah was fifteen she joined him on a summer canoe trip in the North Maine Woods that he had helped organize to train Jewish outdoor educators. Their guide, Ray Reitze, met them at the airport, and Ashirah remembered the one-hour drive to Ray's home as life changing. He told them about his childhood in southern Maine, where his mentor was a Mi'kmaw tribal elder who resided on the acreage of the Reitze family's farm. The man had taught Ray "his skills and philosophy of living with the land," Ashirah explained. She remembered listening to Ray's stories and trading glances with her father, both of them "thinking this person is amazing." For the rest of the trip, as Ray introduced them to the ponds and waterways around Allagash Mountain, he embodied a completely different kind of human existence from any that Ashirah had known or imagined. "I had no idea that there were people who knew how to live off of the land, period," she said. For the first time in her life, she drank water from a spring. She marveled at the edible plants Ray would pull from the side of a path. He was also the first person to teach her about "this idea of inner vision," which she described as a conscious sense that "conveys information or guidance we'd otherwise have no way of knowing." This sense was "often accompanied by a physical sensation" such as "a twisting in the heart or in the stomach." In the context of a decision, one felt "a light or a lightness when considering one option versus a darkness or a heaviness when considering the other."

By the end of the trip Ashirah was "such a wreck" thinking "there's no way I can possibly go back to the city after this." Her father was so enlivened by the trip that he began to use some of the basic skills and knowledge he learned from Ray in his own teachings. Ashirah remembered Gabe demonstrating how to light candles for holiday ceremonies by using friction fire. On another occasion when he had seen some roadkill, the carcass of a deer, he made use of it to show what a split hoof looked like as part of an instruction on kosher dietary laws. Gabe also suggested that Ashirah return to Maine with him later that year on a personal trip to spend more time with Ray. When they did, he invited Ashirah to apprentice with him and his wife, Nancy, the following summer at their Earthways School of Wilderness Living in central Maine. Ashirah knew she wanted to learn everything the Reitzes could teach her, which "was not going to happen over just a one-week trip." She decided to leave high school early and move to Maine. Her parents were supportive on the condition that Ashirah would earn her general education diploma the next year.

Around that time, word of Ray's philosophy and teachings also reached Chris Knapp, a seventeen-year-old Mainer who had just come back to the state after spending a year at a folk school in Norway that taught students traditional handcraft techniques, organic farming, and other skills for developing self-reliance. At that time Ray was building a shelter to use for overnight programs, and Chris volunteered to help. He recalled that when he learned the Reitzes were hosting an apprentice who was a girl, the words *I'll probably marry her* passed through his mind. Chris added: "Then I thought, well that was a really weird, arrogant thought. I haven't even met her and don't even know this character [Ray]."

Ashirah recalled having had a similar experience a few months before she met Chris. She had been feeling lonely for a life partner and was "putting that intention out to the universe." One night when she was alone in the Reitzes' home, the words *you'll find a husband in the fall* came into her head. Ashirah had been working with Ray on learning to recognize her inner vision and remembered feeling a mix of happiness and acceptance. But when she met Chris for the first time, "it wasn't love at first sight for either of us." He had been going through a phase of feeling "very down on society, the modern world, and very judgmental of it," she explained. "That was a hard aspect of him for me." Chris's memory of that time was that he was bent on proving himself, while Ashirah seemed much more attentive to her limits. "I remember thinking, well, maybe not her," he admitted, "but then we ended up spending a bunch of time together."

He asked the Reitzes if he could study with them, then spent the next few months learning side by side with Ashirah. She remembered an evening when she realized their relationship had changed — she had been sitting beside a pond near a beaver lodge where she liked to practice quiet observation when Chris came and sat beside her. "That kind of thing started to happen more and more," she said. Ashirah moved in with Chris that winter, sharing a dwelling he had built on the Reitzes' land, where they stayed until they were in their early twenties. In that time, they learned to provide for themselves from the land, completing a 150-day expedition in northern Maine that they spent "trapping, hunting, and living with the forest."

The Knapps were married on a warm night in October 2001. At their reception they served turkey, focaccia bread, and carrot cake that "ended up being way too sweet," all of it grown or made locally. They ended the evening with contra dancing to fiddle music. Ashirah recalled that the moon had been full that night, which she felt was a good omen until a rain shower passed through. The newlyweds opened their school in Temple three years later and expanded their class offerings over time. By the start of the COVID-19 pandemic, they were teaching about a hundred students each year. They provided day and weekend community courses, overnight and multi-day immersion experiences, a weeklong stay for families, and apprenticeships of at least two months. At that time Ashirah and Chris were both forty-one. "We do joke that there are 2 months and a foot between us," she said. "I'm 5', Chris is 5'10" [and] our birthdays are . . . two months apart." Ashirah was petite but muscular, with short brown hair. She had a distinctly maternal presence — observant and reassuringly calm, if potentially fierce. Chris was tall and lean, with dark hair and a whimsical face. He seemed confident and essentially unfettered. Their children, Owen and Pamela, were thirteen and ten years old, respectively, when the first COVID-19 cases in Maine were confirmed in mid-March 2020.

The Knapps closed their school in compliance with the governor's orders, and within weeks the family was living on capital they had saved for improvements to their facilities. The world was about two months into the pandemic when Ashirah sent her third letter of support to Governor Mills. "The black flies are thick in Temple," she lamented in the first sentence, after her usual preamble thanking the governor and her staff "for all that you are doing!" It was the last week of May, and the Knapps were planting beans and corn. In nearby Farmington certain businesses had been allowed to operate again, and Ashirah had heard that some locals saw the reopenings as "a light at the end of the tunnel." She disagreed: "I think that's the train coming at us." Ashirah assured Governor Mills that the Knapps would remain vigilant. She and Chris emphasized for their children that they were helping curb COVID-19 by continuing to miss out on some activities and pleasures. Ashirah also told them that "six months (or eighteen months or two years, more likely) really isn't very long in the greater scheme."

She went on in her letter to lament "an undercurrent" of ageism during the pandemic — a notion she had heard "that we shouldn't bring down the economy for a bunch of old, sick people because they are living outside the bounds of the natural world anyways [*sic*]." Ashirah was "so shocked and sickened" when she realized "there were people touting this" in social media posts and other public forums. At the Blaine House protest on April 20, when thirty-four people in Maine had died of COVID-19, nearly all of whom were over age seventy, one of the cars that joined the protest carried a sign that read 34 DEAD ≠ 90,000 LOST JOBS.[4] Ashirah saw "value and validity in every life," as she told the governor. She explained that she had "worked in senior-care for several years," and the medical office she currently worked for provided "services to a marginalized population." She felt that "we humans should be able to make allowances for those among us who need help." Ashirah did not "want to think that part of the answer" to the pandemic "needs to be bringing our population back within the laws that govern the natural world." She paraphrased her husband's view on the subject, which had been "the greatest comfort" to her since the pandemic started — Chris believed that humans, "as a species, have so much power that we can direct . . . enough that we can take care of each other and still be OK." If we overburdened our resources, we could "use some of our incredible human ingenuity to restructure our systems so that is no longer a problem." The world did not "have to say that our elders should die for our economy," he told Ashirah. "We have to change our economy."

Ashirah ended her letter by setting the scene in Temple: "My son is metal-detecting around the yard, my daughter is painting, my husband is drawing, and I am off to exercise." Lastly, she told Governor Mills that "we usually work hard but today is Sunday." It was also Memorial Day weekend, with the holiday the next day. The governor had used her radio address earlier that week to honor Maine servicemen and -women who had "served and fought with determination and great hope for our collective future," she told listeners. She also invoked the wartime leadership of President Franklin D. Roosevelt, paraphrasing his call for Americans to "speak with one voice, one heart, with determination, and dignity, showing what our nation is capable of as we fight against a formidable foe and formidable odds."

Governor Mills had recently seen *The Roosevelts: An Intimate History*, a 2014 documentary mini-series by Ken Burns that PBS was rebroadcasting early in the pandemic on Thursday evenings.[5] The governor noted in her journal that she had found the series "captivating." In several different entries she made long lists of quotes and historical details that resonated with her, including the fact that the Roosevelts "received between 5,000 and 8,000 letters a day." She also mentioned that the "power of [FDR's] personality made people believe he stood to greet them when he never did"; that "Eleanor allowed only women reporters to her press conferences because only men were allowed at Franklin's press conferences"; and the fact that the Roosevelts' five children had nineteen marriages. During one episode centered on World War II, Governor Mills wrote: "Why do certain moments create exactly the right human beings," such as FDR and Winston Churchill.

On Memorial Day, as the nation marked both the holiday and the start of the summer season, an unarmed Black man named George Floyd died in Minneapolis, Minnesota, during his arrest by a police officer. A bystander had filmed the altercation, and the footage showed the officer, Derek Chauvin, kneeling on his suspect's neck for nearly nine minutes while George pleaded that he could not breathe.[6] His death, as the *New York Times* reported, "unleashed one of the most explosive trials of American racism in modern times."[7] During the ensuing days protests were held around the world. There were demonstrations in all fifty states and Washington, DC, with "looting and brick throwing and violence in some cities, and kindness and understanding in others," as Governor Mills wrote in her journal. She was concerned that too many people in the crowds were "ignoring social distancing and COVID precautions," including those in several Maine cities and towns. "But now, on top of all that, a president who incites violence with heated rhetoric and self-centered speeches." She was referring to the weekly White House phone call with the nation's governors, which President Trump joined a few days after the demonstrations began. He had "started right out on a virulent diatribe, calling the governors 'weak' and telling us we needed to 'dominate' the protesters." He went on to say:

"You're going to arrest all those people and you're going to try them."[8] Governor Mills remembered thinking that he was having some kind of breakdown. She called out to her staff to come into her office and bear witness.

By then she had learned that the president was planning a trip to Maine a week later to tour a century-old family business that was one of only two companies in the world manufacturing the specialized medical swabs needed for coronavirus testing.[9] The other factory was in northern Italy, which was battling rampant COVID-19. During the call with the president Governor Mills told him that his planned visit could present "security concerns," implying that the tone of his rhetoric might incite violence.[10] President Trump retorted that she had "tried to talk me out of it. Now I think she probably talked me into it." He added: "She just doesn't understand me very well, but that's okay." The next day the governor held a press conference and asked the president to "check the rhetoric at the door" when he arrived in Maine.[11] She urged him to "abandon the divisive language that sows seeds of distrust." The governor added that she was speaking "as someone who is responsible for the health and safety of 1.3 million people, including those who support and believe in you."

Ashirah wrote her next letter before the president's visit to Maine, but she had seen news headlines about his incendiary rhetoric on the conference call, including his exchange with Governor Mills. "My husband and I thank God every day that we have you as a governor during this time!" Ashirah wrote. "I don't think I could take Trump and [former Governor] LePage at the same time. It is discouraging enough already." The Knapps did not have a television, but they read the news online or listened to Maine Public Radio. "We did make the decision to tell our kids about George Floyd this week . . . and how especially being a Black man in this country puts you in greater danger of being killed by the police," Ashirah told the governor. It had been "a sad and difficult family discussion, of which we seem to be having many these days," but she did not want Owen and Pamela to "live a sheltered existence" due to their race, class, or nationality. She had also lamented in a Facebook post that day that there were "a lot of families that have to teach their children from an age younger than mine [that] the color of their skin puts their lives in danger."[12]

She went on to explain that life in Temple was increasingly busy now that the growing season had arrived. "We planted the rest of our garden, our second goat came into milk, we wrapped up school with the kids, and continued to reach out to our neighbors and friends to see how everyone is doing and offer our help." Ashirah confessed to "such a heavy, sorrowful feeling" that no matter how much good she tried to do in her community and beyond, there was "absolutely no way I can alleviate the amount of hurt that is happening around the world." She felt comforted by a reminder from her father that small amounts of good add up. To that end she enclosed "a little humor to help brighten the day of anyone who sees this" — a page of black-and-white photos of animals on the homestead with handwritten signs explaining "the havoc they wreaked." One photo of three ducks was captioned: WE GOT A RUNNY ONE ON THE ONLY NEW L.L.BEAN COAT MOM EVER OWNED. In another picture, one of the family's goats stood behind signs that read: I ATE MOM'S GOAT-THEMED BARN CALENDAR AND AN APPLE TREE. YUM!

In the governor's office, Martha Currier found herself looking forward to Ashirah's letters as they continued to arrive. "Golly this person is committed," she remembered thinking. It was "kind of like escapism" to read about whatever was happening in Ashirah's world. The letters were "just so positive and civil," Martha said. "We seem to be in a place of a lack of civility, just a lack of patience to hear what someone else is saying — where their thoughts are coming from — and there should be more of that." By then Governor Mills had realized the same woman was writing from Temple every week and asked her staff to make sure that Ashirah's dispatches reached her.

When President Trump arrived in Maine, about two hundred protesters met him at the airport.[13] Police had cautioned that armed supporters of the president were expected to gather in Guilford, where he planned to visit the medical swab factory. Some of his critics assembled in the tiny town despite the warning, chanting "Black Lives Matter" not far from a group shouting "four more years."

Local news reports estimated there were "hundreds" on both sides, who mostly kept to opposite ends of town. Sheriffs' deputies were sent from nearly every county in Maine but made no arrests.[14] One man who was standing with a pro-Trump crowd told a journalist that the president had "been fighting for the people who see through the lies."[15] Others in that group brought weapons, including assault rifles.

The factory the president visited had been working to double its output to help fill the country's shortage of COVID-19 testing supplies.[16] "Now our nation has turned to you," he told about 150 workers there.[17] Earlier that day he had also met with a group of commercial fishermen to "say congratulations" because he was planning to give them access to a protected area off the Gulf of Maine — the marine national monument was beyond the range that most of them fished.[18] He also told them they had "a governor who doesn't know what she's doing." He derided the Mills administration's phased plan to reopen the state's economy, telling his audience "she's like a dictator."[19]

The governor used the national spotlight to amplify her response. "I have spent the better part of my career listening to loud men talk tough to disguise their weakness," she said.[20] "That's what I heard today. I don't care what the president says about me, I care what he does for Maine people, and that's not very much." She ignored the presence of Paul LePage, who met the president at the airport and accompanied him for part of his visit; her predecessor had been increasing his visibility in Maine since declaring that he planned to seek another term.[21] During his eight years in office he had infamously vetoed more than 640 pieces of legislation, topping the combined total rejected by the state's governors over the previous century.[22] Many of the bills were written with bipartisan support, and sent to him for his signature while his own party had a majority in the legislature. Governor LePage had campaigned on his conservative values and promises to cut taxes and shrink state government. He had also drawn attention for his dramatic upbringing, which the press covered widely after a strategist billed him as "the only candidate who had a compelling life story."[23]

Paul LePage was born in Maine, the oldest of eighteen children. He escaped an abusive father by leaving home at age eleven and claimed to have survived by begging, sometimes sleeping in horse stables and a "strip joint."[24] After spending two years homeless, he lived with people in his community and found jobs, graduated from high school, and earned an MBA. He became general manager of a chain of discount stores and served on the city council of a small town in central Maine, later becoming the town's mayor. His ethos and brash leadership style resonated with then powerful Tea Party Republicans, the far-right movement that organized during the 2008 global financial crisis partly in opposition to some policies of President Barack Obama.[25] In 2010 the audience at a GOP forum in Maine applauded candidate LePage after he told them "government should be working for the people, not the people working for the government." He added: "You're going to be seeing a lot of me on the front page, saying Governor LePage tells Obama to go to hell."[26]

While in office Governor LePage routinely made national headlines for his offensive, if not outright racist, sexist, and otherwise incendiary rhetoric. His most notorious remarks included his comparison of the removal of Confederate statues in the South to "taking down the monuments of those who perished in 9/11"; a quip about drug dealers "with the name [sic] D-Money, Smoothie, Shifty," who he claimed were coming to Maine to "sell their heroin" and "impregnate a young, white girl before they leave"; and his critique of a Democratic state representative as "the first one to give it to the people without providing vaseline."[27] The governor also left a voicemail for another Maine House Democrat, calling the representative a "little son-of-a-bitch, socialist cocksucker" for accusing him of racism.[28] In 2016, ahead of that year's presidential election, he embraced comparisons to the eventual GOP nominee. "I was Donald Trump before Donald Trump became popular," he quipped after endorsing the controversial candidate, despite having recently implored the Republican Party to disavow him.[29] Governor LePage left office in 2019 with a 40 percent approval rating. He announced that he was moving to Florida and declared that he was "done with politics. I've done my eight years. It's time for somebody else."[30]

Governor Mills mentioned the LePage legacy, if not his name, during her press conference on that day in early June 2020, when he came back to Maine to shadow President Trump. After dismissing the latter's cameo as "a rambling, confusing, thinly-veiled political rally," she told the assembled reporters that since taking office she had worked to "restore civility and normalcy in our state." She touted that she had hired "the most qualified and highly respected public health professionals" to rebuild Maine's "decimated" healthcare system "far before we knew there was a pandemic on the horizon" — the state's CDC had more than one hundred vacant jobs at the end of her predecessor's second term, after years of his health department budget cuts.[31] On the day Governor Mills took office she used her first executive order to expand the state's Medicaid program.[32] Voters had approved the expansion by statewide referendum in 2017, but Governor LePage refused to implement it over cost objections. More than fifty-five thousand people had since been granted coverage, including some twelve thousand since the pandemic started.[33] Now, after nearly three months of pandemic restrictions and precautions, Maine was still among the states with the lowest COVID-19 case numbers per capita in the country — by the start of the second week in June there had been just over twenty-five hundred confirmed cases and ninety-nine deaths.[34] In closing her press conference on President Trump's visit, Governor Mills told reporters that she was accelerating business reopenings in all but three of Maine's sixteen counties, except for those where cases had increased. "My responsibility is to protect the health and wellbeing of Maine people and to support our economy, and I will continue to strike that balance," she said. "I urge the President to take his own responsibility to protect the health of all Americans as seriously."

Ashirah cheered her on from the woods of Temple. "It's been a pretty rugged week, hasn't it?" she wrote to open her next letter. "We are grateful and proud of how you stood up to the President . . . and were impressed with your decision to use such strong language with him. Go Governor!" Life was comparatively quiet on the homestead — June was usually the leanest time of year, with the root cellar almost empty and the gardens only recently sown. Sometimes there were wild greens left from the bounty of May, but for much of that month the Knapps bought most of their fruit and vegetables from local co-ops or supermarkets. Ashirah confessed that she also bought "quite a lot more treats than Chris" on those trips — namely, potato chips and chocolate.

Her children were out of school and the weather was warm enough that they needed cooling off. Ashirah often took them to jump in nearby streams "that nobody would go swimming in other than us." Those had turned out to be good opportunities to write to the governor. "I continue to be flabbergasted by my fellow humans' selfishness and capacity to hurt," Ashirah fumed. "There are so many brilliant and loving people in the world right now, but it often feels like there are a lot more hurtful and violent ones. It doesn't feel like all the little actions will ever be enough, yet it's all we can do." She had been "playing with the thought that, though bad seems to spread easily and readily . . . people can be turned away from it, while the slow little acts of love maybe really sink into a person's soul and leave a lasting mark." She had recently asked her parents, who were in their early seventies, whether "they had ever lived through another time that felt this hard" — Vietnam, the Cold War, or the emergence of HIV, perhaps. Her father's answer was President Trump's election. "Not very encouraging, but I appreciated his honesty," Ashirah wrote.

Buried toward the end of the letter she mentioned that it had warmed her heart to receive a response from Governor Mills that week. "I'm glad to know my support is getting to you and that it means something," Ashirah wrote, adding that it was also a good experience for her children "to see that one *can* reach out to one's representatives and have an interaction." She noted that her daughter had "immediately appropriated" the card for her signature collection. Governor Mills had recently started writing back to as many of the people who sent supportive cards and letters as her schedule allowed. She had mailed her note to Ashirah at the end of May, handwritten on official stationery, and in cursive script, thanking her for her "words of support — they mean a lot to me." The governor thought the Knapps' business had "a very good chance of success and will become even more attractive once the worst of the pandemic is over." Meanwhile, she appreciated Ashirah's "patience and words of support" and asked her to please "stay safe." Ashirah ended her letter in response by reminding the governor to "please stay strong in your convictions no matter how loud the criticism gets." She added: "You still know the truth, even when other people are telling you you're wrong. I hope that helps bring you solace."

Indeed, critics were still registering strong opposition to the Mills administration's pandemic response, including a Republican state representative who had recently called for the governor's impeachment.[35] Other GOP Maine lawmakers had sought to revoke her emergency authority.[36] In late May the US Department of Justice filed a statement of interest in support of a group of Maine campground owners who were suing the state in federal court over pandemic restrictions for out-of-state tourists.[37] In a press release the DOJ called the rules unconstitutional "discrimination" that was "inadequately tailored to further public safety" and "imposing devastating economic costs." The governor publicly acknowledged divisions over her leadership, reiterating her openness while dismissing some criticism as "partisan political chatter."[38]

She was also hearing from confused, concerned, or disapproving constituents in writing, usually by email. "Whoever was handling correspondence would sometimes write back to them, or sometimes we would just deal with it on TV, in the news conferences," she explained. Dr. Shah made a point of responding to Mainers' most frequent questions, and he took care not to patronize people, particularly when he was debunking pandemic myths. By June he was hosting most of his CDC briefings alone and remotely, though the state's health commissioner, Jeanne Lambrew, often joined his video conferences to help answer reporters' questions. For the first six weeks of the pandemic Dr. Shah had made most appearances with the governor at his side. She remembered that "there was constant news," and they "were trying to project . . . confidence, trust, hope." They would "try to find some hook with people," she added, so they could relate what was happening to Mainers' lives. "And that's why we kept quoting from, like, Mr. Rogers or you know

[Disney's] *Frozen 2*, 'Do the next right thing,'" she said. Dr. Shah's briefings drew a following almost from the start. Mainers trapped at home tuned in obsessively, and a Facebook page called "Fans of Dr. Shah" quickly drew more than thirty thousand followers.[39]

Nothing about his résumé hinted at celebrity potential. He had degrees in both medicine and law from the University of Chicago, studied economics at Oxford University in England, and worked for the Cambodian Ministry of Health during the SARS epidemic.[40] He was forty-two years old and came to Maine in the spring of 2019 from his native Midwest, where he ran the Illinois Department of Public Health for four years. During that tenure Dr. Shah had been one of several state officials accused of mishandling an outbreak of Legionnaires' disease that caused the deaths of thirteen residents at a veterans' home.[41] When that controversy followed him to Maine, Governor Mills publicly defended her administration's decision to hire him. "He was kind of a victim of politics," she said. "You know, new administration, they clean house obviously." She mentioned the first time she "saw him at work," when more than two hundred asylum seekers from Africa arrived in Maine the summer before the pandemic.[42] "They were all sleeping on cots in the expo building in Portland and there was Nirav doing medical exams with these people and checking them out, the little babies, seeing if they had any problems," she said. "I could see he was compassionate and methodical — I thought, this is a good man."

When they started holding COVID-19 briefings in mid-March 2020, Dr. Shah tried to be both relatable and memorable in every appearance, especially when explaining safety practices. He felt that "public policy is important, but what the public does is even more important."[43] He spoke casually and candidly and minimized medical and political jargon. He had the wit, timing, and deadpan delivery of a talented stand-up comedian, and cracked jokes whenever possible, often using vivid analogies to play up important points. In one briefing, less than a week after Maine's CDC confirmed the state's first case of COVID-19, Dr. Shah stressed that handwashing "with intensity" was a critical precaution: "The best way I've seen this described was to wash your hands as if you have just sliced a bag of jalapeño peppers and now need to take out your contact lenses."[44] He would subtly weave song lyrics that echoed pandemic talking points into his briefings, including riffs by Prince, Coldplay, and Rick Astley, without breaking a smile.

Dr. Shah felt that even his "lame attempt" at "corny" jokes could bring people together.[45] He allowed himself to go off script or laugh during briefings when there were technical difficulties or other mishaps, and he let his humanity show. When viewers noticed that he took sips of Diet Coke between questions from the press, he acknowledged the habit as his "sole vice," adding "at least for now I'm going to stick with it."[46]

Dr. Shah was honest with Mainers, even and especially when delivering bad news, and he earned respect for his willingness to acknowledge shortfalls or failures. Governor Mills believed that his credibility and rapport with the public was saving lives — that Mainers trusted him, and that their appreciation for his shtick increased adherence to pandemic restrictions. "There should be a whole book of Niravisms, honest to God," she said. "That stuff got people's attention, people of all ages." She added that Dr. Shah was "extraordinarily patient," particularly with the press. "He'll take questions and sometimes they'll be offensive or offbeat and he'll just take it in stride. Me, I'd be throwing something." By early May the governor had reduced her appearances at Dr. Shah's briefings. "What did I have to add?" she explained. "People loved him!" Charlie Miller was among those who noticed her absence. "My friends know Janet and I are friends, and they all had the same complaint . . . 'where's Janet?!'" he said. He emphasized that Dr. Shah was "over-the-top-fabulous" on his own; Charlie also knew the governor was in constant communication with her top health officials, but he recalled urging her to make sure that her constituents knew she was "the driving force . . . making the decisions" — to make herself "first and foremost in this." He added: "She did not want to do that. It's not in her DNA to take credit or, in a sense, to lead in that way."

In mid-June the daily number of new cases in Maine was declining and hospitalizations were at their lowest point since April.[47] The state was receiving fewer applications for both food assistance and support for needy families after a spike in the number of appeals at the beginning of the pandemic.[48] Its leisure and hospitality industries had lost more than 42,600 jobs, but restaurants in most counties had reopened for indoor dining and were among the many businesses on a path back to normal operation.[49] Governor Mills acknowledged ongoing fears for the state's economy but advised continued caution in a radio address. "Boy, I can think of nothing worse . . . than an outbreak or resurgence of this deadly, untreatable virus at the height of tourist season," she told listeners. In the neighboring states of New Hampshire and Vermont, COVID-19 case numbers were holding steady at levels similar to Maine's, based on population, so she announced that residents of those states could visit without a two-week quarantine.[50] Starting July 1 out-of-state visitors could skip that requirement if they provided proof they had tested negative within seventy-two hours of arriving, but some in the hospitality industry complained that testing options were still too limited for the change to be a boon.[51]

Toward the end of June some news reports began calling out Maine businesses that were not strictly enforcing mask mandates. Governor Mills used another radio address to admonish them to "please strictly adhere to all health and safety protocols."[52] Continued precautions were "the most effective way to make sure that we don't have to put on restrictions again." She implored business owners to deny entry to anyone not wearing a mask, an offense punishable by a $1,000 fine and up to six months in jail. Her sister Dora understood why some people mistook the governor as "dictatorial" at times in the pandemic when she had to "do the right thing, for the common good." Dora explained that their parents raised them with "a very strong moral compass," but she added that the governor also had a "soft side" that "does not like to give orders."

Ashirah continued to appreciate the governor's "choice of strong statements and language," as she wrote in her next June letter. In her opinion Governor Mills was "not rude" but gave her positions "without pulling punches or getting swayed." Ashirah added: "I am also relieved, as a citizen of this state, to hear you speak the way that you do because it takes away my concern that you will change your stance because of pressure." She did not know many people who disagreed with the measures the governor had taken to manage the pandemic so far. She had only one acquaintance who was "strongly opposed" but "at least had the grace to say he honestly didn't know what he would have done differently, just that he would have." Ashirah thought that "if people looked deeply enough into themselves, a lot of them would find that they are frustrated, angry, scared about the situation" and "displacing those feelings onto you or others when actually there really was no other sane choice" for how to keep people safe.

She did not have much family news for that week's letter, other than having taken her children to the dentist for cleanings. She thought "the office did a good job with safety" and, "just as important," the hygienist had said "she felt well taken care of" by her employer. Ashirah thought it seemed "possible to open a lot of life back up with precautions" except for the fact that there were "a whole lot of Mainers who are choosing not to take precautions!" This was where the governor's restrictions were "coming in to save people's lives, because they don't have enough sense to save their own." Ashirah added that she was not referring to people who were "living in group situations and can't social distance" but those who "consciously decide precautions aren't necessery [sic] because they haven't gotten sick yet!" To end her letter "on a happy note" Ashirah shared a joke she had seen recently in her social media feed: "Can we start taking showers again or should we all just keep washing our hands?"

One of the problems Ashirah had mentioned — the lack of isolation options for Mainers living in groups, especially those who tested positive and had no place to quarantine — was greatest in Maine's urban minority communities. The state was working to provide more virus testing and alternative housing in those areas, after a report in mid-June showed that Maine had the country's highest racial disparity for COVID-19 infections.[53] In particular, the COVID Tracking Project had found that Black residents, who represented less than 2 percent of the state's population, accounted for almost 24 percent of positive cases.[54] Dr. Shah called the disparity "categorically unacceptably high and unacceptable to every single person who's working on the response."[55] He noted that many of those affected had been among the African asylum seekers he met a year before when they arrived in Portland soon after his own start in Maine. They were "now, in turn, helping *us* on the front lines . . . playing a critical role in our economy during this time, working in places like grocery stores and other parts of the essential food supply chain, such as in meat processing plants, under very difficult conditions." Dr. Shah acknowledged that "much more work" was ahead to end the racial disparity, and "we should not feel complacent, but we can at the same time feel pride about where we have come, given where we started."

Overall, Maine was succeeding in controlling the pandemic while cases were rising in about half of the other states — a "disturbing" surge, as Dr. Anthony Fauci, director of the infectious disease division at the National Institutes of Health, told Congress in late June, the same day that President Trump said the "kung flu" was "going away" during a campaign event.[56] In contrast, Governor Mills touted that Maine had the seventh lowest number of cases and ninth lowest number of deaths out of forty-two states that were reporting the figures.[57] Toward the end of June, Ashirah wrote to say she wished "that everyone in the world had the same safe place right now." She reported that most people in her area were wearing masks in public and some stores had "very good shields set up between customers and cashiers," as well as "signs encouraging social distancing and directing the flow of traffic." She had felt comfortable taking her children for "an experiment with social distance swimming" with their friends. "All the kids did great so I think it is something we can repeat," she wrote. Ashirah also mentioned a neighbor who was organizing car parades for local people who were celebrating birthdays.

Meanwhile, the Knapps' garden was suffering from brutally hot and dry weather unlike any period of drought that Ashirah or Chris could remember. They were watering all their plants by hand, carrying hundreds of gallons in buckets from a tiny pond nearby. As they watched the pond's level drop "by inches a day" Ashirah worried that "there may be another smaller disaster for farmers in Maine on top of COVID this year." She was comforted by watching "the natural world continue to go about itself," especially after dark. "At night the tree frogs and bullfrogs create a cacophony, the fireflies are out, and we watched a bat zipping around last night." She thought she might have lost a new duckling to one of two "gigantic" snapping turtles looking for nesting sites on the homestead. Her parting dose of humor for the week was to share that her cat was "having the time of her life hunting chipmunks and squirrels and eating all but the tails, which she leaves for us to find."

Ashirah's letter reached Augusta on the same day that Governor Mills wrote in her journal: "Reading notes from constituents in the evening brings tears to my eyes." She mentioned one that came with a drawing of a kestrel. The sender had written that "like the hummingbird, the kestrel is one of the only birds who has mastered the ability to hover in one place without beating her wings. She is a swift and aggressive hunter, yet she is also capable of mastering great stillness and patience." Another card featured a quote by the Christian motivational writer and speaker, William Arthur Ward: "Feeling gratitude and not expressing it is like wrapping a present and not giving it." In the governor's entry for that day she also included a quote of her own choosing, as usual with no context or comment other than having been moved to put it in her journal. In this case the author was Charles Addams, creator of *The Addams Family* cartoons, who had written or said: "Normal is an illusion; what is normal for the spider is chaos for the fly."

In the governor's final radio address for the month of June, she told Mainers that if they continued to protect themselves and one another, the state could proceed with a return to something resembling pre-pandemic life, if not normalcy.[58] Her administration was preparing to launch the third stage of her Restarting Maine's Economy Plan on July 1, which would allow spas to reopen, as well as water parks, arcades, movie theaters, and other indoor and outdoor amusement facilities, under strict health and safety protocols. Governor Mills reminded listeners that it was "possible, if not likely even, that the changes we are making will result in an uptick in cases" as was happening with tragic consequences in so many other states. "Don't let down your guard now," she warned. "It is up to every one of us."

CHAPTER THREE

"The pandemic grows long here . . ."

Americans were buying more fireworks than ever before and setting them off in the weeks before Independence Day. As the summer of 2020 began, the US was reporting more than forty thousand new COVID-19 cases per day,[1] and hundreds of cities and towns had canceled their annual Fourth of July pyrotechnic displays so as to avoid large gatherings. A frustrated nation found new ways to celebrate the holiday, throwing impromptu parties on front stoops or fire escapes and in scaled-down backyard barbecues, with family members and friends from social bubbles, or six feet apart from their neighbors at outdoor block parties — at least in regions of the country where people were still taking precautions.

The virus infection curve was rising in forty states after many governors had loosened or rescinded pandemic restrictions, with the worst spikes in the West and South. In Texas hospitalizations more than quadrupled after the state reopened its economy in May. By late June its governor, Republican Greg Abbott, had paused the state's reopening.[2] On the second day of July, he imposed a statewide mask mandate by executive order, reversing his earlier view that governments could not force individuals to wear masks.[3] As the long weekend set in, the Northeast was one of the only regions where COVID cases were declining.[4] In Maine a total of 105 people had died of the virus, the ninth lowest number in the country, adjusted for population.[5] The number of confirmed cases, 3,294, was the nation's seventh lowest count, but it had risen slightly for the first time since mid-May, due in part to more testing. State health officials also believed that young people were spreading the virus as a taxing school year ended and they let loose for summer vacation.

That summer in Maine was also unusually hot and ominously dry. Most of the state saw drought conditions intensify in July from moderate to severe.[6] The potential consequences ranged from people gathering unsafely at beaches and pools to cool off to farmers suffering major crop damage or losses. In a radio address just before the holiday, Governor Mills repeated her calls for calm and caution: "This year's celebration of our nation's founding will be unlike anything we've ever seen in our lifetimes." She went on to under-score the strangeness of the times: "Boy, when I ran for governor I never envisioned I would have to tell people in Maine to stay home, to wash their hands, to stay six feet apart from others at all times, to wear a cloth face covering." She regretted that some people "have tried to make this pandemic political" over precautions they felt were threats to their personal liberty. "But then again, are any of us truly free while this pandemic rages on around us?" She invoked the Declaration of Independence and called on Mainers to "pledge to each other our lives" as its authors had. "Let us remember in this difficult time that our fortunes and futures are bound together."

Ashirah wrote from Temple to share that her family marked the country's birthday by watching young descendants of Frederick Douglass deliver excerpts from his 1852 speech "What to the Slave Is the Fourth of July" in a new short film.[7] The historic address, given to a women's anti-slavery group in New York, was an unflinching indict-ment of America's hypocrisy in perpetuating slavery. "Your high independence only reveals the immeasurable distance between us," the former slave had told his audience. "The rich inheritance of justice, liberty, prosperity and independence, bequeathed by your fathers, is shared by you, not by me . . . You may rejoice, I must mourn." National Public Radio made the film amid ongoing protests around the country following the murder of George Floyd. At the end of the production, one of the descendants, fifteen-year-old Isidore Dharma Douglass Skinner, talked of the dangers of pessi-mism in the pursuit of racial justice. "I think we are slaves to the notion that it will never get better," she told viewers. "I think it's important that we celebrate black joy and black life and we remem-ber that change is possible, change is probable and that there's hope."

Ashirah found the film "very powerful" and told the governor "the words hit right into your heart." The Knapps were watching TV or movies as a family a few nights each week and had recently been choosing episodes of *The West Wing*, a fictional NBC drama series that originally aired from 1999 through 2006 and was set in the White House during a Democratic administration. "It was almost painful to watch such an achingly beautiful portrayal of what a good government in Washington could be," Ashirah wrote, adding that her children were "willing to watch the more serious and educational programs as long as we mix them in with *The Golden Girls*, *M*A*S*H* and *Star Trek!*" Owen and Pamela were thrilled to be out of school and spending more time with friends, meeting for more socially distant swimming or Dungeons and Dragons sessions. "Not sure what we'll do when it's too cold to be outside with other people," Ashirah mused. Her thoughts were already turning to the fall, especially the question of whether she and Chris would risk sending their children back to local classrooms if and when their school reopened. President Trump dismissed any other possibility the week after Independence Day. "We're very much going to put pressure on governors and everybody else to open the schools," he declared as he hosted a White House event on the issue, arguing that keeping kids home would cause more harm than COVID. "Everybody wants it," he pronounced. "It's time to do it."

The school the Knapps ran on their homestead was arguably a sort of test case for what a return to classroom learning might be like for students and educators with the pandemic still surging. By July, Ashirah and Chris were legally allowed to reopen and invite students and apprentices back to the homestead, but they felt that strict COVID protocols "would severely impact the quality of the experience" their school offered. "A lot of our work involves being right next to people because we're showing them 'here's how you hold this tool, here's how you move,'" Ashirah explained. "It was going to be really difficult to do something where we had to be right next to someone and yet we were trying to not be right next to someone." The communal experience of cooking and sharing meals was central to much of their programming, but social distancing guidelines meant the Knapps would have to move meals and classes outside during months when mosquitoes and biting flies were thick and relentless. The return of students also meant potential COVID exposure for their children, who had compromised respiratory health — Owen struggled with severe asthma, and Pamela had bronchomalacia, a congenital condition that left her susceptible to developing pneumonia. The Knapps had decided to postpone restarting classes at least through the summer, so July on the homestead was unusually quiet, if typically hot and buggy. In comparison with winter — when there was always work involved with staying warm, inside the house and outdoors — Ashirah enjoyed the ease of the warmer months. "There's all the appreciation I have for the fact that I can just get up in the morning and I don't have to start a fire to be warm," she explained. "We also have no way to cool our house down because we don't have that kind of electricity. We don't have ice cubes, we don't have a way to keep things frozen to get ourselves cooled down. So we really feel the heat of the summer, the good and the bad of it."

Ashirah had recently started writing some of her letters to Governor Mills on nature-themed stationery instead of lined notebook paper. "A neighbor had given Pamela her old scrapbooking stuff," Ashirah remembered. She went through the box and chose everything she thought was "appropriate to send the governor" and "not completely contradicting who I was, like I probably took out the ones with the little flying ice cream cones and things like that on them." She would choose a different print for each letter — a pond surrounded by a pine forest, crisscrossing animal tracks, a collage of leaves and acorns or sunflowers and strawberries — and fill the blank side of the stationery with her thoughts, sometimes spilling over onto lined paper when she ran out of space.

Her letters often took more than a week to reach the Blaine House from the day she mailed them: Ashirah's dispatch for June 29 was stamped as received by the Office of the Governor on July 9. "My daughter says she wants to tell you thank you for being such a strong woman model and that she wants to be a governor one day," Ashirah wrote. "My son says to tell you we are going to keep being careful even though people all over are getting lax." That week Ashirah and Chris were preparing for the latest in "an ongoing bunch of difficult talks" with members of their social bubble. She understood that some of them "felt like we forced our protocols on them" but "then there were things they just stopped doing that we had all agreed to do and they never told us." The lack of communication, Ashirah felt, made the process of finding consensus "gut-wrenchingly emotional" because someone was always "taking offense and feeling hurt and disrespected."

She went on to mention her father's theory that there was "a second virus out there besides COVID" — a mentality plaguing people who "can't fight back" at the pandemic, so they "latch onto whatever they *can* fight about." Ashirah admitted to feeling that impulse herself, "and I'm a pretty even-keeled person, so I can only imagine what this is doing in people who don't spend as much energy getting themselves straightened out internally before looking at the world each day." Ashirah thanked Governor Mills for "working from the top" and assured her that there were "lots of us out here still working from the bottom who are with you" and "prepared for the marathon and not the sprint."

By then Ashirah had been sending supportive letters for three months. Her initial motivation for writing every week, she explained, had less to do with "making a difference" than wanting to show her support for a controversial leader whose decisions made sense to her, however drastic. Ashirah decided that one letter would not be enough because the governor "was going to be getting the shit from people all the time, and so I needed to keep giving her something positive all the time." She could understand "why somebody would be more upset" at that early point, if they were still "thinking 'everything is fine, this thing isn't such a big deal, she's just putting all these constraints on my life, I hate her.'" Ashirah felt a need to apologize to the governor, who was "trying to save these people's lives" — people who were "too stupid to do it themselves, and now they're angry at you for it . . . like a bunch of toddlers."

In early July the Mills administration stoked fresh controversy by adding tourists from New York, New Jersey, and Connecticut to the list of states whose residents could come to Maine without quarantining or testing negative for COVID-19 within the previous seventy-two hours. Visitors from New Hampshire and Vermont had previously been approved, but Governor Mills had left the restrictions in place for residents of Massachusetts, Rhode Island, and other states outside the Northeast where case numbers and positivity rates were increasing or higher than Maine's.[8] At that time, most states had issued various restrictions on travelers, sometimes jointly, for both their own residents and out-of-state tourists.[9] Many states extended those restrictions well into summer or beyond.

In response to Maine's restrictions, the *Bangor Daily News*, one of Maine's largest newspapers, printed a pair of contrasting opinion essays that denounced the governor's decision from both sides. One was submitted by the owners of three small businesses in the state, who felt that "the rush to reopen Maine" was "troubling on multiple fronts" and told tourists "we would rather you wait to visit until we are out of the thick of a global pandemic that threatens all our lives." The author of the second piece was a man who grew up in Maine but had moved to Pennsylvania and was forced to cancel a beloved annual family vacation to his native state that summer to comply with the governor's "unreasonable" restrictions. "Not in my worst nightmare did I dream that watching the sunrise from atop Cadillac Mountain or . . . feasting on a lobster dinner . . . would make us criminals," he wrote. "But that is the reality of summer 2020 under Maine's governor."

A *Boston Globe* columnist found humor in the restrictions: "We used to be friends, Maine," he wrote in a spoof column, complaining that Governor Mills had "just announced to the entire world that every person in Massachusetts has the cooties."[10] Maine had been "letting out-of-state visitors from New Hampshire and Vermont just waltz in the door and eat an overpriced lobster roll like the coronavirus never happened," he quipped, adding that he was "sure tourists from Massachusetts aren't a central part of your economy or anything." In 2019 travelers to Maine spent $6.5 billion, and more than a third of one-day visitors were from Massachusetts, the second largest group after in-state tourists.[11] Despite concerns that travelers and Fourth of July revelry might spread COVID, the number of cases in Maine declined the week after the holiday. The state's hospitalization rate was holding at its lowest point since Maine started reporting the metric in mid-April, and a total of 110 people had died of the virus.[12]

Nonetheless Governor Mills was unwavering in her messaging about the ongoing threat of the pandemic and the imperative of taking proven health and safety precautions "intended to protect the health of all Maine people."[13] On July 8, 2020, she issued an executive order requiring restaurants, lodging establishments, and large retail stores in more populous cities and coastal counties to enforce the state's mask mandate. The measure strengthened a previous order that allowed businesses to deny entry to customers not wearing masks. "I know it may be inconvenient for some," the governor recognized. "I also believe that Maine people care about each other, and this simple gesture is a small price to pay for knowing you could save someone's life."[14] In a Maine CDC briefing that same day, Dr. Shah took "a step back" and put COVID's transmissibility in stark perspective — he reminded viewers that six months earlier "there wasn't even a single confirmed case" in the US, but within a hundred days the nation's count had spiked to one million; forty-three days later it reached two million; and as of that afternoon's briefing, there were more than three million cases nationwide.[15]

The seemingly endless onslaught of such dire statistics prompted countless internet memes, starting in the early days of the pandemic, as people satirized COVID messaging to cope with quarantines, rote safety protocols, the sudden normalcy of mass global mask-wearing, and unprecedented uncertainty in general. During the week of Dr. Shah's somber briefing, Governor Mills reposted a meme on her personal Facebook page that used crafting hobby terms to explain the contagiousness of COVID: "You and nine friends are crafting. One is using glitter. How many projects have glitter?" That week, Ashirah's letter from Temple mentioned another Facebook post that was circulating at the time, "reminding people that Anne Frank was two years in that attic. I guess there's nothing more to say, after that."

The rest of Ashirah's report was similarly bleak. "The pandemic grows long here," she wrote, admitting that she felt "overwhelming uncertainty" about its potentially lasting effects on the Knapps' business and their children's education. Owen and Pamela were "bickering constantly," and Chris and Ashirah's marriage was "strained," mostly because they disagreed about the COVID protocols their family should practice. "I will admit I was on the far end of caution," she remembered. "I think through all the details, which tends to make me a lot more cautious. It also means I get less done in life, so that's the other side." In recent weeks they had "been through hell" with members of their social bubble, she told the governor. In the midst of so much conflict Ashirah found herself questioning her decisions. "It's hard to hold one's ground when everyone else is letting go," she wrote. She mentioned some "informative" talks with neighbors from Connecticut who owned summer homes near the Knapps' homestead — they had "seen COVID up close in a way we have not here." After their conversations Ashirah "set a goal of one more year to be strong and there will probably be a vaccine by then." As the nation's case and fatality counts kept rising she had told herself she was "not imagining all this." She felt "frustrated that our president has not stopped this thing and we're in for a long, hard time."

With the country's general election now fewer than four months away, Governor Mills was focused on Maine's approaching primary. She had postponed voting day from June 9 to July 14, despite the likelihood of even lower turnout than primaries usually drew, to give state and local election officials more time to streamline COVID safety procedures for in-person voting.[16] She also extended the deadline for requesting and submitting absentee ballots until polls closed on election night. State primaries that year were crucial test cases, ahead of the 2020 presidential election, for whether voting could be done safely, efficiently, and legally, with an unprecedented number of Americans expected to vote absentee in both contests. More than half of the states held primaries from June through August.[17] Maine's was one of six that took place in July. "I usually vote in person," Governor Mills told residents in her radio address two days before precincts opened. "I enjoy seeing folks at the polls. This year however, I voted absentee, and I urge everyone else to vote absentee as well." More than two hundred thousand voters requested absentee ballots, nearly six times the number in the previous primary and a record for the state. The governor's deadline extension caused problems in some precincts, including Portland, Maine's largest city, where a wave of absentee ballots submitted on Election Day prevented officials from announcing results until the next day. "November's going to be a different game," Maine's secretary of state told the Associated Press, predicting exponentially higher turnout.[18]

On the afternoon of the primary, Governor Mills used her Twitter account to amplify the news that Maine and neighboring New Hampshire were the only two states reporting a decline in coronavirus cases, based on a seven-day average.[19] "That is, of course, welcome and encouraging news," she wrote. "But I want to be clear: it cannot be cause for celebration, as much as we want it to be." The "deadly virus" was "still lurking in our communities," and "the best thing Maine people can do for our health and our economy is stay vigilant." She had tirelessly preached caution for four months, and forced her constituents to take precautions, all the while "trying to avoid a police state." If she felt an emotional or physical toll from that sustained effort, her journal entries during that time only occasionally hinted at the personal cost of her job. On March 28, 2020, the day after she reported the state's first death from COVID-19, a man in his late eighties, she had written that the announcement "was a bit emotional. Not so very hopeful, but with dire warnings to the Maine public to stay away from other people." Three days earlier she had ordered essential businesses "to immediately employ strategies to reduce congestion in their stores," but as she drove past a Walmart in her hometown of Farmington, she had seen "no precautions, no warnings, no limiting of customers, etc. Very upsetting. I should just close them down."

In late spring, "after an exhausting, topsy-turvy week," the governor spent "a lovely evening" with two friends on a small island in midcoast Maine that belongs to painter Jamie Wyeth. She wrote in her journal that he had greeted them "with cannon fire" as they walked along a path made of crushed oyster shells to his home, a historic lighthouse built in 1857 with an attached keeper's residence, its "windows half open to invite an ocean breeze."[20] The trip lasted for only a few hours but felt like "a great escape" during a "controversial, stressful" time. In the course of her career to that point, Governor Mills had adapted to having only short intervals to unwind. "I've always had pretty full time jobs, *more*-than-full-time jobs," she explained. "I never took vacations when I was district attorney." Later, during her second term as attorney general, she "had a sick husband." The longest getaway the couple took during nearly three decades of marriage was a five-day trip to Bermuda. During the weeks between the governor's election and inauguration she and Charlie drove to New Brunswick, Canada, and back down the coast of Maine. After that, and until the pandemic, she had traveled only to conferences in other states, but did not take "a vacation vacation . . . My husband's gone, and the kids are grown up and have their own families. Who am I going to go with?"

Instead the governor looked forward to spending "weekends at camp" — a modest lakeside cottage in central Maine that she had bought just before she was elected, from her late aunt's estate. The house had a screened front porch where she loved to sit and watch sunsets and "shooting stars in the night sky over the lake." During the summer of 2020 she would gather there with her stepdaughters and their children, "the 'grandgirls' — always keeping our distance as best we can, staying outside," as she wrote in her journal. "Good to see other people, share a laugh and a meal with good friends." Sometimes she stayed for just one night; she needed only a few deep breaths and a swim before heading back to Augusta. She welcomed the long car rides that Maine's "you can't get there from here" geography infamously imposes. A member of her security team always did the driving, whether her outings were official or personal, and she usually spent the commutes returning work calls and emails.

A few days after the state primary election in mid-July an Economic Recovery Committee, which Governor Mills had created in response to the pandemic, warned the crisis had "pushed many otherwise healthy Maine businesses to the brink." The group added that residents who "struggled with inequity prior to COVID-19 now face immense challenges." Those dynamics urgently increased "the economic and social importance" of supporting childcare providers and sending Maine's children back to classrooms in the fall. The panel told the governor that Maine's portion of the $1.25 billion allocation from the Coronavirus Aid, Relief, and Economic Security Act — a $2.2 trillion economic stimulus bill President Trump signed in March 2020 — would cover "a fraction of what . . . is needed," including the extra funding the state's public schools would have to spend to safely restart in-person learning.[21]

Two days later Governor Mills announced Maine's guidelines for that process. She took a personal tack, telling teachers, school staff, and parents of school-aged children that she was "very sensitive to their needs" as "the daughter of a woman who taught in the public schools in Maine" for almost four decades, and "as someone who brought up five daughters who attended and graduated from public schools."[22] She hosted a virtual press conference, joined by her top education and health officials, to explain a tiered, color-coded system that schools would use to decide whether to teach students in person, remotely, or some combination of the two, based on their counties' health metrics.[23] "This is what several other states have also done," Governor Mills told reporters. "There's never been a playbook for this pandemic," she added, and she knew there would be concerns and "Monday-morning quarterbacking" but promised that her administration was "doing the best we can." While on camera she held up some of the letters she received from children "saying they're bored at home, they want to see their friends, they want to have play dates again." She read aloud from one of them, sent by a young girl who missed having recess and had written that "people are thinking [COVID] is the end of the world — no it is not. I want to go back to school."

By then Ashirah was seriously considering homeschooling her children in the fall. "Several of us parents hit a wall this week," she wrote to the governor on the day before the Mills administration's school reopening announcement. "We're all planning for a difficult time, then I realized . . . [the pandemic] could actually be gone by Sept[ember] if everyone in this country pulled together." Ashirah had safety concerns about sending her children back to classrooms. She also felt that, because she had the time and resources to teach Owen and Pamela at home until the pandemic eased, she could "take some of the burden off" the school system by teaching them at home. "None of this is what I wanted or had planned for myself," she added, "but that needs to be set aside until we get through this."

Ashirah confessed that she was resting all her hopes on vaccine development. "I certainly wouldn't be pulling out of worldwide medical efforts, as our president has been doing," she added, referring to the Trump administration's abrupt decision in early July to withdraw the US from the World Health Organization.[24] "I wish it felt like we were in this together, making the sacrifices and doing the hard things." She had realized that "some of us will always remember this as a scary, sad, difficult time," while others would "sail through" without getting sick or changing their behavior and "look back on it as the big hoax." Ashirah closed that week's dispatch "with a little humor" — she had ordered some custom-made bumper stickers that read REAL MEN WEAR MASKS and was giving them away to friends. "Let me know if I should mail any to Augusta," she wrote, adding a smiley face before she signed off.

By the time Ashirah's letter arrived in Maine's capital a few days later, the nation was mourning the loss of Georgia congressman and civil rights icon John Lewis, who had died of pancreatic cancer on July 17. Governor Mills called him "a hero who taught us to hope and fight for a better future, even in a sea of despair" and ordered that US and Maine flags in the state be flown at half-staff for two days.[25] The next week some Maine business leaders repeated calls for the governor to drop "embarrassing" restrictions on tourists from Massachusetts and Rhode Island. She refused, citing those states' COVID-19 positivity rates, which were the highest in New England.[26] A Republican state representative joined the outcry, calling Governor Mills an "authoritarian" in a weekly radio address for the Maine House Republicans caucus. "Many listeners are no doubt familiar with George Orwell's dystopian novel 1984," the representative warned. She then made a point-by-point comparison of the book's fictional government and its strategy for "keeping people in a constant state of fear" with the Mills administration's handling of the pandemic. "State government now has us under surveillance," she concluded, "and is encouraging Maine citizens and businesses to police and inform on each other," in a reference to contact tracing and other measures.[27]

Governor Mills gave an address that day too, about "the parallel pandemic of substance use disorder," at her second annual opioid response summit.[28] She had created the event five months after taking office; it gathered people who were battling addiction, and their supporters, to meet with health providers, state law enforcement officials, and national experts for a daylong event to "foster collaboration on the state's ongoing response to the opioid crisis."[29] The 2020 summit was held virtually, a week after Maine's attorney general reported that 258 people had died of drug-related overdoses in the state in the first half of that year, a 26 percent increase over the previous six months. The "vast majority" of those deaths had been caused by at least one opioid.[30]

In the governor's address to the summit, she compared the isolation she had imposed on Maine residents in the first four months of the pandemic with Superman's Fortress of Solitude in the comic books she had read when she was in grade school. Governor Mills knew that among "those who stayed at home" because of her executive order, there were "good people who had come to rely on friends, therapists, programs and groups to support them in kicking long term habits and dependencies" but were "suddenly" unable to rely on those relationships and "fell through the cracks" because of COVID-19. "We have not forgotten you," she told them. "Come out of your fortress, because you are not alone."

She also thanked the "heroes and helpers" who "saved lives" — the state's outpatient methadone clinics had "pivoted" to doubling the number of take-home doses of treatment they provided for narcotic addiction. Governor Mills noted that "this change does not appear to have resulted in a single death." She also praised recovery centers in Maine for quickly transitioning patients to telehealth visits and moving support meetings onto virtual platforms, which "increased access to much needed treatment, especially in rural areas." At the addiction medicine clinic where Ashirah worked part-time, she recalled its doctors planning to use telemedicine long before they had to stop seeing patients in person for several months. The smooth transition to telehealth, she explained, had helped reduce disruptions in treatment that could be traumatic for patients.

In Ashirah's final letter that July, she railed to the governor that "too many of my fellow Americans are idiots," sounding off on pandemic skeptics and deniers. "In the face of all the news, all the science, all the personal stories, still there are people I know personally saying this is all a lie and they're not wearing a mask because that is their right, damnit." She felt that those people should "commit (I never know if I spell that word right!) to not going to the hospital" if they got sick. Maine had so far avoided the severe outbreaks that were overwhelming other states' healthcare systems that summer, while managing to reopen its economy. Ashirah believed that Maine was "doing so well" because people were spending so much time outdoors. She worried that too many had stopped taking precautions and, come fall and winter, they would "move their same sloppy habits inside and we'll start getting sick."

Two days later a coalition of state Republican lawmakers and tourism groups appealed to Governor Mills to drop restrictions on tourists from Massachusetts and Rhode Island and give Maine's hospitality industry "a chance at salvaging part of the tourism season." Many hospitality businesses in the state had hired fewer workers or shortened hours of operation, bracing for a predicted 30 percent decline in tourist travel nationwide and a 45 percent decrease in spending.[31] The GOP lawmakers proposed a plan that would allow visitors from any state with a COVID-19 positivity rate of 5 percent or less; Maine's was 0.998 percent at that time. They also called on the governor to increase the size of gatherings allowed in the state from 50 people to 150, indoors and outside, with social distancing enforced. They argued that their plan would give Maine's event venues an edge over those in some neighboring states where limits had already been raised.

At a press conference, one of the sponsors of the Republicans' plan, state senator and assistant GOP leader Jeff Timberlake, stressed that "the folks from Massachusetts . . . spend a lot of money, and we need to welcome them back to Maine." Senator

Timberlake contended that his party's plan was "based on science and facts" and was not "something that's radical or off the wall."[32] In a notably sharp rebuke the governor called the proposal "a Donald Trump–style assault on the very public health measures that have successfully protected Maine people." She reiterated that not only were tourists from Massachusetts and Rhode Island welcome to visit, but both states were among those that had "followed Maine's lead in adopting a seventy-two hour negative COVID-19 test as an alternative to quarantine" for tourists. "For the life of me," the governor retorted, "I cannot understand why Republicans care more about Massachusetts money than the life of a Maine person." She did increase the crowd size limit to one hundred people, but for outdoor gatherings only.[33] Having made that sole concession, she urged the GOP lawmakers, instead of asking her to "sacrifice the public health measures that have kept Mainers safe thus far," to join her "in calling on Congress and the President to pass another round of economic support."[34] The US government had sent Americans $1,200 "economic impact payment" checks, and a federal program that supplemented unemployment benefits for millions of Americans by $600 per week was set to expire at the end of July.

Governor Mills also urged the GOP leaders to join her administration's efforts to "brand Maine as a safer state" for residents and visitors, including a $2 million summer advertising campaign targeting tourists in states that were exempt from her quarantine and testing restrictions. That week the Maine Tourism Office reported that the new ads and the agency's website were "getting more views than expected."[35] By late July many tourism business owners had come to embrace the state's strict safety protocols as selling points. "It wasn't something they were used to doing," the governor recalled, but she pointed out that tourists "came here because of that." She added that employees also "wanted those protocols because they wanted to be safe from customers, and from other staff." More than three thousand hotel and restaurant workers in Maine had completed a pair of new online courses to earn a "micro-credential" in COVID-19 "readiness" that had been developed by Maine's Community College system and Hospitality Maine, a nonprofit industry trade group. "We wasted no time," the group's CEO explained in announcing the free courses. "There was an urgency to educate an entire industry workforce on new ways of operating safely and consistently."[36]

The idea for the course had been suggested in the spring by a retired Republican state senator who owned a seafood restaurant in Maine for more than twenty-five years. He felt that it was "incumbent on the industry to turn around and kind of self-regulate" and "do our part to make things better."[37] The training taught procedures for sanitation, cleanliness, and social distancing. Employees earned digital certificates, and employers could then advertise that their staff was certified. In late July — the same week as Maine's Republican lawmakers called for the governor to unleash more tourism — the online course developers launched a second set of tutorials on "stress management and the foundations of de-escalation." They reported that the state's hospitality workforce, "known for creating relaxing environments for others," was facing "a new anxiety: working through a pandemic." That paradigm included "social distancing, incessant cleaning and the debate over face coverings," new sources of stress that could "damage mental and physical health."[38]

Another new worry loomed for Maine residents who were facing eviction, with a pandemic-related federal moratorium set to expire at the end of July. Eviction filings in the state had dropped sharply under that protection — just over 900 in the first half of 2020, compared with an annual average of 5,801 before COVID-19. Housing advocates warned that if the moratorium expired, the state could see "an eviction crisis" that "could result in severe harm to tenants, landlords and Maine communities on a mass scale."[39] In the face of that "housing cliff" Governor Mills issued an executive order to increase the notice period for eviction from one week to thirty days. She also announced that the state would use $5 million in federal pandemic aid funds to double month-by-month payments to landlords who agreed not to evict tenants.[40] "Homes are more than brick and beams and mortar," the governor had said when she first launched the rent relief program in April 2020. "Home is where my husband and I raised five girls. It's where we sat at the kitchen table, helping with homework, paying bills. Where we slept safely each night." Now, in her final July radio address, she told Mainers: "The last thing people need to worry about in the middle of a pandemic is losing their home."

That same week the governor also directed $1 million from the federal pandemic aid package to local nonprofit groups "to significantly and quickly expand services to help reduce the disproportionately large racial and ethnic disparities in COVID-19 in Maine."[41] The state's public health commissioner, Jeanne Lambrew, explained that "the different part of what we're doing today is working in partnerships, because what we have heard loud and clear is that the community members *can* identify these needs . . . and we want to take down barriers." When Governor Mills took office she had welcomed immigrants to Maine, after former governor LePage called asylum seekers "the biggest problem in our state."[42] The new funding followed recent complaints, from community leaders in cities with Maine's largest Black and immigrant populations, that the Mills administration had not done enough, or reacted too slowly, to address racial inequities the pandemic exposed.[43] Incidentally, now private citizen LePage had returned from Florida that month to reestablish residency, after teasing a bid for reelection.[44] "I registered to vote last week and today I picked up these shiny new plates for my car," he wrote on his Facebook page. "So glad to be officially back home here in Maine."

Ashirah's word to describe the last week of July was "rugged," but the entire month had been tumultuous. "Every time I think we have reached the epitome of disaster in this country," she wrote, there was "some new outrage" that developed or was "perpetrated on us." In the last few days of the month the US government reported a nearly 33 percent crash in the country's gross domestic product since April — the worst quarterly dive since records started in 1947;[45] President Trump suggested postponing the November election, claiming on Twitter that it would be "the most INACCURATE & FRAUDULENT in history" due to "Universal Mail-In Voting";[46] and the country's pandemic death toll reached 150,000, the highest in the world, with states in the South and West setting daily records for pandemic fatalities.[47]

In Maine both the number of cases and the state's positivity rate had risen slightly for the second straight week, with new outbreaks traced to a medical center and a blueberry processing company. Thirty-eight cases in July were confirmed in visitors from other states.[48] In a shocking end to the month, a woman from New York City, who had long summered in Maine, was swimming off the coast of a town called Harpswell on July 28 when she was killed by a great white shark.[49] It was the first fatal shark attack in the state's recorded history, and some locals felt the tragedy had changed the area permanently.[50] Scientists noted that the shark likely mistook the woman for a seal — great whites were increasingly drawn to warming waters and the food source of the thriving seal population off the New England coast.[51] Warnings were posted at beaches, but one swimmer who had braved the waters in the area near the incident explained to a newspaper reporter: "There's so much fear, and I personally have so much fear in my life." This had been her "one day off," she added, and it was "a beautiful day."[52]

The next week a local independent movie theater canceled planned outdoor screenings of the 1975 film *Jaws*, about a fictional island community's complacency after a series of deadly shark attacks.[53] The woman who ran the theater explained that "given the circumstances with the recent shark attack" she felt that it "wasn't a necessity to screen the movie." Instead, she added more showtimes for *Jurassic Park*. The business had shut down indoor screenings due to pandemic restrictions but used "Yankee ingenuity" to set up an improvised drive-in theater nearby, with help from a transportation museum in the area. The shows had been set to end in July but were so popular that they were extended through the rest of the season. Their theater's proprietress noted: "We may be behind masks but . . . we get to come together in a way that is safe at this time."

CHAPTER FOUR

"Deep breath . . . I can do this . . ."

The first week of August 2020 was another sultry one, in the waning Dog Days of Maine's third hottest summer since records began 126 years before.[1] It was also one of the driest, with the worst short-term drought in about two decades. There was rain in the weather forecast, but in the potentially dangerous form of Tropical Storm Isaias, which was expected to pass over New England later that week. Its path was still uncertain, but a hazardous weather outlook was in effect for most Maine counties, a first test for emergency managers in planning storm shelters where people could congregate safely in a pandemic.[2] The state's COVID-19 positivity rate was still less than 1 percent, compared with the nation's weekly average of 8 percent. Based on that and other data, the Mills administration had just cleared all of Maine's public school districts to reopen full-time, subject to precautions.[3] That weekend, the governor left Augusta to spend a night at her camp with her niece. "It was good to have company," she wrote the next day, August 3. "Today would have been my thirty-fifth anniversary with Stan." She added that she had recently gone to the cemetery where her late husband was buried, to check on his grave. "The bowling trophy from 1972 that I planted there on Memorial Day is still there keeping him company."

Janet Mills married Stanley Kuklinski on August 3, 1985. They had met two years before, when she took a tennis lesson from Stan at the racquet club he ran in one of the three counties where she was district attorney. "I was a single woman in my mid-thirties," she remembered, and tennis was "something to do" in a part of Maine where "the social life . . . wasn't exactly sparkling." There was no romance at first — Stan was married, and his wife had advanced cancer. She died in early 1984, leaving him with five daughters between the ages of four and sixteen. Later that year Stan asked DA

Mills to have dinner with him. "You'd expect that I'd find some lawyer, or politician or something," she mused. "I couldn't date lawyers, for all intents and purposes, because I had cases against everybody in town." Her connection with Stan felt "comfortable" in part because they had such different vocations. She found him "very loyal, and caring and hard-working," and he seemed to be a good father, however overwhelmed by the task of raising five young girls on his own. "They were ordering out for pizza every day," she remembered.

On one of her early outings with Stan, he asked DA Mills to help him buy some clothes for his youngest daughter, Lisl, who went with them to a local department store. "He kind of used that kid to get to me, I think," the governor quipped, adding that the child was "sweet" but "obviously very clingy" with Stan. Soon after their shopping trip Lisl convinced her father's new girlfriend to buy a grocery cart full of junk food. "She would go, very innocently, 'my mommy always got us these.'" The trailblazing district attorney suddenly found herself mid-learning-curve on child-rearing: "My role, in good part, was just trying to organize things because it was emotionally and physically chaotic. The laundry, the groceries, all that stuff." Her close friend Janice David, whom she had met when they were both volunteering for Ted Kennedy's ill-fated 1980 bid for the Democratic presidential nomination, remembered DA Mills needing tips on running a household. "She always lamented that her mother never taught her any homemaking skills so I generally laughed at her for what she couldn't do," Janice recalled. "Her mother and father had her prepared for other things, more important things than sewing on buttons. But she'd call me and say, 'How do you cook a roast pork?' I mean it would be something like that, and I'd just go, 'Oh my God.'"

Within a year her friend had married Stan, moved in with the family, and become a full-time stepmother, sharing the one bathroom in the house with five girls whom she was still getting to know. "Each of them was having their issues with their mother dying," she remembered, "but we got to be friends." She spent the most time with the youngest girls and "would go take them out and play minigolf or something," but Stan's two older daughters were more independent. When discipline was called for, he usually did the enforcing of rules because DA Mills turned out to be "a softy" in that realm; she often took Lisl to work when the child refused to go to daycare or preschool. "She got to be almost a mascot at the courthouse," the governor remembered, smirking at the thought of a favorite anecdote that, she confessed, she had told "over and over again"— as DA she had come home from work one day to find Lisl dressing a Barbie doll in a designer gown: "I said, 'Oh Lisl, Barbie's getting all dressed up, where's she going tonight?' And she said, without a hitch, 'Well, Barbie had grand jury today and tonight she's going to a Democratic fundraiser' . . . I go, 'Oh wow, you can't say anything in front of these kids.'" Decades later, Lisl worked for a law firm as a paralegal, until she had two children, but told Governor Mills that she did not want to go to law school. "She said basically 'I'm making good money, I have good healthcare, time with my husband . . . I have what I want.' Smart kid." None of the governor's stepdaughters followed her path into politics, and two moved to other states, but she remained close to all of them, as well as her five grandchildren.

Her twenty-nine-year marriage to Stan had "ups and downs in the relationship, like everybody does," she explained, adding that he was "kind of a messy person in the house, which drove me crazy." Stan loved sports and had played them his whole life, starting with baseball when he was young. He was "a good tennis player, of course" and became "a great golfer" who was infamous for buying a new golf club "every time he went to a pro shop, which made him the laughing stock of his golfing buddies," she said. Toward the end of Stan's life he "rejuvenated" a local high school boys' tennis program.[4] "Coach K," as his players called him, was known for his trademark warm-up suits. "They were red, white and blue," the governor remembered. After Stan died she found "fifteen or twenty of the exact same [suit] . . . maybe they got dirt on them — he'd buy a new one." At Christmastime that year she made gifts of a few of them to the boys he had coached. "They loved him and they're all running around with his warm-up suit now." Her husband "enjoyed a good joke" but "wasn't a good storyteller." She also described him as "a loyal family person." Stan had grown up in Utica, New York, and his parents divorced when he was a small child. "The father just left," she explained, and Stan "shined shoes at the bus station when he was a little kid, to help his mother get by." He finished high school but did not go to college, instead becoming a contractor. Stan built his mother and stepfather a new house, among dozens of other homes, until he changed careers, married his first wife, and relocated to Maine.[5]

In 1994, when his second wife, District Attorney Mills, launched her ill-fated run for Congress, Stan was "not all on board" with her decision. He had become a real estate developer, and the couple also raised horses on the historic farm where they lived after "the girls had all gone off to college." The governor remembered that Stan "went along" with her first campaign for a federal office, "but he wasn't excited about it." The seat in Maine's second of two districts had opened after GOP congresswoman Olympia Snowe announced her bid to replace retiring US Senator and Democratic majority leader George Mitchell. DA Mills finished third in a primary crowded with eight candidates. From her friend Janice's point of view, the campaign suffered from a lack of money and a candidate who "didn't want to go into debt." Janice added that "Stan was a factor," noting that he "liked it when he was in the reflected glow of her but he didn't like the reality of it — Stan couldn't take care of himself. He wanted her to come home and make his dinner." Janice explained that her friend's husband "just never had the reality of a woman who had her own career." His first wife "had five children, and what she did was take care of Stan and take care of five kids. That was his experience, and he had a Polish mother who doted on him." DA Mills had "really tried, too," Janice added. "I remember her getting home at 7:30 . . . and trying to get him dinner and being concerned if she didn't do that he was going to run over to the local convenience store and bring home garbage and live on pizza. Which he did — if she wasn't around to take care of him, that's what he did."

After the primary loss, DA Mills finished her term and joined her brother Peter in private law practice for the next fourteen years.

Peter was also serving in the Maine legislature as a Republican senator. In 2002 both siblings ran for the state's House of Representatives
and won. "It was fun, we'd pass back and forth a lot" in the halls of
the statehouse, the governor recalled. She and Peter "agreed on a lot
of things," despite their difference in party. "We didn't have the
extreme progressive left wing [or] the extreme conservative right
wing at that time, although it was after Newt Gingrich came into
power . . . the Contract [with] America and all that," she recalled. By
1999 Republican congressman Gingrich, of Georgia, had served and
resigned as Speaker of the US House of Representatives, having
overseen an aggressive conservative reform agenda that, historians
and political scientists widely agree, catalyzed the polarization of
contemporary American politics.[6]

Maine lawmakers, meanwhile, "did some tax reform stuff, property tax relief measures," the governor remembered. "It was before
marriage equality but we worked a lot on domestic partnerships,"
including a 2004 state law that protected some rights and benefits for
same-sex couples.[7] Representative Mills "didn't feel politically ambitious at that time," but she served in the state legislature until 2008,
when colleagues and staff encouraged her to run for attorney
general. "I thought . . . why *not* me," she recounted. She had already
worked as an assistant AG in the Maine office in her first job after
law school and thought the top job looked "very attractive . . . like
being district attorney, only with broader jurisdiction." She also felt
she had an advantage with her fellow legislators as a candidate who
was one of their own — Maine is the only state where lawmakers
elect the attorney general; most states choose one by popular
election.[8]

Representative Mills won a majority of her colleagues' votes and
was the first woman to become Maine's top legal officer. In a speech
at her swearing-in ceremony, she told her audience: "I ran for office
because I believed I was the most qualified person for the job, and I
hope that history proves it so." She went on to say she had taken the
same oath as "the long line of Attorneys General down through
history," including fifty-five men who had served over the course of
nearly two centuries. In a play on her achievement as the sole woman

to become AG, she deadpanned that she was "the first and only Attorney General — from Franklin County." The line got a few laughs. She also pointed out that both her ninety-two-year-old mother and her six-year-old niece were present, and told them: "We are changing something about what is 'normal,' what is expected and of whom it is expected, here and around our country." In closing she thanked her husband, who had been "so patient and supportive."

Two years later AG Mills lost her bid for reelection in a Republican sweep when the party won majorities in both the Maine House and Senate, and voters elected Paul LePage as governor. Among the candidates he had defeated in the Republican primary was Peter Mills in his second failed gubernatorial bid. Governor LePage appointed him to run the state's Turnpike Authority. Janet Mills, now a private citizen, had loved her job as attorney general and wanted it back, so she became vice chair of the state Democratic Party. Then, while practicing law in the litigation department of a firm in Augusta, she "went around helping to recruit people to run for the legislature to get the majority back." In the next election, in 2012, Democrats regained control of the legislature, which voted to put Attorney General Mills back in office. She was in the middle of her term when her husband had a stroke.

By then Stan had also fought cancer three times. His health declined over the next year until he died in September 2014, exactly a month before his seventy-fourth birthday. In the course of his illness, the governor became "all too familiar with the ups and downs of the healthcare and health insurance system[s] in Maine."[9] She realized how well equipped she had been to manage it all, despite her grief. "Now, I am a lawyer. The Attorney General. I am no shrinking violet," she wrote in a speech two years later, as she looked back on the experience. "But what about other people who are faced with this paperwork, these phone calls, these nuisance denials intended to wear you down at a time when you are least able to cope with a crisis? What about those families?" She was determined to reform that system, to make healthcare in Maine more accessible and affordable, however many politicians had tried before.

Some of her earliest actions as governor would deliver on that goal, but the idea of running for higher office had yet to strike her in the first few months after Stan's death.

That December, during her first holiday season as a widow, AG Mills focused on her bid for reelection to a third term. When she accepted her party's nomination, she told state lawmakers in a speech that "we have the raw materials . . . this year, in this *citizen legislature*, to paint things of great beauty, despite non-unanimity, despite differences."[10] AG Mills had recently seen an exhibition of Jamie Wyeth's paintings and was struck by the way the artist chose simple subjects, "rocks and boxes, pigs and rams, barns, horses and seagulls," and made "masterpieces" from his interpretation of them. She saw a parallel between the work of running the state and Jamie's particular process of using raw materials to make his art. "What lesson can we learn from this master of multimedia?" she continued. "A man who crushes pearls to paint a starry sky; who mixes real straw with expensive oils to draw a bale of hay . . . a champion of the common thing?" She felt that the metaphor might be "a stretch" but deployed it fully nonetheless, as she often does in speeches. She concluded by sharing a personal story. "My husband Stan, the tennis player, who left us seventy days ago, told me every day, 'Just hit the ball over the net one more time,'" she told her colleagues, "so I am asking you for another term."[11]

She won reelection despite an even party split in the House and Senate by then, with Independent legislators tipping the vote in her favor.[12] She had also faced opposition from Governor LePage, who, she claimed, refused to swear her in publicly.[13] "Eventually somebody told him he had to," she recalled. "He did it off in some corner of the Cabinet Room somewhere." Governor LePage and Attorney General Mills had clashed repeatedly since her reelection two years before. She saw his refusal "to do the constitutional duty that he had," administering her oath of office, as part of his "frustrating" pattern of "unnecessary chaos and unnecessary lines in the sand being drawn." That pattern fueled her own interest in running for governor. "He would create these crises, one after another," she remembered, "and it frustrated me, as someone who believes . . .

that government can do good things — that anybody would purposefully obstruct the process of government and the integrity of public office just seemed unnecessary."

In turn, Governor LePage, who had campaigned on promises to curb state government, felt that Attorney General Mills had held him back repeatedly "from carrying out duties" that he judged to be "in the best interest of the people of Maine." In 2017 he sued her for declining to back his administration in several high-profile legal matters, including his attempt to block a federal requirement that the state provide Medicaid coverage for about seven thousand needy young adults. She had felt his argument in that instance "lacked legal merit" and sided with the federal government. The LePage administration lost the case and a subsequent appeal to the US Supreme Court.[14] AG Mills also joined an amicus brief with states that opposed President Trump's 2017 ban on travel to the US by residents of some predominantly Muslim countries.[15] Governor LePage supported those restrictions. The attorney general's actions, he argued, amounted to a "clear abuse of power."[16] In turn she dismissed his lawsuit as "frivolous" and reminded him that she was "an Independent Constitutional Officer" with a "duty to represent the public interest," citing a Maine Supreme Court ruling.[17]

Despite stark differences between the two politicians, they shared some defining ideology, as AG Mills pointed out in a speech after she was sworn in for her third term. "It's true, you probably won't catch Governor LePage and me sitting down sharing a glass of Chardonnay, eating Brie and watching *Downton Abbey* together," she quipped. "But I do respect the Chief Executive, and I do think we have some things in common: We both like 'straight talk.' We both speak our minds. We both believe in action. We both get upset when people steal from the public purse. We are both determined to end domestic violence. We both despise the drug dealers that are killing our youth. We both oppose the scams that rob our veterans of their hard-earned dollars. Like the old Jimmy Cliff song says, we've got 'many rivers to cross . . .' But we both believe, fundamentally, in the Rule of Law — the knowledge that our country is governed by laws, not by individuals."

A year and a half later, in the summer of 2017, she was in the midst of her third consecutive term as AG when she announced that she was running for governor. Eight other candidates had already joined the race, including Republicans, an Independent, a Libertarian, and a member of the Green Party.[18] "I'm the better qualified person of that group," she remembered thinking at the time. "That was it. Why not me? Not that I was born to run for governor or anything like that. Just the timing felt good . . . the opportunity, time and place." Part of that timing, as she told reporters when she launched her campaign, six months after Donald Trump was inaugurated as president, was her belief that voters wanted "leadership that brings people together . . . that doesn't divide them, doesn't polarize them."[19] She could not have conceived of one day having to make the choice to literally separate Maine people from one another to protect them from a global pandemic, a crisis that most Americans believed "only exacerbated existing political polarization" — in August 2020, a majority thought the country "had become more divided" because of COVID-19 "and the racial and social justice protests sweeping the country."[20] The Battleground Civility Poll, an annual bipartisan survey of the nation's registered voters, found that "seventy percent . . . sympathize with the cause of the summer protests" but "majorities of Republicans (61%), Independents (63%), and Democrats (55%) all thought politics grew less civil over the summer. And, most voters (59%) think things have gotten less civil during the COVID-19 crisis overall."

Some opponents of the Mills administration had dispensed with civility before the pandemic, freely and obscenely expressing their discontent in forms and forums ranging from bumper stickers, license plates, and T-shirts printed with various iterations of FUCK MILLS to a Facebook group called "Janet Mill's [sic] Memes" that drew more than ten thousand followers to its posts, which paired photos of the governor with messages that were vulgar or critical, or both.[21] When criticism of her leadership broadened and intensified during the pandemic, she understood people's frustration but rejected any implication that she relished imposing restrictions on their lives. "Who wants to be the governor who shuts down funerals and weddings and graduations and Fourth of July parades and . . . picnics and bars? Nobody wants to be that person." Those judgment calls were precursors, moreover, to some of the most difficult and controversial decisions she knew she would have to make, including plans to distribute vaccines that were still in development, as well as who would be first to receive them and how to overcome potential public resistance.

The subject of civility weighed heavily on Ashirah's mind when she wrote to Governor Mills on August 1, 2020. "Thank you so much for your strong leadership at this time, and thank you to your staff," the letter started. Touching on the controversies of July, Ashirah mentioned that she knew a sea kayaking guide whose scheduled trip with the governor had recently been canceled, "but what he wanted to tell you was that he appreciates your saying what needs to be said and not worrying about reelection." She added that she "certainly" hoped Governor Mills would "run again and be elected again" despite the fact that "the things we all say and do now will echo for years." That week Ashirah had gotten "very good pointers" from an older man she respected, on "when to speak up . . . or to not rock the boat." He advised her to know her "purpose in speaking, know the audience [and] allow the other side to save face," as well as to "be kind if possible." Ashirah came away from the conversation feeling emboldened to trust her own instincts. "My whole adult life I have been very conscious of seeing everyone's side and speaking deliberately so as not to offend anyone," she wrote. "At the risk of being conceited, I think I've got that lesson and now I want to focus on using my voice more."

She also mentioned in the letter that she had just ordered a homeschool curriculum for her children, who were "really looking forward to doing more challenging work this year." The local school system had "not been doing that for our kids," Ashirah explained, with the caveat that she knew the district was "constrained, as most schools are." She knew the loss of "the social part" would be difficult for Owen and Pamela, but the Knapps were unhappy with "the safety situation" and worried what might happen "when everyone's shut up inside all day [even] with masks on." They felt that homeschooling was "better in the end" because "the stress of COVID would be incredible." Ashirah had been doing research about reusable masks and face shields to use for shopping in stores and when she returned to work at the addiction medicine clinic. "I also discovered that you can buy adhesive nosebands and I've been offering these so people can tighten the noses on their cloth masks," she wrote. "It's not enough but it's what I can do."

Before the pandemic, August on the Knapps' homestead had been one of their busiest months, between hosting students and apprentices and tending their gardens in the heat of peak summer. In a year with normal rainfall "there's a lot of food coming in" through the month, Ashirah explained, "all the fresh garden food you could ever want." During the summer of 2020, though, some areas of Maine counted a record number of days with no rain. Farmers in much of the state were struggling to salvage crops, especially those with no irrigation, including Ashirah and Chris.[22] In northern Maine some sought emergency approval to graze livestock on conservation lands; others who faced a lack of hay were forced to sell cattle. The drought was also among the factors blamed for curbing Maine's annual wild blueberry harvest, which yielded just over forty-seven million pounds, about half the previous year's bounty.[23] The state produced 99 percent of the wild blueberries sold in the US, and thousands of migrant workers came from in and out of state every year to help pick them.[24] They lived and worked in close proximity, both in the fields and in communal housing, so growers tested workers for COVID-19 as they began arriving toward the end of July. By the 4th of August the state had confirmed twenty-three cases, but those workers were being treated, and a total of fifty were isolated in temporary housing.[25]

Another looming concern was an influx of thousands of students from other states who would arrive at the end of the month on more than thirty public, private, and community college campuses in Maine, bringing increased risk to host towns.[26] Their return would also bring much-needed income for stores and restaurants that depended on student spending. To minimize losses restaurant owners around the state had cut staff, reduced hours of operation, and increased outdoor dining capacity. In turn, cities and towns "one by one allowed the restaurants to expand onto the sidewalks and the streets, which was great," Governor Mills remembered. "That was a different dynamic and a successful one." Many restaurants also took advantage of an executive order she had signed in April that allowed them to sell beer, wine, and cocktails as take-out items. That order helped the owner of a barbecue restaurant in Maine's largest city stay in business — he claimed that 20 percent of his revenue since the pandemic started had come from sales of his signature margarita.[27] Unlike many of the governor's pandemic executive orders, if not most, the take-out cocktail measure was so popular that state lawmakers proposed bipartisan legislation to extend it for two years.[28]

One group of restaurant owners who had sued Governor Mills over pandemic restrictions lost their case in early August when a federal judge in Maine, who had been appointed by President Trump, granted the governor's motion to dismiss the lawsuit. In the judge's decision he acknowledged that the restrictions were "burdensome" but wrote that the plaintiffs had not shown "a present violation of their constitutional rights that warrants injunctive relief; not while the Nation is scrambling to adapt to an unprecedented pandemic that is believed to have killed more than 150,000 Americans in four months and caused debilitating illness for many survivors."[29] The judge added that the "collective crisis ought to have imposed a sense of collective humility given the long shadow cast by all that we do not know about the disease." He then quipped, in a reference to the ancient Greek philosophy that much knowledge is unattainable, "We might hope that Socratic wisdom is making a comeback." The lead plaintiff in the case was Rick Savage, the brewpub owner who had read the governor's cellphone number on national television several months earlier, during his appearance on a Fox News show.[30] He was not among the plaintiffs who appealed the judge's order later that month.[31]

Governor Mills had long since turned her attention from the constitutionality of her administration's early pandemic restrictions to the actions it could take to limit their economic consequences. In early August she directed a second round of federal pandemic aid to dozens of municipalities and tribal governments to help them pay for COVID-19 signage, protective equipment, enforcement staff, and other costs of preventing the pandemic's spread.[32] Another round of financial relief, $200 million in the form of economic recovery grants, was planned for later in the month — "meaningful relief" for "the small farms, the fishermen, the Mom & Pop stores, the diners, the [B&Bs], the motels, stores and local family businesses" that were, the governor said, "the backbone of our economy and the lifeblood of our communities."[33] Meanwhile, she implored Mainers to "step up and be counted" in the 2020 US Census, which would determine federal funding "to begin the long path to recovery" from the pandemic.[34] By that point only about half of the state's households had participated, despite a first-ever online option. Governor Mills warned that an undercount could also affect legislative districts and cost the state billions of dollars for services based on population, ranging from school lunch programs and student loan relief to healthcare and road maintenance. The census was "much more than just a head-count," the governor explained in her first August radio address. "It is a critical measure that will help ensure our state's voice is heard in the years to come."

On the second Saturday of the month, Ashirah wrote to say she was "relieved and grateful" that Maine was "doing so well" at limiting the pandemic's spread. She was "[a] little confused as to why," since there had been "so much movement against mask-wearing here," but she wanted the governor to know that more people were now wearing face coverings in the Temple and Farmington area. That week Ashirah had attended a public meeting by videoconference with officials from her local school district. The Knapps had submitted the required state paperwork to homeschool their children, but Ashirah was impressed by the district's plans for returning students to classrooms that fall. "It sounds like the schools are trying and this is just a difficult situation all around," she wrote. She planned to email the district to ask whether education technicians, who were "at the very bottom of the pecking order," would have the protective equipment they needed to work with special needs students who may not be willing or able to wear face coverings. Ashirah saw this as "an immediate need right here" despite the fact that there was "much valid advocacy to be done in the world." The issue had raised her awareness of "different people's . . . inability to wear a mask," but Ashirah suspected that "this gets used as an excuse not to wear one too often."

Near the middle of August, the world's COVID-19 case count reached twenty million. The number had doubled in just six weeks, after taking six months to reach ten million cases. On that unnerving day Governor Mills took heart from presidential candidate Joe Biden's announcement that he had chosen US senator Kamala Harris as his vice presidential running mate. "She's black, Asian, a woman, oh, and smart!" the governor wrote in her journal, adding that Senator Harris was "a bit of a street fighter, like Biden." The two women had served as their states' attorneys general, concurrently from 2013 until 2017. They both signed onto legal actions against predatory mortgage lenders, schools that harassed student borrowers, pharmaceutical companies that unlawfully marketed prescription drugs, and the Environmental Protection Agency over inadequate regulatory enforcement, to name a few.[35] In public comments on the senator's historic selection, Governor Mills attested: "I know firsthand her leadership qualities, her intelligence, and her commitment to American values."[36] A week later, at the Democratic Party's first-ever virtual nominating convention, Senator Harris became the first woman of color, as well as the first person of Indian descent, to be nominated for vice president.[37]

Around that time, Governor Mills visited her camp to see the results of recent structural work to reinforce the old house. She reported in her journal that the building was "level at last" with "doors that open and close," and closets she could finally use. "The house feels new and good and the karma is good." She remembered a sense that "the camp was saying 'yes, I feel like I'm not tumbling down anymore.'" The governor spent a couple of nights alone there, marveling at the annual spectacle put on by the Perseid meteor showers. "One big one, the largest shooting star I've ever seen, right over my head as I swam off the dock after dark," she wrote.

Ashirah was sleeping under the same starry show that week while camping with Chris and their children in western Maine, beside a lake whose depths held the remains of two ghost towns. In the late 1940s the former settlements of Flagstaff and Dead River had been emptied of their two hundred residents — and the graves of their dead disinterred — so that the Central Maine Power Company could close the gates of its new hydroelectric dam and submerge what was left of the towns.[38] The reservoir that formed in their place, Flagstaff Lake, was the Knapps' base camp for their annual summer vacation, as Ashirah told Governor Mills in a letter. "We found the most incredibly beautiful boat access campsite, with a big pebble beach and lovely swimming," she wrote, adding that she would not be able to mail her letter until she returned to Temple. Ashirah was still resting from a back injury that gave her "new respect and empathy for people who live with constant pain," but she hoped to join the rest of her family for some hiking and biking. She was also reading, and loving, the adventure novel *Kidnapped* by Robert Louis Stevenson, in preparation for teaching lessons on the book that fall as part of her son Owen's homeschool curriculum.

Ashirah had recently arranged for him to take algebra as a remote student with the local school in the fall "because we are not strong in that subject." She had learned that the school would reopen with a hybrid model of both in-person and remote instruction. "I feel less out-in-front alone in my decision to homeschool with the school system itself taking major precautions," she wrote. To end her dispatch, Ashirah reported that "nearly everyone wore a mask" in the town where her family had stopped for groceries and gas on their way to the lake. That changed a few days later, when they moved to a new campsite and biked to the nearest town for ice cream. Ashirah noticed there that most tourists were wearing masks while "the local folks looked mainly like they weren't." On hiking trails, she added, people made an effort at keeping social distance but "hardly anyone seemed to get it fully" — either stepping only a few feet off the trail or standing right beside it, wearing masks but "panting on us as we went by." She allowed that some caution, at least, was "a lot more than nothing," but she could not understand "why six feet is such a hurdle."

That week Ashirah added to her letter every few days, as if she was keeping a journal: "I'm [two-thirds] through *Kidnapped* and having fun reading aloud to the kids here and there." She was enjoying the challenge of interpreting what she was reading "fast enough to emphasize it correctly to help the kids understand the unusual language." The Knapps went back to Temple a few days later and Ashirah finished her letter from the homestead. "It was lovely to leave for a while and now is good to be back," she told Governor Mills. "I hope you get to have some breaks, as well." She dated the letter August 22, 2020, the weekend before Ashirah planned to start homeschooling with Owen and Pamela. She would also still be working from home for the addiction medicine clinic.

She added that her husband was set to resume his graduate studies that fall — Chris was in his "third year of a two-year program" as he joked, "doing a master's in environmental education." He had convinced a liberal arts college in New Hampshire to accept him without a bachelor's degree. "I told them, 'You've got to look at life experience.'" By then he had been an outdoor educator for more than a decade. For his thesis, Chris planned to design an educational experience on the homestead that would "formalize" the Knapps' apprenticeship program into a credit-bearing college semester for young people, ages eighteen to twenty-eight, "who are aware that the world that we're inhabiting is not working out ecologically and socially" and "are searching for ways to apply their values." The course would teach practical skills that have a positive effect on daily life, including small actions like composting human waste. "We're not just pooping," Chris explained. "If we're making thermophilic compost then we have the potential of building the fertility of . . . this little tiny microcosm ecosystem, so that's hopeful. It feels meaningful."

With Chris focusing on his coursework, Ashirah knew her fall days would be long and full. "Deep breath . . . I can do this . . ." she wrote, maybe as much to herself as to Governor Mills. Then she signed off and sent the letter, her longest yet, to Augusta. It crossed in the mail that week with another response from the governor. "Ashirah, I hope you and your family are doing well," she wrote, adding that summer weather, "other than the drought," had "lifted

up spirits across the state." Maine was "still a safe place to be
compared to nearly all other states," she noted. The governor hoped
the Knapps' children were "getting outside a lot" and "reading some
good books." Like their mother, they were "destined to be good and
thoughtful writers."

The note was dated August 25, the same day that an exasperated
Governor Mills pleaded with Mainers not to "attend or organize large
gatherings, indoors or outdoors."[39] A woman from Maine had died of
the virus the week before, after being exposed to one of sixty-five
people who attended an indoor wedding reception in the northeastern town of Millinocket earlier in the month. Guests' temperatures
had been taken and some showed proof that they tested negative for
COVID-19, but they did not wear masks and the inn did not follow
state guidelines for social distancing.[40] A regional hospital tested more
than 360 people who were either guests at the event or had contact
with them — more than 30 were positive, and counting. "We have got
to protect our health and the health of our families," the governor
admonished in her final August radio address.[41] She knew that people
were "getting tired . . . impatient and anxious maybe. We all are. But
we cannot let down our guard." By the end of the month, the wedding
was linked to infections of at least 123 people, including dozens of
inmates and staff at a county jail more than two hundred miles away
from where it took place, as well as employees and residents of a rehabilitation facility for seniors more than one hundred miles away. One
of those residents, an eighty-three-year-old woman, died of COVID-
19.[42] "One little match can spark a big fire that we might be unable to
put out," the governor warned, adding that the end of summer
marked "a new phase of reopening" with the return of students to
classrooms. "Don't take a chance."

The last few days of August brought some light rain to Temple,
as well as some mail from Augusta.[43] "We just received your note,
thank you!" Ashirah wrote in her response to the governor. "I hope
my weekly letters are not boring or burdening and I apologize . . .
for the stream-of-consciousness style!" Her first week of homeschooling had gone well, and she was "so excited to be in control of
the curriculum" so she could "push the kids in areas they need it and

. . . slow down and dig in where they are struggling." She added that she knew a woman who was questioning whether to send her children back to classrooms in the local school. "It was nice to be able to put her mind at ease with [regard] to her ability to homeschool (if that's what they decide)," Ashirah wrote. She thanked Governor Mills for her "ongoing work" and shared a hope: "that you get . . . chances to take time to rejuvenate, so that you can continue to have energy to lead us during this time."

When Ashirah mailed her last August letter, the governor was on an island off midcoast Maine, where she had rented a house through Labor Day weekend. "It was just far enough from shore to feel private, but there [were] people there," she remembered. The island's year-round population was about four hundred, which swelled during summers, and Governor Mills was staying in the town center. It was a working holiday — she made calls, answered emails, kept up with the news — but she took a break from "speech-making, speech-giving, scheduling, Zoom meetings, all that stuff." She added, though, that she had been getting "to do more as governor, honestly, during the pandemic, because we did so much by Zoom," instead of traveling to and from meetings.

By the end of August she was content to do less, if only for a week. She hosted some small, socially distant picnics and dinners for friends. "People were dropping in, sitting on the porch," she remembered. "My staff came . . . and we hung out. It was fun." In theory she could relax and feel proud of her administration and Mainers for having salvaged something of a tourism season while maintaining the country's second lowest COVID-19 infection rate.[44] Still, she knew the pandemic would continue to test her administration, with schools attempting to bring students back to classrooms and the return of cold weather that would drive people indoors, increasing the risk of spreading the virus. Also looming was the unprecedented challenge of holding the 2020 presidential election safely and legally. The closing weeks of the first pandemic summer had been something of a break for most Mainers, after long months of restraint. For at least a few more days their governor needed some peace, and she found it "just sitting there watching the ocean come and go."

CHAPTER FIVE

"... this feels like the end of the world."

September 1 was staff orientation day at a Christian academy in the southern Maine city of Sanford. The school was run by a Baptist pastor, Todd Bell, in affiliation with Calvary Baptist, a church he had started there.[1] Pastor Bell had officiated the August wedding that the Maine CDC was now investigating as a COVID-19 super-spreader event. At some point on that orientation day he wrote in a post on his public Twitter account that it was "thrilling to see how God is advancing in the midst of everything around us! Glory to God! #ChristianEducation."[2] His tweet included a picture of him standing at a podium, addressing more than a dozen people. They sat closely together around long tables facing him. No one in the room was wearing a mask. As a private academy, Sanford Christian was exempt from a new state requirement that all public school educators, staff, and students ages five and above wear face coverings when indoors.[3] In a second post that day Pastor Bell added that while "so many people and so many things are quarantined," he was "glad the word of God is not quarantined!" Later that week the Maine CDC announced a second death from a COVID-19 infection linked to the wedding and dozens of new cases in the same county as Pastor Bell's church.[4] Ten were among his congregation, including his father.[5] State education officials advised the county's schools that the outbreak made it unsafe for them to reopen for in-person learning.[6] Maine CDC director Dr. Shah reported that 144 cases had now been linked "in some way shape or form with that August seventh wedding."[7]

Pastor Bell was usually dressed in a suit and tie in photos of him that were posted on his social media accounts and the websites of his various ministries. He mostly wore one of two expressions: gravely serious when preaching, or an extremely enthusiastic smile, to the point of drastic. He was tall and thickset, with a fleshy face and dark hair that was graying at the sides. He spoke with a strong southern accent, having spent most of his life below the Mason-Dixon line, according to his parish biography.[8] Born in Florida, he was "saved at the age of six" and went on to train and work as a machinist in North Carolina before earning an undergraduate degree in theology there and a doctorate of divinity in Tennessee. In the early 1990s "God called Pastor Bell and his family to the state of Maine" to "plant" churches, including the one in East Millinocket, where he officiated the August wedding.

Pastor Bell and his wife, Amy, had flown to the nuptials in his private plane, a Cessna 310 registered to his "Wings with the Word, Inc. aviation ministry." They made the trip three days after he was a featured speaker at a regional Baptist ministry convention in Rhode Island, where the coronavirus positivity rate was still higher than Maine's.[9] He would not have had time before the wedding to quarantine for the recommended fourteen days. The ceremony was held the next day in East Millinocket, a tiny town in the North Maine Woods, about sixty miles from the US-Canada border.[10] The bride and groom, who had flown in from California, complied with the state's requirement that they test negative for COVID-19 so they would not have to quarantine for two weeks.[11] They exchanged vows at a Baptist church founded by Pastor Bell and his wife in 1996 — the first of more than half a dozen churches the Bells started around the state.[12] The bride's parents were part of its founding congregation, and one of the Bells' daughters was a bridesmaid.[13]

After the ceremony, a reception was held about seventeen miles away at the Big Moose Inn, a complex of sporting camps with a public restaurant. The inn was next door to a trading post and a raft trip outfitter, on a scant strip of land between two lakes. The town had no reported coronavirus cases before the wedding.[14] Its remote location might have given the hundred or so people involved in the ceremony and reception a false sense of invulnerability. Despite the inn's posted signs informing visitors that masks were required, the guests did not comply. By coincidence, on the same day as the event, a Gallup poll was released that found nearly nine in ten Americans always or usually wore masks in indoor settings.[15] The wedding guests also ignored a requirement to maintain social distance, and the venue's staff did not enforce either mandate. The number of guests at the reception exceeded the state's fifty-person limit for indoor gatherings. Some precautions were taken, including mask-wearing by inn employees, but eventually half of those who took part in the events that day, in any capacity, tested positive for COVID-19.[16]

By the end of August, dozens of secondary and tertiary infections — at the jail in the same Maine county as Pastor Bell's church, and the senior rehabilitation facility in another county — had been epidemiologically linked to the wedding, along with the first death, a woman who had not attended the event. The state's CDC was also investigating rising coronavirus infections among congregants at the Bells' church. The agency warned that anyone who had attended services there or at the ministry's Bible school had potentially been exposed to the coronavirus. The county was now at the center of half of Maine's active outbreaks.[17] This was the disaster scenario that Governor Mills and her administration had taken drastic measures of unprecedented proportion to try to prevent. In response to those measures, untold hundreds of thousands of Mainers had radically altered their behavior to protect themselves and others, to say nothing of the sacrifices of healthcare and other essential workers who risked their lives to keep the public safe from the pandemic.

The story of "the Maine wedding" was picked up by national media outlets, both conservative and liberal-leaning, and reported as the latest in a succession of shocking pandemic cautionary tales.[18] It also underscored the deepening ideological divide between Americans who believed the costs of enduring extreme precautions and other disruptions caused by the pandemic were justified by the potential benefits — including lives saved and other outcomes that could never be known or quantified — and those who no longer felt that way, or never had. For many of those who had set aside supposedly irreconcilable differences en masse to fight the same microscopic foe, any rapprochement was brief. By the end of the summer of 2020 the battle against COVID-19 had become a proxy war for the country's polarized political, cultural, and moral factions. As the poet Archibald

MacLeish wrote in a resonant 1956 commencement speech at Smith College, "by shouting that 'those who are not with us are against us'" it was "as if the difference between human liberty and human degradation were no more than a choosing of political sides."[19]

For Pastor Bell, that difference was a question of faith, but his sermons and social media posts had political undertones. "I am going to trust one, who is in all and over all and through all," he told his congregation in a sermon at the end of August.[20] "He's the one that has the power to remove pestilences." He added that "the people of God" should wear a mask, or even "a nuclear fallout suit," if they wanted to. "We will laugh at you, but we will let you wear a nuclear fallout suit." He went on to preach that "if you want to have the liberty to have done your own research," wearing a mask was "kind of like trying to keep a mosquito out of a chain-link fence."[21] He also warned his flock that COVID-19 vaccines, which were still in development, made use of "aborted baby tissue," an inaccurate reference to fetal cells derived from elective abortions, that gave rise to current laboratory cell lines used in vaccine development and testing.[22] Pastor Bell was indignant about media portrayals that he felt mischaracterized him and distorted his role in the outbreak. He told one Maine newspaper that journalists "seek fear and drama not truth!"[23] In turn, the press noted his lack of any expression of remorse for having participated in an event that was confirmed to have spread COVID-19, or even apparent sympathy for those who were sickened or died.[24] As the outbreak grew, Pastor Bell stopped speaking to reporters and hired a lawyer but continued to lead in-person worship services, and his church's choir kept singing, face coverings not required.[25]

Pastor Bell's actions were "very frustrating" to Governor Mills. "On the one hand we had a lot of people who were trying to stay safe and do the right thing, who were just terribly mad and emailing me, wanting me to somehow prosecute him," she remembered. "On the other hand you had his followers who felt he was following his own conscience, or whatever." The governor and her staff "had a lot of discussions about what to do," but the state had "no licensing authority over churches," and the pastor had not yet been found in violation of her pandemic-related executive orders. "He was baiting us," she recalled. "In a very weird way he was baiting us to take him on, and it was a fine line . . . nobody wanted to make a martyr of him." Governor Mills felt that "the guy obviously had an ego" and was "kind of a self-promoter" who "would take advantage" of any action against him to "just enhance his own visibility." Her administration instead scrutinized operations at public facilities where the state had authority "to step in."

The Maine CDC's investigations of wedding-related cases at the rehabilitation center and the jail traced the outbreaks at both facilities to employees who had worked shifts despite having COVID-19 symptoms.[26] The rehab center employee, a parent of a wedding guest, was a certified nursing assistant who arrived for a ten-hour overnight shift and wrote in a logbook that she had chills, muscle aches, a cough, and a sore throat.[27] The log was not reviewed, and the woman did not report her symptoms to a supervisor. State health officials cited the facility for the failures and set conditions for its continued operation, including the potential loss of Medicare and Medicaid funding.[28] The jail employee had attended the wedding, then put in two eight-hour shifts at two separate facilities while showing symptoms of COVID-19.[29] The CDC report found that staff had not been screened daily for symptoms at either location. Neither was mask-wearing enforced. In the outbreak that followed, four dozen inmates were infected, as well as forty-three workers and sixteen members of their households.[30] The state's department of corrections subsequently checked all county jails for compliance with pandemic protocols. Meanwhile, Dr. Shah reiterated to the religious community that "some of the things that can generate COVID-19" were "literally the reasons you go to church for — fellowship, close camaraderie, singing."[31] Governor Mills reminded Mainers ad nauseam about the urgent need to keep taking precautions. She recalled an earlier COVID-19 outbreak in Washington State, in March 2020, when two church choir practices spread the virus to 87 percent of the group's members, three of whom died.[32] "We didn't want that to happen," she noted, "but, you know, there's only so much you can do."

A different Christian organization that housed recovering addicts in southern Maine had sued Governor Mills in the spring to block her pandemic restrictions but lost its case in May. "The state is managing an extraordinary array of issues," Judge Nancy Torreson wrote in her decision, "and it has responded to the challenges raised by COVID-19 by establishing uniform standards and restrictions based on evolving scientific evidence. Upsetting the careful balance being drawn by Maine's governor at this time would have an adverse effect on the public interest."[33] The church's founder appealed, and his case was pending in federal court that fall.[34] His organization and Pastor Bell's were among a minority of religious groups, in Maine and the country as a whole, whose leaders had publicly challenged pandemic restrictions. By late July the US Supreme Court had ruled against two in other states, a Christian church in Nevada and one in California.[35] An August survey by the Pew Research Center had found that eight in ten Americans believed "houses of worship should be required to follow the same rules about social distancing and large gatherings as other organizations or businesses."[36] The poll also noted that "a two-thirds majority of Republicans" shared that view, despite the fact that "Democrats and those who lean toward the Democratic Party are substantially more likely ... to say houses of worship should be required to follow the same social distancing rules as other organizations."

By September most of Maine's religious groups had long since pivoted to providing worship services online in some form, or as drive-in or socially distanced outdoor gatherings, or both.[37] Their leaders recalled facing little resistance to the temporary loss of communal rituals, other than parishioners' disappointment. The president of the Maine Council of Churches found "nothing but support" and "a lot of patience" among her membership, as she recalled in a group interview that spring with representatives from the state's Muslim, Jewish, and Christian communities on Maine Public Radio. She explained that "mainline Christianity basically respects everyone, not only ... in our congregation but the surround-ing community," including nonbelievers. She added that "we take science seriously and we value all lives as precious and worthy of respectful protection from exposure to a deadly, dreadful virus."[38]

The number of COVID-19 cases stemming from the East Millinocket wedding continued to rise through the first week of September, ahead of the Labor Day holiday. In a media briefing just before the long weekend, Dr. Shah told reporters he was "concerned" that the outbreaks had "the potential to spiral" and affect surrounding areas. He emphasized that "really, truly, face coverings coupled with physical distance are two of the strongest pieces that we've got in our armamentarium" for reducing transmission and that "if everyone were to do that, we could get a grip on COVID-19 not just statewide . . . but nationwide." Weather forecasters predicted warm, sunny days through the weekend and the Monday holiday, with no chance of rain to spoil the unofficial end of summer.[39]

In Temple, Ashirah's parents arrived on the homestead just before Labor Day weekend. "It is so wonderful to have them," she gushed in a letter to Governor Mills, admitting that she had "only cried a little" when she first saw them. "We are all soaking up the family time and I will pull energy from it for a long time to come." She noted that they would "be respectful" of the governor's fourteen-day quarantine requirement for out-of-state visitors. Ashirah went on to report that homeschooling had been "going (pretty) well" so far. She was "very happy with the level of work" both children were doing, though they were still adjusting to having her as "a teacher and not 'mom.'" In math lessons Pamela was struggling to master multiplication of double and triple numbers and would protest: "That's not wrong, mom!" When Ashirah showed her the correct answer on a calculator, Pamela was unmoved: "Well, the calculator is wrong!" Ashirah was "laughing now," but at the time she could not believe her "wonderful, smart, strong daughter . . . was arguing with a calculator's answer."

From there her letter turned to something "unforgivable" that Ashirah had seen that day at a local laundry — two women who worked in elder care facilities in the area were "discussing their jobs at less than [six feet] for about ten minutes" without wearing masks. Ashirah fumed that she had been wondering "how in the world" the virus was "still getting into nursing homes" — just before she wrote that week's letter, the state had announced the death of a third person at the senior rehabilitation facility where an outbreak had been linked to the August wedding. "What those women were doing was awful," she wrote. "They have people's lives in their hands!" Ashirah had a tendency to, as she put it, "come up with both fists" when she saw "something wrong" or disagreed with someone, whether that person was her husband or the president of the United States. She did not "go through life seeking out conflict," she explained, but "when you're raised . . . in any form of Judaism . . . you always hear about the Holocaust and you always hear you can't ever be quiet, you have to speak up." Both of her parents, she added, had modeled a willing-ness to take risks that Ashirah attributed to their confidence in their intuition. Her father, she felt, had created a professional niche for himself that combined teaching Jewish laws and traditions with his love of the natural world, "even though it means no job security." She also admired her mother's decision to go back to school in her sixties and upgrade her professional nursing credentials from licensed prac-tical nurse to registered nurse. Ashirah pointed to her own interests, especially in her mentor Ray Reitze's teachings, as having shaped her "strong standpoint . . . about what I think is true in the world." She explained that during her apprenticeship with Ray, whom Ashirah and Chris referred to as Grandfather, he guided her in learning both to recognize her "gut feeling" and "to say 'yes it is true.'" She believed that "a mixture of all of those things . . . make the two fists come up" in the face of injustice.

Ashirah closed her Labor Day letter with a note on "the happier side" — she had seen "people all over . . . wearing masks all the time" on the campus of the University of Maine in nearby Farmington, the governor's hometown. Ashirah had heard the school was "serious about sending people home if necessary" — in early September two schools in the state reported cases spread by off-campus parties where students had ignored pandemic safety precautions.[40] Many other colleges and universities were managing small COVID-19 outbreaks despite screening students and staff on their arrival. As campuses had reopened around the country, the schools' strategies for detecting the virus varied widely. In Maine the public university system reported a

dozen positive cases by the first day of September. One of its graduate schools hosted a webinar about the pandemic that week, featuring the governor's sister Dora, in light of her work in the state's
largest integrated health system and as former director of Maine's
CDC.[41] She warned that reopening so many schools in succession,
from kindergarten through college, was "like putting a little gasoline
on these sparks," adding that "we just want to make sure to keep the
fuel level as low as possible." She also mentioned ongoing outbreaks
stemming from the August wedding in East Millinocket, but she
hailed the state's efforts to limit the spread of COVID-19 as otherwise
"a tremendous success story." She added, on a personal note, that her
mother "used to have us go around at the dinner table at night and
share roses and thorns" — the most positive and negative thing about
each family member's day — "and she always made sure that we
ended with a rose." Dora applied the metaphor to the state's first
pandemic summer: "The thorn is the cautionary tale of the wedding,
but the rose is really that we also had thousands of young people who
came to [four summer camps in] Maine from almost every state in
the nation . . . and we had not one outbreak of COVID-19."[42]

Meanwhile, her older sister's administration was in the process of
establishing another new set of pandemic protections. This batch
sought to ensure the integrity of the November general election and
minimize the risk of COVID-19 infection for poll workers, election
officials, and the higher-than-normal number of voters who were
expected to take part, especially by absentee ballot. A record 185,000
people had voted absentee in Maine's July primary, and the secretary
of state predicted that nearly half a million people would do so in
November. By early September 120,000 requests for the ballots had
already been submitted, about 60 percent of them from Democrats.
Governor Mills used another executive order to further amend some
election protocols, in part due to lessons the state learned in July. At
that time primary voters had been allowed to request absentee
ballots as late as Election Day, which posed challenges for some
precincts; in November the deadline would be five days before the
election. Her order also allowed poll workers to begin counting
absentee ballots seven days early, instead of four.[43]

To help manage the expected influx, and to reduce reliance on an already overtaxed US Postal Service, the governor had in June authorized cities and towns to install official ballot drop boxes for both of that year's elections. More than two-thirds of the states, including Maine, planned to use the boxes ahead of the November general election, despite growing political controversy over security and other concerns.[44] In late August, President Trump had called drop boxes "a voter security disaster" in a tweet that was labeled with a "public interest notice" for violating Twitter's policy against "false or misleading information intended to intimidate or dissuade people from participating in an election or other civic process."[45] The president later encouraged Republicans in California who were facing legal action for setting up unofficial ballot drop boxes.[46] Meanwhile, manufacturers could not keep up with demand.[47]

When Governor Mills heard about the shortage, she believed the boxes could be made in Maine, so she called a friend who taught architectural and engineering design in the state's community college system. "Within, like, forty-eight hours he had one designed," she remembered, "and I thought, what an inventive mind." Early in the pandemic the same professor had designed a device that would allow multiple COVID-19 patients to use a single ventilator, in response to a nationwide shortage of the machines.[48] His mock-up for the ballot drop boxes could be fabricated quickly from folded and welded sheet metal.[49] The boxes could then be mounted on the side of a building or bolted to the ground to deter unauthorized removal. They were also weather- and tamper-resistant, with a narrow deposit slot and two lockable doors. A Maine company that specialized in manufacturing barbecue smokers, Humphrey's BBQ Inc., won an expedited state contract to make the units. Employees at Humphrey's put in "ungodly hours" and "a lot of personal sacrifice" to finish orders for delivery in October.[50] The company "pumped out dozens and dozens" of the boxes, the governor recalled, "and transported them all over the state." She added, with excitement in her voice, that the project "was kind of fun."

The governor took a break from recording a weekly radio address while she was away from Augusta over the long Labor Day holiday weekend, but she returned to local airwaves in the second week of September. Her address laid out a plan for balancing the state's budget for that fiscal year, despite a predicted shortfall caused by the pandemic. Her administration and state lawmakers were also expecting a major decline in revenue from Maine's sales and use tax as a consequence of the governor's restrictions on business operations and tourist travel.[51] In the spring she had asked all state government departments, agencies, and public institutions to find "possible savings in things that could minimize the impact to our hardworking state employees and to the critical services that Maine people rely on." Now her budget chief had also recommended drawing on "higher than anticipated revenue from historic alcohol sales over the years," as well as federal coronavirus relief aid. "Importantly this proposal does not touch the rainy day fund," Governor Mills told listeners, adding that the state would need further "support from Congress . . . to spare our state from more hard choices." She would "continue to join the chorus of governors across the country, bipartisan voices" calling for more federal aid so she could "chart a full economic recovery for the people of our state."

The first official day of fall was still more than a week away, but an inevitable change had already taken place in Maine — that subtle shift in the way the light glinted a little less brightly off the ocean and lakes and the more conspicuous fact of much earlier sunsets. On the second weekend of September 2020 some Mainers woke up to forty-degree weather. In the area near Temple the temperature was thirty-six degrees that Saturday morning. For the Knapps, the arrival of fall had always been "this wonderful time of bringing in the bounty," but the drought diminished their harvest that year. They also gathered acorns in the woods to grind for flour and raked truckloads of fallen leaves for garden mulch. Shorter days meant the family had to "think about electricity more," with their solar energy system generating less power. The arrival of colder weather also meant that Ashirah had to "figure out what the kids [were] outgrowing" and how and where she would "buy their next size up of boots or their next set up of snow gear."

On that first chilly day, September 12, she made time to write her weekly letter to Governor Mills. Ashirah shared that it had been "beyond wonderful" to have her parents visit. She had been enjoying "all the normal aspects of having them here for a long visit," but especially during the pandemic, when she found it "soothing and energizing to really be with other people." Her son had told her that every time he heard "voices coming down our trail" he would remind himself to stay at a social distance, until he remembered "that it's grandma and grandpa and I don't need to!" His observation was "heartbreaking" for Ashirah "as a mom," but she recognized that her family was "really in a good place" despite what her children had "gone through with the pandemic." The Knapps had "plenty of food and water, huge outdoor spaces to spend time in," and "enough money that we can get by without doing anything that feels unsafe," as well as "the ability to homeschool this year" and, "of course, the strength of family and a few good friends." She ended her letter "with a joke from my dad" about the state's new road signs that had been printed with official warnings about Maine's pandemic restrictions. Ashirah had told him she was worried the signs were expensive and would one day "need to be trashed" because "the laws might change at any time." Her father told her to write to the governor and "strongly" suggest that the state "make sure it had invested in some bottles of spray paint" so the signs could be reused. Ashirah added: "That's my dad."

A few days later the Maine CDC announced the deaths of four more people in the state whose COVID-19 infections had been linked to the August wedding. The total was now seven, and none of those people had attended the event. Dr. Shah also reported that members of Pastor Bell's congregation were confirmed to have been among the guests.[52] By then, 40 percent of the positive cases confirmed in Maine since mid-August were in the same county as the pastor's church. The jail where an infected wedding guest had sparked an outbreak was also in that county, which was now the site of half of the state's thirteen active outbreaks. "I am concerned about where we are," Dr. Shah warned in a briefing. "I'm asking everyone else to share in that concern. COVID-19, right now, is not on the other side of the fence. It is in our yards."[53]

At that time about 65 percent of Mainers said they were closely following recommendations for mask-wearing, according to a survey by Harvard, Rutgers, and Northeastern Universities. The same poll found that Governor Mills had an approval rating of 54 percent, a slight uptick from earlier in the summer but still down sharply from her 72 percent rating in April, just before she announced her phased plan to reopen the state's economy.[54] Another indicator, called the "Back-to-Normal" index, from Moody's Analytics and CNN — based on factors ranging from gross domestic product and unemployment claims to real estate listings, travel indicators, and restaurant traffic — found that Maine was "operating at ninety-three percent of where it was in early March," the fastest economic recovery of any state.[55]

In mid-September the governor attended an event in her hometown to mark the first anniversary of a propane explosion there that killed a fire captain and injured four firefighters. After the ceremony, on her Twitter account, she reposted a photograph taken by a local news reporter, in which she was standing apart from a group of uniformed firemen, everyone wearing masks.[56] She wrote in her tweet that the 2019 incident and its aftermath had "once again revealed the character of Maine people, whose outpouring of support sustained our small community through its most challenging moments." The governor also called on her constituents to "recommit to taking care of one another as we did then, rising a stronger people and a stronger state." In a journal entry that day, she wrote that at the time of the explosion she thought "the episode . . . would be the lowest point" of her administration. "Little did I know," she added. "As tragic as that incident was, it certainly pales in comparison to a worldwide pandemic." Little did anyone know anything anymore, it seemed, if they ever had. For those who survived COVID-19, the crisis recalibrated much of humanity's relationship with the inevitability of mortality, regardless of the extent to which people's daily lives were upended. In the First World, whatever had caused people stress before the pandemic now seemed relatively quaint, if not paltry. Likewise, the question "What's next?" had become rhetorical, followed by a collective notion, whenever some escalation did arrive, that "we should have seen it coming."

On the evening of September 18 news broke of the death of liberal Supreme Court justice Ruth Bader Ginsburg. In a posthumous statement released through National Public Radio, Justice Ginsburg expressed her "most fervent wish" that she "not be replaced until a new president is installed."[57] President Trump claimed to have heard of her passing from a reporter, just after he had attended a campaign rally in Minnesota.[58] "You're telling me now for the first time," he responded. "Whether you agreed or not, she was an amazing woman who led an amazing life. I am actually sad to hear that. I'm sad to hear that." In an official statement issued later, the president called Justice Ginsburg "a titan of the law" who had "demonstrated that one can disagree without being disagreeable toward one's colleagues or different points of view."[59]

That night Governor Mills was at loose ends. "God save us," she wrote in her journal. "Ruth Bader Ginsburg died. Six and a half weeks before the most polarizing presidential election of the century." She noted that Senate Majority Leader Mitch McConnell had since announced "unequivocally that the Senate will move on whoever Trump nominates" before the November election. The governor saw this as "an appalling power grab, on top of everything else that is making this . . . election the most important in many decades." Senator McConnell's pledge was brazen hypocrisy in light of his categorical refusal, after the death of Justice Antonin Scalia in 2016, to allow President Barack Obama's nominee so much as a hearing.[60] At that time he had declared that "the American people should have a voice in the selection of their next Supreme Court Justice. Therefore, this vacancy should not be filled until we have a new president."[61] Now that Justice Ginsburg was gone, Republican senators lined up behind President Trump, with the exception of Alaska's Lisa Murkowski and Maine's Susan Collins, who called for the nomination process to wait.[62]

The governor vented in the privacy of her journal that "Trump should be defeated on November 3; he should be indicted on November 4; the Republican Senators should resign regardless of the election; and Melania should file for divorce on November 5." On the day after Justice Ginsburg's death, a Saturday, President Trump announced that he would choose a woman to replace her "without delay." Governor Mills fled Augusta with her "kitchen cabinet," a few women commissioners from her administration, to Maine's southern coast, where they "walked the beach, and walked and walked." The stretch of coastline they chose was "so wide and beautiful" at low tide, with "a sunken boat . . . and a tidal pool, and a stream that comes in and out." The weather was "getting chilly," but it was a day when they all needed "to hit the beach and just commiserate, and we drank a glass of wine to RBG." It was an afternoon of "fresh air, friendship [and] sisterhood" during "such a stressful, stressful time," as the governor described it in her journal. In an official public statement, she called Justice Ginsburg "one of the greatest Americans ever" and "a gracious, tenacious person with great intellect who was devoted to the integrity of the Court and to the rule of law as it applies to every person in our country."[63] Governor Mills had met Justice Ginsburg and "had the pleasure of watching people argue before her in the gallery of the highest court in the land." On behalf of Maine's people, she was grateful for Justice Ginsburg's "service to our nation."

Ashirah felt "like we lost a key soldier," as she told the governor in a letter that week. "I'm walking around with a hole in my gut and a crushing sadness [that] I'm not fully allowing in because it would be overwhelming." She hoped Justice Ginsburg "was at peace in the end" and "did not feel she was failing by dying before the election." Still, a part of her wanted "to wail in sorrow and abandonment: what about the rest of us?" She wondered how to "carry on in the face of all that is our world right now." Her daughter, who had turned eleven that week, was upset by the thought that President Trump could win reelection. "We can't take another four years of him undoing things!" Pamela had lamented. Ashirah responded that "the people in Syria have been living in war for a lot longer than this and you do what you have to do." Despite her pragmatism, Ashirah confessed to the governor that "this feels like the end of the world — the pandemic, the political insanity, the loss of the Supreme Court, the country on fire, and climate change rolling over us all." It had occurred to her that "Roman and Greek citizens probably never

thought their empires would fall either, and this is the fall of the
entire earth." She would "keep trying, for sure," she told Governor
Mills, "and I think the question I will be asking myself now is . . .
how does one fit into an empire that *is* falling?"

With that, Ashirah abruptly changed the subject; the end of the
world was "too sad a note to end on." Instead she offered her family's "duckling saga," a still-unfolding ordeal she was managing after
one of her broody hens laid eggs that did not hatch. Ashirah's daughter had been counting on having ducklings on the homestead, so
they bought a batch, newly hatched, in the hope that the bereft
mother hen might adopt them. "Only she didn't adopt them," Ashirah wrote, "she began attacking them!" The Knapps were left with
ten ducklings that needed to be kept warm for two months until
their feathers came in. "We now have the babies in two plastic bins
in our house, the whole house smells of duck, and on top of that
they're babies so they're *loud*." Ducklings, she explained, "are incredibly messy critters and they stink!" Her daughter's were "three
weeks old, just five more to go!!"

The next week started with the news that an eighth person in
Maine had died of COVID-19 whose infection stemmed from the
August wedding.[64] The state also reported the first outbreak in its
public school system — twelve people had tested positive at a high
school in the county where Pastor Bell's church was located, as well
as the jail where a wedding guest had started an outbreak.[65] Nationwide that week the pandemic's death toll reached two hundred
thousand, the highest of any country. The US also accounted for 20
percent of the global tally despite America's having less than 5
percent of the planet's population.[66] "The world is topsy-turvy,"
Governor Mills wrote in her journal that day, on the autumnal equi-
nox. She was increasingly troubled by the deeply partisan controversy over Justice Ginsburg's replacement. Senate Republicans were
"committed to confirming whoever Trump nominates," she fumed,
"even though the election is only six weeks away." She found it
"more nefarious" that the "newly constituted Supreme Court
would rule on that very election" in the event of legal controversy
to that extent.

In the same journal entry Governor Mills noted that she planned to head for Baxter State Park in Maine's north woods the next day. She had strong personal ties to the place and would be there to mark the sixth anniversary of the death of her husband. During her terms as attorney general one of her responsibilities had been to help manage the park's more than two hundred thousand acres of wilderness. When she was sworn in for her first term as AG, she mentioned the park in her speech, noting that her mother was in the audience: "She is particularly excited that I will be serving on the Baxter Park Authority fulfilling the prophecy she made decades ago, that I would be 'forever wild.'"[67] In 2014, just two weeks after Stan died, a heartbroken AG Mills went to the park with one of her grandsons. She called their trip a "break for the brain, welcome grief relief."[68] Two years later she described the park in an essay as "a place of respite and repair" whose meaning "lies in its quietude, in its broad spaces, in its deep peace." Baxter, she wrote, was a "uniquely noncommercial" expanse of woods where isolation was "a virtue, almost a prerequisite at times."[69] She sought that isolation again in late September 2020, recording in her journal that she planned to spend twenty-four hours in the park without internet or cellphone coverage, and "perhaps find some peace of mind."

Her administration continued the business of governance in her brief absence, with an announcement that the state was dropping its requirement for visitors from Massachusetts to provide a negative COVID test or quarantine for two weeks.[70] The positivity rate in that state had finally come to resemble that of others whose residents had been exempt all summer, explained the Maine CDC. The governor's economic commissioner underscored publicly that "Massachusetts visitors play a key role in our tourism economy," adding that she was "hopeful for a strong fall tourism season as well as a robust ski season."[71] Fall colors had already "emerged rapidly" on the trees in the state's north country, according to Maine's official foliage spokesperson.[72] The transition would "accelerate daily as the entire state starts going toward peak conditions in October" after being "jump-started" by early frost and a lack of rain.

By then the entire state was experiencing moderate to severe drought, with reports in all but one county that some residents' wells had gone dry.[73] The US Department of Agriculture declared a disaster in one northern Maine county that grew 90 percent of the state's yearly potato crop. That harvest generated more than half a billion dollars in annual sales and supported about 6,150 jobs.[74] The drought also presented a hazard for the 955 people taking part in the first of four state-permitted moose hunts that year, an iconic tradition in Maine.[75] "It's dry as hell, and as dusty as all get out," warned a moose biologist at the state's Department of Inland Fisheries and Wildlife.[76] The dust was creating dangerous whiteout conditions for hunters caravanning on unpaved backroads, increasing their risk of crashing. Those who managed to tag a moose would struggle to keep it cool and clean on their way out of the woods. "I don't know how we emphasize this enough for people," the biologist added. "This is the real deal. You've got everything against you this week."

In Temple the drought was "wearing on" the Knapps, as Ashirah rued in her final September letter. "Our garden has sat still all summer — we'll have to buy vegetables this year," she wrote, adding that it was "discouraging to see all the springtime work turn to nothing." Their fields had dried up, leaving little pasture for their goats. "We'll be feeding hay a month early this year." Ashirah confessed to Governor Mills that it had been "a difficult week." She explained that she had spent years looking for a family dog and was "committed to rescues or shelter dogs." Her search had so far been "beyond impossible" because the Knapps needed "a non-shedding breed" that would not aggravate their son's asthma. The right dog also had to be "kid-friendly, cat-friendly and big enough not to freeze in the winter." That week Ashirah thought they had "finally found a very promising prospect" until the owner balked at negotiating the "tissue-thin" adoption contract. "This is probably the twentieth one that I've . . . gotten my hopes up about," she admitted. "It seems a small thing to anyone who's never had a dog, but it is a very large thing for me." Ashirah knew her children "(and myself) would benefit from that unconditional love, especially now." She told the governor that "it hurts so much that I can't provide that for them." In an uncharacteristic flash of self-pity she added: "I just don't understand why it never works out for me."

Ashirah ended her letter with her usual positive tone, announcing the return of apprentices to the homestead; the Knapps were excited to host two women and one man, all in their twenties, for a two-month stay. "It is nice to share the space with people again and my kids are loving the extra conversations and activity." She also celebrated the "really good piece of good news" that the family's well had not run dry. In a final note before signing off for that week, she wrote: "Maybe next week will be better." At the end of September, the global pandemic death toll reached one million, after more than two million new cases and thirty-six thousand deaths had been reported worldwide in just the previous week.[77] In Maine at that time, 141 people had died of COVID-19. The state had the lowest hospitalization rate in the US, adjusted for population, as well as the second lowest coronavirus positivity rate and the fifth lowest death rate, despite recent outbreaks. In the governor's final September radio address she announced that Maine also ranked "first in the nation on the percentage of people tested," due in part to the deal she had secured with test maker IDEXX in May.[78] "Testing alone is not prevention," the governor cautioned listeners. "Don't have big parties indoors or outdoors . . . Don't take a chance, please. We've all read in the newspapers where some have taken those chances and disastrous, tragic results have ensued."

The governor did not specifically mention the superspreader wedding, but Dr. Shah had recently declared that COVID-19 had "now infected virtually every aspect of life" in the county where two outbreaks had been linked to the event. Public schools there were now closed for in-person learning, and outdoor parks had been shut down and cordoned off with yellow caution tape. The city council had imposed a mask ordinance for all indoor and confined outdoor spaces, with a $100 fine for violators. The council had no authority over Pastor Bell's Christian academy, where students were still attending classes in-person and unmasked. He had also continued to hold in-person services at his church. Meanwhile, his son's wedding was set for mid-October at a church in neighboring New Hampshire. It was the only wedding planned there that had not been rescheduled due to the pandemic, according to the church adminis-trator. "I hope Pastor Bell will wear a mask," the administrator told the press.[79] "To ask another person of faith to leave is an incredibly hard thing. But unfortunately, I have to be a hard-ass. If you're not wearing a mask, you're not coming in." Seventy-five guests were planning to attend.

CHAPTER SIX

"... the kick or the hug ..."

O ctober 2 was a Friday, and Governor Mills was planning to "take refuge" that weekend at the home of a friend. She noted in a journal entry that she had two pandemic-related phone calls scheduled for that day, both with the rest of the nation's governors. One of the calls was "to discuss what we're supposed to do about a vaccine distribution plan the feds want from each of us" by mid-October. This was despite the fact that "nobody knows what kind of vaccine may be developed, what temperature it will have to be kept at or how it's supposed to be warehoused and secured." Her administration's draft plan called for first vaccinating healthcare and essential workers and nursing home residents.[1] Next would be Mainers with underlying health concerns, school staff, and prison populations, followed by the remainder of residents. The governor's second conference call that day "was supposed to be with the President but he and Melania both tested positive for COVID." The governor was unmoved: "Trump is only one of about 50,000 people [in the US] to test positive for the virus today alone." The president's symptoms worsened that day, and in the early evening he was flown to Walter Reed military hospital for observation.[2]

Governor Mills left Augusta to meet the friend hosting her on Maine's southern coast for a sunset stroll. As they walked, "a beautiful, full double rainbow" arched across the sky over the bay and "dumped all its gold into the sea." The sight calmed her, as did any amount of time she spent outdoors. "I think the nation is going to be okay," she wrote in her journal, an "intuition" that was rooted in "hope . . . just pure hope," as she later explained. "Because how could it get any worse?" The governor's sadness over the recent death of US Supreme Court justice Ruth Bader Ginsburg was compounded by its ill-fated timing, as if scripted by Hollywood — of *course* one of America's most controversial, polarizing presidents would end up with the opportunity to appoint a third member of the nation's highest court. His pick, federal appeals court judge Amy Coney Barrett, had been a clerk for Justice Antonin Scalia. Judge Barrett had since spent three years on the bench in her sole judicial stint. Her confirmation, which would shift the court's ideological makeup to an enduring conservative majority, seemed all but certain to come before the November election. That contest promised to be one of the most contentious in US history. Now the incumbent, who had been questioning the integrity of the election, and gone so far as to suggest postponing it, was hospitalized with COVID-19 in the midst of a nationwide surge of cases. How could "it" get any worse, indeed; Americans of every political persuasion seemed to be bracing themselves.

Ashirah's next letter, on October 4, ignored partisan rancor and touched on the pandemic only tangentially. She was busy scheduling plans with other homeschooling families in the Knapps' area in an attempt to make new friends, with "mixed results" so far. One group had been "great about wearing masks but didn't pay attention to social distance," and a second group "didn't really hit it off" with her children. Ashirah had "several more meet-ups in the works" and was optimistic about a family whose children shared Owen and Pamela's interests in metal detecting, reenacting, swordplay, Dungeons and Dragons, and the popular card game Magic: The Gathering. "This could be a match made in heaven!" she told Governor Mills. Ashirah was also looking forward to a new homeschooling group she had just joined. Its "very strong focus" was "on decolonizing our personal lives and relating to each other with sensitivity." She was already trading suggestions for good documentary films with other members of the group in their online forum. She had recommended a serious but uplifting one that examined "how women's bodies are used in advertising. It is a movie every woman and daughter *really* should see, which of course also means that every man should see it." Ashirah concluded with an update on mask-wearing in her area, reporting that face coverings were now "the norm" around Farmington. It was "rare to see someone in a store without a mask," she wrote. "We are thankful and hopeful, though it also seems cases are on the rise."

On October 5, President Trump was released from Walter Reed after an aggressive course of world-class medical treatment unavailable to most Americans, including experimental antiviral drugs and constant monitoring of his condition. "Don't be afraid of COVID," he had written in a tweet that day. "Don't let it dominate your life."[3] He returned to the White House and did not wear a mask as he went inside, despite his doctor's express warning that the president was still contagious.[4] That day in the US, state and local health agencies reported 62,413 new cases of COVID-19.[5] Even Maine was barely controlling the pandemic after having salvaged a relatively successful summer tourist season, if less profitable, with no widespread increase in transmission. The state's CDC had just announced an increase of 488 cases during the previous two weeks, almost 10 percent of Maine's total to date. Forty percent of those cases were in the county where initial outbreaks stemmed from the superspreader wedding. The CDC was also monitoring new outbreaks, including dozens of cases at two paper mills, one of which was the largest in Maine. Gone was the routine humor from Dr. Shah's briefing on October 1 — he took a dire tone as he explained that most new cases could not be linked to a known outbreak.[6] The virus was now "spreading and occurring in every part of Maine, from person to person, from family to family." He also warned that younger Mainers were contracting the virus; the average age was forty, down from fifty-one in the spring.

Despite the pandemic's worrying trajectory in Maine, the state was still faring better than most, with the lowest hospitalization rate and the country's second lowest number of positive cases, both metrics adjusted for population.[7] Maine's death toll of 142 was the fourth lowest of any state.[8] Governor Mills acknowledged that the pandemic had been "painful" for a lot of Maine people and businesses, but she emphasized that the state had so far "balanced public health with economic health."[9] At the start of the second week of October she announced that her administration would proceed with the fourth stage of its plan to reopen Maine's economy. Restaurants, movie theaters, and other businesses that offered seated indoor service would soon be allowed to boost their capacity from a maximum of fifty people to one hundred, and bars could reopen for indoor service at the beginning of November.

As part of the governor's "balancing act" approach she also used an executive order to strengthen the state's mask mandate, requiring all businesses statewide to enforce it, instead of just those in coastal communities and Maine's bigger cities. She expanded the mandate's scope to include private organizations and municipal buildings and underscored the consequences for noncompliance. "We've already had, in one instance, a $20,000 fine," she warned during the CDC briefing and in her radio address that week, adding that more than two dozen entities had been cited for posing imminent health hazards.[10] The governor emphasized that Maine's strategy was "fairly consistent with what other New England states are doing." She also stressed the need for people to keep taking the same proven precautions and not "be lured into a false sense of security." That spring and summer Mainers had "worked together . . . to ensure that we could leave our homes safely" and "get back to something of what life used to be like." With winter approaching, she implored, "let us adapt again to keep it that way."

At that point in the pandemic, Mainers' attitudes toward mask-wearing and other safety measures mirrored the nation's spectrum, from extreme to opposite extreme. In one rural county in western Maine that was trying to contain an outbreak at a paper mill, Rick Savage — the restaurateur who had read the governor's cellphone number on a Fox News show in April — continued to flout state guidelines at his nearby brewpub.[11] He told a Maine newspaper that he "never wore" a mask and griped that Governor Mills was "running around the state making it look like there is still a COVID problem so she can keep the state of emergency going."[12] Two hundred miles to the northeast, in the area where the August wedding was held, no new cases had been reported for a month. After the initial outbreak there, more residents had started wearing masks and three affected towns temporarily closed businesses. Schools began the academic year with fully remote instruction. A local official in one of the towns called the wedding "a wakeup call" for people who had been "complacent."[13]

Statewide that fall, all twenty-six of Maine's annual agricultural fairs had been canceled.[14] (The largest one, the Fryeburg Fair, which started in 1851 and drew 225,000 people every year, did hold some marquee events online, including its "Moo-la-Palooza" cow-impersonating contest.[15]) Another indication of broad public concern was the record number of voters who had requested absentee ballots ahead of the November election — more than 261,000 by the first week of October, about a third of the total turnout in 2016. Apart from the challenge of conducting balloting safely and legally, Maine was also set to become the first US state to use ranked-choice voting in a presidential contest. The method allowed voters to choose candidates in order of preference, ultimately ensuring a majority winner; if necessary, last-place candidates were eliminated, and their support was reallocated according to voters' rankings. Mainers had approved the system in 2016 for use in only US House and Senate races. Two years later ranked-choice voting resulted in the upset ouster of a Republican congressman by a Democratic opponent who had collected fewer first-place votes. The system then survived a succession of court challenges, including a bid by Maine Republicans to block its use in the 2020 presidential election. On October 6 their emergency appeal to the US Supreme Court was rejected without comment by Justice Stephen Breyer, who also declined to refer the case to the full court.[16]

A few days later Ashirah wrote to Governor Mills for the first time that month. By then the fall foliage in Temple was already past peak color — Maine's official foliage coordinator, who had done the job for almost three decades, declared the 2020 season "one of the quickest . . . I've seen in all my years of reporting."[17] Mother Nature had "decided to throw in her two cents to prove she's still in charge." On the Knapps' homestead this was always "a really beautiful time," as Ashirah described it, when the weather had "finally cooled off but the days are still long and it's not really cold yet." She also loved "the change of the smell in the air and living right in the forest" through the transition to winter. As she told Governor Mills in a letter dated October 10, Ashirah was thrilled to be witnessing more of her children's learning process, an upside of having chosen to homeschool them. Pamela, who had turned eleven in September, "did a science chapter about food chains," including a section about scavengers and "came up with her own question" — she wondered whether people could be considered scavengers "when we go to the store and buy packaged meat that we didn't kill?"

Ashirah mentioned that Owen, who had recently turned fourteen, had finished reading *Kidnapped*, which she had so enjoyed in August in advance of their lessons. Her son was now "working on his final essay, showing all the parts of the 'hero's journey' in the book with textual proof." She noted that he "hates the textual proof part. I think it's very good practice, though." Owen was also studying the legacy of President Lincoln for one of his history lessons and questioned whether the Emancipation Proclamation was solely about "social justice and human rights." He had learned that the 1863 declaration, which held that "all persons held as slaves . . . are, and henceforward shall be free," was "a political move" aimed, in part, at deterring other nations from involvement in the Civil War.[18] Owen wondered "what other stories I'm being told that are also not true." Ashirah had reassured both children that she was "very proud of them for their original thinking."

That week she too was pondering questions, in her case about an aspect of "homeschooling/unschooling" that she considered "a weakness." She wondered whether it was a mistake to support children "in being whoever they are" in instances when "who they're being is not okay." Ashirah believed that "sometimes a kick-in-the-metaphorical-butt is what should happen," but she felt that "people are afraid of doing it" for fear of discouraging individuality. "So my own question these days," she told Governor Mills, "is what gives one the balance to be able to decide which is appropriate, the kick or the hug?" Part of the answer for parents and children, she believed, was grounded in having obligatory work in life, "like carrying wood, growing food, doing chores — something that just needs to happen when and how it needs to happen."

Her letter only briefly mentioned "the bigger world (as big as this country anyways [*sic*])," which the Knapps continued to "watch in dismayed horror." Ashirah added that "things feel very bad. Not sure there is anything to say anymore." The nationwide upsurge in COVID-19 cases continued as temperatures fell in some regions and Americans spent more time together indoors. For the country's governors the crisis complicated innumerable aspects of the daily business of running their states — Governor Mills had yet to nominate a new chief justice for Maine's Supreme Court, more than five months after the former judge resigned to become dean of the University of Maine's School of Law.[19] The governor made time during the second week of October to meet with three close advisers and continue the selection process. Her chosen successor would be her third appointment to the state's highest court. The nominee would need to be confirmed by Maine lawmakers, along with nominees to lower courts, but the legislature had been adjourned since mid-March because of the pandemic. To boot, the state's courts also had yet to resume some proceedings because of pandemic protocols, as well as a shortage of judges and a backlog of cases.[20]

The governor and her advisers for the nomination stayed at "an old rescue station once manned by the precursor to the Coast Guard," as she described it in a journal entry. They used the outpost, on Maine's northeastern coast near Acadia National Park, to regroup and "make calls about the Chief Justice's position." The group also spent time "talking about the economy and economic recovery . . . and brainstorm[ed] about things generally." Governor Mills wrote that the station had "beautiful views, but cold windy weather." She noticed "how different the light is . . . Islands on the horizon seem to hover above the sea, unattached and unattended." Her company there included her former chief legal counsel, who had just left that role at the end of August. In a statement announcing his departure she had called him "a trusted advisor and cherished friend" whose "wise counsel . . . particularly during this pandemic, has been truly invaluable."[21] Despite his presence in their small party, the isolation her job imposed was heightened by her remote location. "I am lonely," she wrote in her journal, "but it is ghostly-weird and haunting, and the light changes every five minutes."

Governor Mills returned from that brief retreat before the long weekend for Columbus Day. By 2020, Maine was among the fifteen states (along with more than 130 cities) that had renamed the holiday as Indigenous People's Day.[22] She had signed the change into law the year before, calling it "another step in healing the divisions of the past." That Sunday she went to her hometown to hear a folk band perform at the local drive-in. It was a "relaxing event," she wrote in her journal, with "the autumn sun highlighting the woods and hills across the Sandy River." She noted that she had been approached by "a number of people . . . thanking me for keeping the state safe." After the concert, in keeping with her habit of instigating impromptu gatherings, the governor invited the band to reconvene in the backyard of her camp, with her and some of her family members, and play a few more songs. The band added a photo from the encore to its Facebook page, showing its members standing slightly apart from Governor Mills, all wearing masks. They thanked her in the post "for continuing to work hard for Maine in a thankless time."[23]

The next day the governor and her two top health officials met with the coordinator of the Trump administration's Coronavirus Task Force, Dr. Deborah Birx, who was in Maine as part of a tour of college and university campuses around the country to share information. Governor Mills described the meeting in a journal entry as "a pleasant panel-type conversation," referring to Dr. Birx as "cautious" and "noncommittal." The governor also noted that her administration relayed its "complaints about the way the feds are treating the states when it comes to testing materials, swabs, etc., and federal messaging about the pandemic." She elaborated slightly to one of Maine's newspapers, recounting that she had "impressed upon Dr. Birx the importance of providing continued federal resources to small, rural states like Maine, not just hotspots around the country, to support expanded testing so that we don't become a hotspot."[24] The paper noted that Dr. Birx was "asked whether she thinks it's safe for President Trump . . . to resume holding large campaign rallies" such as the one he had held the day before in Florida. Dr. Birx responded that "she would give the same advice as she gives the people of Maine" — to continue wearing masks, distancing from others, and avoiding large groups indoors and outside. "This is when we have to care for one another in a very careful way," she said.

Dr. Shah echoed that advice in a briefing two days later, imploring residents not to "throw away our shot" at preventing the sort of sharp increases in COVID-19 cases that thirty-five states had reported over the previous two weeks.[25] While Maine had been "holding steady" since September, with an average of thirty new cases per day, all of its neighboring states had reported increases, including spikes of 112 percent in New Hampshire, 100 percent in Connecticut, and 70 percent in Rhode Island. On a positive note Dr. Shah explained that Maine was conducting about 50 percent more diagnostic tests than the national average. With that "robust testing architecture" the state would be able to detect small increases in Maine that could "morph" into larger outbreaks. "But why let it get to that?" he asked. "In the same way that no one in Maine would ever conceive of waiting until the ice storm hits before we start salting the roads, we have an opportunity right now to take action to prevent what we see on the horizon." Dr. Shah reminded residents yet again that they should "wear a face covering . . . practice safe socializing," and "know who you're interacting with."

Maine's first winter storm arrived two days later, on the weekend of October 17, leaving half a foot of snow in some parts of the state.[26] That week Ashirah wrote one of her shortest letters yet, filling only one side of a sheet of three-hole-notebook paper, with a few lines to spare at the bottom. She was busy teaching her children, getting a flu shot for her son and herself, and continuing her search for "a possible family dog." That week the Knapps were "trialing" a new candidate whose breed was "not hypoallergenic, so it's a 98% chance we can't keep him." This would be her last attempt at adopting "a shelter or rescue dog" before looking for a purebred poodle, "but before we committed to that, it seemed important to try a 'regular' dog." Ashirah had "plenty of moral questions" about "supporting a breeder, even a good one," and was conflicted about "spending a few thousand dollars on a dog, with our income, and with hungry people in the world." Likewise she knew "how meaningful it would be" for Owen and Pamela "to have a dog during the rest of their childhoods."

Ashirah did not mention national politics or the fact that the November election was now just over two weeks away. By then, the

Associated Press reported, Americans had cast a "record-setting avalanche" of twenty-two million absentee ballots, representing 16 percent of all the votes cast in the 2016 presidential election.[27] In Maine the count was up to 415,000 absentee ballots requested, about 39 percent of registered voters, and more than half of those ballots had been submitted.[28] With polls showing a close race, both the Biden and Trump campaigns were courting the second of Maine's two congressional districts, whose single electoral vote was seen as one of the nation's toss-ups.[29] The candidates' outsized interest was due to yet another unusual Maine law that split the state's total of four electoral votes — two were always given to the overall winner, and the other two allocated to the victor in each district.[30] Nebraska was the only other state that split its electoral votes by congressional district, which did not occur until 2008. That year Barack Obama took one of the state's three district votes despite John McCain's overall win.[31] Maine's vote-splitting law took effect in 1969, when a mill-worker-turned-legislator "hatched" an idea to restore the early-nineteenth-century practice, according to Paul Mills, the governor's brother. The bill's passage was "notably uncontroversial," as he explained in a newspaper column in 2016, the first year the law forced an electoral vote split in Maine. Hillary Clinton had carried the state while Donald Trump took the second district by 10 percentage points, a win his campaign was intent on repeating in 2020.[32]

The second district included the majority of Maine's land area and about half of its population. On October 19, Vice President Pence headlined an outdoor campaign rally there, near Bangor, the state's third largest city, at a family-owned truck stop established in 1967. The company's website proudly declared that its customers could buy fuel, "traditional Maine food," and "almost any item you could possibly want, from souvenirs and snacks to CB radios."[33] The vice president spoke at a podium, standing in front of a fully loaded logging truck hung with a MAKE AMERICA GREAT AGAIN! banner. He kept his distance from the state and local officials who also spoke at the rally, including former governor Paul LePage. Media reports estimated that several hundred people showed up, but organizers claimed that the crowd eventually topped one thousand.[34] Either way the event exceeded the state's limit of one hundred people at outdoor gatherings. Those in the crowd mostly stood close together, and few wore masks.[35] By comparison the Biden campaign required face coverings and social distancing at its public events around the country, and both its candidates and their staff wore masks during their travels.[36] It had also canceled some in-person events in mid-October after the communications director for vice presidential nominee Kamala Harris tested positive for COVID-19, along with two members of flight crews on campaign trips.[37]

The day after the vice president's appearance, an openly exasperated Governor Mills urged Mainers who had gone to the rally to get tested for COVID-19 "because they probably have been exposed to any number of people who are carrying the virus."[38] The governor joined Dr. Shah's now biweekly CDC briefing remotely, from her office in Augusta, and told reporters: "We keep saying please limit gatherings, don't attend large gatherings." After months of composure during the briefings she attended, the governor now shook her head on camera and said she was "saddened" by the vice president's attendance at the rally. During a recent conference call she had asked him "directly" to clarify his panel's position on safety protocols for gatherings. "He paused and he said, 'it is our strong recommendation that people avoid large gatherings, keep six foot distance from other people and wear face masks,'" the governor recounted. "I'm disappointed personally . . . that he did not heed his own advice yesterday." In response to the governor's comments, the leader of the state Republican Party retorted by email to a Maine newspaper: "I guess we'll have to call it a 'peaceful protest.' Gov[ernor] Mills and her pals will be fine then." He was referring to racial justice demonstrations held in the state over the summer — those events had also exceeded the state's crowd limit for outdoor gatherings, though many protesters had worn masks.

The day after the vice president's appearance, a COVID-19 contact tracer for the White House advised at least one local official, who had helped plan and attended the truck stop rally, that he might have been exposed to the virus during the event.[39] The official was not infected, but within a week the vice president's chief of staff and several aides tested positive.[40] On the same day that their cases were revealed, President Trump's chief of staff, Mark Meadows, said in a television appearance that the US was "not going to control the pandemic . . . because it is a contagious virus, just like the flu."[41] He added during the contentious CNN interview that "what we need to do is make sure that we have the proper mitigation factors, whether it's . . . vaccines or treatments to make sure that people don't die from this." His comments incensed Governor Mills, who had asked Mainers earlier that week to "stick with me" and summon the "courage, conviction and resilience" that helped previous generations survive "wars, depression, booms and busts" and the 1918 influenza pandemic.[42] "We're not going to surrender, we're going to use all the tools we have," she had pledged, adding that "each of us must take responsibility for the trajectory of the virus."

Maine was still among the states that had been most successful in limiting the pandemic's spread. By mid-month the number of new cases was at last declining in York County, and schools there had been cleared to return to in-person learning.[43] Meanwhile, a new outbreak had begun in another county, about 130 miles to the northeast, in the state's midcoast area. Its origin was a "fellowship rally" held by a Pentecostal church in the town of Brooks during the first weekend of October.[44] The event included indoor services with sermons by a visiting preacher from Oklahoma. It drew at least a hundred people from the host congregation and churches in two other towns.[45] By the third week of October a Maine CDC investigation had linked forty-two cases of COVID-19 to the Brooks rally. The people infected ranged in age from two years old to eighty, including students at four schools in the area and a Christian academy run by the church, as well as an employee of a senior care facility in another town. The church's pastor, Matthew Shaw, also worked as a security supervisor at a nearby county hospital.[46] Dr. Shah detailed the outbreak for reporters during another uncharacteristically humorless online briefing. "We expect the number of cases associated with this outbreak to increase, perhaps significantly," he warned. Masks had been available during the rally, he added, but they "were not routinely used."

The church suspended in-person services. As the outbreak grew Pastor Shaw recorded a video of himself apologizing to "our community . . . as far as the effects of the virus may have spread" and posted it on the parish's Facebook page. He sat facing the camera, wearing a checkered shirt and a dark blazer, and told viewers that the church had been "encouraged not to make statements" but that "we regret what has happened" and "we ask your forgiveness." He was sorry "for the consequences that maybe the community is feeling," including "the fear that is settling into the hearts of . . . those of you that might have been inconvenienced" or "physically been affected by the virus." He then added a disclaimer that his apology did not apply to people who had "used this opportunity just to voice your opposition against the church," but "rather those of you, for twenty-five years, that we have stood with and stood by" in grocery store lines, at parades, and amid tragedies and beside graves. "You are the ones today — we want to make sure you know that we are sorry." He then preached a twenty-minute "message of hope." By that weekend three people had been hospitalized with COVID-19 infections traced to the church's rally, and the total number of known positive cases was approaching sixty.[47]

The outbreak culminated a week of mixed news for the Mills administration, starting with an uplifting state revenue tally from the summer months that beat forecasts by more than $68 million. The bump came despite major shortfalls for the hospitality industry but was also partly inflated by federal pandemic stimulus funds. Also that week the state attorney general reported that 258 people had died of drug overdoses in Maine during the first half of the year, an increase of 27 percent over the second half of 2019. More than 80 percent of those deaths had been caused by at least one opioid.[48] Governor Mills, who had made Maine's effort to confront the nation's opioid epidemic a major priority, acknowledged that the pandemic had "laid bare challenges in reaching people" who were battling addiction.[49] She added that her administration "must do more to save lives" — it soon dispatched new mobile response teams for every Maine county to distribute an opioid antidote and promote treatment programs.[50] That same day Purdue Pharma, the maker of the painkiller OxyContin, agreed to plead guilty to criminal charges in connection with the opioid epidemic, as part of a more than $8 billion settlement with the US Justice Department.[51]

Near the end of that fraught week, the second and final presidential debate took place. An Associated Press analysis called the proceeding "actually a debate — a brief interlude of normalcy in an otherwise highly abnormal year, and a reprieve for voters turned off by the candidates' noxious first faceoff."[52] With little more than a week left until the election, Governor Mills used a radio address the next day to encourage absentee voting.[53] "Make sure your voice is heard November 3rd," she told listeners, then spent much of the four-minute recording explaining instructions and deadlines for those who had yet to cast ballots. She also mentioned "a little bit of talk" in other states about potential harassment and voter intimidation. "We don't expect a problem with that here in Maine and we do have plenty of tools to address it if it does occur," she said. "Just remember, you have a constitutional right to vote. No one can prevent you. It's your civic right and your civic responsibility." On Saturday the Biden campaign sent Kamala Harris's husband, Doug Emhoff, to Maine's prize second district to speak at two events. Both were invitation-only to limit the crowd size — he toured a potato grower's facility and later spoke at a small rally at an eight-hundred-site campground.[54] News reports noted that about eighty people attended the second event, and all of them were wearing masks.

The next day in the district dawned a calendar-picture fall Sunday, with sunny blue skies and temperatures in the midforties. That afternoon, at the Treworgy Family Orchards in the north-central part of the state, some Mainers who arrived to pick apples or brave the farm's "famous corn maze" were met by the Secret Service. The White House had called the owners the night before to ask if President Trump could make "a small, unpublicized stop," as the Treworgys explained in a note on their website.[55] "Each day we aim to make America a little better by practicing radical hospitality, connecting people together and to the land through agriculture," they wrote. The family was "honored to welcome a sitting president," but the Treworgys were "not endorsing any particular candidate." President

Trump had been in neighboring New Hampshire that morning for a rally announced several days earlier.[56] Word of his last-minute side trip to Maine spread quickly enough that a crowd of supporters gathered ahead of his arrival at both the airport in Bangor and the orchard.[57]

Governor Mills was also in the second district that day, in part to show support for Democratic US Senate candidate Sara Gideon, the Speaker of Maine's House of Representatives, who was attempting to unseat Maine's four-term Republican incumbent Susan Collins.[58] Their close race that year was the most expensive political campaign in the state's history and the second costliest Senate race in the country, with $185 million spent by the campaigns and outside groups.[59] About an hour before Air Force One arrived at the airport in Bangor, the governor spoke at an outdoor press conference nearby.[60] Behind her, supporters wearing masks stood holding blue signs for the BIDEN HARRIS and SARA GIDEON FOR MAINE campaigns. At first the governor spoke calmly. "Three-and-a-half years ago I said, well, Donald Trump has been elected president, I'll give him a shot," she started. "But I am not now, and no one should give him the benefit of a doubt." She called the Trump administration a "complete failure of leadership," adding that the president had "never grown in the job . . . never learned to accept expert advice, wise counsel, even from medical doctors," or "learned to feel the pain of other people." The governor was holding some note cards with planned remarks but mostly ignored them. Her face was drawn with anger, and her voice rose to a strained shout, shaking with emotion at times. "More people than ever before are dying from this virus . . . are sick and hospitalized in ICU wards across this country from this virus, which this president has lied to us about and miserably failed to get under control."

That day Maine's CDC reported the largest twenty-four-hour spike of new COVID-19 cases in the state since May, an increase of sixty-one since Saturday.[61] Despite the Mills administration's relentless warnings about large gatherings, some three thousand people showed up at the Treworgy Orchards to see the president. He did not wear a mask, nor did most of those in the crowd, and social distancing went unpracticed as people crammed together behind large bins of pumpkins set up as improvised barriers.[62] The Treworgys were overrun. "We expected the President to show up unannounced, surprise the few people who happened to be here, and leave with some nice photos of him holding a pumpkin," they wrote in another note on their website, two days later. They copped that their staff had ceded control to the president's security team and could not enforce the farm's policy of mask-wearing and social distancing. "Not only were we surprised," their statement claimed, "but the Secret Service and White House personnel were shocked at the number of people arriving as well." The family did not apologize but declared that they were "concerned about COVID-19's spread" and were "proud that Maine has been a leader on limiting the spread as much as possible."

That night in Temple, Ashirah wrote her final October letter to Governor Mills, after the Knapps watched *The Lord of the Rings: The Fellowship of the Ring*, the first film in the trilogy adapted from J. R. R. Tolkien's fantasy novels. Ashirah started her letter by describing a scene that took place about two-thirds of the way through the film, between two of the story's protagonists, the hobbit Frodo Baggins and his friend the wizard Gandalf. In their exchange Frodo wished that he had never come to carry the powerful ring he had volunteered to destroy, for the good of all life on their Middle Earth, in a perilous, faraway place. Ashirah paraphrased Gandalf's response: "[He] says 'so does everyone who lives to see such times, but it's not up to us what comes to us, only what to do with the time we have.'" She then explained that the wizard's line from the 2001 film had resurfaced "as a Facebook post at the start of the pandemic, and it is still so poignant." She felt that there were "so many parts of those movies that portray the chance to be one's higher self or one's lower self; they're very touching."

Ashirah went on to say that the Knapps were "steeling" themselves for the November election. She confessed that she would "love to go somewhere far away" for the next several months. "I think, whatever happens, it's going to be a shit storm," she wrote. "I wish I could just skip that." Ashirah added that one of the apprentices living on the homestead at that time was the daughter of "a

Trump supporter" who had emigrated from Hong Kong to escape the influence of Communist China. Ashirah could not understand the man's allegiance to a president with a record of racist or otherwise offensive comments about minorities. She was also baffled as to how the man did not "see similarities in restricted freedom / governmental imbalance" under the Trump administration, adding that "if he doesn't see it, I guess it shouldn't be a surprise that so many others don't see it either."

Lest she dwell on troubling thoughts for too long, Ashirah suddenly changed the subject: "But in very happy news, we now have a dog." The long-shot adoptee that she had mentioned in her previous letter, whose name was Clutch, had been living with the Knapps for six days without triggering Owen's asthma. "The dog needs a lot of training," Ashirah lamented. "Also I need a lot of training!" She described Clutch as a "big, black, athletic dog, with a beautiful long-ish shiny coat," who "looked like he had Spaniel in him but we never knew for sure." His placement with the Knapps was "a 're-homing,' meaning he came directly from one person's house to my house," she explained. Ashirah had been dreaming for a decade of finding a match. "Last night I sat down with him and just told him all this, and I cried the hardest I've cried since March," she wrote. "It was really good to get some of that out. It will probably take a few more times, too."

The next day Governor Mills wrote in her journal that "Republicans in the US Senate confirm[ed] Amy Coney Barrett to the US Supreme Court." She noted that Judge Barrett had "practiced law for about three years" and "never tried a case, possibly never appeared in court until she was appointed to the 7th Circuit Court of Appeals three years ago." Maine's Senator Collins had been the only Republican to vote against the confirmation. She then flew home for the last week of her reelection campaign. Her opponent, Speaker Gideon, dismissed the senator's lone vote against Judge Barrett as "nothing more than a political calculation" after she had supported the president's 2018 appointee, conservative Justice Brett Kavanaugh. In 2020, Senator Collins had been the only Republican candidate from her chamber who did not endorse President Trump's reelection bid. She was also her party's only remaining member of Congress from New England. In late October, Senator Collins told the *New York Times* that she had briefly considered running as an Independent "but was quick to note that she couldn't easily abandon 'the New England brand of Republicanism.'"[63] That brand seemed all but extinct ahead of the November election, as polls showed an ominously close race with Speaker Gideon; in 2014, Senator Collins had won reelection with two-thirds of the vote.[64]

In the same late-October journal entry in which Governor Mills mentioned the Barrett confirmation, she noted that the governor of South Dakota, Republican Kristi Noem, had come to Maine "to stump for Donald Trump" in the second district. "She criticizes me for regulating activities to protect Maine people against the virus," she wrote. "At the same time, in her state, hospitals are overflowing with Covid patients." Governor Noem had joined a "Team Trump" bus rally and declared that she had "made very different decisions" in responding to the pandemic "than the governor here in Maine," who, she alleged, had "overstepped her authority."[65] One of Maine's largest newspapers shot back in an editorial that South Dakota had confirmed almost as many new cases of COVID-19 in just the previous seven days — more than sixty-two hundred — as Maine had tallied in the preceding seven months.[66]

That week both presidential campaigns sent proxies to Maine's second district. Governor Mills joined Jill Biden, the Democratic presidential nominee's wife, in speaking to a crowd of fifty people at an outdoor "Get Out the Vote" event.[67] The Trump campaign sent the president's oldest son, Donald Trump Jr., to headline a rally that drew about five hundred people.[68] That event had been moved from its original location after state health officials reiterated Maine's crowd size limitations for gatherings. At the new venue, the grounds of a church whose pastor had sued Governor Mills over pandemic restrictions, attendees had their temperatures checked upon arrival. Masks were made available but few were worn.[69] By midweek, poll workers in Maine had started processing absentee ballots — about 417,000 had been submitted, representing more than half of the turnout for the 2016 election.[70]

Meanwhile, as the state's CDC worked to contain the outbreak caused by the Pentecostal church rally in Brooks, the agency reported more than fifty new cases on two consecutive days for the first time since May.[71] On October 28, Dr. Shah announced seventy-six new cases, occurring in all but two counties, and in eight schools and two long-term care facilities.[72] The number of people hospitalized with COVID-19 in Maine had more than doubled in one week, to sixteen, with seven patients in intensive care units. "Although the numbers remain low, they are significant," Dr. Shah warned in an emergency remote briefing. "The levels we are seeing right now . . . could quickly turn into exponential growth." He explained that the driving factor behind Maine's increasing COVID-19 metrics had changed, from "focal outbreaks in congregate care settings" to "the fact that the virus is everywhere among us . . . hitching a ride and traveling farther and wider across the state, from home to home." Governor Mills joined the videoconference to echo his warning, adding that 1,144 healthcare workers were among those currently infected in Maine. "When you do get sick, whatever risks you take, we may not have enough healthy medical personnel to take care of you, and take care of those you infect," she said. "We're still not doing enough to stay safe, and feeling safe is not the same as being safe."

The next day Maine's CDC reported 80 new cases. On Friday, October 30, the number had jumped to 119. "The surge [is] here," Dr. Shah wrote that day in a post on his Twitter account. "Take action now. For your sake, and for the sake of your family and community, wear a mask and stay apart. This is serious."[73] Governor Mills was reluctant to postpone plans to allow bars to reopen in November or to reinstate previous limits on Maine's residents and businesses. "Nobody wants to further restrict people's liberties," she had told reporters earlier in the week. "Many of the things we're allowing are healthy things, and keeping people sane, for crying out loud." She continued to stress the importance of individual responsibility in curbing the pandemic's spread, but Maine's case count kept rising. As she weighed the situation, she took a few moments to write a short response to Ashirah's first October letter. The governor kept an assortment of letters from constituents in a box beside her desk in her office at the Blaine House and made time to read and sometimes respond to them when she could. "Personal letters made life real again, the daily life of Maine people," she explained. Her note to Ashirah was short but personal: "Thank you for your weekly updates. I am pleased that your family are getting your flu shots . . . and that your kids are taking their schoolwork so seriously and reading a lot despite the social uprooting of this pandemic. Please give them a hug for me."

On Saturday the governor used her final radio address before the election to again urge Mainers to vote. Her administration had alerted the press that she would make an announcement over the weekend about new measures in response to the record numbers of COVID-19 cases in the state. "Like most Maine families, Governor Mills is very apprehensive about the spread of this deadly virus as we face colder weather and holidays that generally encourage gatherings of all sorts," her spokesperson said in a statement.[74] Meanwhile, that day was Halloween, and health officials at the local, state, and national level had been warning for weeks that trick-or-treating posed a risk of spreading the virus. One year earlier Governor Mills had hosted a Halloween reception for families at the Blaine House, featuring authors who read their stories to "an enraptured group of kids."[75] Now the mansion had been all but empty for months. Rooms that had been full of children's voices as they "had treats, laughed and enjoyed costumes" were quiet. The governor reposted some photos from the event on her Facebook page, showing children and their parents dressed up for the holiday. "Great memories," she wrote. "They will return!"

CHAPTER SEVEN

"... a place in my heart that's been closed ..."

Ashirah chose a piece of wintry stationery with a smiling snowman on the front for her November 1 letter and sat down to write while the Knapps were "having some Sunday morning family time." The weather was cold and rainy, but no snow yet, as Ashirah began her dispatch.[1] "My daughter is doing a charcoal drawing of a photo from *Life* magazine's photo collection, my son is carving blue foam into terrain to play a Dungeons and Dragons episode on, my husband is drawing a hot pepper plant we brought in from the garden to keep through winter, and our new dog is beginning to learn how to chew on toys and how to relax with us." Ashirah had realized how much more training Clutch would need before *she* could relax with the dog. "He has such a strong prey drive," she told Governor Mills. "I'm going to have to work hard to have him off leash around our goats and ducks, and have him leave the cat alone." She could sympathize with one of her sisters, who had recently described feeling "like she's treading water" in a new job. "She has a lot of responsibility and opportunity to direct the company, just as she always wanted, but now that she has the job she realizes she's underqualified and trying to learn as she goes . . . I said that's just how I feel with this dog!!" Ashirah did not mention whether her sister appreciated the analogy.

The Knapps had been "watching the alarming rise" in Maine's COVID-19 metrics — the state's seven-day positivity rate, while still among the nation's lowest, had doubled to 0.92 percent in the previous two weeks, and Ashirah was "getting sad and scared again."[2] Summer had brought "a good long break from that kind of fear and stress," but both were "coming back now." She had hoped that her children "would have been fine to go to school" that fall and that all of her "extreme caution and planning would be unnecessary in the end." Now she was "thinking again about supply chains, food, saving money" and "back to feeling for all the people who are more effected [*sic*] by the pandemic" than her family. As usual Ashirah ended her letter on a "humorous note"; this time Clutch had "started whining to go for his walk" at five o'clock that morning. "We usually get up around [six], then work with him on waiting quietly while we start the stove etc.," she explained. The dog kept whining, and Ashirah had started to fret that his behavior "was getting worse instead of better," until she remembered that Daylight Saving Time had started overnight and her clock had changed on its own. "Phew!" she wrote. "The only time I was ever glad that technology is being built so automatically smart."

That same day Governor Mills announced new actions that her administration planned to take that week, "to prevent and mitigate the spread" of COVID-19 in Maine as the virus "explodes across the country."[3] She postponed a plan to allow bars to reopen for indoor service and reimposed fifty-person limits for indoor gatherings as of November 4, the day after the presidential election. She also revoked exemptions from Maine's quarantine restriction for visitors from New York, New Jersey, and Connecticut, and Mainers returning from those states, who would again have to self-isolate for two weeks on arrival or test negative for COVID-19 within seventy-two hours. The rule was enforceable "as necessary" by police and "any governmental department or official" that regulated operation or occupancy of any lodging establishment.[4] The governor recalled feeling "just heartsick" and facing "a lot of pressure to impose customer limits in stores again, and masking, all those things, and I said, 'Jesus, I can't close stores, Black Friday's coming, Thanksgiving.'" In her official statement she told the owners of establishments affected by this new round of restrictions that she was "deeply sorry" she was "forced to make this decision." She knew it would "cause hardship" but pledged that her administration would "continue to do all we can to support Maine's small businesses and hardworking families."

In her next radio address Governor Mills noted that her measures were "very similar to moves made in other states this week."[5] She made that point often, lest critics accuse her of rogue action, as some did early in the pandemic, including President Trump. The nation had so far reported "more than 230,000 deaths, about four times the number of American soldiers who lost their lives in the Vietnam War," she told listeners. "People all over this state are getting sick and dying. People with loved ones, respected members of the community, people who go to your church, your grange, your legion hall." On November 2 the Maine CDC reported new outbreaks at an athletic center, a rehabilitation facility, and yet another church — Pentecostal again, this time in the middle of the state, after offering "revival services" and hosting visiting evangelists from Florida.[6] Meanwhile, the leader of a Baptist parish in Calais, near Maine's border with Canada, was garnering positive attention for his transparency in responding to an outbreak of more than two dozen cases in his congregation.[7] He had been posting regular updates on social media and urging people with symptoms to get tested for COVID-19. "It would have been really a lot easier road for me if I hadn't opened my mouth so much," he admitted to National Public Radio. Now other church leaders were contacting him to offer support and seek advice on avoiding outbreaks. "It's an interesting call to take from someone who wants to know how not to end up like you." The pastor added that his church had been "among the most cautious institutions" in town, limiting the size of in-person services and recommending masks but not requiring them. His congregation had been "willing to play by the rules," but there was "a feeling amongst some people that, 'Why are we doing all this stuff?'"

At 12:01 AM on Tuesday, November 3, Election Day, Governor Mills recorded in her journal that results were in from the hamlet of Dixville Notch in the neighboring state of New Hampshire. "Biden wins all five votes," she wrote. "Clean sweep." It was the first walkover there by any presidential candidate since the town's tradition of midnight voting began in 1960, to accommodate railroad workers who had to be on the job before polling hours. That year Richard Nixon beat John F. Kennedy, nine to nil.[8] Governor Mills's journal entry omitted the results in nearby Millsfield, New Hampshire, which tallied its votes around the same time that night — President Trump had carried the town, sixteen to five.[9] In Maine, the rest of

Election Day brought light snowfall across much of the state, ranging from a dusting to around five inches. Voters were undeterred;
more than three hundred thousand ballots were cast in person and
without incident, save for reports of two-hour lines at some polling
places.[10] By the end of the day, poll workers had also counted 508,918
absentee ballots, more than half of registered voters.[11] Maine's secretary of state later confirmed the total turnout of about 78 percent
was "historic."[12]

The governor was proud and relieved that her state had held "one
of the most controversial presidential elections in history" safely and
legally, despite the pandemic. "We were getting sued," she explained,
referring to a legal challenge earlier that fall against Maine's alleged
"barriers to absentee voting."[13] The plaintiffs, including the Alliance
for Retired Americans, with support from the American Civil Liberties Union, wanted the state to count all absentee ballots that were
postmarked by Election Day, even if they were delivered days later.
"There was this national campaign to do that and we absolutely
resisted," the governor recalled. "It was just sort of encouraging
procrastination," she added, not to mention delaying election
results. Moreover, the governor, a lawyer herself and Maine's former
attorney general, had already done a "really kind of excruciating,
laborious review of the election law statutes" to determine which of
them could be modified by executive order. Her administration
"suspended a couple deadlines" to encourage absentee voting and
facilitate the task of counting an unprecedented number of ballots
submitted by mail or official drop boxes. "We said . . . we don't need
a court to tell us to suspend this law or that law," she recalled. A
superior court judge agreed, and the state's supreme court upheld
that ruling on appeal.[14]

Election Day vote counting in Maine continued into Wednesday,
when Joe Biden was declared the majority winner, avoiding the
runoff element of the state's ranked-choice voting method in its first-
in-the-nation use in a presidential contest.[15] By that night the Democratic nominee had won 53 percent of the popular vote, to his
opponent's 44, and carried Maine's first congressional district handily,
60 percent to 37.[16] President Trump was rewarded for his courtship of

the second district, winning its single electoral vote for the second time. In other Maine election results of note, that record-priced, supposedly nail-biter US Senate race between incumbent Susan Collins and state House Speaker Sara Gideon was not so close in the end; Senator Collins won a fifth term decisively, with 51 percent of voters' support over her opponent's 42. That margin was, however, conspicuously scant compared with the senator's previous win, which she had carried off by 37 percent.

In another plot twist that year Maine's staunchly crimson second district reelected its Democratic congressman Jared Golden, a US Marine Corps veteran. In 2020 he told reporters that by running "on a positive message" he had shown "that voters are hungry for a positive tone, positive leadership, and civility in our public space."[17] As for the Maine legislature, that year Senate Democrats gained a net of one seat to keep their majority, the largest in decades.[18] The party also kept its preponderance in the Maine House of Representatives. Republicans narrowed that advantage but lost one House seat their party had held for decades in a heavily conservative area of central Maine. The Democrat who won it, a surgeon, became the fifth Black lawmaker in Maine's history.[19] "What I want to do is bring us together," he told a regional newspaper, "and I think Maine has a much better opportunity to do that . . . than other places."

Elsewhere in the US, vote counting wore on into November 5, and President Trump continued to stoke rancor and mistrust with baseless claims about the election's integrity.[20] "This is a case when they are trying to steal an election," he told reporters during a press conference, accusing Democrats of corruption but offering no evidence.[21] "They're trying obviously to commit fraud, there's no question about that." That night Governor Mills wrote in her journal that there were still "no results from the presidential, though Biden's pulling ahead in PA, GA, AZ, NC, Nevada . . . Pins and needles. Pins and needles." She noted that the president had made a television appearance "and spewed hate and falsehoods, blaming widespread fraud and ballot stealing." She also mentioned that Steve Bannon had "called for p[eople] like Dr. Fauci to be beheaded." The president's former top aide had made the comment during his podcast that day. "I'd put the heads on pikes," he said. "I'd put them at the two corners of the White House as a warning to federal bureaucrats: Either get with the program or you're gone."[22]

The governor also mentioned that she had talked with Charlie that night. He had pointed out "that countries like Turkey are watching this intently, waiting to see if the 224-year experiment in democracy can work. Whether we can rid ourselves of a dictator peacefully through access to the ballot. Let's certainly hope so." On that day of the pandemic, as the country's steepest infection curve to date continued its ascent, the US had reported 121,349 new cases of COVID-19.[23] In Maine the CDC reported 183 new cases, the state's highest-ever one-day spike. Governor Mills responded with an executive order imposing a statewide mask mandate in all public settings; face coverings had previously been required only when people could not keep six feet apart.[24] She directed all business owners to post signs about the mandate and required large establishments to enforce it. She also noted that her Republican counterpart to the south, Massachusetts governor Charlie Baker, had issued a similar order the previous week.

Ashirah sounded her approval in that week's letter. "We appreciate your recent mandate about masks," she told Governor Mills. "I do think the people choosing not to wear them will continue not to wear them," she wrote, adding that it was "great you're on the record for coming out strongly in support of mask-wearing." Ashirah confessed that she had been wondering "what changed" to cause "such a rise in cases here?" Were too many Mainers shunning face coverings and social distancing? Or were those measures "not as effective as we thought" and people were "getting sick through those safe-guards"? She admitted that she did not "listen to the Maine CDC updates daily; probably the question has been asked and answered." Either way, that week Ashirah had called her siblings, who were "spread out across the country," and "told them to stay safe." She was apprehensive about returning to work at the addiction treatment clinic. The facility would be seeing patients in person the following week, "but then it will be telemedicine until January, which is a relief." She wanted to be at home to manage Clutch, who was "settling in still." That day the dog had disappeared in the woods for "a very worrisome ten minutes" before returning. Ashirah knew his training would "continue to be a ton of work," but, she hastened to add, "it's wonderful to have him! I feel a place in my heart that's been closed beginning to thaw out now." She had been keeping her evenings free so she would "have some time to cuddle with him before bed." She was also thrilled to watch her children "falling in love with him, and him [sic] with them." Her mother had "said it best: 'Dogs are a pain-in-the-ass . . . But, what a dog gives you, nothing else can.'"

Ashirah then changed the subject to Election Day, though she had relegated mention of it to the second page of her letter, toward the end. Four years earlier the presidential election had been "the biggest thing on [her] mind"; by 2020 she had "let go of hoping for a good outcome so it's not so desperate." Ashirah and Chris had felt safe masking up and going to the Temple Town Hall to vote in person. "There's never a line," she explained, "and I've always told the kids we're super lucky because there are people who have to take an entire day off to go vote, and for us you just go in and vote and you're done." That night the Knapps had watched another episode of The West Wing. This time they chose the finale from the show's sixth season, in which a Latino congressman from Texas, played by Jimmy Smits, accepted the Democratic presidential nomination. During his address to the party's convention, he told his audience: "We're all broken, every single one of us, and yet we pretend that we're not. We all live lives of imperfection and yet we cling to this fantasy that there's a perfect life and that our leaders should embody it. But if we expect our leaders to live on some higher moral plane than the rest of us, well, we're just asking to be deceived."[25]

The dialogue moved Ashirah more than it might have if the country's political reality had not been so paralyzed by acrimony and hypocrisy for so long. "What a beautiful speech!" she gushed to Governor Mills, adding that she found herself "weepy all the time these days." She didn't know whether to blame "perimenopause or pandemic / climate change / social justice sensitivity." One "upside," which had taken "thirty years of periods to realize," was that her emotions sometimes came "from seeing such overwhelming beauty in things" that she would "stop trying to fight it and just sit back and enjoy the ride." Ashirah obviously felt a woman-to-woman connection, but she maintained that gender was not a conscious factor in her decision to write to Governor Mills. She did acknowledge her "bias" in having thought, on any level, that she could offer "something in the way of emotional support," or that the governor might "be more emotionally open" to connection, because they were both women. "I should definitely look at that," she added, "the next time somebody comes along who I think, 'I should write to this person' and not just assume that because they're a man, nothing I say will have meaning."

Governor Mills did not dwell on the subject of her gender in any context; with regard to Ashirah's letters, she considered it only in retrospect, when asked directly. "I'm guessing she would not have written to a male governor," she answered. She did not care to elaborate. From the start of her career, it was the inevitable pattern for others to focus on her gender while she got on with the job. After graduating from law school, when she became the first female prosecutor in the criminal division of the Maine Attorney General's Office, she won a homicide case in the state's supreme court against a former police officer who had shot his wife.[26] She had noticed a newspaper reporter in the courtroom and looked for his story that Sunday, only to find it published in "the Family and Society section . . . with the headline, 'The Prosecutor Wore Pale Powder Blue.'" The reporter's story centered on "what a cute thing it was for a 'girl' to be prosecuting a murder case in a room full of men," the governor later recalled. When she became the state's first female district attorney, people often asked her what it was like to be a woman DA. "What a stupid question," she told an audience during a speech to the Maine Bar Association. "I'd say, 'I don't know. I've never been a male DA.'" During her first term in that office she "felt besieged by invitations to speak about domestic violence, child abuse, and sexual assault," from both women's groups and law enforcement. "I finally stopped accepting those invites," she told an oral historian.[27] "I said, 'I want to talk about burglaries, robberies, white collar crimes, arson, manslaughter cases, drug offenses, I do all these other things too, you know.'"

Some of the governor's supporters believed sexism was still a major factor when she took the state's highest office, considering the vitriol she had faced before the pandemic started. "I absolutely think part of why people have been so upset with her and continue to be so upset with her is just because she's a woman," Ashirah said. While she did not consider herself "at all knowledgeable about politics and political realms," it was her "personal feeling" that there was "a certain tone to the disrespect" that was "not relating to her policy." Ashirah recalled some media coverage to that effect during the pandemic. In her social media milieu she often saw "posts . . . calling [the governor] a bitch — I don't think that that same kind of language would be used in the same kind of way talking about a man."

The COVID-19 crisis provided stark new evidence of both the proven ways that women govern differently from men and how their constituents respond.[28] The journal *Politics & Gender* published research in August 2020 that found "a leader's gender has little impact on policy compliance in general."[29] However, the study noted "ample evidence that voters are more likely to exhibit gender-motivated biases toward female political leaders when they belong to the other political party." The governor's friend Janice David recalled seeing offensive anti-Mills yard signs during the pandemic "in the hinterlands" of Maine's politically conservative second district. She was so shocked by the first FUCK MILLS bumper sticker she saw on a passing truck that she called the police. "I just was so appalled . . . Children see this, is this ok?!"

Ultimately Janice felt that "all of these things say more about the people who are putting those signs up" than her friend's personality or leadership. She was surprised and baffled by the suggestion that some Mainers who disapproved of Governor Mills felt she was an inaccessible politician who could not relate to their problems. "She's just a salt-of-the-earth person," Janice countered. "There's no affect to her at all." In the course of their more than four-decade friend-

ship the two women became close despite their "completely opposite" life choices. As a young mother Janice "tried not to" work so
she could stay home with her children. "There was nothing I
desired," she explained. "Janet always had something she desired."
The governor and her friend also had some political differences,
within the same party affiliation — Janice, a progressive Democrat,
attributed the governor's "centrist" lean to the opposing forces that
shaped her ideology, starting with her upbringing in a "Yankee
Republican family," with a father so frugal that he "used to buy his
neckties at yard sales." A teenage Janet Mills was then influenced by
the fraught era of the 1960s, her friend said. "No matter where you
came from, things like civil rights, Vietnam, the women's movement, they all played a part."

Janice was amused by portrayals of the governor as a "wasteful"
spender with an "extreme liberal agenda," as the Maine Republican
Party has described her.[30] "I just crack up . . . This is a family, I mean,
they are downright chintzy," she said of the enduring Mills ethos.
"They don't want to spend a dime they don't have to spend, of theirs
or yours." She added that Governor Mills "wants to have Republicans, as much as possible, supporting stuff she does. She knows how
to compromise." That bent bothered some in the governor's own
party who saw her politics as too conciliatory or tame, especially in
the era of President Trump. In comparison Governor Mills — with
her heartfelt empathy, boundless love of Maine, and idealistic
speeches woven with paeans to the undying pragmatism and perseverance of Mainers — sometimes came across as a toothless romantic. "Janet *is* a romantic," Janice noted. "I do think you have to call
things out. She does, but she's held back . . . Again, as a woman I
think you're in a different position." She pointed to the battery of
incendiary remarks that her predecessor, Paul LePage, made as
governor. "If a woman had said any of those things they would have
condemned her," Janice said. "Not that he didn't get some condem-
nation. It just isn't the same."

Gender and personal conduct aside, the arrival of COVID-19
demanded a profoundly different level of leadership from Governor
Mills than from most of her predecessors, if not all seventy-four of

them. Her equanimity no longer seemed quaint in the face of a global crisis, with dire consequences in every US state, however varied. She was forced to make impossible decisions between "lives and livelihoods" and to rely on her cabinet — chosen when a global pandemic was an unfathomable disaster scenario — to implement them, come what may.[31] By early November 2020 almost a quarter million Americans had died after getting the virus.[32] The case count in the US was climbing toward ten million.[33] Even Maine was watching seemingly every indicator of its hold over the pandemic turn against the state after months of mostly blunting its spread. Janice remembered that Governor Mills "didn't sleep much, literally." Her friend was "just weighing everything back and forth . . . In a state like Maine, where she knows half the people in the state by name, you know that the decisions that are made are affecting people. You know *how* they're affecting people."

In the midst of all that Ashirah's letters kept arriving in Augusta every week. Janice recalled that the governor would sometimes read them aloud to family members, friends, or her staff, often with tears in her eyes. "She felt that this woman was doing so much for her — that that was a big thing for her to sit down and write and be supportive like that, and do it on such a regular basis . . . It really touched her and it *did* keep her going." At the end of Ashirah's November 5 letter, she wished Governor Mills "peace and strength in the long journey we have ahead." After signing her name, Ashirah added a striking postscript: "I haven't said it in a while," she wrote, "but some of the talk around election time got me thinking again: you know that your decisions are right, and a lot of us who have our heads screwed on straight know your decisions are right, and then some folks out there are just totally insane and I hope their comments don't get under your skin!"

On Friday, November 6, Joe Biden was projected as having won the election.[34] Some states were still tallying votes, and he asked Americans to "stay calm," assuring the nation that "the process is working" and "each ballot must be counted." In Maine that day Dr. Shah reported 147 new cases of COVID-19 and several new outbreaks "across the state," including a county hospital near one of the Pentecostal churches that had held superspreader events in October.[35] He also warned that Maine's seven-day positivity rate had more than tripled in the previous two weeks, from 0.54 percent to 1.73. "The risk is everywhere around us," he warned, somehow summoning fresh urgency in his voice when he again recited pleas for people to "do the right thing" and at least wear face coverings. "There's a lot riding on it."

The next morning Governor Mills wrote in her journal that "after four days of counting, the announcement came at 11:30 AM, CNN and all the networks called it for Joe Biden and Kamala Harris." The Democratic nominees had earned more than seventy-five million votes and counting, a record for any White House ticket.[36] Senator Harris had officially become the highest-ranking woman elected to serve in government — the first woman, person of color, and person of Asian descent to be elected vice president. "The nation breathes free again," the governor added to her entry. "Free of hatred and vitriol, [of] mud-slinging from the highest office in the land." In a speech that night, the president-elect asked the nation "to put away the harsh rhetoric" and "listen to each other again."[37] He told both his supporters and voters who had backed President Trump that "to make progress, we must stop treating our opponents as our enemy."

The president, meanwhile, was holed up in the White House and had so far refused to concede. By that point both men had received more votes than Barack Obama's record-setting take in 2008. So far, the Biden campaign's margin of victory was more than four million votes.[38] Turnout in Maine had tied with Colorado and Wisconsin for the nation's second highest, with nearly 76 percent of voters having cast ballots.[39] (Minnesota was number one, with 79 percent turnout.) Sixty-two percent of the votes cast in Maine were by absentee ballot.[40] For Americans who were happy with the election results, that weekend brought overwhelming relief. Governor Mills spent part of Saturday at her home in Farmington, clearing out her barn of old stuff she had been meaning to give or throw away, ostensibly "before the winter." Janice alleged that this had been a much longer-term project, calling her friend "an absolute hoarder" who had

already done "five years of clearing out the barn." In part the governor had always been too busy with her career to make time for
de-cluttering. Janice also blamed "that Maine frugality thing," as
opposed to clinical hoarding associated with depression or personality disorders. "She thinks she's going to give something away that
somebody's going to need," Janice quipped, "and I'm going, 'Nobody
wants that, it's junk Janet' — I'm that friend." On that post-election
Saturday the governor enlisted help from her sister and a different
friend and posted a photo of their trio on her Facebook page, smiling behind their masks, with the caption: "The barn crew hears the
news that a new President is elected." A few more friends stopped
by to celebrate at a social distance, and they drank two bottles of
prosecco, toasting the new administration-to-be. The governor also
posted photos from a hike she took that weekend in the scenic hills
near Maine's capital, and a stunning orange sunset beside a lake. It
was the shortest of breaks before what promised to be the longest
of winters.

On Monday, President-Elect Biden pledged "bold action" against
the pandemic and pleaded with the nation to leave politics out of
that fight. "We could save tens of thousands of lives if everyone
would just wear a mask for the next few months. Not Democratic or
Republican lives, American lives."[41] Both he and President Trump,
who was still questioning the election's legitimacy, hailed the news
that day from the drugmaker Pfizer that its COVID-19 vaccine had
proved 90 percent effective in early trials.[42] Meanwhile, Maine's CDC
reported 172 new cases and more outbreaks, which were becoming
so common that they no longer made front-page news.[43] One of the
largest in the state, at a prison in southern Maine, was still growing,
with 122 inmates and nine employees having tested positive.[44] It was
the second major outbreak at a prison in the state since the department of corrections found inconsistent compliance with pandemic
protocols among its facilities.[45] Criminal justice advocates questioned the Mills administration's enforcement of those guidelines
and reiterated calls made in the early months of the pandemic for
counties not to jail people charged with minor infractions or to
release more of them sooner.[46] That week, by coincidence, a state

oversight group flagged systemic failures by the agency charged with providing private lawyers for indigent clients facing criminal charges.[47] Governor Mills, who had appointed the agency's commissioners, deflected responsibility to them for addressing the failures. She also questioned their recent bid for a bigger budget in the midst of the state's "pandemic-driven shortfall."[48]

In Temple that week the Knapps had finished harvesting the root crops they managed to grow despite Maine's ongoing drought. "Now I'm eagerly awaiting my two dairy goats coming into heat for (hopefully) April babies," Ashirah wrote to Governor Mills, in a letter dated the 10th of November. "Every year I get concerned that the heat won't happen, but of course it always does!" Ashirah had just received the note the governor sent in October. "Thank you for that," she wrote. "I did give both the kids a hug from you." The best part of Ashirah's week seemed to have been her temporary return to the addiction medicine office. She enjoyed seeing her work colleagues and patients for the first time since the clinic switched to telemedicine early in the pandemic. She loved coming home from work each day with a feeling that she had done "something good in the world." After that week the doctors did not plan to see patients in person again until the new year. While Ashirah would "miss the human interaction" she admitted that she was "also happy to work from home, with cases going up." She hoped the reusable masks she had ordered online from a crowdfunded company would be in production by January. "I think one could walk through a COVID ward with those masks and still be safe," she wrote.

Two days later Maine's daily report of new cases reached 197. The state's CDC also reported the deaths of three residents, a toll that was also now increasing by the day.[49] On November 13 a somber Dr. Shah reported a record of 243 new cases and several more deaths. He warned that the state had now tallied more than one-fifth of its all-time COVID-19 case count in just the first half of November, adding that his agency's "gumshoe epidemiologists" could no longer connect the majority of cases to known outbreaks. Maine was now in "an unvirtuous cycle that's building upon itself" — smaller social gatherings were leading to more community spread, which was in

turn making social gatherings even more risky. Dr. Shah told reporters that this was "all the more reason" for people to know how they
could help — "namely wearing face coverings." After saying the
phrase *face coverings* for what might actually have been approaching
the ten thousandth time, he paused and appeared to gather himself,
his eyelids heavy as he took a deep breath and turned to the details
of yet another emerging outbreak.

In the still-unfolding cinematic saga of the global pandemic, it
was as if the montage sequence had begun. In a Hollywood treatment this would have been the point in the story when the drone of
officials and experts reciting the world's spiking COVID-19 metrics
fell away, subsumed by dramatic silence or a gripping orchestral
score. In the US, the next plot point was looming, with the travel-
heavy Thanksgiving holiday less than two weeks away. Would
Americans heed experts' advice to avoid gatherings, or would revel-
ers flout all the guidance en masse? In Maine, Governor Mills made
the decision to bring back unpopular restrictions for visitors from
Massachusetts, citing "alarming" COVID-19 metrics there. Its residents, and Mainers returning from the state, would again have to
quarantine for two weeks or test negative within two days of arriving in Maine. The governor encouraged employers to let people
work remotely and asked residents to "patronize Maine businesses
by ordering curbside and using delivery services."

Would another stay-at-home order be next, as was happening in
Europe? Since late October, Belgium, the Netherlands, France, and
England had gone back into nationwide lockdowns, and Germany a
partial one, as the pandemic's autumn resurgence filled their hospitals.[50] With the US reporting about ninety thousand new cases every
day, a Gallup poll found that Americans' support for another lockdown had fallen sharply since the spring, from a high of 67 percent to
49.[51] When examined along party lines, Republican support dropped
from 74 percent to 40; among Democrats it slipped from 91 to 87
percent. Nonetheless, by mid-November governors from both parties
had put new restrictive measures in place, ranging from mask
mandates imposed by GOP governors in North Dakota and Iowa to
another lockdown by their Democratic counterpart in New Mexico.[52]

Governor Mills was determined to avoid that extreme in Maine, but her administration was running out of other measures to check the pandemic's now rampant spread. Even the tone of her messaging took a frank turn, despite more good news about vaccine progress. "There is no fairytale ending to this nightmare yet," the governor said after Moderna reported that its vaccine candidate was 94 percent effective in early trials.[53] In her second radio address that month she told listeners that some of Maine's mask-wearing guidance to date had been "confusing" — one previous iteration called for face coverings only when social distance was "difficult to maintain." Now the state had "a bright line that says if you are in a public setting, wear a face covering."[54] For the avoidance of doubt, the governor added that it was "just common sense" not to wear a mask while "hiking alone on the Appalachian Trail or hunting in the woods."

Her amended order left in place a broad exception for people with "serious medical conditions or who are otherwise unable to remove the mask without assistance." Only large establishments were required to deny entry or service for noncompliance, but a range of business owners reported confrontations with customers and some employees who claimed exemptions or simply ignored the mandate. That tension point troubled the governor too, as she wrote in her journal. "I have been deeply concerned about putting the burden of enforcement on the clerk at the checkout . . . working solo sometimes late at night and dealing with difficult clientele." So far she had stopped short of requiring smaller businesses to enforce the mandate. The governor raised that possibility during "an emotional meeting" with retail industry representatives in mid-November, held by videoconference ahead of their mainstay holiday shopping season. "I just looked at them and I said, 'What are my choices?'" she remembered. "'I don't want to shut down business . . . when you folks have suffered so much, but tell me what you could do to help save people's lives?'"

For the president of the Retail Association of Maine, Curtis Picard, that conversation was part of a period he found "hard to talk about sometimes." He had led the association for fifteen years and formed personal relationships with "a lot of the people, the small business owners" he represented. "I know what they went through," he said, his voice thick with emotion, "having to lay off people through that period, worried about their economic survival." Curtis was also serving on the governor's Economic Recovery Committee, which by the end of that month planned to release its final report on how to stabilize and rebuild the state's economy post-pandemic. He knew that Governor Mills had to "make incredibly hard decisions every single day" but said his members "pushed constantly for additional guidance whenever there was a new executive order" — he explained that "the intent" of those orders "was sometimes different than what was written." He appreciated that the governor fostered meaningful collaboration. "We were all [just] brainstorming how we could try to keep businesses open as much as possible, because you're trying to weigh the health security . . . and the economic survival of Maine people. It was not easy. That's an understatement."

Curtis briefed his members on the discussion and sent Governor Mills a long email listing their concerns, starting with the mask mandate. "Please be clear with Maine people that there really are no medical exemptions," he wrote, adding that "even people who claim a medical exemption can wear a plastic face shield." He also implored the governor not to limit store operating hours, much less shut them down, except as "a last resort." In turn retailers suggested further reducing customer limits — over the summer they had cut store traffic to five people per thousand square feet, or about 40 percent of normal capacity. Then winter arrived, and the industry's hope of recouping losses during the holidays disappeared, Curtis said, "like in the span of two weeks . . . once it started getting cold again and the [COVID-19] numbers started going up." He remembered thinking, "I'm glad we still have five per thousand square feet and [are] not shut down completely." His members pointed out a "flip side" to capacity limits, that more customers would be "queuing up outside of stores in colder, darker weather," as Curtis explained to the governor. "Businesses will need to be concerned with ice or snow falling from roofs as people are waiting in line. Again, no easy answer."

By the third week of November the Maine CDC was so inundated with reports of possible new cases of COVID-19 that the agency had to bring in twenty members of the state's National Guard to help with contact tracing and outbreak investigations.[55] That month had already been more deadly than the previous three combined, with two dozen lives lost to the virus.[56] Some Mainers kept ignoring the Mills administration's constant pleas to take precautions and disobeyed laws despite recent tragic evidence of the consequences. If they needed reminding, a lawsuit had just been filed against the inn that hosted the August superspreader wedding. The business was sued by the estate of a woman who died after contracting COVID-19 from an employee of her nursing home, who had been a wedding guest.[57] Incidentally the ceremony's officiant, Pastor Bell, shared a Twitter post at the end of November to update his followers on his plans to expand his ministry. "Continuing to use #aviation to reach #others with the #Gospel," he wrote, adding that he was "praying about where to start another church in the coming months!"[58] He also posted photos of his new office and a new pickup truck, both gifts from his parish.[59] None of his posts that month mentioned the pandemic. Also in late November, Rick Savage indicated that he would comply with a judge's order to close his brewpub, avoiding a fine of $5,000 a day.[60] The restaurateur's license had been suspended earlier that month, and he was found in contempt of court for flouting pandemic restrictions.

Governor Mills reiterated her reluctance to impose another stay-at-home order, especially in the absence of federal stimulus funds, including supplemental unemployment benefits that were set to expire at the end of December. The governor all but begged Mainers not to travel or gather for Thanksgiving: "As you make your plans . . . please consider whether any in-person gathering is at all necessary."[61] She also issued a curfew for movie theaters, casinos, restaurants, and other businesses that offered seated food and drink service. They were now required to close by 9:00 PM through the first week of December.[62] She noted that most other Northeast states had done the same to discourage long evening outings "at a time when many students and family members are returning to Maine and . . . social gatherings are more common." The curfew came with only one day's notice, angering hospitality industry leaders and some state Republican lawmakers who questioned its effectiveness. As similar measures were put in place across the country, President Trump appeared to acknowledge, in a series of tweets, that he had lost the election "in the eyes of the media." He repeated, again without evidence, that the vote was "rigged" and he would "concede NOTHING!"[63]

As if to underscore how much the world needed reasons to smile, a tech-savvy Maine lobsterman was also making headlines, for one of his recent posts on the video-sharing app TikTok.[64] The clip showed Jacob Knowles and his crew rescuing a tiny bird from drowning after it had been "blown offshore" and feeding the "poor little guy" potato chips while it dried off. The bird sat on Jacob's head as he steered his boat back to Winter Harbor on Maine's northern coast, where he set it free. "See you later buddy," he called out as the bird flew away toward the shore. The post had six million views by the time Maine media outlets picked up the story.[65] One newspaper editorial lauded the fifth-generation lobsterman for helping "make this bad year a little better."[66]

A few days later Ashirah sent Governor Mills some comic relief. "I told my husband this morning that I would have to up my humor in my letters to you because your life and job are probably getting much harder with COVID expanding in Maine," she wrote. Her entire dispatch for that week consisted of three short vignettes from Wednesday morning "in the Knapp household," starting with an exchange Ashirah had with her son — she was on the first floor of the house and had called upstairs to say that Owen had neglected to brush his teeth and clean up breakfast. "Uh, I'll come down," he answered from his bedroom on the second floor. A few minutes later Ashirah called up to him again: "Why are you back upstairs? You brushed your teeth but didn't clean up breakfast!'" Meanwhile, Chris was in the next room reviewing math homework with their daughter. "But dad, I *understand* fractions," Pamela had told him. "Well you must not understand everything," Ashirah had heard him respond. "You got five out of the last six wrong." As all this played out Ashirah had been sitting at her desk with Clutch at her feet —

the dog had gotten into her sourdough bread starter the day before and eaten several cups of the fermented culture, which could be harmful to dogs, before he was thwarted. He was now "having digestion issues" and making Ashirah's work area "quite . . . odiferous." She drew a smiley face at the end of the sentence. "Good thing I love each of them so much," she added, then wished the governor "a good holiday" and signed off.

Ashirah's letter was dated November 20. That day, a Friday, Governor Mills revealed that her administration would help launch a plan to build the nation's first floating offshore wind research farm in the Gulf of Maine.[67] One of her major goals since taking office was to establish Maine as a key player in the country's growing offshore wind industry, despite vehement opposition from many of the state's commercial fishermen over potential damage to key fishing areas. The governor promised to engage them meaningfully in planning the project and billed the small-scale array as a "measured, deliberative approach." It was a start, she argued, toward securing the state's economic future, especially its post-pandemic recovery. The project would also deliver on her administration's promise to generate more renewable energy in the fight against climate change. The goals were just two of the sort of pre-pandemic imperatives that America's governors were juggling with the complex, urgent process of allocating and disbursing federal pandemic relief funds ahead of a December 30 deadline.[68] During the same week as the wind farm announcement, Governor Mills directed more than $6 million in federal coronavirus aid funds to expand and extend the state's relief program for Mainers who could not afford to pay their rent because of COVID-19.[69] Her administration also put a similar amount toward extending high-speed internet access to more than seven hundred students in rural Maine and allocated a second round of pandemic recovery grants to small businesses and nonprofits.[70]

On Saturday of that weekend, the governor put on a blaze-orange coat and hat — it was the middle of Maine's hunting season — and went for a half-mile hike near her camp, to a ledge overlooking the lake.[71] She sat there for a while under a sky streaked with lead-gray clouds and took in the familiar view across the lake toward a spine of dark-blue hills to the west. Later she posted photos from the trail on her Facebook page, including shots of two hand-painted signs nailed to some trees she passed in the woods. One was lettered with a sentence from the first published work by John Muir: STORMS, THUNDERCLOUDS, WINDS IN THE WOODS, WERE WELCOME AS FRIENDS.[72] The naturalist wrote that line after an encounter with a rare orchid in a Wisconsin bog had made him weep with joy. The other sign held the final verse from the 1866 poem *Flower-de-Luce*, by Maine native Henry Wadsworth Longfellow: O FLOWER OF SONG, BLOOM ON, AND MAKE FOREVER THE WORLD MORE FAIR AND SWEET.[73] The governor's walks and hikes, however short, were usually enough to revitalize her, or had to be, for the next stretch of running the state. In Augusta one of her favorite evening strolls was the third-of-a-mile route from the Blaine House to the end of the city's Capital Park across the road, where an obelisk marked the mausoleum of her nineteenth-century poet predecessor Governor Lincoln. "There's nothing poetic about the place though," she quipped. His grave was in "a spooky, dark corner" of the park, she explained, "but then you find out that in 1991 they dug up the crypt and there was nobody there." Oddly enough the former occupant referred to his own "silent tomb" in the final lines of his lengthy poem *The Village*; the minor nature epic ends with a wistful lament for its author's "vain dreams" of "worthier offerings" as a bard, which he had forsaken "to toil in Law and climb its rugged way."[74]

On the Tuesday before Thanksgiving, Maine's CDC reported the deaths of twelve people from COVID-19 and 258 new cases. Both were one-day highs, as Dr. Shah noted in a post on his official Twitter account, adding tersely that "these are not the kinds of records we want to be setting."[75] On Wednesday a winter storm brought snow to much of Maine as Governor Mills made her final appeals for her constituents to skip holiday gatherings or take precautions to hold them safely. She was echoing the same message from President-Elect Biden, who had finally been allowed to begin the transition to his administration, including making plans for his pandemic response. A federal official appointed by President Trump had delayed that process, citing "recent developments involving legal challenges and certifications of election results."[76] When the official eventually gave her approval, the president responded on Twitter that the decision was "in the best interest of our country" but added that he would "keep up the good fight" and believed he would "prevail."[77]

Governor Mills spent Thanksgiving at the Blaine House. She wrote in her journal that it was a "small, quiet day with just a couple of family . . . safely distanced." In Temple the Knapps skipped their tradition of spending the holiday with Chris's "big extended family." Ashirah recalled that everyone was "luckily . . . in agreement that we shouldn't get together because of COVID." His parents, though, had been part of Ashirah and Chris's social bubble, so they came to the homestead for dinner. "I had a surprise right before the meal," Ashirah told the governor in a letter a few days later. "I went to do animal chores and found one of my goats unable to lower her head and stagerring [sic] around her pen." Some quick internet research had suggested three potential problems, but Ashirah "only had medication on hand to treat two of them." She gave the goat both treatments and "miracle of miracles, by the end of the evening she was improving." The goat turned out to have had a thiamine deficiency that could be fatal if untreated. "I thought for sure she'd die that night," Ashirah wrote. "She's prone to medical issues and not a great milker, but the sweetest goat you'd ever want to meet."

During the family's Thanksgiving dinner Ashirah was also anxious about Clutch, who spent most of the meal whining, rather understandably, "because he smelled the food the whole time." The Knapps were still "at the very beginning of training with him and trying to understand him," she remembered. Chris's mother was nervous too — she was allergic to dogs and also had "a real fear" of them "because of events that happened when she was little." All those factors "made it . . . less relaxing of an evening," Ashirah admitted. The next day Clutch attacked one of the Knapps' other goats after it escaped from its enclosure. "No damage was done, but I was pretty shaken-up," Ashirah told the governor. She added, as if to reassure herself, that "the dog comes from working herding lines so he should be trainable."

From there Ashirah turned to her "last story of the week" from her trip to town that day, where she had overheard a man "speaking unhappily" to a female laundry attendant. Ashirah had realized that the man, who was not wearing a mask, "wasn't just unhappy, he was laying into her about the Americans with Disabilities Act and how he couldn't be treated any differently than anyone else and he was going 'to sue the shit' out of them." Ashirah being Ashirah, she "couldn't just leave it at that" — she felt "a societal responsibility" to try to "diffuse [sic] the situation." She asked if the woman "needed any help, as a way of letting her know she wasn't alone." The attendant had said the police were on their way, so Ashirah asked the man if she could assist with his laundry. His response was "something rosy" about wanting to "get that woman fired." Ashirah had left as the police arrived so she "didn't see how it ended," but she was "proud" of having spoken to both people involved. "It was also something that was only right and reasonable to expect anyone to do," she told Governor Mills.

The episode was another signal that the enforcement problem retailers had complained about earlier that month was broadening. By the end of November, Maine had recorded sixty-seven deaths from COVID-19 and nearly half of the state's cumulative case count.[78] The state's seven-day positivity rate "sadly continued to climb," as Dr. Shah reported on the last day of the month. The metric had jumped to almost 4 percent, up from 2.6 the week before.[79] In fact all of the metrics Maine's CDC was using "to keep tabs on" the pandemic's spread in the state had risen. On the eve of December, the only one that seemed sure to decline was the count of available beds in Maine's intensive care units.

CHAPTER EIGHT

"... in the midst of hope there is horror..."

I am in quarantine," the governor wrote. It was Tuesday, December 1, and she was isolating in the Blaine House, "having had 'close contact' with a person who tested positive for the virus, namely one of my security guys." In her journal entry for that day Governor Mills noted the irony that she had been in the car with the infected officer for only a few minutes while she took "a long conference call about COVID." They had worn masks and, so far, she had no symptoms. She recorded a two-and-a-half-minute video message to tell her constituents that she would be working from home while waiting to see if she tested positive for the virus. "I'm still taking the same steps that other Maine people are taking to keep others safe," she added, underscoring that "no one is immune" from the pandemic. "Please take this seriously. Tell everybody else [to] take this seriously too." Her video was less polished than her other on-camera appearances, which she usually made from behind her desk at the statehouse, with technical support from her staff. This time she was alone in her office at the governor's residence. She sat a little too close to the camera, presumably so viewers could see a photograph on the wall behind her of a lobster boat with the name HOPE on the side of its hull. "We are Maine strong," she said with a smile and a resolute toss of her head. "Please keep the faith and stay safe," she added. "I look forward to talking with you later this week."

The next day President Trump released a forty-six-minute video about the results of the November election.[1] It was recorded without an audience and posted only on social media. The president stood at a lectern in the White House Diplomatic Reception Room and started: "This may be the most important speech I've ever made." He went on to repeat claims of "great voter fraud, fraud that has never been seen like this before."[2] All he omitted was evidence. The president mentioned the pandemic four times but only in the context of the election — he accused Democrats of using COVID-19, "sometimes referred to as the China virus, where it originated, as an excuse to mail out tens of millions of ballots" and to make "destructive changes to our election laws" that "were not a necessary response to the pandemic." That day the number of new cases reported in the US in the previous twenty-four hours topped two hundred thousand for the first time. The count of people hospitalized with the virus also reached a record of more than one hundred thousand.[3]

In Maine that day Dr. Shah held a remote briefing to report 232 new cases. In the previous forty-eight hours, he added, there had been twenty-four deaths and eleven new outbreaks.[4] Governor Mills was a few minutes late to join the conference, again from a computer in her Blaine House office, now on day five of her quarantine. "Sorry, I was having trouble getting connected, doing this on my own," she said with a self-conscious laugh. She told viewers that she was still symptom-free and gave an update on the state's vaccine distribution planning, calling the process "a monumental undertaking, nothing simple about it."

She did not elaborate at the time but recalled privately that she had been "so ecstatic that there *was* a vaccine," then immediately faced the reality of having to "decide who should be first in line" to get it. Most states were starting with front-line health workers, but Maine had the country's oldest population. The governor had "some really hard heart to heart conversations" with Dr. Shah, and her other top health officials and their departments made recommendations, but the final decisions were hers. "Everybody's going to be exposed to the virus [and] thinks they need the vaccine — who among us is more likely to get very sick and die when exposed?" she considered. She "had friends who were getting cancer" but would have to wait their turn, depending on her judgment. "I'm not God," she remembered thinking; religious leaders were among those outside her administration who advised her. The whole dilemma "became so simple, ultimately, but so complicated — how fast could we get as many people [vaccinated] as possible," she recalled.

Now, with the start of that process imminent, she leveled with Mainers watching that day's briefing that the federal government had, without explanation, halved the number of vaccine doses planned for its first allocation to Maine and some other states. The governor also warned her audience that "a very concerning perfect storm" was forming, with federal pandemic aid set to expire at the end of the month, including unemployment benefits for tens of thousands of Mainers, and Congress had yet to approve a second relief package. She pleaded with her constituents to take all precautions to protect themselves and one another from the virus. "We sound like a broken record," she said. "The holidays are upon us, we want to pretend that everything's back to normal, ho ho ho, but it's not."

She then took a question from a reporter who asked whether there were "any other staffers, or people who have been around you, quarantining . . . and can you say how big that web is?" The briefing was broadcast on public radio, and Ashirah's husband had been listening in Temple — Chris thought the reporter's question was "somewhat aggressive," as Ashirah related in that week's letter to Governor Mills. "He said you answered it really well by pointing out that . . . your office practices social distancing and mask wearing so no one else would have been exposed!" Ashirah mentioned that she and Chris regularly checked on an elderly woman in their community, who had told them that her home health aide "does not wear a mask" and was "sick + coughing" during a recent appearance. "Excuse my language but WTF?!" Ashirah wrote. Maine was among the states with a persistent shortage of direct-care workers that the pandemic had magnified beyond crisis level.[5] The Knapps had notified the woman's relatives about the aide's alleged transgression, which was only the latest example of broader personal irresponsibility that troubled Ashirah: "I should have known we, as a society, would choose not to take individual action but would instead wait for the 'big fix' to save us — in this case the vaccine." She lamented that this was "the same behavior we show with climate change and most other problems . . . rather than also looking at our own actions."

Judges and lawyers call that behavior willful blindness, or "the idea that there is an opportunity for knowledge, and a responsibility to be informed, but it is shirked," as author and former CEO Margaret Heffernan defined it.[6] She encountered the concept when reading about the 2006 trial of Enron executives Kenneth Lay and Jeffrey Skilling, who were convicted on charges of fraud and conspiracy for massively inflating the value of their energy company. The judge in their case had instructed the jury: "You may find that a defendant had knowledge of a fact if you find that the defendant deliberately closed his eyes to what would otherwise have been obvious to him."[7] In Margaret's 2011 book *Willful Blindness: Why We Ignore the Obvious at Our Peril*, she argued that the condition "originates . . . in the innate human desire for familiarity" — it "seems innocuous and feels efficient" but can "put us in peril," with consequences ranging from obesity and failed marriage to medical malpractice, genocide, and global warming.[8] Likewise, she pointed out, the fact that blindness can be willed "is what gives us the capacity to change it," individually and in society.[9]

By early December the first COVID-19 vaccines were expected to be available in the US within weeks. Meanwhile the states faced a deadline of December 4 to submit their distribution plans to federal officials.[10] Maine's finalized proposal called for inoculating nearly thirteen thousand healthcare workers first, starting with those in hospital intensive care units, emergency departments, and inpatient COVID-19 wards.[11] Ashirah had strong views on the vaccination hierarchy and shared them with Governor Mills. "After frontline health workers (which better include the housekeeping staff at hospitals) the next group in line should be essential workers," she wrote, adding that "we should be thanking and protecting the people risking their lives for us." Ashirah hated to "put the elders after them" but she felt that residents of nursing homes and other congregate care facilities could be protected with strong safety protocols. "People just need to stop screwing [that] up," she added.

As the pandemic worsened, Ashirah continued to think of "all the people . . . who do not have the open land at their fingertips that we have." In describing each of the seasons in Temple, she had talked of a dramatic transformation in the colder months that turned the Knapps' land into "this gigantic playground outside." Winter was "the best example of the beauty and the harshness" of their home-stead, especially on mornings when she woke up to temperatures well below zero. Ashirah found exposure to that season's elements perennially "invigorating and exhilarating in a way that nothing else is." After the heat of summer, she and her family loved "having the world change so much and being able to walk on water" so they could go cross-country skiing, snowshoeing, ice-skating, and sled-ding. She also mentioned "things that are difficult" about wintering in the woods of Temple that made the season "just straight-up more work" that "gets to be a lot in the end." After snowstorms the network of pathways around the homestead needed shoveling, between the house, the barn, the root cellar, the classroom, and the car, which the Knapps kept parked halfway down their long drive-way. A neighbor cleared the road with his tractor, but Ashirah was "always thinking about whether the car will start" or if she should carry the battery charger down the icy driveway just in case. Temperatures that could drop to twenty degrees below zero meant that outdoor work and farm chores were more difficult, in addition to "having to constantly dry out wet mittens and wet hats and wet boot liners."

As December 2020 began, Ashirah wondered whether the dark-ening days and the frigid cold would be harder to endure with the pandemic's grim metrics "going up and up and up." She felt "so grateful to be tucked away in a quiet corner" but was struggling with the continued "ups and downs of training" Clutch; the dog at least provided plenty of comic material and dramatic incidents for Ashirah's letters. At the end of her first one for that month, she shared the story of a recent encounter with hot popcorn, which Chris had taken off the stove one night and poured into a bowl. "A few kernels popped out and the dog went to investigate," Ashirah wrote. "He pulled back very fast when he realized how hot they were!" Her son had laughed while taking his own handful of popcorn, until he burned himself too: "Then we all started laugh-ing at *him*." However trifling some of the content Ashirah chose for her letters, they had become a singular source of communion for Governor Mills. They were also a sort of universal tether to her constituents, despite Ashirah's uncommon lifestyle, or, perhaps, because of it —after all she was just as unique as each of the governor's more than 1.3 million constituents. She was, however, the only one who sent the governor a letter *every week*.

On the same day that Ashirah wrote about the popcorn incident, Governor Mills extended Maine's 9:00 PM curfew until January 3 for bars and other businesses that served food or drinks to seated customers. The curfew was a "targeted step . . . in public settings where we know folks are more likely to let their guard down and expose themselves and others to this deadly virus." The governor added that it allowed businesses "to stay open for the majority of their operating hours." She again mentioned that the curfew was "in line with actions taken by other states." The leader of a hospitality industry trade group told the press that, with COVID-19 cases spiking, the curfew extension was less surprising to his members than its initial imposition before Thanksgiving. Still, they were "skeptical of the impact" the measure would have, now that "most cases seem to be originating in private gatherings."[12] He was referring to a shift in guidance from state and federal health officials earlier that fall after more Americans had returned to indoor activity. To his knowledge, he added, his members were "adhering to the state's strict safety standards, because they understand the risk that failure would mean to their employees, customers and the future of their businesses."

The governor's decisions, nine months into the pandemic, continued to aggrieve some Mainers but reassure others. That paradox was "part of the nature of this crisis," said US senator and former Maine governor Angus King. "The problem Janet had," he believed, "and what made her response so remarkable, and important, was that she had to make decisions that would have direct impact on people's lives." If, for example, her "order for a curfew . . . shut your bar down and you lost money, or maybe even lost your bar, you knew it," Senator King said. "What you didn't know is that she may have saved your mother's life, but it takes real guts to make decisions that have an overt negative political implication, on the abstract proposition that it will save lives." Senator King attributed some of the criticism aimed at the governor — and any of her counterparts who had made similar or more cautious decisions — to "the coarseness of our current political world . . . and leaders who have enabled and encouraged that."

Many of Governor Mills's actions in response to COVID-19 were not just unpleasant for her to take but unpopular, to say the least. "All the politics pointed in the other direction — to open the schools sooner, to take away the mask mandate sooner, to not do the curfews," Senator King noted. "She did it the way she did it because she thought it would help Maine get through this and save lives," he added. It remained to be seen whether the pandemic's trajectory would corroborate the governor's overabundant caution, if it ever could. John F. Kennedy spoke of a parallel conundrum, if a different degree of threat, in a 1953 speech on "the unrelenting efforts of the Soviets to build irresistible military strength" through the development of nuclear weapons.[13] The then senator Kennedy said it was "an obligation of the most pressing sort, to inform the American people of the severity of the threat to our security and the sacrifices that must be made to meet it. This is not an issue, I think, on which the Democrats can win elections, for only disaster could prove that correct."

On December 5, Governor Mills announced that her COVID-19 test results came back negative. "Masks work!" she trumpeted to Mainers, adding that she "firmly" believed she would have tested positive if not for the face coverings that both she and her infected security officer had been wearing when she was with him.[14] She clarified that she would stay in quarantine for the rest of the ten-day period following her exposure. The governor took the occasion to make yet another plea for people to "hang on" and take precautions. "We have entered the darkest days of this pandemic," she noted, "but hope is on the horizon." That evening she wrote in her journal that she was "watching the first snowfall from the Blaine House" as she wrote a short poem:

> *Grumbling plow*
> *plodding through town*
> *A headache of wind*

> *teasing tree tips*
> *Petty creatures hole-hiding*
> *barely taking breath*
> *Bent to an anonymous fate.*
> *The world gravity downed,*
> *Peace-hunting,*
> *Mist-wrecked,*
> *Sleep now*
> *Fog bound on*
> *bowed ground.*

By morning almost a quarter of the state had lost power as heavy, wet snow fell across New England and wind gusts topped gale force.[15] In the central Maine town of Troy the storm caused a small dairy farm's barn to collapse, trapping eighty cows inside.[16] Neighbors rushed to help, and all but six of the cows were saved and relocated to another farm nearby. "I thanked God it wasn't any worse, and it could have been," one of the farm's owners told a reporter. He explained that he and his wife had already been struggling to stay in business despite the pandemic and dramatic fluctuations in milk prices, compounded by the state's ongoing drought. "Maine people were born tough," he said, adding that "they can take a lot, but they do break."

The next day Dr. Shah reported 427 new cases of COVID-19, a one-day record that he called "a surge on top of a surge."[17] The Maine CDC had been "hiring and hiring," he added, but its personnel were so overwhelmed with lab results that the agency could no longer give a full case report to every person who tested positive. It would instead prioritize those who were most vulnerable to serious infection or at risk of spreading or getting the virus in congregate settings. On December 8 the United Kingdom became the first Western country to begin vaccine distribution; Russia and China had started inoculating their citizens with vaccines that had yet to finish late-stage trials.[18] Two days later a US government advisory panel ruled that the vaccine developed by Pfizer and BioNTech was safe for widespread use, leaving only the US Food and Drug Administration's emergency use authorization outstanding.[19] The next day, Friday, December 11, President Trump pressed the FDA via his chief of staff. He also wrote Twitter posts calling the agency "a big, old, slow turtle" and urging its commissioner to stop "playing games and start saving lives."[20] The FDA gave its provisional approval before the end of the day, and by Sunday shipments of freezer-packed vaccine doses were on their way to the states.[21]

The milestone of the first vaccine approval in the US coincided with the beginning of Hanukkah, which the Knapps celebrated each year in addition to Christmas, in keeping with Ashirah's Jewish faith. "The kids have a lot of fun decorating the whole house for whatever holiday is coming," she said. For each night of Hanukkah they sang songs and said the traditional blessings over their menorah as they lit candles and exchanged gifts. "Another piece that we have added in, which I really enjoy and we have all found meaningful, is thinking and talking about the idea of having light in the darkness," Ashirah explained. Governor Mills touched on that theme when she marked the start of the Jewish holiday in 2020 in her radio address for that week.[22] She talked of the "light that exists in the hearts of people" as "beacons who guide me through the toughest times." The governor also told listeners that while their celebrations "may look different this holiday season," they remained "as meaningful and spiritual as they did through other, darker times — through wars, depressions, storms and hardship." By then her administration had committed all of the $1.25 billion in federal pandemic relief funds, two weeks before the government's deadline.[23] One of those allocations sent $600 checks to many unemployed Mainers that month, which the governor hoped would be "a lifeline" through the holidays."[24]

That weekend she presented a new outdoor display of fourteen Christmas trees around the perimeter of the Blaine House, each one decorated by the staff of a different state agency, with a central theme of resilience. "The Department of Marine Resources had lobster pots on theirs, Fish and Wildlife had, you know, snowshoes and traps and fishing gear, and it was kind of cute," the governor said. She had not done much to decorate the interior of the house because it was still closed to the public, so she liked the idea that "people could drive by slowly and see the trees." Before long both the trees and front lawn were found to have been redecorated with dozens of disposable face masks. "Protesters would come almost every Saturday, and . . . started throwing masks at the trees," the governor recalled, laughing with the little snort she sometimes gave when she was genuinely amused or, for that matter, unamused. "Kind of a cheap shot," she added. "It's Christmas trees, for chrissakes."

The gesture was most likely in answer to her stern announcement, the day after the Blaine House tree unveiling, that she was "simplifying and strengthening" the state's mask mandate by requiring enforcement.[25] She had issued a new executive order stipulating that the "owners and operators of all indoor public spaces, regardless of the type of entity or size," would now be required to deny entry to anyone not wearing a face covering. In a long media release accompanying the order, the governor explained that "claiming a medical exemption" was no longer "an excuse" to enter any sort of establishment without a mask. "This comes in light of reports from retailers of individuals abusing the exemption," she explained, noting that there were "reasonable" alternatives to masks for people with disabilities. The statement included a quote from the leader of the advocacy group Disability Rights Maine, whose community rejected "recent attempts to misappropriate our identities and misuse our vitally important and hard-fought civil rights protections, as a form of misguided civil disobedience," adding that a "vast majority of Maine people with disabilities wear face coverings . . . because it is safer, and it is smart."

In the statement Governor Mills leveled with Mainers that her administration was "running out of available public health tools" to curb the pandemic. She reiterated that imposing another stay-at-home order and closing schools and businesses was "the last thing I want to do." Her announcement also noted the penalties for noncompliance, including trespassing charges, fines, and prison time. The intention behind her new order was clear, but the "Exceptions" clause again left room for misinterpretation. It allowed that masks were "not required" for people who had "trouble breathing or related medical conditions," as well as those who were "unable to put on or remove the mask without assistance" and people with "a developmental issue that is complicated or irritated by a face covering," but the clause went on to say that "no accommodation may make it permissible for any person to enter or remain in any indoor public setting without a face covering." The order prompted requests for more clarity almost immediately, and the governor vented frustration in her journal: "Another tough day . . . People think it is easy to issue these orders and make these decisions. But each of these executive orders is heart-wrenching, drafted after much brainstorming, with great deliberation and detail to words." By then she had issued sixty-two of them in the nine months since she proclaimed a state of emergency, compared with just thirteen during her first year in office.[26]

Governor Mills had typically drafted executive orders related to the pandemic in consultation with her chief legal counsel and her commissioner of health and human services, Jeanne Lambrew. Commissioner Lambrew had been unanimously confirmed to that post after serving in the Clinton and Obama administrations.[27] As a senior aide to President Obama, she had helped design and implement the Affordable Care Act — one of the law's main authors called her "the master of the fine details," adding that "no one in the executive or legislative branch knew as much as she did."[28] Commissioner Lambrew had a PhD in public health and was known in her field as something of a celebrity. She lived in Maine from the age of nine, in a family of medical professionals who spent holidays arguing about healthcare policy.[29] Young Jeanne was moved by their passion for the subject, if not their exuberance, deducing that "the arguments were all about this: How do we care for each other?" She was the first person Governor Mills named to her cabinet, a choice the governor declared was "the most important appointment" she could make.[30] She added that Dr. Shah accepted the job of running Maine's CDC in part because he had wanted to work with Dr. Lambrew.[31]

The governor came to regard both hires among the wisest and most fortuitous of her administration. Apart from Commissioner

Lambrew's expertise, she had a steadying effect on people she oversaw or was charged with informing during the pandemic. She spoke
daily with Dr. Shah and the governor and held countless conference
calls with nursing home administrators, physicians' advocates,
hospital CEOs, state lawmakers, and myriad other stakeholders. "It
was so important to quell the level of potential panic and make sure
they knew what we were doing," Governor Mills recalled, "and say
'here's what we're thinking, what do you think?' Even if they didn't
like it." For Commissioner Lambrew, the job was "by far the most
public-facing" of her career, and that was how she described it *before*
COVID-19, in an alumni magazine profile published in January 2020
by Amherst College, her undergraduate alma mater. At that time
she explained that she had "always struggled with the limelight" and
that "being interviewed makes her feel like a turtle who longs to
retreat into its shell." That spring, when she started regularly joining
the Maine CDC's remote pandemic briefings, Commissioner
Lambrew did look turtlish on camera as she read stiffly from
prepared remarks, often without looking up to acknowledge those
who might be watching. While some might have appreciated her
lack of flash, she was usually upstaged by Dr. Shah.

By late fall, his broadcasts had turned somber as he recited grim
and growing metrics of the pandemic's toll. Somehow, he always
summoned gravity and sincerity, especially in announcing deaths —
he withheld names but read out each person's home county, gender,
and age, slowly and deliberately, then offered condolences to those
grieving, before moving on to the rest of his update. He did not
break from that routine even on the morning of December 14, when
the first vaccine shipments were finally delivered to three of Maine's
largest hospitals.[32] "Let's not forget the storm even as the sun is
emerging," he started, channeling Governor Mills, whose remarks
were often replete with nature metaphors. Dr. Shah went on to
report 2,574 new cases and thirty-two deaths in just the previous
week. He spoke for nearly six minutes before he allowed a touch of
tongue-in-cheek humor as he turned to "the big item of discussion."
He acknowledged that the milestone of vaccine distribution was "a
light at the end of the tunnel" then deadpanned to viewers that it

was "important to remember that you're still in a tunnel." He added that "hard decisions have been made to get us here," but fewer than 2,000 vaccine doses had arrived in the state out of the 2.6 million needed for the "massive undertaking" of fully inoculating Maine's population. "In the same way that our spirits are lifted when we see the first buds on the trees . . . in the spring," he leveled, "we all know . . . it will be many months ahead before the snow fully melts." In the meantime, Dr. Shah warned that it was imperative for Mainers "simply not to let your guard down" but keep taking precautions, especially over the coming holidays. "COVID-19 has not been vanquished, in Maine or across the country."

Governor Mills echoed him in a Twitter post, allowing that the vaccine's arrival was "a much-needed beacon of hope."[33] Scores of Mainers had also turned to the holiday season for hope that month and found ways either to reimagine their traditions within pandemic parameters or create new ones. In Portland, the state's largest city, locals could sign up for a new Secret Santa program that paired them with strangers to swap gifts that they were encouraged to buy from local businesses and artisans.[34] In midcoast Maine, an annual holiday light display at the largest botanical garden in New England was "transformed" from a walking tour to a driving route, with tickets at $40 per carload.[35] Farther north, the city of Bangor canceled its annual holiday parade and organized a light display contest for the public to vote on. More than sixty homeowners and businesses in the region signed up for a chance at the $500 prize for "Best Overall Display."[36] Even the Calvary Baptist Church in southern Maine, led by Pastor Bell, appeared to embrace socially distanced celebration. In mid-December the parish held a "drive-thru caroling spectacular," posting an invitation on its Facebook page for "everyone to drive through our parking lot as we safely sing about the true reason for the season."[37]

Despite Mainers' efforts at merriment, the state's COVID-19 metrics rose relentlessly, and confusion prevailed in the week after Governor Mills issued her mask mandate enforcement order. Retailers, in particular, complained to her administration that people were still abusing the medical exemption. "We were adamant that they needed to be clear that there were no real medical exemptions," said Curtis Picard of the Retail Association of Maine. He urged the governor "to do more than issue an executive order and press release." In addition, his members had "legitimate concern about how the mask enforcement was really going to work, and whether it was going to put workers in harm's way for having to enforce it" — the order stipulated only that owners and operators "must require all persons to wear face coverings in publicly accessible areas." Meanwhile, Curtis remembered, "rumors were rampant that shutdowns were coming, and grocers in particular were concerned about panic buying again and empty store shelves."

Four days after Governor Mills issued the enforcement order, she amended it to remove any mention of medical conditions.[38] One day later her administration reissued a three-page document titled "Guidance on Enforcing Face Covering Rules in Public Settings," complete with Roman numerals, bullet points, and a tone of thinly veiled exasperation.[39] The memo updated an earlier version that Maine's attorney general had issued jointly with Commissioner Lambrew just before Thanksgiving. At the outset they reiterated that mask-wearing was "key to keeping our businesses open." They also emphasized that state law gave Governor Mills authority to impose the order, which law enforcement could uphold with criminal charges. "The Governor has asked people to use their common sense in complying with the face-covering requirement," the document noted, adding that the state had "no interest in taking action against people for honest mistakes or minor violations." Individual violators faced a $1,000 fine, while entities whose owners failed to rout scofflaws could be charged $10,000. As for medical exceptions, the guidance flatly specified that people with disabilities had options such as wearing face shields instead of masks, or using curbside pickup and personal shopper services, but that *all* indoor public facilities were closed to anyone without a face covering. On the matter of enforcement, the AG and Commissioner Lambrew directed anyone who faced resistance from scofflaws to call the police. One could almost hear the document's authors banging their heads against the walls of their home offices.

The next day Maine's CDC reported 619 new COVID cases, another twenty-four-hour record, and Ashirah wrote her weekly letter to Governor Mills. "In the midst of this terrible rise . . . there is the hope of the vaccines," she started. "Or vice versa, in the midst of hope there is horror. I'm not sure which it is." She confessed to having "plenty of fears" about the safety of the vaccines but told the governor she was willing to get "whichever brand" when the time came, as her "contribution to a nationwide trial." Ashirah went on to say her children had been "particularly challenging" that week, but they were "enjoying ice skating on the pond at the edge of our land." The weather had turned cold enough for strong ice to form, she added, "and whole new play options have opened up!" They had also started cross-country skiing with a local group "so they see other people every day."

Ashirah added that her daughter, who was "thinking of going into politics," wanted the governor to know "that she really appreciates having a strong female political figure to look up to." The dog did not get much mention that week, except that he had "continued to be very difficult" around the goats and "completely insane" if the cat was in sight. Otherwise Clutch was "coming along enough" that Ashirah was "starting to have mental energy again in and around homeschooling and working from home." She also loved to write and had gotten "pretty far into a romance novel" that she was hoping to finish drafting soon. Ashirah admitted that it had taken her "a long time to be able to tell that to people with a straight face!" The longer she had worked on the book, the more she loved writing "about people caring for each other, and . . . everything that I think is important in a relationship."

That weekend Governor Mills did her Christmas shopping at "all the little stores" in Farmington. In a journal entry on Saturday, she wrote that she had met Charlie for dinner at the Cumberland Club, a private social club founded in 1877 in Portland.[40] He had "shaved off the facial hair he grew during the presidential campaign" and was "wearing a jacket, white shirt and tie and beautiful brown leather Italian shoes." They shared "an elegant meal" and "a couple hours of good, honest conversation" in the front banquet room, where they had "the tall, white Christmas tree" to themselves. The club had been the governor's "favorite haunt of late" when she wanted some "privacy and good ambience and good food." It was housed in a Federal-style brick residence built in 1800. The organization's website noted that "national players," from Civil War general Joshua Chamberlain to President Franklin Roosevelt and Hillary Clinton, had found it a "warm place to relax." When Governor Mills was elected, she was given a complimentary membership, a fitting, if ironic culmination of her father's work half a century earlier to end discrimination by private clubs in Maine — many had excluded women, people of color, and Jews until Sumner Peter Mills proposed barring the clubs from selling liquor.

In 1969, during his term as a Republican state senator, he sponsored and won passage of a bill that denied a state food or liquor license to any organization that withheld membership or services on the basis of religion, race, or ethnicity.[41] "If you are going to serve the people of the state you must do so on a fair and honest basis," Senator Mills said in explaining the bill's purpose to his fellow legislators. "But if you are going to occupy a fine building on one of the main streets of one of our prominent cities, and you are going to tacitly bar people of the Jewish race, or a different color than yourself, then you can't ask for the privileges of the state of Maine to do it." The law faced opposition from the state's attorney general on due process grounds, and some critics called it a government overreach.[42] In a newspaper opinion piece another detractor argued: "Even if the one Negro among forty applicants is the only person rejected, where is the proof? The assumption may be overwhelming but laws must not be enforced on the basis of assumptions."[43]

The Cumberland Club did not accept female members for another decade, at which point its president explained the decision as both "long overdue" and "right for our time."[44] No male members resigned over it and only two expressed objections, but a new house rule reserved some rooms exclusively for male use between certain hours. Some forty years later, Dora Mills was at the club with her sister, just after the 2019 election, when they remembered their father's complaint that his regular invitations to speak at the club had been discontinued after his bill passed. "So we were all kind of laughing how he'd remind us of this on our way up High Street in Portland, and the manager came over with this big book," Dora remembered. "He said 'governor-elect, would you sign?' He said 'it's the membership book — we always give a complimentary membership to the governor of Maine.'" Dora added: "So when he walked out of the room I said, 'Oh come on, we've gotta drink to our dad!'"

In December 2020, the day after the governor's festive dinner at the club, there was reassuring news from Washington that congressional leaders had agreed to pass a $900 billion pandemic relief bill after months of partisan wrangling.[45] Their bipartisan deal would extend supplemental unemployment benefits and send a $600 check to most Americans. President Trump called the package "a disgrace" — he felt the individual stimulus payments were "ridiculously low" and called for Congress to "get rid of the wasteful and unnecessary items from this legislation ... or else the next administration will have to deliver a COVID relief package."[46] He added — despite having lost the November election, along with dozens of subsequent lawsuits contesting the results in battleground states — "Maybe that administration will be me."[47] His objections called the bill's fate into question only a week before benefits were set to end for millions of Americans, including tens of thousands of Mainers. Also that week the state's labor department reported the highest number of new jobless claims since early July.[48]

Vaccine distribution in Maine continued on the 21st with some six thousand residents of long-term care facilities and their twenty thousand care providers. Meanwhile, the state's daily COVID-19 case counts continued to set records. Two days before Christmas the number spiked to about 750, and Dr. Shah thought it might have peaked.[49] He wrote off some of the increase, saying his agency had staffed up and was processing more cases. Other key metrics had "ticked downward" in the last week, he added. The pandemic was "with us and in every corner of the state," but it was not accelerating. Dr. Shah practically chirped that "if anything, it shows signs of stability and maybe even signs of contraction."

That same day Governor Mills issued an official proclamation granting Santa Claus an exemption from the state's travel restrictions. Nonetheless she stipulated to "all Maine children: with Santa on his way, be sure to practice good social distancing by staying all snug in your beds so he can go about his essential work!" She also appeared in a short group video with her Republican counterparts in the neighboring states of Vermont, Massachusetts, and New Hampshire, each of them recording portions of an upbeat holiday pandemic safety message.[50] Over a soundtrack of jingling bells they lauded their constituents' famed toughness and resilience, reminding them to "mask up, and happy holidays." Some of Maine's most renowned retailers put their leaders on camera too, as part of their "Let's Be Kind" campaign.[51] The presidents of outdoor outfitter L.L. Bean, the regional grocery chain Hannaford, and the Renys department store franchise asked shoppers to "be patient" and "wear a mask" in their stores "until we get through this."

By coincidence, on the same day that both videos were released, restaurateur Rick Savage lost a bid to keep the liquor license for his brewpub, despite having turned over management to his brother.[52] The state official who decided the matter issued an eleven-page decision calling the establishment an "imminent threat to public health" due to its owners' repeated violation of pandemic restrictions, including failure to enforce mask-wearing and social distancing. In turn their lawyer accused the state of unfair scrutiny, calling the pub "the most inspected restaurant, probably, in the United States," and claimed the business was now in compliance. "We desperately want to protect the livelihood of the fifty-eight families that depend on operation of the restaurant," he told the press.

The weather on December 25 made for a wet and unseasonably warm Christmas in some parts of Maine, with a record high temperature for that day of fifty-seven degrees at a National Weather Service station near the border with Canada.[53] Governor Mills celebrated the holiday that evening with an intimate dinner at the Blaine House, sitting six feet apart around the state dining room table with only her sister Dora and Dora's two children. One of them, the governor's exuberant niece, Julia Mills Fiori, had recently moved into the mansion for the rest of that school year — she was a freshman at a college in Maine where she had struggled through a lonely first semester of mostly remote learning, isolated in her single dorm room. To reduce the potential for COVID-19 transmission, the school alternated which classes were allowed on campus for the second half of the year, and first-year students had to vacate. Julia wanted to keep some semblance of her college experience, as opposed to living with either of her parents, who were divorced. She had "always been super close" with her aunt, so it "just felt natural" to ask if the governor wanted a housemate "to kind of shake up the world a little bit, and annoy her in the most loving of ways." They had dinner together on most days and often did their work at night in the same study, despite all the empty rooms in the house. "I think we both really needed to have the other one there," Julia explained, adding that "when you're so busy like she is . . . trying to run a state that is just going through such massive difficulties, it can be kind of nice, I think, to have someone just be like, 'yeah I got a really bad grade on calculus.'"

On December 26, Ashirah wrote to the governor to report that Christmas Day was "difficult." The Knapps had spent most of it with Chris's parents, again in lieu of his family's traditional big gathering with all of his aunts and uncles. He and the children had spent the night on Christmas Eve, and Ashirah joined them in the morning with Clutch — she had stayed behind in Temple to look after the animals, including the dog, who was still too needy to be left alone on the homestead. Neither did he wish to be sequestered on the in-laws' sunporch, where the two families exchanged gifts. Ashirah had driven through a downpour and arrived "soaking wet . . . dripping on the floor, the dog's dripping on the floor, everything is dripping on the floor," she remembered, laughing as she recalled the scene. Fiasco loomed as Clutch kept seeing Chris's parents' cat through the glass doors to the house, which the dog did not seem to regard as a barrier.

To everyone's relief no drama ensued, but Ashirah omitted most details of the episode from her letter to the governor, instead recounting the next day's relative serenity. "Today just the four of us went for a nice long walk on the logging roads on the side of Spruce Mountain (the one that shoulders up to Mount Blue)," she wrote. Owen had found "an old cellar hole homestead," so he had planned to go back to the site with his metal detector in warmer weather. When the family got home Clutch was "good and tired," and both Owen and Pamela had gone upstairs to play Dungeons and Dragons remotely with some friends, leaving Ashirah and Chris to have "a supper alone" downstairs — they had not spent "much (any!) time together" since the pandemic started, she explained, "so it was a lovely experience." She ended that week's letter on the subject of vaccine distribution, which left the Knapps "hopeful each time we hear things." Nonetheless they were prepared to "tamp down harder as we learn more about the new COVID strain" — researchers had recently detected a mutated variant of the virus in the UK. Within days US health officials had warned that the new variant might already be circulating in the country and was potentially "more rapidly transmissible than other circulating strains."[54]

On December 27, President Trump signed the relief bill that Congress passed just before Christmas, leaving lawmakers in both parties baffled by his last-minute objections the week before. His volte-face came after a pair of emergency unemployment benefit programs expired, causing delayed payments for millions of Americans.[55] That news shared column inches in Maine newspapers with myriad upbeat end-of-2020 feature stories, including a young toilet paper company's "banner" year, after having opened a new factory just before the pandemic.[56] When a nationwide run on toilet paper ensued, Tissue Plus had pivoted successfully from processing products for commercial clients to supplying panicked consumers in forty states. In another year-end story, Bob Duchesne, who authored a column called "Good Birding" in the *Bangor Daily News*, reckoned with his failure to meet one of his resolutions for 2020 — the year before he had spotted 327 different species in the state and he had aimed to best that by identifying 3 new ones.[57] While Bob had seen a rock wren, which was "a mega-rarity" in Maine, his number one "target," a boreal owl, had eluded him. Its home was "confined to the thick forests of Canada," he wrote, which had closed its borders to nonessential travelers early in the pandemic.[58] "Fifty years ago, Americans went to the moon," he wrote. "Now we can't even go to Canada."

On the 30th, Governor Mills turned seventy-three but spent her birthday isolated in the Blaine House waiting for results from another COVID test. "Running a low fever for a couple days," she wrote in her journal. "Had both a nurse and a doctor do house calls yesterday . . . They rushed the COVID test through the [Health and Environmental Testing Lab] and it was negative." That day Dr. Shah reported 590 new cases and one death, for a total of 334 lives lost that year, acknowledging "those 334 families who will be entering the new year without the loved one that they lost this year to COVID-19."[59] He also warned that Maine's positivity rate had increased to 5.4 percent, a concerning jump of almost a full point during the previous two weeks, or one full virus incubation period. This was a worrying sign, he explained, because it signaled "increased and increasing levels of transmission statewide." In response, Governor Mills extended the state's nine o'clock curfew for certain businesses, including bars and restaurants, "until further notice."[60]

That day, in the tiny Maine town of Fort Kent, which sits across the St. John River from Canada, the owner of a cocktail bar called Crossings told customers in a social media post that he was closing permanently, after about a year and a half in business.[61] "The latest order with the curfew has hit us hard and we can no longer continue," wrote Dr. John Hotchkiss, an entrepreneurial army veteran who was also chief of the radiology department at a nearby hospital.[62] "We made it through 2020, but cannot sustain operations with all the guidelines in place." His post said Crossings would shut down on New Year's Eve at 9:00 PM "per the Governor's orders." He described his bar as "a revival of an iconic local pub" that offered "a unique experience in Northern Maine," with a lounge style, live music, craft cocktails, and "New American cuisine."[63] Fort Kent was home to just over four thousand people, including about sixteen hundred undergraduate students per semester at the University of Maine's outpost there.[64] Dr. Hotchkiss said his business was near enough to the population center of Edmundston, Canada, just across the border, to draw customers "occasionally" from that city of about 16,500, until the border was closed because of COVID-19. However, businesses in Fort Kent were "far enough removed to be relatively unimpacted by the reduction in cross border commerce," he added. "By far the lion's share of Crossings' business came from the local communities with scattered groups of snow machine and fishing derby enthusiasts also in the mix." He maintained that new businesses in the town were "an uncommon thing" and that "when you lose those jobs it is really hard to replace them."

Dr. Hotchkiss felt that Governor Mills had "probably made the best decisions she knew how to make" in managing Maine's pandemic response, but her restrictions took a disproportionate toll in "rural, far-flung parts of the state like Fort Kent." Such extreme measures as business closures seemed heavy-handed, he explained, in a town where COVID-19 cases were rare until November 2020. "Janet Mills didn't close my bar, but the actions that she took were insurmountably painful and destructive to the finances of the business." He had laid off some employees and personally covered the rest of his payroll "for months toward the end." By late December "there was not enough money coming in to even cover utilities," he remembered. "Finally I just had to say this dog will not hunt." Here was the "problem" that Senator King described, in which a business was lost as a consequence of the same leadership choices that might have saved lives. Dr. Hotchkiss took issue with that logic: "No one has ever saved a life, we've only prolonged life or delayed death." He felt that "the sort of currency that was utilized to make decisions in this entire situation was very narrowly focused on COVID numbers [and] deaths." He was quick to add that when those decisions were being made, no one would have "wished to trade places with the governor" or any bureaucrat, but he felt "the fundamental premise that somehow we can limit death" was "kind of foolhardy." Pandemics were "part of existence," he added, and "if we maybe bear that in mind, we can make better decisions for those of us that are not yet dead."

Ashirah's final December letter was dated the 30th, only four days after her previous dispatch. "There is lots of uncertainty in my household," she told the governor, "around my job, my husband's work, the kids' schooling." She was also concerned about "protocols for the bubble" that her family shared with others, and "how the rocky period will go as some people are vaccinated and want to relax precautions." Ashirah explained that some of the impending change had been "a long time coming," such as Chris's evolving plans for their school, now that he had mostly finished coursework for his master's degree. "To be fair, it's not all because of COVID," Ashirah added. The pandemic had "condensed everything, the good and the bad, and catalyzed it into its next iteration." As for the world beyond the homestead, she felt growing anger toward Americans who were still flouting pandemic precautions; if they wanted to "get them-selves killed, let them!" she wrote. "They want their rights and don't want to be 'sheep,' let them!" Then she unleashed a breathless, unprecedented tirade, telling the governor that "those people can go home and die alone, suffocating in their own bodies, the way [an] older person would have had to do, who didn't get an ICU bed because there weren't enough, and we needed to triage who's most likely to survive."

Ashirah had recently explained to her daughter that the country was "already at the point in many hospitals of having to decide that someone gets care and someone else doesn't." In early December, as the nation's pandemic metrics spiked post-Thanksgiving, the *New York Times* reported that more than a third of Americans lived in areas where hospitals had "fewer than fifteen percent of intensive care beds still available."[65] For those in "a large swath of the Midwest, South and Southwest" the *Times* had found that fewer than 5 percent of ICU beds were open, and in some places, there were none. Hospitals in some states were preparing for the possibility of having to triage care, while harrowing stories came from states where doctors had already done so, having had no other choice. As the month progressed, California had become the epicenter of the pandemic in the US, the first state to report two million coronavirus cases.[66] Ambulances were lining up outside ERs, gurneys were set up in hospital waiting rooms and gift shops, and overflow patients were treated at a former prison.[67] On Christmas Eve the state reported forty-four thousand new cases. Its death toll of 319 for that day alone was 8 more than the total number of COVID-19 deaths in Maine to date. "It feels harsh to say it," Ashirah told Governor Mills, but she felt that if "we can't save everyone anymore, let's save the people who didn't go out and choose to get COVID like dumb-asses."

Ashirah grasped at social media that week for source material for her usual end-of-letter humor. She chose a friend's "very funny post along the lines of 'I just can't decide what to wear to New Year's Eve in my living room. I don't know, maybe I won't even go.'" The joke was apropos — on the 31st Governor Mills was still not feeling well and had learned that another officer on her security team had tested positive for COVID-19. He was asymptomatic and they had not had recent contact, but the governor isolated again that day as a precaution. "I am alone upstairs in the Blaine House all day," she wrote in her journal. "A pretty palace. The downstairs and upstairs security quarters are being disinfected with some defogger." She added: "On the good side I had a house call from the nurse again this morning and my vitals were okay." She had taken a second COVID test that was "rushed through" within hours and came back negative.

The governor had spent part of the day recording New Year's Eve messages in multiple media to her constituents. In her final 2020 radio address, she recalled that "a year ago we counted down from ten and watched the ball drop, fireworks explode, and confetti fall."[68] Now she was feeling "grief and gratitude," she told listeners. She acknowledged their losses of family members and friends, jobs and savings, major life milestones and celebrations. "We grieve the lives we were living," she added, "and the ones we wanted to live, before we ever heard of COVID-19." The governor felt gratitude "for the people who sacrificed so much to keep us safe," including medical professionals and first responders, educators and business owners. She thanked the "grocery store clerks, gas station attendants, restaurant workers, fast food cashiers, delivery drivers, utility crews and plow drivers . . . who never stopped making sure that we had food to eat, warm homes and safe roads." She announced that more than twenty-seven thousand Mainers had been vaccinated so far and repeated pleas for precautions that she had been making for months. "Remember, too, that even in normal times, the holidays can be a difficult time for many," she said, asking listeners to "check on our neighbors, help those who are struggling, and extend a hand in kindness. Simple things can make a difference in the lives of others."

On her Facebook page the governor posted a video of herself — a little off kilter again, like the one she had made in quarantine in early December — asking Mainers not to let their guard down.[69] "There's a reason there won't be hordes of people tonight in Times Square, no celebrations in cities across the state of Maine," she said. "So don't worry about missing out on anything by staying home tonight and just lying low. Connect in other ways . . . Pick up the phone and talk to a family member or friend. Get some exercise. Watch a good movie. That's what other people are doing." The governor wrote in her journal that night that it was "a scary New Year's Eve." Indeed, there were new pandemic challenges looming in 2021; distribution of vaccines had been sluggish so far, with signs of persistent skepticism of their safety, including among healthcare workers, and the new virus variant had just been detected in the US for the first time on the 29th.[70] Despite her age Governor Mills had chosen to wait to be vaccinated until state health officials determined her eligibility as part of Maine's distribution plan.[71]

She spent the final hours of 2020 "escaping by watching episodes of *The Crown* on Netflix in the Blaine House library." The fictional television series, based on the historic reign of the UK's Queen Elizabeth II, had recently released its fourth season, which also portrayed the country's first woman prime minister, Margaret Thatcher, and Lady Diana Spencer, who became the Princess of Wales. Perhaps it was not escapism she sought that night, in the drama of the British royal family, but the safety and reassurance that only the past can provide — she knew how the story ended and, as in any fairy tale, its heroine had never faltered unrecoverably, no matter what went wrong in the world.

CHAPTER NINE

"... the highest possible level of lunacy ..."

A new state law took effect on the first day of January — before the pandemic Maine's legislature had passed a bipartisan measure that required many year-round businesses with more than ten workers to offer paid sick leave. When Governor Mills signed the bill in 2019 she called it a "forward-looking policy" that balanced the interests of employers while protecting 85 percent of the state's workforce.[1] "I don't know anyone who hasn't gotten sick or had a child who's gotten sick," she said at the time. "That's just life, and such unexpected circumstances should not break the bank for working Maine people." A year and a half later, on New Year's Day of 2021, the state's CDC reported seven hundred new cases of COVID-19, which had taken the lives of 347 Mainers. That day the number of cases in the US topped a record twenty million, having doubled since early November. By then the virus had killed more than 345,000 Americans, or one out of every 950.[2] The US economy had suffered its worst contraction since the end of the Second World War.[3]

Suffice it to say the principle of paid sick leave had new import by the time Maine became the sixteenth US state to codify the benefits as law.[4] People with sore throats, runny noses, or low fevers were no longer simply discouraged from going to work, as before the pandemic, but barred from doing so, in some cases by law — Maine required employees of prisons and licensed medical facilities to be screened for COVID-19 symptoms. Nationwide, an experiment with paid sick leave had effectively been under way since April 2020, when some Americans became eligible for the benefits under the emergency federal Families First Coronavirus Response Act (FFCRA). That program might have helped blunt the pandemic's spread by alleviating fears of lost wages or jobs, especially among low-wage workers, who might otherwise have gone to work while sick.[5] The FFRCA was not renewed in the second federal relief package that

President Trump signed in late December, and the nation's trial period with paid sick leave had ended on the 31st, just as Maine's new law took effect.

Around that time the state's lawmakers, led by a Democratic majority, had submitted nearly seventeen hundred new bills to be drafted for consideration during their next session.[6] The legislature had convened in December for the first time since the early weeks of the pandemic, taking their oath of office in a thirty-two-thousand-square-foot auditorium of a convention center in Augusta so they could maintain social distance, masks required.[7] Some members expressed frustration over plans to hold public hearings and some committee meetings remotely for that session, with only minimal use of the statehouse. "What am I supposed to say to these front line, low paid workers as to why I get to stay home as their 'representative' and they have to go outside and work?" one Independent legislator vented to colleagues in an email thread.[8] A Democratic representative noted that the session would be "unique," as her colleagues adjusted to making deals online instead of in the halls and back rooms of the statehouse.

The range of the 130th legislature's proposed new measures included an act to reduce the age at which rabbits could be sold in Maine (from eight weeks to six), as well as a resolution proposing an amendment to the state constitution that would establish a right to food.[9] One measure sponsored by a state senator from Maine's northeastern coast sought to "provide that a forestry operation that conforms to accepted practices may not be declared a nuisance."[10] The assistant House majority leader put forth bills that would "enact significant police reform" and "alleviate the disproportionate impact" of COVID-19 on people of color. Other pandemic-related measures proposed surveying students' mental health, suspending property revaluations and meals and lodging taxes, and extending a moratorium on evictions. A slew of bills pertained to Maine's election laws, with some aimed at restricting access while others sought to expand it.[11] That push-and-pull was happening in dozens of states following record voter turnout in the presidential election, according to the nonpartisan Brennan Center for Justice.[12] The center's roundup for January found that more than a hundred restrictive bills were introduced, prefiled, or carried over that month in twenty-eight states, more than triple the number put forward by that point in 2020. Lawmakers in thirty-five states had put forward more than four hundred bills to expand voting access, about twice as many as the year before.

In Maine, legislators had submitted eleven bills pertaining to the governor's authority during a state of emergency, with several aimed at curbing its scope. In particular, Republican leaders had objected to lawmakers' lack of involvement in Maine's pandemic response, almost from the beginning.[13] Governor Mills reflected on those long months in a journal entry on January 3. "Happy New Year," she started wryly. "Many [Facebook] posts shout how lousy 2020 was. The TV shows reviewing the events of the past year bring inevitable tears." It had been a parade of "injustices one after another; the thought that it just couldn't get any worse, but then it does, day after day, week after week." She lamented the "inevitability of bad news, horrifying headlines . . . presidential debates that were embarrassing for our country, the ineptitude and rudeness of the sitting president." She went on to mention a recording released by the press that day of President Trump's phone call to Georgia's secretary of state imploring him to "find" enough votes to overturn Joe Biden's victory there, or face a potential "criminal offense."[14] "Give me a break," Governor Mills wrote. "Thirty times the President of the United States claimed on this call that he'd won the election. This guy has long outlived his tenure and any usefulness he had to democracy."

That day both of Maine's US senators, Independent Angus King and newly reelected Republican Susan Collins, joined eight of their colleagues in issuing a bipartisan rebuke of the president's actions, though they did not mention him by name.[15] "The 2020 election is over," wrote Senators King and Collins, together with Democrats Joe Manchin of West Virginia, Mark Warner of Virginia, Jeanne Shaheen and Maggie Hassan of New Hampshire, and Dick Durbin of Illinois, as well as Republicans Bill Cassidy of Louisiana, Lisa Murkowski of Alaska, and Mitt Romney of Utah. They added that "challenges through recounts and appeals have been exhausted," and "further attempts to cast doubt" on the legitimacy of the election were "contrary to the clearly expressed will of the American people." They went on to say it was "time to move forward" and that "Congress must now fulfill its responsibility to certify the election results."

That process was set to take place three days later, on January 6. "A new morning in America!!" wrote Governor Mills in her journal entry for that day. "The sun is shining in Maine and in Georgia and across the USA," she added, referring to unofficial results of Georgia's US Senate race that showed both seats were likely to flip from incumbent Republicans to their Democratic challengers. In that case Raphael Warnock would become the state's first African American senator, and Jon Ossoff its first Jewish one, giving their party the narrowest of majorities in the Senate.[16] Later that day, Governor Mills added to her journal entry that modern American history had now come to include a deadly insurrection incited by a sitting US president, with the goal of overturning his defeat in a legitimate election. Donald Trump had spoken at noon "for more than an hour to several thousand supporters outside the White House," she wrote. The president had repeated "false claims that illegal voters cast ballots in Pennsylvania, etc., urging his supporters to go down to the Capitol and speak their minds, more or less." She noted that his "message was clear" and the crowd "marched down to the Capitol, stormed the building and broke into the Senate and House, disrupting the proceedings to certify the results of the Electoral College. It was chaotic, and Trump refused to concede the election or discourage the crazed mob."

That afternoon Governor Mills was in her office at the statehouse, watching news coverage of the attack with her staff. "People came in and we just sat there and stared at the TV. Could not believe what was happening." The House and Senate recessed and the Capitol went into lockdown. The vice president and members of Congress who had been inside were evacuated as the violent throng ransacked the building. Senator Collins was the only member of Maine's delegation in the chamber at the time.[17] In a newspaper op-ed a few days later, she recalled being "taken through the tunnels under the Capitol, with the police urging us to 'hurry, hurry!'"[18] She noted that she had "chosen to wear high heels that day so it was hard to run." The senator and her colleagues "spent many hours in a 'secure location' in the complex, watching on television in disbelief" as intruders "roamed around the Senate Chamber, with one thug sitting where the vice president had been presiding and others rummaging through our desks." She mentioned that lawmakers "were brought some salads, sandwiches and water, but no one was allowed to leave." Senator Collins had tried to reach contacts at the White House in the hope of urging the president to tell the mob to disband, only to watch him "completely undercut that message . . . telling the rioters that he knew how they felt." She decried his response as "terrible, especially since he incited them in the first place."

That night, after the Capitol had been secured, the senator and her colleagues were led back inside the building "with lots more law enforcement, including FBI tactical teams in riot gear, and the National Guard" escorting them to finish certifying the election results. Shortly before four o'clock in the morning, Vice President Pence declared that Joe Biden had won a majority of the Electoral College.[19] Senator Collins spent what was left of the night at the home of Senator Murkowski, whose "husband had built us a nice fire and had glasses of wine awaiting us." She returned to Maine the next day feeling "saddened and outraged" that rioters had "temporarily taken control of the symbol of our democracy." She had also felt "a sense of pride that . . . the forces of democracy had prevailed."

Among the casualties of the insurrection, a Capitol Police officer, who was injured during contact with rioters, died the next day, and four other officers who had served that day later took their own lives.[20] Four people in the crowd had died during the onslaught, as Governor Mills noted in her entry. She condemned the violence in public comments, stating that she did not believe it was "sanctioned by most Americans; nor do I believe it represents the true character of the American people." It was, rather, "a clear and troubling reflection of our fractured nation." The governor had reserved her thoughts on the president's leadership for her journal. "Trump is simply repulsive," she wrote. "I cannot think of anyone in public office who has demonstrated less dignity, less integrity, and who has had so much greater a love of self than of the nation."

At some point that day Ashirah wrote her first January letter to Governor Mills. "Oh my holy god!" she started. "Every time we think we've reached the highest possible level of lunacy, it goes higher!" Between a global pandemic and the first mass invasion of the US Capitol since the War of 1812, her children were "certainly getting an amazing look at history-in-the-making," she told the governor.[21] Owen and Pamela had "both expressed concern" about their eventual post-pandemic return to public school "and dealing with kids who are Trump supporters." Ashirah was at a loss for what to tell them, until she remembered "a eulogy given for a journalist who worked in areas of unrest and war" who believed that "there are *not* two sides to every story" but that "sometimes things *are* black and white, right and wrong."

Ashirah said no more about the attack on the Capitol. She might not have had time — in the days before January 6, she had slaughtered and butchered two goats and finished preparing taxes for the Knapps' school, which they had recently converted from an LLC to a nonprofit business. She had also started planning her children's homeschool lessons for the rest of that month, all between the "hours each day of dog exercise and training" she was still doing with Clutch.[22] She kept her letter short, confined to the inside and back of a small note card that had a charming illustration of a hedgehog on the front. The only personal news she shared was about her job at the addiction medicine office, which had canceled plans to see patients in person that month due to the ongoing COVID-19 surge. "It's another pay cut for me (I'm down to one-third of my pre-COVID salary now)," she wrote, adding that "being home and safe is worth it."

During the next forty-eight hours, President Trump announced that he would leave office on Inauguration Day but would not attend the ceremony. By then Twitter had "permanently suspended" the president's account "due to the risk of further incitement of violence." In turn he posted a statement on the platform through a member of his staff.[23] "Even though I totally disagree with the outcome of the election, and the facts bear me out," he wrote, "nevertheless there will be an orderly transition on January 20th."[24]

Meanwhile, Democrats in Congress threatened to impeach the president. At least two members of Maine's delegation joined calls to invoke the US Constitution's Twenty-Fifth Amendment, which allowed for the removal of a president who "is unable to discharge the powers and duties of his office."[25] Senator King called the insurrection "a deeply disturbing abdication" that raised "serious concerns about the coming thirteen days."[26] In Augusta, Maine, and other US capital cities that week, security protocols at statehouses were scrutinized and, in some cases, police presence increased.[27] The state police team that guarded Governor Mills enhanced her security markedly. Her niece, who had settled in at the Blaine House by then, was "quite relieved to see that the troopers have amped up their protection." On January 9, Julia wrote in her diary, as she referred to it, that she was "worried about what could happen between now & the inauguration . . . What a crazy time."

The governor focused on governing, submitting a nearly flat budget proposal to Maine lawmakers for the next biennium, telling them it would "keep the ship of state steady as we weather this storm" and "chart a path out of the pandemic."[28] Her $8.4 billion plan relied on federal pandemic aid and spending cuts to fill a projected revenue shortfall, while adding $61 million to the state's rainy day savings fund "as a hedge against future fiscal crises." She avoided tax increases and limited any new outlays to education and healthcare services, calling her plan "a no nonsense, no drama document." The staff of the conservative Maine Policy Institute agreed, calling it "not groundbreaking by any stretch of the word" with the consequence that it was "likely to attract sufficient bipartisan support to pass" despite doing "little to prepare Maine for an uncertain economic future."[29]

In a journal entry on January 13, Governor Mills wrote that President Trump had been "impeached for the second time," adding that he was "the only president ever to earn this distinction." Ten Republicans had joined Democrats in Congress, including Maine's two representatives, in charging the president with "incitement of insurrection," putting him on course for a Senate trial.[30] At the same time his administration announced major changes for COVID-19 vaccine distribution under its "Operation Warp Speed" project, led by Vice President Mike Pence. Federal health officials began prioritizing dose allocations to states that had been most successful with inoculations so far and urged them to expand eligibility, promising to release millions of doses from the nation's reserves.[31] In a radio address that week Governor Mills told listeners that the vice president had "recognized Maine as one of the leading states nationwide in rapid distribution of the vaccine."[32] By that point just over sixty-two thousand doses had been administered in the state in the first month, enough to protect only about 7 percent of the population.[33]

The governor expanded vaccine eligibility to emergency first responders, as well as seniors aged seventy or above. The "updated strategy" also "focuse[d] on adults of all ages with high-risk medical conditions" that increased their risk of getting seriously ill or dying from COVID-19.[34] In a candid statement the Mills administration warned Mainers that the US government was "purchasing vaccines and distributing with only a week's notice," and the supply was "limited, unpredictable, and inconsistent." In fact, the state learned, the Trump administration's promised stockpile did not exist, as the governor explained two days later.[35] "My administration and all the other governors are still trying to find out about this," she added. Meanwhile, Maine's CDC reported four deaths and a record of 824 new coronavirus cases that day, in a wave of post-holiday infections that had yet to crest.[36]

Maine's death toll of 453 was still among the nation's lowest, adjusted for population, but the subject of lives lost was one that Governor Mills "kept coming back to" in conversations with Julia, her new housemate, as that winter progressed. Her niece remembered hearing the governor arrive each evening from her office across the road: "'What's the kid up to today?' That was always what she'd say when she came in the door." They talked as they ate dinner together or if they converged afterward in the same room, where the governor would keep working or respond to mail from constituents while Julia studied or watched movies for her film class. "I don't think there was a moment where she wasn't thinking about how many people have died this week, how many people are in the hospital right now, how many people died last week," Julia recalled. "She'd describe what it was like to get that first phone call, of the first death in the state of Maine, and I think that weighed on her quite a bit." Her aunt was "not someone who was quick to cry," but she "would come back to that [call] every so often" and "get emotional about it."

Julia repeatedly described the governor as "a very empathetic person" who had "experienced grief" and could genuinely relate to Mainers who lost people they loved to COVID-19. "You don't necessarily see that as much with her but that's why I'm trying to bring it forward," Julia said. "If you don't know her from before she was governor it's kind of hard to figure out who she actually is, I think." The answer was not to try, her niece seemed to be suggesting, but rather to allow that her aunt was the rare politician who lacked artifice — that when *this* governor filled seemingly every speech, press release, social media post, and pandemic briefing with some soaring overture of devotion to the people of Maine, she meant every sappy word. Likewise when she issued stern directives or leveled with her constituents, as she did in a mid-January radio address about vaccine distribution.[37] "My fundamental goal throughout this pandemic has been to save lives, plain and simple," she told listeners. "My question, every step of the way has been, who is . . . most likely to suffer and die if they don't get the vaccine right off."

As the number of vaccinated Mainers continued to grow, albeit at less than warp speed, Julia sensed that her aunt had taken "a little bit of a breath" — that her "worry was still there for sure but it was a little bit less" now that she had "a way to combat this disease and before we hadn't had that." The governor got her first vaccine dose on January 15 and promptly shared the news across her various public platforms, including a photograph of her smiling behind her mask as a doctor knelt beside her, gloved and masked, administering the shot. "I have the utmost confidence in the vaccine," she said in a press release.[38] "It is safe. It is effective. And it will save lives." Also on that Friday, Dr. Shah reported more than eight hundred new cases of

COVID-19 for the third consecutive day.[39] He told reporters that Maine's vaccination count had topped seventy thousand, but that effort could be constrained "for the foreseeable future" after the state had learned "that there were no second doses sitting on the shelves." He leveled with Mainers that there were "more questions than there are answers," especially with the coming change of presidential administrations, but he promised to "keep everyone updated based on what we know, and specifically how it affects you, and where and when you may be able to get vaccinated."

The next day Ashirah gushed over Dr. Shah in a letter to Governor Mills: "I've been very impressed by his briefings. He is such a good public speaker!" She noted that this was "so rare to come across (I certainly wouldn't be in the category)." Ashirah felt that Dr. Shah was "very understandable" and "well spoken," and he had given her "more confidence" than she would have had "if he was poor at it." She realized that "public speaking has nothing to do with job ability," but it was "always a pleasure to hear someone doing well." Ashirah added that she was hoping and praying "for continued strength for you and all the people who are directly dealing with" the pandemic. She could not see how those in the medical profession would "come out of this without deep scars" and was "so sorry for the hell that so many" had been through already. "I don't know how they are keeping their sanity and I imagine many are not keeping it," she wrote. "I feel this cold dread when I look ahead at the more contagious variant(s) and what's going to happen in this country." She was not surprised to see others relaxing how strictly they followed safety precautions, pointing out that "we humans are amazing at not looking at what's really scary out there, like climate change."

Ashirah assured the governor that "there are many of us still being careful." She also reported that she had gotten her first vaccine dose that week "as part of the addiction medicine clinic I work in where I have direct contact with patients." She later had a sore arm, then "started to feel very tired, upset stomach, 'brain-fogged,' woozy," though she allowed meekly that her symptoms had coincided with another minor disaster involving Clutch. Ashirah had been walking the dog on a leash in the woods when he took off after a squirrel.

"The next thing I knew I was flying through the air," she explained. She had collided with a tree, head-and-shoulder-first, and "slumped to the ground in a groaning puddle," at which point she finally "let go of the stupid leash!" After a "self-assessment" she decided that "everything was attached and somewhat working" and retrieved the dog. "We made our ginger [*sic*] way home," she wrote, "where I immediately lay down with ice and Advil." The next day "the whiplash set in," and she "started to get really scared" that she had a concussion or a brain hemorrhage. She added a parenthetical, "because I think about these things," and drew a smiley face. After doing some reading about COVID vaccine side effects Ashirah decided she was not near death; between having gotten her first shot and the dog debacle, her body was "putting up a good, strong immune response." In a self-effacing coda she added that she would hold the dog's leash differently from then on "so it hopefully rips out of my fingers" the next time Clutch fancied a bit of spontaneous squirrel hunting.

That weekend Governor Mills had "retreated" from the Blaine House with her niece after "vague threats" were "issued by a handful of idiots against state capitals across the nation," as she wrote in her journal. "A rainy, windy day but . . . nice to be away from both Augusta and Farmington," she added, downplaying a bizarre array of potential security concerns that ranged from remote to extremely local. To start with, the FBI had recently warned that armed protests were "being planned at all 50 state capitols . . . and at the US Capitol" through President-Elect Biden's inauguration on January 20, according to news reports.[40] In Maine's capital, security was duly enhanced around the statehouse, and Governor Mills put the National Guard on standby "out of an abundance of caution."[41] In announcing the move she noted that many other states had done the same "based on what we saw last week at the US Capitol." She added that she respected "the right of all Maine people to speak their minds in a peaceful and lawful manner." The governor had also agreed to send National Guard service members to Washington, DC, to "support federal agencies . . . during the inauguration."

In the midst of those measures, an independent news magazine called *Mainer* published damning screenshots and other content from a personal Facebook account belonging to the chief of Maine's Capitol Police force, Russell Gauvin, including a November 7 post declaring that he had "zero confidence in the reported results" of the election.[42] In a post the next day he said Facebook was driving him "crazy" and he was "trying Parler," referring to the controversial social network known at that time for attracting conservative members to its relatively unmoderated platform. The network had been suspended by its hosting service a few days after the January 6 attack on the US Capitol due to reports that some rioters had used Parler to coordinate their siege.[43] The *Mainer* report also claimed that in July 2020, Chief Gauvin had "expressed sympathy with the views of a former Maine police officer who called for deadly violence against Black Lives Matter protesters and the immediate prosecution of government officials nationwide for 'enabling' the demonstrations against police brutality."[44] In another post that summer, Chief Gauvin had reportedly mocked the use of face masks as a pandemic precaution, writing: "In my opinion we are all being played. Where are the legit scientific studies on this?" Governor Mills and her public safety commissioner were "troubled and concerned" by the report, they told the press, noting that "the matter" would be reviewed for any violations of state policy.[45] They added that Chief Gauvin had since "assured them of his commitment to upholding his duties and responsibilities, regardless of any personal beliefs."

By then the chief had also removed his social media accounts.[46] The nature of his posts would have been concerning even if the events of January 6 had never taken place. After that day much of the country's already exhausted population had been suspended in a state of existential shock that had few comparisons in modern US history. Would President Trump keep his word that he would transfer power peacefully to his successor on January 20? How many of his supporters were the sort of unhinged, violent extremists who had just tried to thwart democracy in a deadly insurrection, and could they, indeed would they, attempt some sort of nationwide coup? Had the wave of anti-government vitriol that predated the pandemic crested on January 6 or was it gaining momentum? Were such questions reasonable or the overreaction of alarmists? What were the consequences of all this for the future of American democracy?

At the state level, President Trump's decision to delegate much of the fight against COVID-19 to governors had brought sustained national attention to their authority, especially Democrats. They had faced a new ilk of coarse criticism in an era of apparent impunity that the president had arguably catalyzed during his candidacy and capitalized on while in office. In one extreme example, in October 2020 the FBI had charged thirteen men with conspiring to kidnap Michigan's Democratic governor Gretchen Whitmer as part of an alleged plot to incite civil war. In reaction to the arrests, Governor Whitmer told reporters she "knew this job would be hard" but "never could have imagined anything like this."[47]

In comparison the backlash Governor Mills experienced in Maine had been almost wholesome. Protests against the state's pandemic restrictions continued through the fall of 2020 and into that winter, including a run of daily demonstrations outside the Blaine House by one woman who used a megaphone to convey her grievances. She obtained several consecutive permits from the Capitol Police for weeklong activity that she described as "talking with people . . . and carrying signs and flags. May play music. Letting Governor Mills know she has become a dictator and refuses to hear the people."[48] In that same time period other frustrated residents regularly picketed on weekends in the area near the mansion, with some driving around it in their cars while they shouted angry complaints. One man who obtained several permits specified that he represented the Maine Freedom Fighters, a group described on its Facebook page as "a Pro-American, Anti Socialism/Communism Coalition" whose "common shared goal" was to unite unenrolled Independent and Republican voters in Maine "into an active Coalition to defeat ALL Democrat [sic] candidates." Records provided by the Capitol Police also showed that "a small number of single permit requests" were filed by "various persons who protested masking or other political matters."

Governor Mills often left Augusta on weekend days to escape the din of protesters' disapproval. Her niece mentioned one exception, when the governor "got so tired of hearing them yell so loudly" that she played the Rolling Stones song "You Can't Always Get What You Want" at top volume on the house stereo. The protesters "couldn't hear it from the street," Julia remembered, "but it was great because it drowned them out." On the day before the inauguration, news broke that the governor's state police protection unit was investigating vandalism in a midcoast county, where the words KILL MILLS had been spray-painted on some roadways and the entrance gate to a state park.[49] The governor and her administration were focused on managing vaccine distribution, including the first day of expanded eligibility. The state's largest hospital system had logged some eighteen thousand calls that day as Mainers seeking appointments overwhelmed doctors' offices with inquiries.[50] "It's a great sign that there is so much robust demand for vaccine in Maine," Dr. Shah told reporters.[51] He asked Mainers to "bear with us and bear with those hospitals and clinics" and "don't get upset with the person on the line when you get through." Further compounding Maine's supply shortfall, he added, the state's CDC had recalled forty-four hundred doses of the Moderna vaccine after sensors showed the vials had exceeded temperature requirements at some point during their shipment to thirty-five sites in Maine. Dr. Shah acknowledged the news was "concerning," but he stressed that checks in the system had worked to ensure that every dose was "safe, effective and viable before it goes into any arms." Meanwhile, major outbreaks continued to grow at long-term care facilities filled with residents who were now in the state's open vaccine eligibility categories.[52]

On Inauguration Day a temporary leader took command of Maine's thirteen Capitol Police officers, after dozens of state lawmakers called for Chief Gauvin's suspension over his social media posts.[53] (Seventy Republican lawmakers criticized the suspension as an attempt at "ideological conformity."[54]) Governor Mills went to her office at the statehouse, where she edited her response to a group of fishermen who had signaled possible opposition to the offshore wind research project her administration had announced in the fall. She also learned that a judge had approved a deal that would effectively acknowledge the state had rectified its historic failure to provide adequate mental health care for Mainers, dating back to a 1990 class-action lawsuit.[55] The governor was heavily guarded while she worked, with police outside securing every entrance. At least three protesters showed up with signs or flags and demonstrated peacefully. None approached the statehouse, which had been closed to the public since the pandemic started.[56] All three told a reporter they believed the election was stolen. "I could be wrong," one man said. "But I have a right to be wrong."

Joe Biden and Kamala Harris were sworn in that afternoon in a heavily secured ceremony that took place without violence or other disruption. In public statements Governor Mills praised President Biden for speaking "eloquently to the divisions that have plagued our nation." She pledged to work with his administration to "turn back the coronavirus pandemic" and "chart a more prosperous future for all." In the privacy of her journal, she let loose: "What a huge national sigh of relief just went up." Just before the inauguration the governor had gone back to the Blaine House with some of her staff "for a small (Covid appropriate) watch party," and they "popped open some champagne as soon as Joe had taken the oath." She noted that President Trump had skipped the inauguration, but that was "okay" because he didn't "have the class" to attend "without acting boorish and offensive."

She noted that "the ceremony was simple, an hour long, with Lady Gaga singing the National Anthem, Garth Brooks singing something else, and Biden delivering a 'surprisingly normal' speech — 'patriotic normcore,' as *The Atlantic* called it." Her own opinion was that the inaugural poet, twenty-two-year-old Amanda Gorman, "stole the show with a perfect delivery of her wonderful poem, 'The Hill We Climb.' That poem really was in fact the inaugural speech." Governor Mills found the poem's text online for discussion that night with her niece — they had "always shared a love of poetry," Julia explained. "I think I love poetry as a result of her, to be honest." As they ate dinner together, she and her aunt had "ruminated" on Amanda's poem and "got into the more nitty gritties of, like, how did she craft it and what did this mean." Later that night the governor mentioned in her journal that she had been exchanging text messages "back and forth all day" with her stepdaughters, reminiscing about their visit to Washington, DC, a few years before. One evening during the trip they had come out of their hotel to see "the Capitol shining under a full moon, like a beautiful wedding cake." The governor added: "Well, that's how my heart feels right now, in love again with my country."

In Maine the tougher forms of her affection continued to rile some of her constituents, including the chief elected officials in two counties, some of whom had begun to take action in recent days to formally oppose the state's mask mandate.[57] The three commissioners of the least populous county — Piscataquis, in Maine's conservative second district — wrote and adopted a formal "Resolution of Protest" demanding "the mandates and the lock-down" be lifted.[58] The measure was rife with misinformation, referring to COVID-19 only as "the Wuhan Virus" and claiming that mask-wearing could "cause respiratory disease."[59] The authors noted a coincidence between "the apparent change in the Presidential administration" and the end of some state "lock-downs . . . lending credence to the belief that these edicts were not driven by science but by political animus."

Despite flagrant falsehoods and thinly veiled hostility toward Governor Mills, there was empathy and desperation in and between the lines of the resolution, which mentioned disagreements over pandemic restrictions that the commissioners claimed were "turning neighbor against neighbor." They also felt that the governor's "edicts" had "disproportionately depressed rural counties" at a time when "rates of suicide, drug abuse, domestic abuse, alcohol abuse, and depression" were "on an alarming rise throughout our country." Within a week, in the more populous county of Androscoggin in southern Maine, four out of its seven commissioners and an administrator did not wear masks when presiding over a contentious debate regarding the statewide mask mandate.[60] One commissioner complained: "This has gone too far and trampled our constitutional rights."

In the case of either county, if commissioners wanted their convictions validated by those with more influence they could look to the state legislature, where some Republicans had ignored the mask mandate during a meeting earlier that month in the statehouse. A resulting squabble had since intensified after two other GOP lawmakers wore absurdly inadequate mask substitutes at hearings in the building.[61] By that point in the pandemic more than 250 lawmakers around the country had become infected with COVID-19 and at least seven had died, according to an "ongoing tally" by the Associated Press.[62] Among them was the seventy-one-year-old speaker of the House of Representatives in neighboring New Hampshire. He died unexpectedly in early December, only a week after he was sworn in as speaker, and was found to have had COVID-19. The AP tally found that in 2021 some state legislatures with Republican majorities, "from Montana to Pennsylvania," were planning "to hold at least part of their sessions in person, without requiring masks." In Maine, leaders of the Democratic-controlled legislature moved to clarify and strengthen their mask policy. "I have to be completely honest," lamented its House Speaker, "I never anticipated that when we said face shields were an acceptable alternative, that anyone would wear a face shield that covers only half their face."[63]

On the Friday after President Biden's inauguration, Governor Mills was on her way to meet Charlie for dinner when she stopped to visit some of her grandchildren. One of them, a four-year old, picked up a book the governor had brought two weeks earlier, and started reading it to her. "What a miracle when a child begins to read," she wrote in her journal that night. "So proud and happy." In her entry for the next day, the governor mentioned that she had gone ice fishing with some friends, one of whom had "brought everything we needed," including baitfish, rods, and a heated portable shack, plus "food and bottles of booze — [F]ireball to warm the throat and soul." At some point in the middle of it all — between the governor's horrified disbelief at watching Americans attack their own Capitol in a deadly rage on live television, and the "big joy" she felt as her granddaughter read *Green Eggs and Ham* for the first time — the pandemic's worst surge in Maine to date began to recede.

On January 28, Dr. Shah reported that there were 284 new cases that day and the state's positivity rate was down to 3.6 percent, about half its height three weeks before.[64] He added that Maine's count of vaccinated residents had risen to 128,704 (out of 1.35 million). Two days earlier President Biden announced that his administration was boosting vaccine purchases and would increase shipments to states by about 16 percent in the coming weeks, with a goal of fully protecting three hundred million Americans by the end of the summer.[65] Dr. Shah welcomed the news but warned that in the next three weeks the state could hope to vaccinate less than half of residents aged seventy and older. He also noted a "concerning" trend that "many individuals" vaccinated so far "declined to provide their racial or ethnic background, or it hasn't been reported up to us." He clarified that health officials needed that information, in this case, to "make sure we are reaching populations that have been disproportionately affected by COVID-19" because of race, ethnicity, geography, or age. "We can't know where we're going and whether we're getting there unless we know where we are," he said.

That week Dr. Shah also made a "sobering and saddening" point of reminding Mainers that COVID-19 was still a dire threat, with a death toll in the US of more than 422,000. "Where we go from here as a country and as a globe squarely depends on us," he said, urging continued "care as we are going through our days." Governor Mills joined his briefing to echo that the pandemic was "far from over," but she added that Maine was "beginning to round a corner on that post-holiday surge." She cited the state's improving pandemic metrics in her decision to end the nine o'clock curfew for businesses, starting February 1. "We really wanted to keep those businesses viable, but at the same time protect the public from the virus," she added in a radio address. She again noted that the curfew was "similar to what other states have done."

That weekend Ashirah wrote to say "our hearts are a little lighter" with the pandemic "seeming to ease off a little (at least to not be growing exponentially right at the moment)." She admitted that she had been feeling "a little glum" until she talked with her husband that morning. Ashirah had realized that "trying to work, home school and train a high-needs dog all at the same time" left her feeling like she was "doing a poor job at all three." She and Chris had "worked out a plan" for the two days each week when Ashirah needed to do remote work for the addiction medicine clinic. On those days he would "do the homeschooling" and the kids would "help with the dog." The Knapps had learned that week that Clutch was "somewhat . . . aggressive towards strangers. Not a pleasant thing to find out." Ashirah closed her letter with an invitation for the governor: "This Friday we'll be cutting ice for our ice house (which provides all our refrigeration). Want to come?" She explained that Chris was tying the annual job into the monthly outdoor programming he arranged for students from a local charter high school. "Usually we invite lots of neighbors and have a big potluck," Ashirah added, "but that will have to be next year instead."

Governor Mills did not receive the letter in time to accept or decline. She spent part of that weekend attending a cookout at the home of her cabinet education chief on Maine's southern coast. She relished some time to "hang out with the lady commissioners" and "try to spy the full 'Wolf Moon'" — the governor marveled at the full moon every month and often made an elaborate effort to find the best vantage point to see it. She wrote in her journal that during the drive to the cookout she "got a call from New England Patriots' owner Robert Kraft" asking her to "pick four healthcare workers to go to the Super Bowl next week and be flown down and back in the Patriots jet!" The National Football League team was planning to host seventy-six vaccinated healthcare workers from all six New England states, "to recognize and thank a representative group" from among the "countless healthcare superheroes" in the region and "spread the important message of getting vaccinated."[66] Governor Mills enlisted two of the state's leading health industry advocacy groups to collect applications from front-line healthcare workers and draw four names from the bunch the following week. For now, hope seemed closer at hand as she headed south for a breath of downtime that Sunday. It was the last day of January, and Maine's CDC had reported only 156 new cases of COVID-19, the lowest count since mid-November.[67]

CHAPTER TEN

"... the continued slight let-up ..."

A slow-moving blizzard was heading for Maine on the night of February 1, after burying Manhattan under seventeen inches of snow, more than the city's total the previous winter.[1] In the Blaine House that evening Governor Mills wrote in her journal that she was savoring "the anticipation of a coming snowstorm — cozy, anxious, apprehensive but strangely comforting." Much of New England was due for more than a foot of snow, raising concerns that COVID-19 vaccine shipments would be delayed and potentially compromised.[2] Medical facilities in some parts of the state had already canceled coveted appointments.[3] Apart from the imminent danger and inconvenience of such a big storm, the governor found poetry in the stillness that preceded it. "A beautiful snow approaches, curious crows amassing on the tallest treetops," she wrote. "Big crows perched on thin twigs ... squawking at the nearing squall, flirting with wind, objecting to a change in flight plan."

The storm advanced into Maine that night and lingered through the next day, as Dr. Shah held another CDC briefing, including an update on the state's vaccine program. He looked very much in need of a nap as he told reporters that, to date, more than 158,000 "total shots in arms" had been given and just over 3 percent of residents were fully vaccinated.[4] That effort, he explained, would take "a significant leap forward" as the first of many "high-throughput, public-facing community vaccination sites" opened in Maine. Two of the state's largest healthcare networks planned to start mass clinics that week, the first in a convention and event center where rallies had been held for Donald Trump and Hillary Clinton during the 2016 presidential race and the second at a defunct horse-racing track.[5] The clinics' operators planned to administer at least nine hundred vaccine doses per day from the start, with the potential to expand to more than five thousand daily.[6]

Dr. Shah also noted that the state's COVID-19 metrics had continued to improve, including a 25 percent decline in the hospitalization rate since mid-January. When a reporter asked if that progress was "a reason for optimism," Dr. Shah sucked his teeth, groaned, and shook his head. "Gosh, you know . . . I am at my core an optimist," he hedged. "It's hard in this situation because so much of me wants to say things are getting better and indeed, numerically, there's no doubt that they are." He noted that the daily number of new cases had remained "quite low" and the state's positivity rate had "come down significantly," but there was no telling "how permanent or durable" those gains would be. "Or let me frame it even more starkly — I am concerned that these findings . . . are in fact a pause rather than a stop." The new strain discovered in the UK had since proved to be especially contagious and was now circulating in more than two dozen American states.[7]

Ashirah shared Dr. Shah's wariness, referring to the improving metrics in her first letter that month as "the continued slight let-up of the pandemic." She took more solace in "the return of the light" as each day grew a little longer and temperatures warmed to the twenties and thirties, bringing relief from January's subzero grip. In turn her children were restless for their weeklong winter vacation from school. "We parents are trying to make it fun and special," she wrote. "A little challenging for sure." The Knapps were also "beginning to dream" about warmer weather and "the ease of visiting people that summer allows." Meanwhile, they kept in contact with friends and family on Zoom calls — the videoconferencing platform had become a ubiquitous substitute for in-person connection since the pandemic started. That week on Friday they had joined Ashirah's extended family by Zoom "for a coming out party" for one of her sister's children, who had "decided that they are gender-fluid." Ashirah added: "I am very proud of how everyone is handling the news and it's only what I would have expected of my family."

Compassion and consideration were in shorter supply in other parts of Maine as the pandemic wore into its eleventh month. In the midcoast city of Belfast, home to about seven thousand residents, a group of anti-mask protesters had come to dominate a busy downtown intersection on Sundays.[8] The area had a pizza shop, a record store, and a toy seller called Out on a Whimsey. It was also known as Resistance Corner for its history of occasional occupation by demonstrators — a Black Lives Matter group had recently changed venues to avoid the anti-maskers, whose vulgar signs and shouting through a bullhorn were also blamed for repelling customers from local businesses.[9]

A two-hour public meeting over the protesters' aggressive tactics grew contentious, prompting Belfast's mayor and city councilors to call on "all residents and visitors to enhance and restore all forms of civility."[10] A few days later a woman wearing a mask and brightly colored hospital scrubs stopped her car near the group, got out, and approached the protesters to "share" her "fucking feelings."[11] One of them filmed the scene as the woman told a police officer monitoring the corner that "these people are assholes." She announced that she worked in a "COVID-positive unit" and appeared to have a brief physical altercation with one member of the group while another shouted, "Don't touch me, I feel threatened!" The woman answered: "But I want to touch you, you don't have a mask on!" Police charged her and one of the protesters with disorderly conduct.

That same week in another part of Maine, about seventy miles to the southeast of Belfast, commissioners in Androscoggin County were the latest to propose resolutions formally rejecting the state's mask mandate. Some on the panel opposed the measures, which were tabled after two hours of public debate. Onlookers called the commissioners "cowards." Two days later Maine's attorney general sent letters to the Androscoggin group, as well as their counterparts in Piscataquis, reminding them of their legal obligation to enforce executive orders Governor Mills imposed.[12] He noted that municipalities had "no authority to exempt themselves . . . and any effort to do so would be of no legal effect." For the avoidance of doubt the AG also assured them, "as Maine's chief law enforcement officer," that the governor's orders were "constitutional and . . . enforceable through both civil and criminal processes." A few days later some residents filed paperwork to recall the Androscoggin commissioners who had backed the anti-mask measures, prompting two of them to drop the effort. The third was unmoved. His colleagues called his views "an embarrassment to Androscoggin County."[13] He eventually resigned, at which point the chairwoman acknowledged his years of public service as "a strong and passionate voice for those who shared his firmly held beliefs."[14]

As all these local dramas played out, Governor Mills made an unusual entry in her journal on the 5th of February. In one breathless paragraph she chronicled everything she had done that day, most of which was unrelated to the pandemic she was also managing. In the morning she had given a "Chamber of Commerce breakfast speech (by zoom)" followed by a meeting with the chancellor of the University of Maine system. Next, an interview with a veteran public radio journalist about the major court settlement the governor had mentioned in a late-January entry, over state-run mental health services. The deal to resolve a decades-old lawsuit had now been made public. "This consent decree has gone through five governors, seven attorneys general, three or four court masters and many Superior Court judges throughout the last 31 years," the governor told the reporter.[15] "It is time to put it behind us."

After the interview she had held a cabinet meeting that included "discussion of vaccines and indoor capacity limits for houses of worship and other indoor facilities"; her administration was poised to increase those limits modestly the following week. She had then met with the granddaughter of labor leader and civil rights activist Cesar Chavez, Julie Chavez Rodriguez, the White House liaison to state, local, and tribal governments on issues including the federal pandemic response.[16] To follow, the governor had met with her commissioner of public safety "about investigations of people involved in the Jan[uary 6] insurgency"; a man from Maine had just been arrested in connection with the Capitol riot and faced charges including assault on a federal officer, violent entry, and disorderly conduct.[17]

Near the end of the day Governor Mills had spoken with former Maine legislator Sara Gideon about the "leftover" funds from her unsuccessful bid for the US Senate in November against Susan Collins; the campaign had a post-election balance of more than $14 million and had begun donating some of the money to charities and other Democratic candidates.[18] After that call, the governor had worked on draft press releases about forthcoming appointments to the state's court system, the Maine Indian Tribal-State Commission, the state's Human Rights Commission, and the boards of trustees for the state's community college system and the University of Maine. The last item she mentioned dealing with that day was her proposal that the state collect income taxes on federal pandemic aid to Maine businesses — she explained this as "a tax on whatever was left once the business had deducted the expenses paid by the loan. It was not a new tax, just an effort to prevent a double dip." The governor had backed off the idea after facing strong criticism in late January and was working on a compromise. "No, I'm not busy, not me," she wrote at the end of the entry.

Governor Mills often put in a few hours of work in the evening after full days at her office in the statehouse or long road trips to engagements around Maine. During the months when her niece was living in the Blaine House, the governor would usually "wander through the door" for dinner around seven o'clock, as Julia recalled. They often ate together in the kitchen "just munching on whatever was there" or took their plates into the mansion's state dining room and sat at opposite ends of the long formal table. For dessert their ritual was to open Dove chocolates and read each other the corny sayings printed on the inside of the foil wrappers. "We'd just be laughing . . . over these really stupid phrases," Julia remembered, "like 'the day is what you make of it' or just silly things like that." The governor's distaste for cliché was one of strikingly few differences between her private and public personas; she avoided banality in conversation and much of her writing, including her journals and especially her poetry, but she often laced her public remarks with quaint or timeworn phrases and popular aphorisms. "The things that she puts into her speeches, I think she really believes those," Julia said. "Those ones on the Dove chocolate wrappers — can't stand. It's so funny."

After dinner the governor usually went back to work, sometimes staying downstairs in the kitchen while her niece did homework upstairs. "She'd be down there, like, writing speeches for the next day or whatever, or talking on the phone with people about what was going on," Julia said. "No matter what house she's in, the kitchen is always where she gravitates towards, which, like, is not necessarily great for stereotypes, but she just does everything in the kitchen. It's how she's always been." The governor also used her small office upstairs or brought letters from constituents into a TV room to read while Julia watched movies for her film class — she remembered her aunt "sitting there going through all of the letters and all of the thank-you cards from the past week or so and she'd respond to them . . . I don't know how she had time to do this, but she just did. She *made* the time for it because for her it was really important."

In particular, the governor still looked forward to Ashirah's letters. She usually read them as soon as they arrived, then passed them to her niece. Julia recalled that the governor "loved these letters so much that she had this compulsive need to share them with everyone that she could." This was revealing, she noted, because her aunt was "not someone who dwells on things." Neither did the governor openly share the depth of her feelings, but she talked about Ashirah's letters so often that Julia could quote passages from some of them from memory. "Those letters are just beautifully written . . . and they're subtle in their beauty," she said. "They're simple but they get the point across and they really bring to the reader this woman's deeply rooted empathy for the world and desire to see things turn better." Julia felt that her aunt and Ashirah had "a lot of similarities in that regard and that really just kind of connected them through these letters" particularly because the governor "was getting so much backlash from so many people over the pandemic."

Governor Mills planned to mention Ashirah's dispatches in her annual speech to lawmakers at the end of February, which she and her staff had started drafting early in the month. "I think several of us were making notes, drafting outlines," she recalled, "a lot of brainstorming about what we wanted to cover and how." In late January legislative leaders had sent her the customary written invitation to deliver the speech but asked that she do so "in writing accompanied by a video stream to be shared with the Legislature and the public" because of "new and necessary" pandemic safety precautions.[19] The governor agreed to give the speech virtually on the 23rd and planned to pre-record it the night before. "I care about the people of this great state with all my heart," she wrote in her acceptance letter, "and I look forward to paying tribute to them and sharing how I believe we can turn back this pandemic and emerge a stronger, better state."

She was *not* looking forward to reading the speech to a camera instead of the live audience she had in 2020. At that time, when she gave her first State-of-the-State address, titled "Readiness, Resilience," the notion of a global pandemic was still the stuff of Hollywood science fiction. She had lamented the "deafening" noise of the country's divisive political culture, including a rancorous presidential election that was "turning us away from the security and saneness of our own small outpost." Full of vitality and ambition, she had called on Maine's legislature to come together to help accomplish her agenda, which included improving the state's healthcare and education systems and battling the opioid epidemic, domestic violence, and climate change. Governor Mills had also mentioned a factory explosion in her hometown that had killed a fire captain. At that time she believed the tragedy would be the low point of her first term. The next day the World Health Organization had held an emergency meeting to decide whether a flu-like virus that was spreading in central China, South Korea, Japan, Thailand, and Singapore posed "a Public Health Emergency of International Concern."[20] Now, just over a year later, the governor was drafting her second annual state speech, again touting the resilience of Mainers, but this time her theme was "perseverance" against a rampant virus that had taken millions of lives around the world.

Her staff provided talking points, but she wrote much of the speech herself, working on it as time allowed. She had rarely relied on speechwriters at any point in her political life. Apart from her writing talent, a broad review of her past speeches suggested both an ease with the medium and a willingness to express herself in writing in a way that she otherwise would not, or could not. Moreover, no speechwriter could (or would) have included as many lengthy, detailed accounts of personal experiences as the governor tended to do in public discourse throughout her career. In her speeches as attorney general she often mentioned cases she had tried when she was a DA, especially one that still haunted her decades later. "I remember Emma Waters, a courageous woman, victim of domestic abuse, who came to me for help," she said in a 2009 address on the National Day of Remembrance for Murder Victims.[21] "With her cooperation, I indicted her husband, while she took refuge first at one shelter, then another, then one in another state to be sure she was safe, because, under the laws at that time, he had made bail." A few days later, she had added, Emma's body was found beside a road in New Hampshire, shot in the head. AG Mills went on to say she was soon called to appear as the leadoff witness in the murder trial of Emma's husband.[22] "I got to see what it was like to sit outside a courtroom for hours and hours, then finally be sworn in and asked to identify the victim from a photo that was bereft of her person-hood, totally lacking her soul." A month later, in a speech to a group of Maine prosecutors, she emphasized how important it was "not to personalize cases" but to apply the law, "punishing the deed without condemning the offender's soul." Every case was different, she had added, "and you live with your successes, you live with your disap-pointments. And you live to fight another day."

Another trademark of the governor's oratory was her habit of digressing into effusive odes to Maine's natural splendor. In a 2019 speech to the United Nations General Assembly about climate change — she was the first sitting Maine governor to address the UN — she described the range of her state's landscapes, from its "3,000 miles of bold, rocky, jagged coast" to the "rolling hills, fertile farm-lands, mighty rivers and deep ports."[23] The tendency endeared her to many of her constituents but made some, including devoted family members, eye their watches. Her sister Dora pointed to the gover-nor's 2019 inauguration speech: "She started talking about the Sandy River . . . and I thought, 'Oh my God here we go.'" At that point in the speech Governor Mills had been setting up a metaphor for the importance of progress and cultural connection, telling her audi-ence that waterways sometimes change course but ultimately linked distant places and their people.[24] "Many days I awake to see the mist rising from the Sandy River as it steers its course to the Kennebec, the winter's breath unveiling a new day in my hometown, a new day in this state," she told the crowd, pouring on the reverence. "Then I hear the familiar sounds of chickadees, church chimes and Jake Brakes," she quipped, raising a laugh from the audience. "This is home in Maine," she added wryly — it was another key element of her success as both an orator and a politician that she usually knew not to take herself too seriously.

She also had a raconteur's sense of irony and talent for delivery, including a forte for retelling the same crowd-pleaser anecdotes as if for the first time. In one early-pandemic vignette that she loved to reenact during press conferences and stump speeches, she recalled getting a letter in early December 2020 from a constituent who had written: "Thank you for all you're doing . . . you know Sister Rose is right, gratitude is the highest virtue." Governor Mills had no idea who Sister Rose was. A short time later she mentioned the comment to Dr. Shah, who reminded her that she had quoted the ancient Roman philosopher Cicero during a COVID-19 briefing just before Thanksgiving — the governor had told those watching that there was "much to be thankful for" despite the trying year and that "Cicero said, 'Gratitude is not only the greatest of virtues, but the parent of all others.'" Perhaps the constituent was hard of hearing, or mistook the quote's author as Sister Rose Thering, an activist nun and professor from Wisconsin who fought anti-Semitism in the Catholic Church and whose life was the subject of an Oscar-nominated documentary.[25] Either way, from then on, whenever the mood around the governor's office got too serious or some conundrum came up, she or someone on her staff would crack: "What's Sister Rose got to say about that?"

The energy of an audience, especially laughter, would be missing when Governor Mills gave her state speech at the end of February, save whichever aides stayed in the room when she recorded it. Under those conditions there was the potential for her to seem affected, the opposite of her nature; when on script, and especially on tape, she sometimes sounded overly sentimental, like a 1940s actress in a maudlin screen test. This might have been an upside in a state with a preponderance of residents born when Old Hollywood was still new. Either way her annual speech to lawmakers was one of her highest-profile appearances of the year — she was effectively already running for reelection. She had yet to signal that intention publicly, but nearly a year had passed since her predecessor, Paul LePage, declared that he was "going to challenge Janet Mills" in 2022.[26] In December a reporter from the *Bangor Daily News* had asked Governor Mills if she was planning to seek reelection. "I can't give you a reason *not* to right now," she hedged. The possibility was "certainly likely," she added, but she was "so singularly focused on trying to save lives" that she had not begun to consider a second term.[27] The newspaper ran the story with the headline: "Janet Mills 'Likely' to Run for 2022 Reelection as Showdown with Paul LePage Looms."

On February 10, 2021, Maine health officials announced that one of the coronavirus variants, the blandly named but dreaded B.1.1.7, with its "increased transmissibility," had been detected in the state.[28] In a briefing the next day Dr. Shah explained that a variant was a virus with a "constellation of mutations" caused by genetic errors during replication.[29] "Now, I know that when I use words like mutation and variant it presses all of the scary buttons all at once," he added, noting that many of the "hundreds if not thousands" of variants "pop up, get characterized and then . . . disappear." He acknowledged that the latest research showed B.1.1.7 was between 20 and 50 percent more contagious than previously identified coronaviruses and was more likely to lead to serious illness and death. Dr. Shah reiterated that "the bedrock principles that we've talked about" for about a year — wearing masks, washing hands, keeping social distance, getting tested, avoiding gatherings, and staying home when sick — would "help prevent the spread of the garden variety COVID as well as these new variants."

Dr. Shah added that both vaccines the state was in the process of distributing were effective against B.1.1.7. By then Maine had vaccinated just under 216,000 residents. Its CDC was expecting 22,475 doses to arrive the following week, in addition to those expected through a new federal program launched that day, which would send more doses directly to pharmacies nationwide.[30] As that parallel effort rolled out, nine governors wrote to the Biden administration on behalf of the National Governors Association, appealing for more and better coordination with states, especially amid changing guidance from the US CDC.[31] Likewise, the states had each been handling vaccine distribution differently, and reports of confusion and frustration mounted nationwide.[32]

Maine health officials told the public repeatedly that it was difficult to predict changes to the state's vaccine dispersal plans because supplies were limited and unpredictable. Moreover, scientific knowledge was evolving, and federal guidance kept shifting. Nonetheless the Mills administration faced growing criticism for providing too little information about its decision-making process and for issuing eligibility criteria that seemed inconsistent or contradictory.[33] Other states were resorting to gimmicks to expedite progress, such as a "companion" system in neighboring Massachusetts.[34] In mid-February that state, which had so far permitted only residents of ages seventy-five or older to get vaccines, started allowing younger residents to have the shots if they arrived with an elder.[35] Almost immediately there were reports of opportunism that the governor of Massachusetts found "pretty disturbing," including online classified ads promising various incentives for eligible seniors willing to partner with strangers.[36] One of the least creepy posts offered $100 cash and a ride in "a very clean Toyota Camry" with "a friendly conversationalist" who would allow their passenger "to choose the music and show me all the pictures of your grandkids!"

The same day that Massachusetts launched its buddy program, Governor Mills got her second vaccine dose and released her weekly radio address, telling those listening that it was "just a matter of time" before everyone in Maine would be vaccinated.[37] "I have said it before, but I will say it again — everyone in this state is essential." She explained that her administration was "targeting our limited supply of vaccine to save the most lives" and asked her constituents to "please keep the faith." The next day, a Saturday, the governor joined Dr. Shah on his second trip to one of the state's mass vaccine sites, in the northeastern city of Bangor, where 160 clinic volunteers were giving hundreds of Mainers their shots. Everyone had "joy on their faces, in their eyes," she remembered. "It was just incredible." She told reporters covering her visit that she was impressed by the clinic's "caring" atmosphere and efficiency. "People are not anxious, they're not angry. They haven't been crowded into a room with other people."[38] Dr. Shah added that what he had witnessed that day was "a sign of hope and optimism" and "the pathway out of this pandemic for this state."[39]

After touring the clinic, the governor made "an obligatory visit" to the nearby Bangor Police Department to pose for a photo with its eminent mascot, a taxidermied wood duck that a public information officer had dubbed the "Duck of Justice."[40] Sergeant Tim Cotton, a longtime detective who believed that "humor is the universal language," had rescued the duck from a district attorney's trash can.[41] "No one wanted him," he had told a reporter. "I'm sort of a picker and I thought I could find a use for him."[42] Starting in 2014 Sergeant Cotton had helped draw more than three hundred thousand followers to the department's Facebook page by posting photos of the duck atop police cruisers, in the arms of new recruits, even at Stonehenge during a colleague's trip to England.[43] The posts, along with the sergeant's wry missives on police work, endeared Bangor's officers to their community and made the duck "marginally world famous." Its antics drew national media coverage, and fans started showing up at the department to pose for photos beside the duck's pedestal, ranging from locals and tourists to celebrities, including author Stephen King, a Bangor resident.[44] Governor Mills posted a selfie with the duck on her Facebook page, showing both of them wearing masks. She felt it was important for people to see her lighter side when opportunity allowed, especially during the pandemic, when she was seeing so much less of her constituents and using social media to stay connected.

That night she wrote in her journal that former president Trump had been acquitted in his second impeachment trial — the vote in the US Senate earlier in the day had fallen short of the two-thirds margin needed to convict him on the sole charge that he incited the January 6 insurrection in the Capitol. Governor Mills noted that

Maine's two senators, Republican Susan Collins and Independent Angus King, were among the fifty-seven who voted to convict. "Trump, predictably, issues a statement of vindication," she wrote, "boastfully predicting a big future for his MAGA movement and indicating not a scintilla of remorse, regret or responsibility for the insurrection . . . Jesus." The governor added that it was now "up to the prosecutors, the justice system, the tax investigations and the civil suits to bring this monster to his heels [sic]."

Ashirah spent part of that Saturday on a revelatory walk with Clutch, whom she had taken off his leash in the woods for the first time.[45] The experiment was successful, due mostly to the two feet of snow on the ground that kept the dog from bolting. That weekend was effectively the start of her children's winter break from school, and Ashirah was "very happy to have a chance to catch up on lesson plans," as she wrote to Governor Mills. As part of Owen and Pamela's homeschool curriculum, Ashirah's mother, who was "[all but dissertation] in English," was "doing a novel with each kid" over video chat to give Ashirah "a literature break" — her parents had recently sent the gift of a tablet device for making video calls that "actually allows us to see their faces."

The biggest news in that week's letter was Ashirah's decision to give notice at the addiction medicine clinic that she would be leaving her part-time job there in the spring. She explained that the Knapps' school was "headed in a good direction" but needed "a lot of work to get off the ground." She wanted to support her husband as he launched a range of new programs, including some that offered students multiday experiences on the homestead. She also felt it was important for her to be fully present for their children that summer, come what may of the pandemic. "Someone needed to be at home with the kids mornings and evenings, keeping our family rhythms going while Chris was involved teaching for days at a time," she explained. Ashirah felt "terrible" leaving the clinic's doctors to find a replacement for her, but she believed it was the right time to move on: "Someone is out there for whom it will be right to step in."

Her choice to forgo that income, however paltry, so she could invest more time in the Knapps' business, was an act of optimism considering the emerging threat of COVID-19 variants and the continued slow pace of vaccine distribution in Maine and nation-wide. The Biden administration had dropped the name Operation Warp Speed in January and had yet to title its own effort, though aides on the president's team had a new mantra of a sort, to "over-whelm the problem."[46] By the middle of February a mere 12 percent of Americans had received their first vaccine dose and just 4 percent were fully inoculated, amid reports of racial disparities and growing resistance to vaccination, notably among healthcare workers and military service members.[47]

In a Maine CDC briefing on the 16th, Dr. Shah — sporting a conspicuously short new haircut since his last appearance — told the press that nearly 250,000 shots had been given around the state, with one in eight residents having received a first dose.[48] He reported only ninety-one new cases that day, the first time that metric had fallen below one hundred in three months. The state's seven-day positivity rate had also dropped, to its lowest point since November. Dr. Shah warned that a second case of the B.1.1.7 variant had been confirmed in Maine. "Because we are actively looking for these cases, we expect to find more and more . . . not just this variant."

As the vaccine program entered its tenth week, the state announced that doses would soon be distributed based on new "performance metrics."[49] Health officials also issued strongly worded "guidance" reiterating that Maine's criteria for distributing vaccines were "binding."[50] That rebuke followed press reports that the state's largest healthcare system had vaccinated employees who had no contact with the public while working, as well as some out-of-state consultants who had been hired to dissuade nurses from forming a union.[51] The company was "protecting infrastructure," its CEO explained.[52] Another major hospital group had offered doses to a small number of donors.[53] Maine's attorney general responded that he would "consider seeking legal and administrative sanctions" against "behavior" that flouted CDC protocols and undermined public trust, such as "giving vaccine doses to wealthy donors who cut the line" or "allowing out of state union-busters to receive doses which should have gone to Mainers."[54]

The governor wrote in a journal entry on February 20, now just two days before the speech to lawmakers, that she had spent most of that weekend making changes to the text with her communications director and her press secretary. One new addition was her opening line: "There's never a better time than a Maine winter night to look up at the stars. It was my grandfather, a man from Ashland who looked like Gary Cooper, who showed me how to find Orion in the night sky." Her staffers, both of whom were about half her age, asked: "Who's Gary Cooper?" The governor, incredulous, had told them "to go watch *High Noon*, one of the best Westerns ever," adding that her reference to the actor was "staying in this frigging speech!" The grandfather she was referring to had been a potato farmer through the Great Depression in Maine's northernmost county. She went on in the speech to extol his perseverance as the virtue Mainers most needed "to see us through these times, no matter who we are or where we live." From there the draft text chronicled the pandemic and other historic events of the past year. "Everything we have known, everything that was familiar, so much was canceled, modified, restricted," she wrote. The world had changed and "we had new words to define it," from quarantines, social distance, and curves that needed flattening to surges, positivity rates, and superspreader events. Other words had "taken on new meanings and popularity: pivot, variant, 'you're on mute,' and, of course, zoom."

The world's population had also been forced to bear an ever-increasing toll of lives lost to the pandemic — the governor's speech noted that half a million Americans had died so far. "In Maine, we have lost more than 650 people — friends, loved ones, neighbors, each with a life that had meaning and purpose," she added. She had mentioned a few by name, including eighty-seven-year-old Kerck Kelsey, the first Mainer confirmed to have died of COVID-19, in late March 2020. At that time the governor had noted in her journal that the man's son had thanked her by email for her "kindness and dedication" to the state. He had added: "There's a long tradition in our family of public service in Maine. We are Washburns. Like you, Israel Washburn, my third great uncle, was governor of Maine during a national emergency, the Civil War." For the state's first

death to have been in a historic family had made the pandemic feel
at once terribly real and all the more surreal for Governor Mills.

She had also mentioned "Ron Johnson, father of five, former
Major League baseball player, coach and manager of the Portland
Sea Dogs" and Dr. Jim Paras, a World War II veteran "who dropped
out of high school to join the war effort and later enjoyed the big
dance bands on the Old Orchard Beach pier." Then she digressed to
talk about a "great hero" the nation had lost that year, among notable deaths not related to the pandemic — baseball legend Hank
Aaron had died about a month earlier at age eighty-six.[55] She touted
his legendary 1974 home run that had broken Babe Ruth's record.
This drew another blank stare from one of her aides, who admitted
to being unfamiliar with the legacy of "Hammerin' Hank." The
governor opted to keep him in the speech as well, exalting what she
felt was his "greater accomplishment" — a career tally of 2,297 runs
batted in, which was still the highest in baseball more than forty
years after his last game. Here was a player who "did not just revel in
the solo performance of home run hitting" but had also loved "the
reward of bringing his teammates home, one after the other." The
governor's speech pointed out that while home runs "may win a
ballgame on occasion," more victories came from "the steady work
of base hit after base hit — an effort driven by many, rather than just
one." This was "the story of Maine as well: one team of many," she
wrote. Her constituents had "helped our state succeed" during the
pandemic "despite risks to yourselves and the adversity of our time,
and through courage, compassion and perseverance."

The governor had centered more than half of her address on the
pandemic, her administration's response, and her argument that
the "collective efforts of our people and their government, for now,
are working." She included the state's latest pandemic metrics,
adjusted for population; by that point they showed that Maine
ranked second lowest in the nation for total hospitalizations, had
the third lowest total case count, and the fourth lowest number of
deaths from COVID-19. As for vaccine rollout, Maine was now
"among the top twenty states in the nation for getting shots in
arms," she wrote.

The rest of the speech detailed her recent biennial budget proposal to lawmakers, which she described in her journal as "a sleepy one . . . no new programs, no new taxes." Nonetheless the legislature had found cause for excitement, as she noted in the speech. "Now, I have heard the calls of those who say we should enact sweeping budget cuts," she wrote. "I have also heard the calls of those who say we must spend a lot more, even if it means we must dip into our savings." In the end, she explained, neither extreme was wise. "When you have a fever . . . you don't say, 'Now, get up and run laps and do a hundred pushups,'" she wrote, adding that "getting back in shape" was "not immediate, its course not always predictable."

The governor's budget was "focused on recovery" to ensure "basic continuity, consistency and stability" while the state worked to "beat back the pandemic . . . maintain a stable economy and get people back to work." Toward that end she mentioned a new $25-million bond proposal that she was excited about. The funds would pay to "train skilled workers to fill jobs" in manufacturing, clean energy, and other "high-growth industries" in partnership with Maine's community colleges and trade schools. She was also bent on meeting the state's obligation to fund 55 percent of the cost of public education from kindergarten through twelfth grade, which no governor had done since voters approved the mandate in 2004.[56]

Toward the end of the speech she included her customary ode to Maine's "bold, rocky coast, the tall pines, and the rolling fields" in a passage on the importance of preserving the state's "heritage industries" of farming, forestry, and fishing. She then recalled the "hundreds, if not thousands, of handwritten notes" she had received since the start of the pandemic from Mainers who shared "their stories, their hopes and their heartaches." Some of the messages had stayed with her "long after" they arrived. "One young mother writes every week," she wrote. "She is busy teaching her children, keeping a small business going with her husband and training the new family dog." She went on to mention the letter Ashirah had sent at the end of October, describing the scene from the first film in *The Lord of the Rings* trilogy. The governor explained that the story's hero, when at a low point, wished that "none of this had happened." Her speech then borrowed the analogy: "None of us wished to see the times we have seen these last twelve months, but that is not for us to decide." She believed that Maine was "pushing through" and would "rise a better, greater state for all that we have endured and all that we have learned, all whom we have saved."

Lastly the governor returned to her recurring theme, noting that "Perseverance" was the name of a NASA rover that had landed on Mars less than a week earlier. "That Rover's fiery entry through the Martian atmosphere was made possible by heat shield materials produced by a company in Biddeford, Maine," she boasted. Perseverance, she added, was "also our prerequisite for the future, our password to success, our passport for getting our state back on track." Her closing flourish was unabashedly hokey: "As we look up at the stars tonight, as I did with my grandfather many years ago, we will tell our children about American ingenuity, about Maine's place in the future, about the beauty of our world and our state and about the perseverance of our people."

That weekend, while the governor was finalizing her speech, Ashirah wrote to say she was "so thankful every day to see the numbers going down" as the state's pandemic metrics improved. "I'm also glad to hear the vaccines seem to be effective against at least some of the variants." She mentioned that some "really excellent" face masks she had ordered from a new crowdfunded company had been "delayed and delayed" but might be ready before the next school year. They would "still be useful" because Owen and Pamela wanted to "try public school again . . . and we would feel very confident sending them in with these masks." Ashirah added that it was "nice to be able to tell the kids they can definitely go to school next year even if Covid isn't gone."

Pamela had recently "brought up at supper that she didn't want everything to go back to how it was before" the pandemic — she "wanted to see changes in the world" and was "worried there wouldn't be any." Ashirah also mentioned a recent conversation with her sister-in-law. "We agreed that, bad as Covid is, it has brought about huge personal and intra-family growth for both of us. I certainly feel like about a decade of self-realizations got squashed into one year." Ashirah would have "traded that . . . for a world that didn't need to go through this," but that was "not an option of course." Her parting words for that week were positive as usual, if a non sequitur: "Two months until the milk goats are due to kid. It's getting exciting."

Two days later Governor Mills stood behind a podium in the cabinet room of the statehouse and presented her speech to a camera. "It was so weird," she remembered. "It's so much better in person." She spoke for about thirty-five minutes, and her minor flubs were left in the recording. The final product distributed for broadcast had obviously been edited in a few places, but production value did not seem a priority. The speech aired on local television channels and was streamed online. Immediately after it ended, Maine's public broadcasting network livestreamed a Republican response from state senator Jeff Timberlake, who had been elected his party's minority leader in November.[57] Senator Timberlake had been among the Maine GOP lawmakers who, in mid-summer of 2020, had challenged the governor's economic reopening plan as too limited. Now, as he was introduced to reply to her speech, he suppressed a smirk, as if he were about to launch into a smug lambasting of the address. He started talking but was unaware that his microphone was still muted. After about ten soundless seconds the host cut in to ask him to "touch a button there" so that the audience could hear him. He unmuted his voice and blushed a little as he said he would "start over now . . . the usual thing with Zoom." The host answered: "The world we live in; an unusual State of the Budget Address and an unusual Republican response."

Senator Timberlake started again, noting that he had not seen the speech in advance — he had written down some points for rebuttal while he was watching, but his comments were offhand. At first he praised the governor for acknowledging that "we have a lot of people who are hurting." He added that "every one of us recognizes that . . . whether they be Republican, Democrat or Independent." He then lamented that he "didn't hear much talking about how the governor and the legislature was [sic] going to communicate moving forward." This had been his chief grievance since the early months of the pandemic, when GOP leaders pushed repeatedly to revoke the emergency executive powers lawmakers had granted Governor Mills to manage Maine's COVID-19 response.[58] In their view at that time, the governor had failed to consult the legislature in using her "decision-making authority." It was therefore the chamber's "obligation to rescind" that authority "and establish a new process . . . that involves all parties to better serve Maine."[59] Senator Timberlake had elaborated in a talk radio interview in May that "a lot of people that serve in the legislature are doctors and lawyers and businessmen and farmers — some of us are businessmen *and* farmers who have some expertise in how to deal with crisis situations . . . and maybe they can help."[60] Senator Timberlake was co-owner of Ricker Hill Orchards, his family's ninth-generation farm.[61] At that time the governor responded that she had consulted lawmakers, including through an online portal her administration had created solely for their suggestions.[62] Senator Timberlake had countered that he did not "know of anyone she consulted with," adding that the state's fourteen Republican senators represented about half a million Mainers.[63]

Evidently, he was not among the lawmakers from both parties who had met "secretly" with the Mills administration in a series of meetings held "in apparent violation of state law," as the *Portland Press Herald* alleged.[64] The newspaper had reported in April that cabinet members had facilitated nine remote briefings to answer legislators' questions in the first month of the pandemic. The story accused the administration of failing to give public notice and claimed the governor's staff "made no attempt to document or record" the meetings. Her spokesperson explained then that COVID-19 had "temporarily shifted the way that government business is conducted." The administration had postponed further meetings until it could "work with the legislature to determine the best process to respond to their questions in a transparent way as we all work to adapt to changes driven by the virus."

The pandemic had also drawn new and sudden attention to the role of the country's governors; many now continuously exercised authority that their constituents had previously seen them wield only on extremely rare occasions, such as Massachusetts governor Deval Patrick's citywide lockdown order during the 2013 manhunt for one of two Boston Marathon bombing suspects. When the pandemic started, Maine lawmakers had united in bipartisan consensus to grant Governor Mills broad emergency powers. The longer the crisis continued, the more their unity curdled, unsurprisingly along party lines.

In late February 2021, in Senator Timberlake's response to the governor's speech, he echoed his contention about the sidelining of the legislature — she had "talked about baseball and everything else," he said, referring to her Hank Aaron metaphor. "Well I think it's time the legislature and the executive office plays [*sic*] as a team." His voice was full of frustration, but the overall tone of his remarks was heartfelt, notably civil, and surprisingly personal. "I was elected to represent, you know, basically almost 40,000 people and I don't feel that I've had the chance to represent them as well as I should because we haven't been in there." By then the legislature had not met for most of the previous year while the Mills administration managed the state's COVID-19 response. "If I hear anything up and down the street when I'm out going to . . . the local market it's, you know, when are you going back to work," he said. In particular he took issue with the number of executive orders the governor had issued, more than seventy in the nearly twelve months since her first one related to the pandemic. "I think it's time that we find the solution to that," he said, and called on Governor Mills to "make us part of your discussion, and part of the team and until that happens it's going to be hard."

Senator Timberlake raised few objections to the proposals in the speech, but he did note some concerns that he felt the governor had not addressed. First, he believed that Maine's public schools needed to be "encouraged" to return students to classrooms full-time, echoing a growing nationwide chorus.[65] "I've got a grandson who's 15 years old who told me this week it's time for him to get back to school five days a week," he said. "I think it's important socially, not just for the learning but for the social aspect." That decision now rested with school administrators — a week earlier the Mills administration had cleared all Maine counties to allow in-person learning under the state's color-coded system for assessing the risk of COVID-19 transmission. By then the rate of new cases among school staff and students was thirty-six per ten thousand, less than half of the statewide average, and just 5 percent of Maine's 610 schools had open outbreaks.[66] The Mills administration had been actively encouraging schools to bring students back, as was President Biden, whose proposed stimulus package included $130 billion to help schools pay for pandemic-related costs.[67] Final decisions on classroom instruction versus remote learning were left to local school leaders, as in many states. Superintendents and school boards around the country were facing increasingly intense scrutiny from those opposed to continued closures, as well as parents and teachers who opposed reopening while they were still unvaccinated and uncertain of when they would become eligible.[68]

Another concern on Senator Timberlake's list was a lack of interaction among his colleagues that "really hurt the legislature," which he felt was "more partisan this year on both sides." This was a problem especially in committee work, he added, when groups of lawmakers met to reconcile differences over bills — they were meeting mostly by videoconference due to pandemic safety protocols. "Because we're on Zoom everybody gets to hide behind the camera," he explained. "You don't get to say 'hey can you step out in the hall with me for a minute' and you have a conversation with somebody and then you come back with a solution to the problem." Senator Timberlake contended that he was not "pushing to rip the mask off and just go out"; he felt that if "all these huge companies have figured out how to bring their employees back to work" safely, then Maine's legislature should be able to meet "mask-to-mask" so they could "get back together" and "make better laws." One upside of masks, he added sincerely, was "learning to make people read your eyes better than they used to, instead of just your facial expressions."

Governor Mills wrote in her journal that night that her speech had been "well received." She did not mention Senator Timberlake's rebuttal or statements from some of the state's Democratic leaders praising the speech and her commitment to Maine people. Her niece wrote about the speech in her diary, describing it as "good" but noting that "of course many people are being super negative about it." Julia did not elaborate on who those people were, but the Maine Republican Party was among them. The group posted a hyperbolic response on its Facebook page that claimed the governor had "burned through every taxpayer dollar she could find, including depleting the budget surplus built by Governor LePage."[69] In fact Governor Mills had rejected calls for spending, as she had said in her speech. She had also proposed a budget that would add $61 million to the state's savings over three fiscal years, which would increase its balance to a record $320 million.[70]

A political analyst for one of Maine's local television news stations offered a more constructive take on the address.[71] He praised the governor as "incredibly competent at her job" and "somebody who understands government" but said that he had "seen her give speeches that were much more emotionally connected than this one." He also felt "the speech really needed more vision," adding that people wanted to know "what is the state going to look like a year from now when we are done with this, and what are some of the initiatives she's putting in place." Apart from that "disappointing piece" of the speech, he defended the governor's characterization of how her administration handled the pandemic. "She has been all over it," he said. "Clearly Maine people recognize that and they appreciate her for it."

By the end of February more than 60 percent of residents over age seventy had received their first COVID-19 vaccine dose, and Governor Mills was weighing how and when to expand eligibility. "The vaccines are a blessing," she wrote in her journal. "But there are limited quantities . . . All sorts of people are wanting to be first in line — grocery store workers, teachers, firefighters and EMTs." According to one major Maine newspaper, more than "65 people or groups representing hospitality, transportation, food sanitization, chemicals manufacturers and organ donor services reached out to the Mills administration from early December to mid January."[72] In that same period, the report also found, the governor received some seven hundred emails and letters from constituents about Maine's vaccine rollout. She had consulted with medical experts, her staff, and her cabinet, as well as a religious ethicist, who confirmed the governor's "research-based inclinations" — that research included Dr. Shah's, which he had based on state and national data that showed age was a stronger indicator of the risk of serious illness or death from COVID-19 than any other factor. In Maine, 85 percent of pandemic deaths to that point had been among people aged seventy and older.[73]

At the end of the last week in February, Governor Mills announced that the state would scrap an initial plan to use "complicated" vaccine eligibility rules that were based on profession, age, health problems, and other factors, and instead deploy a solely age-based system.[74] Starting in early March, Maine planned to expand eligibility to more than two hundred thousand people ages sixty and older. The following month the minimum age would drop to fifty, then forty in May, thirty and up in June, and so on. The governor warned that demand for vaccines still exceeded the nation's supply. If that changed the state could potentially move faster through age groups.

Maine joined only Indiana, Nebraska, Rhode Island, and Connecticut in making the switch to age-based eligibility by that point.[75] Connecticut had also given priority to all teachers and childcare workers regardless of age. The lack of priority for teachers in Maine's program caused controversy, especially considering the push to return children to classrooms full-time. A Gallup survey in mid-February found that 79 percent of parents favored in-person learning for students in kindergarten through twelfth grade, about one in three of whom did not have that option.[76] "Of course, the teachers are upset that they're not at the head of the line," Governor Mills wrote in her journal, adding that "people with 'comorbid conditions' such as diabetes, obesity, etc.," were also subject to the age limitation. Her administration planned to set up dedicated vaccine clinics for educators, though they would still be subject to the age restriction, leaving many ineligible almost until the end of the school year.[77] The governor emphasized that the new eligibility plan was in line with her "fundamental goal throughout this pandemic . . . to save lives and protect Maine's most vulnerable people."[78]

In one embarrassing flub, a state agency that oversaw emergency medical services had approved ski patrollers for vaccination in

December, only to revoke permission after consulting with the governor.[79] Hospitality industry leaders felt their workers deserved priority, having been in high-exposure roles for months and considering their role in the state's economy. The Retail Association of Maine's Curtis Picard felt the move to age-based eligibility was "understandable," but he called for more clarity on safe behavior for those vaccinated. Curtis added that the governor should go "out and about a little bit more in the public," now that she was vaccinated, to help build confidence that it was safe to do so.

Governor Mills had already begun to make more public appearances. On the last day of February, a Sunday, she visited the newly renovated Saddleback ski resort in the remote lake district of northwest Maine called Dallas Plantation.[80] The resort had recently reopened after a five-year closure; its owners had struggled to find funding for upgrades, and a series of potential buyers came and went. Saddleback was the biggest independent ski area in the region, which was otherwise dominated by major resorts owned by out-of-state corporate groups. The governor had long supported its reopening as one of the area's largest employers, with plans to create more than two hundred jobs, including dozens of year-round, full-time positions and generate much-needed business and tax revenue in an otherwise economically stagnant region.[81] In a 2018 Twitter post, then as a candidate only weeks from winning election, she wrote that having grown up in Franklin County, "Saddleback was in my backyard" and "as Governor" she would help "get the resort back on its feet." Ultimately her administration "was instrumental in getting them off the ground with loan guarantees from the Finance Authority of Maine," she explained.

Three years later, after an $18 million overhaul, the mountain had reopened for the winter of 2021 in the midst of the pandemic's first major surge. In addition to enhanced snowmaking and a new high-speed chairlift, skiers were met with COVID-19 safety measures ranging from touchless technology to outdoor food tents.[82] Saddleback's developers were also dealing with a new dilemma, as a pandemic-induced real estate boom caused a shortage of workforce housing, forcing them to consider building their own.[83] On the day when Governor Mills visited with her economic and community development commissioner, the pair toured the mountain's upgraded lodge and had lunch in its café. She mentioned the outing in a Facebook post, calling Saddleback "a happening place."[84]

The governor also noted the visit in her journal that night, writing that she had been shown around by the resort's general manager "and his operations guy . . . a lifelong Rangeley resident with a lot of local history." Otherwise she focused her entry on a discovery she had made earlier in the day — that morning, on her way to the ski resort, she had stopped by her home in Farmington, where she came across an "old folder of poems, journal entries and jottings" from the late 1960s and early 1970s. "Tonight, back at the Blaine House, I read through the whole thing," she wrote. "Pretty sad, all in all." There was "much longing" during a "wistful separation" from a boyfriend she pined for while she was studying abroad in Paris. This was the man she later lived with when she was working as a paralegal in Washington, DC, the alcoholic who held a loaded gun to her head.[85] She first mentioned the confrontation publicly during a gubernatorial debate in 2018, after "being accused of not being for gun control," she recalled. She had told those watching that she was "one of the lucky ones" who survived domestic violence. "I packed my bags and I left that place," she said, "and I never turned back."

Now, on that last night of February 2021, Governor Mills wrote that she had found "no joy or jauntiness" in any of her old writings. "Maybe I was happier than I reflected in these notes, using the poems and journal to pour out the worst of my feelings and get them out of my system." She called them "worthwhile but flawed." Lastly in that night's journal entry, she mentioned that she had also joined a birthday party by Zoom that evening for a lawyer friend who had turned eighty. "I reminded him how I threw him a surprise party for his 40th birthday in 1981 at my third-story apartment on Frye Street in Lewiston, when I was DA," she wrote. "None of us could climb those steps today to get to any party." On that lighter note, the year's shortest month ended at long last, heralding both the approach of spring and the first anniversary of the pandemic's arrival in Maine.

CHAPTER ELEVEN

"... we all readjust at different speeds."

In 1841, Henry Wadsworth Longfellow wrote one of his best known poems, "The Rainy Day," at his boyhood home in Portland, Maine.[1] In one verse he described the wind as "never weary." He was writing metaphorically about the inevitability of "dark and dreary" periods in life, but he would have known well his home state's meteorological tendency toward bluster, having spent the first third of his life there.[2] When the wind moved through Maine's gigantic white pine trees it could make a huge, fierce sound, deafening and incessant, hounding one's nerves when it blew for days on end. In 2021, on the night of March 1, an arctic front swept across the state, and Maine residents woke up to wind gusts that topped sixty miles per hour and some of the coldest temperatures yet that winter.[3] The storm knocked out electricity to tens of thousands of households. It caused whiteouts and multi-vehicle pileups in the mountains where snow squalls had formed along the front.[4]

The wind kept up through the next day as President Biden announced that the US was "now on track to have enough vaccine supply for every adult in America by the end of May," two months ahead of schedule.[5] Pfizer and Moderna had increased vaccine production, and in late February the Food and Drug Administration had approved a one-dose vaccine made by Johnson & Johnson.[6] Its rival, Merck & Co., had since agreed to help produce the shots. The president noted that this was "the type of collaboration between companies we saw in World War Two." With the country's vaccine supply constraints poised to ease dramatically in the coming weeks, the president urged states to make plans to increase the number of doses they could administer. To help expedite students' return to classrooms he also directed states, and retail pharmacy chains that were participating in a federal retail vaccine program, to start inoculating teachers and licensed childcare providers.

Governor Mills duly announced that Maine had "updated" its vaccine program "to make pre-K-12 school staff and childcare providers, regardless of age, eligible immediately."[7] President Biden's directive added 36,400 teachers, as well 16,000 childcare providers, to those who could now get their shots in Maine. The governor instructed pharmacies in the state that were part of the federal program to "give available appointments exclusively to school staff and licensed child care workers of all ages." Her administration promised that more state-approved clinics would do the same "as soon as they are able." Meanwhile, the state "did have special clinics for teachers after the president said they had to have precedence," Governor Mills noted. She was frustrated that those clinics, organized in partnership with more than two dozen healthcare organizations throughout the state, "were very poorly attended."

President Biden's vaccine supply announcement was cause for optimism, but he and Dr. Anthony Fauci, the US government's top infectious disease expert, checked Americans' expectations about when the country might return to some measure of pre-pandemic normalcy.[8] The president hedged that he had "been cautioned not to give an answer to that because we don't know for sure." Dr. Fauci warned that "herd immunity" was a fantasy until about 80 percent of the country's population was vaccinated, versus the current rate of about 8 percent. Progress in Maine was marginally better, with 9 percent of residents fully inoculated.[9] That day, in Dr. Shah's first briefing for the month, he warned that the state's positivity rate had "started to creep upward a little bit after hitting a low point a week and a half ago."[10] He added that it was too soon to tell whether another surge was coming. Meanwhile, Maine was among the states preparing to start lifting pandemic restrictions, despite the Biden administration's appeals for continued caution. On March 5, Governor Mills announced a plan she called "Moving Maine Forward" that would keep some safety protocols in effect, including the state's mask-wearing and social distancing rules, while increasing capacity limits for indoor gatherings "to support economic activity" through the coming tourism seasons.[11] The model employed a new standard with "straightforward" percentages of capacity instead of "hard caps." The limits could be raised "on a clear timeframe" to help businesses plan ahead or "dialed down" in response to pandemic metrics. The first increase was set for the end of March, when indoor service at bars could resume. The second round, just before Memorial Day weekend, would allow stores and restaurants to open at 75 percent of their indoor capacity and 100 percent outdoors.

The plan also immediately lifted test and quarantine rules for visitors from neighboring states. It also exempted those from any state "who have either recently had COVID-19 or been fully vaccinated." In late January a federal judge had upheld Maine's quarantine, affirming a lower court's ruling against the campground owners who had sued the previous spring — with support from the US Department of Justice, under the Trump Administration — to block the fourteen-day isolation rule.[12] As of May 1 the state would adopt a "more targeted approach" to its travel restrictions by shifting to an "all states exempt, unless included" model. The governor's press release provided a chorus of approving quotes from retail, hospitality, and tourism industry leaders, who called the changes "a big step forward for all of us" that would "help return us to some sense of normalcy." Curtis Picard's Retail Association of Maine was even more effusive in a Facebook post reminiscent of the governor's own oratory.[13] "A year ago, the light at the end of the tunnel was a freight train," the post said. "This year, it is a Maine lighthouse guiding us to better days ahead."

Governor Mills announced the changes on a Friday. That day in her journal she wrote that she had spent much of the week doing "TV interviews, all concerning the first anniversary of our first case of COVID-19 in Maine," which was coming up on March 12. "Pretty emotional," she added, noting that she "didn't watch any of them." In Temple that weekend, Ashirah was also "finding this year-anniversary to be pretty hard."[14] On Sunday she wrote in an outspoken Facebook post that "everything" was "a trigger taking me back to the time we didn't know what would happen to the world, and to all the fear and anger that came after (and in some ways are still going on)," both in her own life and "the greater scheme." She added that she "wanted to come through with integrity, whatever that ended up requiring" and felt "for the most part" that she had. "There were times I bit my tongue when I shouldn't have and I really regret those." Likewise she would "never feel the same about" some people she knew "because everyone showed their cards last year and some of them were ugly."

Ashirah wrote that she and Chris had learned from Ray Reitze, the mentor they had apprenticed with before they were married, that when they faced "conflicting paths" they should "choose the most loving and that will be the one that is true." When the pandemic started, to Ashirah's mind that path was "so obvious — wear a mask, social distance, keep people alive," yet she had "heard people saying things like, 'Let's not bring the entire economy down for the sake of old people,' and 'Fuck the governor for making a mask mandate, we're doing fine in Maine.'" She added that she was "not going to go into" her response to those people, "except to say I'm not worth shit if I don't care for my elders, and I have been writing to the governor every week in support of her work." Ashirah did not know how she or "we" would "come out of this," but she guessed that was "something we'll all be learning together."

The next day the US CDC announced that fully vaccinated Americans could gather "with other fully vaccinated people indoors without wearing masks or staying six feet apart."[15] That group was also cleared to visit "with unvaccinated people from one other household indoors" without masks or distance if those from the other household had low risk of severe disease. The CDC called the new guidance "a first step toward returning to everyday activities in our communities" but warned that "the vast majority of people" needed to be fully vaccinated before precautions could "be lifted broadly." Also that week, Congress gave final approval to President Biden's nearly $2 trillion pandemic relief bill.[16] The measure provided $1,400 payments to most Americans, the third round of direct federal relief funds, and extended supplemental unemployment payments through the summer. It also included tax breaks for families with and without children, as well as hundreds of billions of dollars for state and local governments, including more aid for schools, and grants and loans for businesses.[17] Early estimates showed that Maine's portion could amount to more than $6 billion.[18] Two members of the state's congressional delegation, Republican senator Susan Collins and Democratic congressman Jared Golden, voted against the bill. Senator Collins called it "a bloated . . . package stuffed full of provisions that have nothing to do with fighting the coronavirus."[19] She accused Democrats of rejecting a "targeted" $650 billion measure she had proposed, the "appropriate size" in her view, so they could "ram through a partisan bill using a partisan process."

Congressman Golden gave a less rancorous explanation for his vote. He represented Maine's conservative second district and was one of only two Democrats in the House who stood against the bill. He felt it "did not go far enough" to "reduce the number of wealthier households" that would receive relief checks.[20] The congressman also objected to the removal of a minimum wage increase and the reduction of unemployment benefits. Beyond those points he had "concerns with the overall size and scope of the bill" when combined "with the over $4 trillion we have already spent battling the coronavirus." Independent senator Angus King, who "proudly" supported the measure, agreed that it was "expensive" but added that "as we've seen over the last year, the cost of inaction is even higher."[21]

Partisan divides were also on display at the state level that week, as Maine's majority Democratic legislature convened for its first full session of the year. One of the chamber's first actions was a vote on the latest GOP-backed attempt to end Maine's ongoing state of emergency.[22] The bill sought to limit the executive powers the governor had been using to manage Maine's pandemic response.[23] Its language objected to her continued renewal of an emergency declaration without providing lawmakers "sufficient scientific rationale or justification." Governor Mills had renewed the declaration every month, as required by state law, since she first issued it in March 2020. Nearly a year later emergency declarations were still in effect in all but one state — only Michigan's order had ended in October 2020, after its supreme court overturned a 1945 law that Democratic Governor Gretchen Whitmer had invoked to manage the pandemic.[24]

The Maine Republicans' measure also made the preposterous claim that "the lives of Maine citizens, local jobs and small businesses, and activities that promote health and well-being have been lost without due consideration." One GOP leader was at least civil in defending the bill, telling a reporter there was "no longer a reason for the chief executive to have to act alone . . . to deal with the pandemic."[25] The House majority leader responded that the governor's emergency powers "diminish not one word of our constitutional authority or our responsibility" but allowed Maine's government "to continue to respond swiftly . . . to changing conditions." The bill was defeated by a vote of eighty-one to sixty-seven, mostly along party lines, though one Republican voted with Democrats and three Independents sided with the Republicans. The next day the proposal also died in the Senate. Maine's legislature was among forty-seven across the country in 2021 that considered some three hundred bills or resolutions to give their chambers oversight or direct involvement in governors' responses to COVID-19 or other emergencies.[26] Eventually lawmakers in all fifty states proposed similar measures and at least twenty-six states approved them.[27] Most were backed by Republicans, in some cases seeking more oversight of governors in their own party.[28] One Democratic state representative got more movement on his proposal to designate the Suciasaurus Rex as Washington's official dinosaur that session than another bill he had backed — after complaints from constituents who had lost jobs and businesses — to limit the Democratic governor's emergency orders to 30 days.[29]

On March 11, Dr. Shah gave only a brief summary of the state's pandemic metrics during his briefing.[30] He focused on the record number of vaccines given in the previous week, noting that a supply shortage continued to limit progress. Next he told those watching that he wanted to "take a moment to step back and think about where we are as a state." He sighed heavily as he added: "Tomorrow marks one year since the first case of COVID-19 was confirmed in Maine. One year since we all began this long day's journey into night. One year during which the unfathomable became the commonplace, with frankly unnerving frequency."

He went on to list "some numbers" that, for him, told "the story of COVID-19 up to now."

The first, Maine's current death toll of 723, could not "begin to capture the sorrow, the grief, the loss" that those people's families and friends had experienced. "Worse yet . . . how the process of dying itself has changed during COVID," he added. Pandemic restrictions had made death "a solitary affair" for many whose lives ended, as well as those who were prevented from sharing their grieving process with others. A national poll released that day showed that one in five Americans had lost a relative or close friend to the coronavirus, especially those who were Black, Hispanic, or in low-income households.[31] The next figure Dr. Shah cited, 1,967,728, was the number of COVID-19 tests conducted in Maine to date, showing "just how many people have been tested for COVID [and] had to endure some of the anxiety that comes with being tested."

Next he mentioned the role of prevention in the state's relative success against the pandemic's spread. Maine's Transportation Department had made more than ten thousand deliveries to distribute 4,648,080 pieces of personal protective equipment. "The early provision of PPE is one reason why Maine was able to avoid some of the scenes in healthcare facilities that played out in other parts of the country." Another mark of the pandemic was "scarcity," he said, of "basic necessities like food, healthcare and even friends." In particular, elderly Mainers had "struggled with things that many of us might take for granted, like their next meal." Since the pandemic started 1,056,258 meals had been delivered to older and disabled residents, triple the number in an average year. Dr. Shah felt that figure was "really illustrative" of the collaboration that brought the state "together at its core, rather than coming apart at the seams." COVID-19 had "worsened challenges" for people across Maine who were "already just trying to get by, to have food and a roof over their head every single day." The state had provided "some degree of social support" for nearly six thousand people "who needed help with quarantining or isolation or just an extra hand getting by."

Dr. Shah went on to acknowledge "the unbearable sameness of it all" that everyone living through the pandemic had endured. "It's almost as if March of 2020 just blurred into March of 2021 with little recollection of the year in between," he said. "I think this is a function of how little we've moved, both physically as well as metaphorically. So much of our lives, whether it's work meetings, conferences, parties, reunions, family dinners, even funerals, all occurred in the same physical space, on that same cramped screen, from that same chair." He noted that Maine's increasing vaccination rate would be "critical" to the return of variety in Mainers' lives. In closing, he gestured to the corner of his screen, where an interpreter for the hearing impaired had been translating the briefing into American Sign Language — she was one of several who had done so for the nearly 170 briefings the Maine CDC had held by then. Dr. Shah thanked her and colleagues for their "partnership" on behalf of "many hearing impaired and hearing challenged Mainers."

After he delivered his remarks, Governor Mills wrote in her journal that "Nirav was brilliant today." She recalled his briefing as "so compassionate" and her reaction as "very emotional." Her own message to Mainers was much shorter, a pre-taped two-and-a-half-minute video that was posted online on March 12.[32] She tried to rouse her constituents to face whatever was left of the pandemic by invoking the country's longest-serving First Lady, who had led alongside her husband, President Franklin Roosevelt, during his four terms in office.[33] "During World War II Eleanor Roosevelt told the American people, 'You gain strength, courage and confidence by every experience in which you really look fear in the face,'" Governor Mills said. "You must do the thing you think you cannot do during this pandemic." President Biden also gave a speech to mark "one year since everything stopped because of this pandemic."[34] He issued an ambitious new challenge, calling on "all states, tribes, and territories to make all adults . . . eligible to be vaccinated" by May 1. His goal for the country was to "mark our independence from this virus" by the Fourth of July. The next day Governor Mills announced that she was "accelerating" the schedule of Maine's vaccine program to meet the president's deadline, based on an increase in the supply of shots.[35]

That weekend Ashirah wrote to say that it was "such a wonderful relief to see the pandemic lifting." By then the daily average number of new cases in the US was about fifty-five thousand, down from about a quarter million two months earlier.[36] Ashirah admitted that she had not "dug into foreign news to see how things are going in less developed countries," adding that her son thought the US "should start shipping vaccine right now to places that won't have it otherwise." Owen felt that this was the right thing to do and was "also important for everyone's health in this country." Ashirah "didn't disagree" but had told him she "didn't think that would quite fly yet." She went on to report that she had a sore knee and had been to see a doctor, "who thought it was a kneecap strain or something innocuous sounding like that." She added: "A nice name for the stupid injury that's keeping me from being with my dog as much as I'd like to be." She knew it would heal with some rest but found the downtime "frustrating and discouraging." As for Clutch, Ashirah had hired a trainer in a town about forty miles northwest of Temple, next door by Maine standards. She hoped the man could help with the dog's "prey drive" — Clutch was "okay" around other dogs, but "as soon as there's another animal moving in front of him he 100% loses his mind!"

Ashirah also mentioned that she was "feeling grateful for the latest COVID relief package" that President Biden had signed into law on the night of his pandemic anniversary speech. The Knapps had decided to use some of their federal aid money to pay off their car and help cover expenses for a trip to visit Ashirah's parents that summer. In addition to direct payments, the president's American Rescue Plan included the largest ever Child Tax Credit.[37] Ashirah planned to use "some of the extra money for children . . . to buy some more science kits" for Owen and Pamela "and not feel bad about it."

She closed her letter with a New Englander's perennial gripe about one of the region's infamous harbingers of spring. "What an incredibly muddy mess life is this time of year," she wrote. "Not just muddy but hard to move through the woods, as the snow is either soft and letting go under snowshoes or it is frozen over so hard it's too slippery for snowshoes." By that point in March, winter had begun its stubborn retreat from the woods of Temple, a long, fickle process of melting by day and refreezing overnight. One upside was maple sugaring season. "We usually put taps out in early March," Ashirah explained. "The trees are all around the edges of our clearing and also up a hillside." The Knapps collected sap from sixty or seventy maple trees to boil down for syrup, ending up with seven to ten gallons, depending on vagaries of weather. With those fluctuations came mud season, interminably boot-caking, car-miring, and floor-coating. "I read a wonderful quote from a trapper's biography," Ashirah told Governor Mills. "Something like, 'Spring is something to look forward to, or look back on, but not to actually enjoy while it's happening!' I agree." She drew a smiley face and added: "My floor will be clean again in May."

That day Governor Mills attempted to hike one of her favorite wooded trails on a nature preserve just south of Augusta, but she found it "entirely too icy." Instead she went home to Farmington to "check on the house and mail and walk . . . around the track at the Fitness Center" with a friend. Later on, back at the Blaine House, she hosted a birthday party for one of her granddaughters "with a safely-distanced small group of family members." She wrote in her journal that her niece was "ensconced upstairs studying." Julia emerged later that night to finish watching the Netflix series *Bridgerton* with the governor. "We didn't watch things a whole lot, and even when we were, it would always be both of us, like, doing work as well," Julia remembered. "But it was always fun to . . . take that bit of a break and just kind of spend some time hanging out together." That night in a diary entry Julia noted that her spring break was coming up and she would be away for two weeks. "I've been thinking that . . . when I get back here it will be halfway through the semester & thus halfway through my time living with Janet here," she wrote. "I need to make sure to take ample time to appreciate it, since when am I ever likely to spend this much time here — or even with her — again? It's been so incredibly special to get to do this and I think both of us really enjoy being with the other."

That same weekend the governor also took a "field trip" to midcoast Maine, where the former presidential yacht USS *Sequoia* had been "under wraps all during the pandemic and patiently awaiting" a complete four-year restoration at a boatyard in Belfast.[38] She wrote in her journal that she "got to climb inside under the plastic wrap and tour the grand dame," a 104-foot wooden yacht built in 1925. The *Sequoia* had served eight presidents, from Herbert Hoover through Gerald Ford, until it was sold in 1977 during cost-cutting by the Carter administration and to end the era of "the imperial presidency."[39] Many remarkable historic events occurred on the yacht, including a trip when President Roosevelt and General Eisenhower were said to have planned the 1944 D-Day landings. Queen Elizabeth II spent a night aboard during her visit to the United States in 1957. In 1963, President Kennedy celebrated his forty-sixth and last birthday in the *Sequoia*'s salon. Just over a decade later a disgraced President Nixon was on board when he told his family he would be resigning his office.[40] The yacht was designated a National Historic Landmark in 1987 and operated privately. It was later neglected during a legal dispute and eventually became infested with raccoons.[41] Governor Mills noted that *Sequoia*'s hull was "especially rotted." Nonetheless she was transported: "How fortunate I am to have walked through the hall, decks and staterooms . . . in the well-worn steps of Presidents." The shipbuilder leading the restoration "had set out black & white photos of FDR & Eleanor, of LBJ and of JFK's birthday party aboard this elegant vessel . . . We walked through history."

While the governor was in Belfast she had also shopped for clothes at her favorite boutique and bought gifts for one of her grandchildren at the toy shop near "Protest Corner." If the vociferous anti-mask demonstrators were in residence that day, the governor did not mention having noticed them. Incidentally, a week later the city council voted unanimously to update Belfast's noise ordinance to prohibit megaphones, which exceeded the new limit of twenty decibels.[42] The city's attorney explained that the changes aimed "to make clear that the council was cognizant of how this combined excessive noise that we have in our city has the effect of degrading the quality of life and impacting health, safety and welfare." Only one person spoke during a remote public hearing held by videoconference, but her question pertained to the use of ATVs and target practice on private property. Both activities were exempt from the ordinance, one councilor explained, along with special events and such "run of the mill, normal things" as church bells and tugboat and lobster boat operation.[43]

On March 16, Dr. Shah reported 189 new cases of COVID-19 and "notable" increases in both the state's seven-day positivity rate and the number of hospitalizations during the latest virus incubation period. He mentioned some "areas of concern," including Piscataquis County, whose commissioners had adopted the January protest resolution against restrictions the state was using to control "the Wuhan Virus." Since the beginning of March seventy-six cases had been confirmed in the county, nearly twice the number in the area the month before. Elsewhere in the US, Dr. Shah explained, the "significant decline in cases" since the end of January had "started to stall out," and other parts of the world were "starting to see an uptick" in pandemic metrics. "All of this is a reminder that we are not out of this," he warned. He added that Maine's vaccine program had recently passed the mark of more than half a million shots given. In anticipation of supply increases the state was "activating more channels," such as retail pharmacies and hospital and community vaccination sites, to build "as much headroom . . . so that when we get vaccines we can fill up to capacity every single day."

The next day Governor Mills signed thirty-four newly approved bills into law, ranging from an act that required racial impact statements as part of the legislative process to a measure that would extend an early-pandemic provision allowing bars to serve alcohol to-go.[44] She also signed a $258 million supplemental budget lawmakers had approved recently, after two days of protracted "and at times arduous" negotiations, as the governor described them publicly. In her journal she called the talks an "excruciating exercise in what should have been an easy review." Republicans eventually forced the majority Democrats to abandon the governor's plan to tax federal pandemic loans and fully exempt the benefits, among a few other concessions.[45] The House majority leader called the final deal a "victory" for bipartisanship. In the end Governor Mills commended both sides for the "sensible compromise" that got the bill "across the finish line."[46] By then lawmakers had overstayed their time slot at the convention center they had booked so both chambers could safely meet in person, potentially delaying the reopening of a vaccine clinic.[47] With most Mainers still waiting for shots, that was one headline neither party wanted to make, least of all while the state's pandemic metrics were rising.

In Dr. Shah's next briefing he warned that the "notable" increases in metrics he had mentioned two days earlier had now gone up even more.[48] "Of course we are hopeful that it doesn't turn into the beginning of a spike," he said, adding that "hope is not one of our actionable strategies in public health." He told those watching that if they were "in that group that is just tired of COVID" and "ready to chuck your mask in the trash, now is not the time to do that." In contrast President Biden sounded giddy when he addressed the nation that day to announce that his administration was "way ahead of schedule" on his vaccination plan.[49] The president would meet his goal of "100 million shots in 100 days" after just fifty-eight days in office. Within ten weeks the country would have "enough vaccine supply for every adult American . . . months earlier than anyone expected."

Governor Mills again accelerated Maine's vaccine timeline for every age group.[50] She pledged that all residents aged sixteen and older would be eligible for shots within exactly a month. To date more than 26 percent of the total population had been given at least one dose, the sixth highest rate in the country at that time, and all six New England states were in the top ten.[51] Unlike the supply of vaccines, eligibility to receive them had been the responsibility of states to determine from the start, and their decisions varied widely. Those that rushed to make more residents eligible sooner reached smaller percentages of their populations when demand exceeded supply, among other factors.[52] Seven out of the ten lowest-performing states — Georgia, Tennessee, Texas, Florida, Mississippi, South Carolina, and Missouri — had made larger-than-average numbers of residents eligible, according to the Associated Press.[53] The same review found that half of the ten top-performing states had "more restrictive eligibility." Going forward Americans would increasingly shape the next chapter of the pandemic themselves, to the extent that vaccine hesitation grew or eased as supplies scaled up, and the risk of serious illness or death from COVID-19 declined.

In Ashirah's next letter she reiterated support for continued caution. "I imagine that there is starting to be pressure to let up on the mask mandate," she told Governor Mills. "Just wanted to pass along that we've spoken to a few families in the last few days who all support continuing to wear masks!" She mentioned one couple who "had a funny story" about some new neighbors who had "moved in as part of the real estate boom in Maine" with children who would be "fully remote students" because of the pandemic. Ashirah's friends had made "their own family decision" for their kids to learn remotely "based on concern about still getting sick" and "thought they might all get along." They soon discovered that their new neighbors were "keeping their kids home because they were staunchly against wearing masks!"

That week the Knapps had spent "some of our (anticipated) child tax credit" to order a small solar setup for their son's bedroom as part of his homeschool science curriculum. Owen had learned how to calculate energy requirements "and transfer that to an under-standing" of what size solar panel and battery he would need to power his lights, fan, iPod, and metal detector. When those components arrived he would "do the wiring and fusing" so his room "would be its own setup, separate from the rest of the house" and he could track his own usage. "A bit pricey for us, but what good hard-skills [sic] to give him!" Their daughter's "next [science] block" would be to assemble a demonstration kit to learn about hydraulics. "Honestly I never got it myself until I did a similar kit with our son when he was little," Ashirah confessed.

That week's canine news was that Clutch's new trainer had "reassured" Ashirah that it was "just his breed and personality to be regal and intense" and she "wasn't doing anything to make the dog unhappy." Meanwhile, spring was continuing its advance in Temple. "Our road seems to have passed through mud season already," she wrote. "It's a little hard to believe . . . but it would be lovely if it's true." She lamented having to "time errands when one has to figure in loading the truck to get out to where the car is parked at the black-top, parking, reloading the car, etc., then reversing it all on the way home." It was "really impossible" to avoid getting her "town clothes muddy somewhere along the way, too." As usual her parting thought was upbeat: "Here's to hoping the next stage of the pandemic can not be too painful as we all readjust at different speeds."

That weekend warmer temperatures lured Governor Mills out of Augusta with a premature eagerness that tends to afflict New Englanders after a long winter, which all winters in the region seemed to be. "Too lovely a day at sixty degrees and the first weekend of spring, but wanting some beach time proves unrealistic," she wrote in her journal. She had indulged her wanderlust with an hour's drive south instead, picking up lobster rolls to have for lunch with Charlie in his garden. From there she visited her youngest stepdaughter, Lisl, and Lisl's two daughters "to hang out with the little girls and see them chase each other down the sidewalk on their little bikes."

The governor had a reputation in her family for making lots of stops on long drives. "Don't ever get in a car with her without taking a good book to read," her sister Dora griped lovingly. "One day . . . she said 'oh, come with me, I'm going to go to this event, some cookout down in Lewiston' or something, and I didn't take a book. We went to the cookout, but we went to five other things . . . No matter what town we drive through, she's always, 'oh yeah we'll stop and see so-and-so I haven't seen in a long time.' I'm like, well I don't know your friend so-and-so." On that springlike Sunday in late March, Governor Mills was on her way back to the Blaine House when she stopped at the home of some friends, a novelist and her husband. "We sit in the chilly air on the knoll next to their apartment . . . and chat politics, Maine history and literature," she later wrote in her journal. She had a pattern of revitalizing herself with good conversation, even in small doses, and the company of others was still a novelty after the isolation of the early-pandemic months and continued precautions since then.

On March 24, the daily number of deaths from COVID-19 nationwide fell below one thousand for the first time since November, but new cases were holding above fifty thousand per day.[54] "I'm often asked, are we turning the corner?" Dr. Fauci told the nation at a White House briefing. "My response is really more like we are *at* the corner. Whether or not we're going to be turning that corner still remains to be seen." By then the US was administering up to three million shots each day. In Maine that week Governor Mills had opened vaccine eligibility nine days ahead of schedule for people aged fifty and older.[55] The state's vaccination progress, coinciding with the change of season, seemed to raise her spirits. "Spring is here," she wrote in her journal that night. "No tulips, no buds on trees yet. But birds are filling the trees and bushes, the air is warm, the streets clear of ice at last." She was also delighted that her long malfunctioning laptop keyboard had finally been replaced. "I was getting so terribly annoyed at having to retype nearly every word because of repeat letters." Her entry mentioned a mass shooting the day before, at a supermarket in Boulder, Colorado, that had left ten people dead, "including the first police officer who responded — this, a week after eight people were shot to death in Georgia in three different massage parlors, six of them Asian American women, setting off a flood of protests across the country regarding bias against . . . Asian American Pacific Islanders." She did not share her personal reaction to that news, other than by way of including it in her entry; the recording of facts often seemed to be her way of indicating she had felt a strong emotional response to something, either of joy or sadness.

The next day a fresh-faced Dr. Shah hosted a CDC briefing wearing a crisp white shirt and a lime-green tie with blue and white stripes.[56] He raised an eyebrow as he reported another increase in new cases, 218 since the day before. Maine's positivity rate had now topped 2 percent, mirroring a slight increase in cases nationwide. Despite that upward trend he was cheered by the fact that the state had "gone more than thirty days without a single death, that we are aware of, from COVID-19, in a long-term care facility." He explained that the state's focused effort to vaccinate residents in those facilities in December and January was "the primary reason why deaths have dropped so significantly and thankfully across the state." Dr. Shah also reported that one out of every three Mainers eligible for vaccines at that point had completed their series of shots. Overall, more than 17 percent of the population was now fully vaccinated.

Governor Mills celebrated the state's momentum privately in her journal that night: "Everyone is getting vaccinated. We're about thirty percent of our total population who have now had at least one shot." She also mentioned that competition for vaccine progress among the state's participating healthcare systems was "fierce but healthy." The rest of her entry was an odd mélange, ranging from a joke she had seen on Facebook — "I asked my mom if she felt any side effects from her second vaccine shot today and she said 'an acute appreciation for science'" — to her transcription of a long quote from Ernest Hemingway's 1929 novel *A Farewell to Arms*:

> If people bring so much courage to this world the world has to kill them to break them, so of course it kills them. The world breaks every one and afterward many are strong at the broken places. But those that will not break it kills. It kills the very good and the very gentle and the very brave impartially. If you are none of these you can be sure it will kill you too but there will be no special hurry.

In a radio address the next day, Governor Mills reminded listeners that bars were now allowed to reopen for indoor service and the state was increasing capacity for indoor and outdoor gatherings. "Summer is fast approaching and the finish line is on the horizon," she said. "Got to keep our foot on the gas, keep people getting vaccinated, keep people alive and healthy, and get back to normal sooner." She urged Mainers to "keep doing the basic things that keep us healthy. Get a vaccine if you're eligible. Please, don't hesitate. It is safe." The relaxing of the gathering rules coincided with her niece's birthday later that week, so the governor hosted a small party for Julia at the Blaine House. "I've never had a better birthday in my entire life," Julia remembered. "I mean it couldn't have been more than six or seven of us and we all wore masks and everything, and some of us were vaccinated by that point. But . . . it was the first time when I really got to be with everyone since the pandemic." Julia treasured a photograph that someone in the group had taken while she was opening presents, sitting on the couch with her aunt. "My head's just resting on her shoulder and we've got masks on and stuff. It's adorable because it was really, like, the first time that we'd allowed ourselves to, you know, have those moments."

Ashirah, meanwhile, had spent part of the afternoon "sitting in the truck with the dog" while Chris and the children had lunch with his parents, as she reported in her final March letter. She had excused herself from the meal because "the dog can't be left alone for long periods in the car yet." She was also reluctant to repeat the holiday season fiascos of Clutch smelling food and seeing the cat through the glass door, combined with her mother-in-law's allergies. As for that week's news she and Chris had finally "sent off" their application to designate their school as a tax-exempt nonprofit organization. "Our fingers are crossed! I really have no understanding of how hard it is to get nonprofit approval," she wrote, noting that the application had been "so many hours of work on my husband's part!" Ashirah added that they "did have help from someone who does this as a side job, so we'll see what happens."

The Knapps were planning to relaunch their school's programs that spring and to welcome apprentices back to the homestead. "It's still awkward, with Covid," Ashirah felt, adding that she and Chris were "feeling much more confident being outside with people" and "not being as concerned about surfaces." Some of the students who had already signed up for courses were vaccinated. "I'll get Chris in, too, as soon as I can," she added. Ashirah felt that the world might face "a long, messy time coming out of this pandemic" in part because it was still unclear how effective vaccines would be over time. "On top of that, with all the people who will choose not to get it I'm just not looking forward to the difficult decisions we'll all have to make." She was "very thankful" that all of her family members and friends planned to be vaccinated "so I won't have to deal with that immediate level of stress, just a broader level." In closing, for her weekly offering of humor, Ashirah paraphrased a social media post she had seen recently with a photo of a person wearing a mask over just their mouth. "The caption reads, 'If you're still not pulling your mask over your nose it's been almost a year now. It takes less time to potty train a toddler.' (Or something close to that.)"

About a hundred miles north, a few unruly Mainers were still ignoring the state's mask mandate altogether. In Piscataquis County, its commissioners' "Protest Resolution" against pandemic protocols had as yet gone unchecked, inspiring some residents to form an advocacy group to oppose the measure. The Piscataquis Regional Organization for Action pledged that it would "pressure" the commissioners to "rescind" their resolution and "compel" them to hold "safe, accessible meetings" in compliance with state laws.[57] A retired physician who joined the group told a reporter from the *Bangor Daily News* that she had never engaged in county government proceedings until that year.[58] The newspaper reported that more than 60 percent of candidates for county commissioner in Maine since 2010 had run unopposed. In Piscataquis, one of three commissioners had faced a challenger in his most recent bid. By the end of March, the panel's anti-mask resolution was still in place regardless of its lack of effect, other than to have inspired civic engagement. Two of the commissioners also voted to deny a local nonprofit theater a letter of support for a federal grant application after its leader opposed their resolution.[59] The theater had not only followed COVID-19 restrictions but also had gone to the apparent extreme of posting a message on its marquee in regional parlance: STAY WICKED FAH APAHT.

On March 30, President Biden and the director of the US CDC, Dr. Rochelle Walensky, warned the public in separate appearances that the country's pandemic metrics were rising dangerously and Americans were risking a fourth surge of COVID-19.[60] "I'm going to lose the script, and I'm going to reflect on the recurring feeling I have of impending doom," Dr. Walensky said. She reported that the numbers of hospitalizations and deaths were up, and case numbers had risen 10 percent that week. The nation had "so much promise and potential of where we are and so much reason for hope," she said. "But right now, I'm scared." The president echoed his recent appeal for continued precautions. "Now's not the time to celebrate," he warned. "It is time to do what we do best as a country: our duty, our jobs, take care of one another."

In Maine that day, Dr. Shah reported more new cases and two deaths but focused on the state's "steady and sustained progress" with vaccinations.[61] He seemed to struggle to restrain his sense of urgency as he announced that the state was receiving more than seventy-two thousand doses that week, a nearly 50 percent increase over recent allocations. "Please do not let this opportunity go," he told those currently eligible for shots. "Don't let the virus get to you before a dose of vaccine does." In one of his most impassioned monologues to date, Dr. Shah then called the vaccines a "stunning scientific success," adding that "so many of you have been waiting" to get shots. "Maine, I need you to make it happen," he said, then invoked the state's license plate slogan. "We all want to get back to being 'Vacationland,' but first we have to become vaccination-land, and this is the week to do it."

CHAPTER TWELVE

"The needs of the many . . ."

Ashirah was writing her first April letter on a Friday evening when her daughter "came over for a quick cuddle good night. Eleven years old and still the cuddliest kid ever." It was the second day of a new month, and Ashirah was feeling upbeat about Maine's progress against COVID-19. "More and more people we know are getting vaccinated," she told Governor Mills. Whenever she saw "an elderly person out and about" she wanted to "cry and celebrate" that they had "made it" through the pandemic, so far. She added that her family would "proceed with extreme caution as we have been doing." Her letter that week was short, filling only one side of a page of three-hole-notebook paper. She noted that the dog was "doing amazing [sic]," but Ashirah's sore knee was still a problem and now the other one was aching. "I really hope that's just because . . . it's taking more weight than normal," she wrote, adding that she was going to try some physical therapy. This was the first time an injury had made walking difficult for her and she was "worried [it] would keep getting worse."

She also mentioned that she had received a friend request on Facebook from "a profile with the name Janet Mills." At first Ashirah had thought, "Oh, that's nice!" Then she had realized "it wouldn't be a difficult thing to fake." Her next thought was that "someone would notice" if a fake account was trying "to undermine" the governor. (The friend request was legitimate — the governor had sent it from her personal account, not her official profile.) Ashirah quipped that her "caution" was both "a strength and a weakness, and something that drives my husband nuts." She also gave an update on mud season — the mire was "drying up, so that helps." She added that it was "lovely to feel the springtime. Every single warm day we have, I value." Ashirah had noticed over the past few years that early April in Temple was when she started "hearing the sound of water again" as the snow melted a little more each day. Before long there would be spring peepers too; the smallest frogs in Maine, no bigger than an inch and a half, signaled their perennial return to the state's ponds, marshes, and swamps with their onomatopoeic breeding call, beloved by many.[1]

Early April was also when the state's population of some thirty-six thousand black bears, the largest in the eastern United States, began to emerge from their dens before there was much vegetation to eat.[2] That spring a state wildlife promotional coordinator warned Mainers: "Dumpster diving, devouring bird seed, grappling with grills, and raiding camping gear are some of the ways bears will seek food in an attempt to obtain 5,000 calories a day to restore their fat reserves lost over the winter months." Similarly, humans in the Northeast ventured from their homes around the same time, after months of dark days spent mostly indoors, and headed for the region's forests and mountains. Some were unprepared for dangerous weather and needed rescuing. Inevitably a few were reached too late; reports came every year of hikers with all levels of experience who ignored or misjudged unpredictable threats and did not survive, in either case having endangered those who went to their aid.

In late March 2021 a young man and woman from Massachusetts were found dead in Acadia National Park, on Maine's northeastern coast, after falling nearly a hundred feet from a steep, icy cliff.[3] During the first week of April, rescuers retrieved a "severely hypothermic" hiker from the Appalachian Trail in extreme northern Maine after he fell into some water and was unable to warm himself.[4] A game warden said the thirty-eight-year-old man, from the state's southern coast, "did not have appropriate clothing or hiking gear" and probably would not have survived if he had not reached out by text message to a friend, who in turn alerted rescuers. That same night the warden service rescued a family of five, all adults from New Jersey, who became stranded near the 3,074-foot summit of Tumbledown Mountain, not far from Temple, where snow and ice had obscured the trail. "With the sun going down, improper clothing, and not enough food, water or lighting to attempt to climb down the mountain, they called 911," the warden service said.

It was perhaps with the human tendency toward willful blindness in mind that on the first day of April, Governor Mills warned Mainers: "Spring is here but the pandemic is not over." She had joined Dr. Shah's remote briefing to announce that, in a week's time, the state would expand vaccine eligibility to residents ages sixteen and older. She noted that the change was almost two weeks ahead of schedule, and in response to a "significant" supply increase.[5] "We're still in a race," she said, "a race of vaccinations versus the variants." The US CDC had reported an increase in COVID-19 cases nationwide that week, noting that a growing number were caused by "variants of concern," including the predominant B.1.1.7.[6] The governor told those watching that mutated versions of the virus were "in western Maine, they're in southern Maine, they're spreading to every region of the state." The variants were "more transmissible and potentially much more dangerous," she added, "so please get vaccinated and stick with the precautions that we've had all along." She asked residents for their "continued patience" while the state worked to make appointments more available, especially in rural areas.

Dr. Shah explained that the recent addition of the single-dose Johnson & Johnson shots would magnify Maine's "ability to turn vaccines into vaccinations." They did not require such strict storage conditions as the Moderna and Pfizer vaccines, or follow-up doses. That allowed more providers to administer them, such as EMS technicians at pop-up clinics that could be dispatched to remote places. In theory, more Mainers could now be fully vaccinated in less time. Meanwhile, Dr. Shah reported five more deaths and 283 new cases since the day before, the highest daily jump since February.

The country had reached a complicated but pivotal point in the pandemic — vaccine supplies and eligibility were increasing exponentially across the US, but the virus was mutating. At the same time, more states were lifting pandemic precautions while still rushing to increase their residents' access to shots. A reassuring study released that week by the US CDC found that full vaccination reduced the risk of infection by up to 90 percent.[7] The agency also announced that it was now safe for fully vaccinated Americans to travel without testing or quarantining.[8] So far only about a fifth of

Maine's population had been fully vaccinated since the first dose in the state was given in mid-December.[9] About a third had received just one shot. Nationwide just 17 percent of Americans were fully vaccinated while about 30 percent had partial protection.[10]

All those factors coincided with Easter Sunday and the last day of Passover, on April 4, the first major holidays since the US CDC advised that fully vaccinated Americans could safely gather. Consequently there were no urgent pleas from the Mills administration that Mainers avoid group celebrations, despite a continued rise in COVID-19 case numbers and the state's positivity rate. Governor Mills gave a radio address on Friday, April 2, "to thank everyone who's gotten vaccinated for taking this important step to protect themselves, their loved ones and our communities."[11] She repeated the news that Maine was opening its vaccine program to all adults starting with sixteen-year-olds. The governor also asked for her constituents' patience as more vaccine sites opened and added staff. Unlike her addresses ahead of Thanksgiving and Christmas, she did not explicitly link her reminder for caution to that weekend's holidays. "Keep your distance from others outside your immediate family," she said. "Remind everyone to wash their hands and wear a face covering." Then she wished happy Easter and Passover to those celebrating, "and for everyone, happy spring."

In the span of about four months, her administration had relaxed the whole architecture of its pandemic management, easing its posture of extreme caution. Governor Mills had now loosened some of the state's cornerstone restrictions and shifted Maine's focus to mass vaccination. Daunting questions remained that could be answered only in time: How many more lives were in the balance despite the arrival of vaccines? Would enough people get vaccinated before some variant caused another surge? Could the governor and her administration convince those who were still hesitant about the vaccines' safety? As this new chapter began Governor Mills took solace in the company of her family, hosting a small holiday dinner at the Blaine House on Easter Sunday. She gathered with her sister and two of their brothers, all four siblings fully vaccinated, plus Julia and her brother. Their voices in the halls and rooms marked another striking change, as Julia noted in her diary that night. "I've gotten so used to having Janet to myself and I've so cherished it because she so rarely has the time for so much one-on-one time," she wrote. "Now that people are getting vaccinated and things are starting to be more normal, I know that Janet will likely be back to the campaign trail and [hosting] events this summer and the small Thanksgiving and Christmas we had . . . will be no more."

If Governor Mills had mentioned campaign plans with her family, she had yet to elaborate publicly on previous comments about whether she would seek reelection. Coincidentally, in early April the Maine GOP posted a submission form on its website, seeking voters' input on its presumed candidate. The party had been "asked to get your feedback for Governor Paul LePage to read as he considers his return to run for Governor."[12] The message also decried the incumbent's "overzealous, job-killing government regulations," accusing Governor Mills of "massive, unsustainable" spending and putting "liberal, special interest politics before the people of Maine." The party promised it would "quickly share all of the notes we receive" with its prospective candidate. No indication was given as to how many Mainers replied, but a companion post on the party's Facebook page received 493 likes, out of about 17,000 followers. Whatever the response, at some point in April state GOP leaders signed a letter indicating that Governor LePage would run unopposed, a formality that allowed the national Republican Party to provide material support.[13]

On April 5, Governor Mills posted some photos on her personal Facebook page that she had taken during "late winter wanderings" in Maine's capital.[14] It was notable and revealing that she had found her way to a small graveyard, located about two miles by foot from the Blaine House. Two of her photos showed a monument there, inscribed in memory of OVER 11,600 PATIENTS who had died at the Augusta Mental Health Institute (AMHI). The facility was founded before the Civil War, in 1840, and closed in 2004, a period spanning vast changes in the country's understanding and treatment of mental illness.[15] After decades of deinstitutionalization of psychiatric patients nationwide, the deaths of five AMHI patients during a heat wave in 1988 prompted legislative hearings on its operation, and a class-action lawsuit.[16] Two years later a consent decree was imposed, which governed the provision of mental health services statewide in Maine until January 2021, when a judge deemed that its standards had been met. Governor Mills had noted that milestone in her journal that day, and again in February after the state had agreed to "measurable performance standards . . . that, if met, could potentially end the Consent Decree within two years."[17]

Now she stood in front of the memorial for the first time and read its inscription, which ended with an admonition: THE LOCATION OF THE BURIAL GROUNDS FOR MOST OF THOSE PATIENTS WHO DIED AT AUGUSTA MENTAL HEALTH INSTITUTE . . . WERE NOT KEPT OR HAVE BEEN LOST. MAY THIS STONE SERVE AS A MEMORIAL TO THOSE PATIENTS WHO DIED AT AMHI. MAY IT ALSO SERVE AS A REMINDER THAT THEIR LIVES HAD VALUE AND THAT THEY WERE DESERVING OF DIGNITY BOTH IN LIFE AND DEATH. The granite monument was placed in the city-owned cemetery in 2015, opposite the hospital's grounds, where a new state-run psychiatric facility had since opened.[18] The original buildings had been added to the National Register of Historic Places in 1982 as the remains of "one of the oldest and most architecturally intact nineteenth century mental health institutions in the country."[19] Historical accounts noted that the facility's location, "directly across the Kennebec River from the State House" had been selected "in order to place the new facility in sight of legislators at work in the Capitol, so they would not forget the needs of Maine's mentally-ill."[20] As Governor Mills discovered nearly two centuries later, the site — now including the AMHI memorial — was also within wandering distance of the Blaine House, should its occupant need reminding.

The Mills administration started the second week of April 2021 by announcing a "groundbreaking Mobile Vaccination Unit" developed in partnership with the Federal Emergency Management Agency (FEMA).[21] The unit was only the second of its kind in New England at that time, funded and staffed by FEMA, with the goal of delivering vaccines primarily "to people in rural and under-served communities across Maine." It was not as slick or cinematic as the acronym MVU suggested — when set up, the unit looked more like a crime scene with a forensic investigation under way. It consisted of an unmarked trailer flanked by white vinyl tents, some folding tables and chairs, and lanes marked by orange traffic cones.[22]

FEMA chose eleven communities for the unit to serve, based on the US CDC's Social Vulnerability Index, which used census variables to identify localities that needed support during and after natural disasters. Planned locations ranged from Biddeford, a city of more than twenty-two thousand people in Maine's southwestern corner, to Madawaska, the northernmost town on the state's border with Canada, with a declining population of about thirty-seven hundred.[23] The MVU would spend four days in each place, aiming to vaccinate at least 250 people per day, mostly with the one-dose Johnson & Johnson vaccine, "in order to maximize efficiency." At an on-site press conference to launch the unit, Governor Mills practically shouted, "Don't wait, all of you who are now eligible to receive a COVID-19 vaccine!"

That night she unwound at the Blaine House with a novelist friend who was visiting for a couple of days. "We entertain ourselves with poetry," the governor wrote in her journal — they spent evenings reading poems to one another over dinner. She had chosen "The Lanyard" and "The Death of the Hat," both written by two-term US poet laureate Billy Collins. At some point they called one of Maine's former poet laureates, the governor's friend Wesley McNair, to join their session by phone. He read "a couple of his poems, one regarding delivering fresh bunches of rhubarb to neighbors, some gone; the other, another lovely poem about life in a small town." In turn the governor had read him a draft of a poem she was working on, titled "Slack Tide." Its explicit subject was a small coastal island once owned by the painter Andrew Wyeth and his wife, Betsy, until it passed to their son Jamie. The governor and some friends had relished a visit with him there, nearly a year earlier. One verse of her poem hinted at the lure of the island's sanctuary:

> A restless diaspora of ducks,
> feathered fatherlings,
> interrupted the dusk, while

an anchor the color of grit
waited for the sea to claim it,
and drew me once more back to the land.
How long would I stay.
One more day
One more day.

On April 7 vaccination sites across the state started giving shots to Mainers as young as sixteen. The next day Dr. Shah told reporters that Maine's allocation of doses for the next two weeks had been cut substantially due to a "fluctuating" supply of the Johnson & Johnson vaccine. The state had hoped the one-dose vaccine would dramatically expedite Maine's inoculation progress. Meanwhile, the number of new COVID-19 cases had continued its ominous run of consecutive daily increases. The whole country was "in the fourth week of an upward trend," the US CDC reported, noting a 2 percent rise in the seven-day average since the last week of March.[24] The agency pointed to the "lifting of social distancing and mask mandates in some areas" and "the presence of more contagious variants" — B.1.1.7 had been detected in all fifty states and was now causing more than 27 percent of cases nationwide.

Ashirah's next letter started with her concern about "the uptick in case numbers" in Maine and nationwide. "It would be nice to just be moving through this one," she wrote, "but I think it was pretty clear from all the evidence that the more virulent variants were going to gain a foothold." She told Governor Mills that it was "a little like an awful deja vu to be thinking about Covid getting bad at the same time there's lots of news coverage about . . . Derek Chauvin." The former Minneapolis police officer's televised trial in Minnesota had begun in late March. During opening statements a prosecutor showed the jury devastating footage of the arrest and then alleged murder of George Floyd.[25] Ashirah wrote that she and Chris had shared "some brief clips of the lawyers' opening remarks" with their children. They had also listened together to an interview that aired the day before on National Public Radio, in which Minneapolis civil rights lawyer Nekima Levy Armstrong detailed the effects of the trial on her community so far.[26] During the segment Nekima mentioned the "great deal of stress and anxiety surrounding watching what happened to George Floyd and hearing him say, I can't breathe, nearly 30 times. Not to mention the anxiety that's created from watching the bystanders plead with the Minneapolis police officers to release George Floyd." When asked what changes seemed possible in the aftermath, Nekima said: "We are hoping that in this case, an officer will be convicted for what he did. Beyond that, I think that people are cautiously optimistic in terms of what the future holds. They're watching, they're sharing information, and my hope is that it leads to results in terms of transforming the way that policing happened in Minneapolis."

The Knapps had since been having "some gritty family discussions about ethics, due process, voting the truth versus voting your conscience, etc." Ashirah wondered if "someday there will be a world in which these tough issues no longer need to be discussed because the incidents that precipitate them simply don't occur" — a world in which "people just choose to be their higher selves, not their lower." That world was "a possible future, several generations down the line," she thought, adding, "I can see it." She noted that she was writing that week's letter on Israel's Holocaust Memorial Day. "I grew up in a Jewish family and there is a definite racial memory in me," she told Governor Mills. Ashirah had always felt "a burning desire" to "speak out against injustice," an urge that "comes from . . . knowing the cost of silence."

By that point in the letter Ashirah had filled one side of a page of lined notebook paper. For the next page-and-a-quarter she sounded off on the "frustrating" dynamics she faced in her part-time job of helping the addiction medicine clinic's patients get vaccinated for COVID-19. "So many of our patients are leery of the vaccine and say they won't do it," she wrote. She had spent all her spare time during a recent shift at the clinic's front desk "searching the Internet for the right fliers" — she had "finally found some good ones" that she felt were written clearly and understandably and "answered some of the fears we were hearing." Patients had been asking what was in the vaccines, how they were "made so quickly," and what proof there was of their safety. "This wasn't just about people in recovery," Ashirah explained. "It was a microcosm of everywhere. Everywhere people were a little scared of this new thing. I was scared of it and I was a strong supporter of vaccines." She compiled a list of pharmacies and hospitals the clinic's patients used, that also offered vaccines. Then she "hit a big roadblock" that she found "pretty upsetting and which shoots us in the foot" — vaccine appointments could not be scheduled "more than a few days or maybe a week ahead of time" and few of the clinic's patients could "just head in at short notice."

Ashirah understood that supplies were inconsistent and unpredictable but she thought there should be provisions for people to plan further in advance. "Especially with the way the second shot can really make a person ill. That's something that would be nice (or even necessary) to plan for." Her concern was that "people will try a few times to sign up . . . and then give up when they keep getting the notice that there aren't any appointment openings." She had found that "websites don't even explain that there will eventually be appointments available and that you need to keep trying." Then, in a nod to the fact that Governor Mills was ultimately responsible for the vaccination effort, Ashirah added: "While I realize this is a massive undertaking whose scope I barely perceive, it's also something we knew was coming, and sensible websites that offer information and explanation are not hard to design."

She started the next paragraph "on happier and less serious notes," sharing the news that "one of the goats' udders is beginning to bag up pre-kidding, which is exciting." By then the spring peepers were "singing everywhere" and the weather had been warm enough that Ashirah could let the family's free-range ducks into the garden each day. Raised for eggs and meat, the ducks were allowed to roam "all over the field and the two farm ponds" during the day. At night the Knapps locked the small flock into a predator-proof coop. "We've lost fowl to raccoons and ermine in the past, so we've learned to tuck them in safely each night," she explained. The next step was "working with the dog to leave them alone." Ashirah ended that week's letter with a jumble of updates: "The kids look forward to

spring break approaching, my knee is improving and we're beginning to plan our drive to . . . Ohio to visit my family in June."

The following week Governor Mills joined Dr. Shah's Tuesday
briefing, on April 13 — unlike the early months of the pandemic,
when they often co-hosted press conferences, by this point her presence was usually an indication of some consequential development,
for better or worse. Dr. Shah started the briefing by announcing
further increases in Maine's pandemic metrics, including 571 new
cases that day. He was quick to add that most of those had been
reported to his agency over several days but exceeded what it could
process in a twenty-four-hour period. He added that Maine's positivity rate had also gone up, to just over 3 percent. Then he took a deep
breath and calmly explained that the US CDC and the FDA had
recommended a "pause" in administration of the Johnson & Johnson vaccine "out of an abundance of caution." The agencies were
reviewing six cases among women who had developed blood clots
after their doses.[27] Meanwhile, Maine had directed all vaccine providers to stop administering the shots. "What we are talking about
today is extremely rare," Dr Shah emphasized. "Again, six cases that
have been detected across the country, out of 6.8 million doses of
J&J vaccine that have been administered." For the avoidance of
doubt, he added: "That's fewer than one in every million."

Dr. Shah described the potential symptoms of a blood clot and
assured Mainers that there were no reports that any had been caused
by the Pfizer or Moderna vaccines — the state's delivery of both was
"continuing unabated," he said. "Getting vaccinated remains one of
the best things that you can do right now." Then he introduced
Governor Mills, who assured Mainers almost too enthusiastically
that the state was working to ensure uninterrupted access to the
other vaccines. "One of the words I've heard most frequently in the
last thirteen months is 'pivot,' so we pivot today," she told those
watching. Case in point, Maine's mobile vaccination unit would
shift from giving mostly the Johnson & Johnson shots to administering the other vaccines. The state would then help coordinate logistics for scheduling the second doses needed with the other vaccines,
while the MVU moved on to the next town. "I've talked a lot about

perseverance over the past twelve, thirteen months," the governor added with a self-deprecating smile. "Today is another example of it." Logistical challenges were "to be expected," and she admitted that this one would "certainly take some more effort." Nonetheless she asked Mainers to "stick with us" as her administration carried out "the largest logistical effort made by the state or the nation in generations."

If it was a feat for Governor Mills to project calm that day, she showed no trace of the effort, despite the perilous limbo the state had entered with the pandemic. She had started loosening restrictions before even a third of the population had been fully vaccinated. Now the frightening blood clot risk, however minuscule, threatened to erode support for vaccines in general, while causing major supply disruptions. Meanwhile, variants were proliferating, and cases were rising ominously in rural areas and among young people, most of whom were still unvaccinated or not yet fully protected. Coincidentally it had been almost exactly a year since the governor cried out to her staff: "When are the locusts coming?!" At that time she had just learned that there was an explosion at a paper mill in Maine, after a "bomb cyclone" spring snowstorm had buried much of state under a foot of snow, a few weeks into Maine's pandemic lockdown, leaving thousands with no heat or electricity. A year later, in the thick of an exponentially more complicated morass, she made her way home to the Blaine House, arriving not long before sunset. According to her niece's diary the governor announced "that she wanted to go for a walk. So we did."

Afterward they lingered outside the mansion near the garden, enjoying the ever-warmer spring weather. Julia sat in the swing the governor had installed before the pandemic and played a favorite song, Bobby Darin's 1959 rendition of "Beyond the Sea," from her cellphone. Governor Mills stood nearby, and they "watched the final rays of the sun glint off of the [statehouse dome] and reflect upon the big green lawn," as Julia wrote later. She added that "it all just felt very peaceful and joyful." It was late April now, and the days were getting longer and warmer. The ice had recently gone out on the lake where the governor had her summer camp. Maine's bird population was about to swell, according to *Bangor Daily News* birding columnist Bob Duchesne. "This is the week the floodgates open," he wrote. "Up until now, there has been a steady trickle of birds migrating back into Maine. From here on, all heck breaks loose."

Two days later the state's COVID-19 positivity rate was up to 3.5 percent, and Dr. Shah reported 579 new cases.[28] He had recently taken to breaking that number down in every briefing, in addition to his regular list of metrics, presumably to minimize alarm. "Of those cases, 124 were individuals diagnosed yesterday . . . 251 were individuals from the thirteenth," and so on. However, Maine's daily average of new cases that day was almost as high as it had been the day before Christmas Eve of 2020 — the upward April curve had so far mirrored the steep climb in cases Maine experienced over the holiday season, which had peaked at a daily average of 625 cases.[29] "We're also seeing that those who are hospitalized are younger than they were before," Dr. Shah said, adding that the average age of those infected was now thirty-five, down from forty-three at the end of 2020. "All of this shows how opportunistic the virus is," he explained. "As older parts of the state . . . have been vaccinated, the virus is now spreading more rapidly among younger populations." He reminded those watching that vaccines were now "available in Maine to anyone over the age of sixteen" and that getting shots remained "critical."

Ashirah wrote to the governor the next day, starting with news that her husband had gotten a dose of the Johnson & Johnson vaccine, four days before the "pause." The Knapps had since talked with their children about "the potential problems." Ashirah admitted that she had "consciously skewed" the risks at first, so Owen and Pamela "wouldn't be scared for Chris," by explaining that only women had developed blood clots so far. She told them that "one's chances were less than one-in-a-million . . . but also how it doesn't help when you are the one." The family had then discussed "the quote from Spock about 'the needs of the many out weigh [*sic*] the needs of the few, or the one,' and what did we feel about that." Ashirah was referring to a famous quote from the 1982 film *Star Trek II: The Wrath of Khan*, which was based on a storyline from the original

1960s science-fiction television series.[30] In the film, Mr. Spock — a
leading character who was part human, part alien, and lived by strict
adherence to logic and reason — told the ship's captain: "Logic
clearly dictates that the needs of the many outweigh the needs of
the few." Captain Kirk added: "Or the one." Spock eventually sacrificed his life to save the starship USS *Enterprise* and its crew. The
Knapps' goal in talking with their kids about controversial subjects
throughout the pandemic was "more to encourage critical and
open-minded thinking than to resolve these discussions with
answers," Ashirah explained. "We generally ended with some
version of, 'Wow, there are many layers of complexity here. It's
really good to take all of this into account, then we do the best that
we can do.'"

In the rest of her letter she vented more frustration over Maine's
vaccine rollout, at least as it was progressing in her region. In another
page-long rebuke she called "the scheduling aspect . . . a huge
ball's-up [sic]," noting that there were "not enough public service
announcements as to how to go about getting vaccinated" and that
those she had seen were incomplete. "It feels as though no decision
was ever made about whose responsibility it would be to make sure
vaccination happens," she wrote. "The addiction medicine office I
work in is contacting all its patients, but that's because the doc[tor]s
there are very proactive and decided to take it upon themselves."
One patient's primary care doctor had been administering only the
Johnson & Johnson vaccine and told the woman to "wait and call
back when she heard that it was being used again." Ashirah "about
went through the roof!" she told the governor. "I tend to get worked
up about things I care for when I see someone else doing a bad job,"
she added in a parenthetical. She contacted the patient herself and
gave her information about finding an appointment for one of the
other vaccines. "We don't know how long J&J will be 'on pause' or
if it will ever be used again! And they should have put her on a list
and said 'we'll call you' (I didn't tell her those last two sentences,
those are just what I was thinking)."

Ashirah's experience was something of a bellwether for how the
Mills administration's vaccination program was going in other thinly

populated areas. Maine was the most rural state in the country, with more than 60 percent of its residents living outside urban centers.[31] Those people tended to have less access to healthcare or faced greater challenges in seeking it, or both.[32] Many rural parts of Maine also lacked broadband access at a time when the Internet had become a vital source for pandemic information. Governor Mills had been working to expand the reach of broadband in Maine, which she considered "as fundamental as electricity, heat, and water."[33] Her administration had "bought $9.3 million worth of at-home learning devices," during the pandemic, "for more than 21,000 students who were trying to learn remotely but didn't have internet access." A state Broadband Action Plan released in January 2020, just before the pandemic, found that more than eighty-three thousand addresses in Maine did not have access.[34] "In reality, that number is most likely to be greatly understated," the authors noted. Their estimate for the cost of expanding broadband to those areas was "at least $600 million."

The paused Johnson & Johnson vaccine had been a key element of the Mills administration's planned push to reach more rural Mainers. Meanwhile, there was minimal vaccine hesitancy in the state so far, and little disparity, at least in that regard, between residents of urban and remote counties. A federal survey in mid-April found that less than 13 percent of the state's adult population was wary of getting the shots, the eleventh lowest rate in the country.[35] Wyoming had the highest rate at nearly 31 percent. Governor Mills credited Dr. Shah in large part for boosting Mainers' confidence in the vaccines. "He's just very patient," she said. "He knows you have to meet people where they are, in public health especially." Not to diminish the crucial contributions the rest of her administration had made, she emphasized that Dr. Shah's was one of the most public-facing roles, mainly through his press briefings, and one he happened to be innately well suited for. "That was why we had one of the highest vaccination rates in the country . . . it's public education and it's Nirav messaging."

By the weekend of April 18, half of Maine's eligible population had received at least one vaccine dose, and 38 percent were fully vaccinated.[36] In announcing the milestone the governor claimed the state was now number one in the nation for "the percentage of its total population that is fully vaccinated," according to a Bloomberg tracker. She kept up the tone of optimism in her radio address that week, telling listeners that Maine's economy had "added more than 4,000 new jobs . . . last month alone, the largest gain since September."[37] Conversely there had been little change in the state's jobless rate, just under 5 percent in February compared with more than 6 percent nationally.[38] "Jobs are available right now," she said, "and many people may not realize they can work and still receive partial unemployment benefits." Taking the tone of a stump speech, she added that her administration was "focused on training skilled workers to fill jobs" and "making education more affordable and accessible." She soon planned to detail how the state would use the next round of federal pandemic aid "to get our economy up and running at full speed," which could not happen "without healthy people." She asked Mainers to "be extra careful" when they traveled for spring vacations, and "for crying out loud, wear the mask."

Governor Mills spent some time with her young granddaughters that weekend, visiting a farm that had some newborn goats. She also went for a short hike with Julia, who wrote in her diary that Sunday that she was enjoying the archery range her aunt had let her set up on the grounds outside the Blaine House. Julia had asked in late winter, "half-joking," if she could hang a target somewhere in the yard so she could practice her hobby. The governor "was like, 'oh sure,'" Julia said. "She knew how much it meant to me." The state police unit that provided the governor's security approved Julia's setup, which consisted of a target attached to a tree, with one side of a barn for a backstop. She caused a minor incident when the Augusta Police, who had not been alerted, passed by on patrol while she was practicing one day in late February. After some initial confusion as to why someone appeared to be shooting arrows near the governor's residence, the matter was quickly resolved with the requisite paperwork. "Now I have a permit to discharge a bow within the city limits of Augusta," Julia wrote in her diary later that day. "Who knew?"

On Tuesday, April 20, Governor Mills made another dizzying, day-in-the-life entry in her journal, similar to the one she had written in February. She chronicled back-to-back Zoom calls with various lawmakers, as well as members of her staff and cabinet, including a weekly meeting "about COVID-19 vaccine distribution and the lack of the one-shot J&J vaccine." She mentioned preparing for, then joining a remote panel discussion on climate change with the governors of Hawaii and Washington. There was also a call with the president of CSX, the North American freight rail company that planned to acquire a regional railroad in New England, including three hundred miles it operated in Maine. The deal promised to upgrade rails and improve freight and passenger service, among other benefits, and CSX was seeking the governor's support.[39] Before she wrote any of this in her journal that night, she recorded the day's biggest news, albeit with the stoic parlance of a former prosecutor: "Minneapolis Police Officer Derek Chauvin is found guilty of all three charges" in the death of George Floyd. "Murder 1, Murder 2, and Manslaughter by the jury after about ten hours of deliberations." In Temple that afternoon, after the verdict was read, Ashirah "went outside and cried for a while," as she wrote in a Facebook post.[40] "Obviously this isn't joy that someone's headed to jail. I don't think anyone is feeling joy. Just relief and the sense that a tiny, tiny bit of sanity has returned to the world."

Two days later Dr. Shah reported that Maine's positivity rate had "come down a bit" to just under 3 percent.[41] "For context, one week ago that number stood at three and a half percent," he explained. "The fact that it's come down is encouraging. Let's hope it stays that way." He also mentioned "so-called breakthrough cases," which reporters had started asking him about earlier in the week. He explained that 453,000 Mainers had been fully vaccinated since December, and of those, the state's CDC knew of only 109 instances when someone then became infected. "Let me put that differently — 99.98 percent of people who got vaccinated . . . have not gotten COVID," he said. "To me that is about the best and most ringing endorsement of the COVID-19 vaccine as you can find." The US CDC reported a total of six thousand breakthrough cases so far, or less than 1 percent of those who were fully vaccinated, which was now one in three Americans over the age of eighteen.[42] Lastly that week, Dr. Shah acknowledged that Maine's emergency preparedness team had delivered its six millionth item of personal protective equipment and thanked its members. "A year and a month ago, when we started these briefings, one of the things that I did every day was read out exactly how many N95 masks and how many pairs of surgical gloves we have," he recalled with a laugh. "It seems a little trite and quaint to look back on those notes now. It's also a reminder, though, of how far we've come in the past year; even though I don't read out . . . the number of gloves that we've delivered, that work hasn't slowed down."

On May 1, now just over a week away, the state would start to loosen pandemic travel restrictions for visitors from out of state. Preparations for Maine's summer tourist season had been under way for months. In one early harbinger, campgrounds were taking reservations at a record pace, with weekend sites already booked from the end of May through mid-September at more than half of the state parks that allowed advance reservations.[43] Many businesses in the hospitality and retail industries throughout New England had begun to raise concerns over shortages of both seasonal workers and workforce housing.[44] Meanwhile, a spring nor'easter had extended the ski season in Maine, bringing half a foot of snow in the mountains.[45] The state's two biggest resorts stayed open through the last weekend that month. The owners of Saddleback Mountain announced that they had secured $1.5 million in new funding for continued renovation after the resort's successful return to operation. The long winter had done little to alleviate the previous summer's severe drought, which had qualified some farmers to seek federal aid. Now abnormally dry conditions had already returned in more than half of Maine's land area. The state activated its Drought Task Force to monitor groundwater and reservoir levels, soil moisture, and other factors in all but one of sixteen counties.[46]

On April 23 federal health authorities lifted the pause on the Johnson & Johnson vaccine after eleven days. In that time they found a total of fifteen women who had developed blood clots after getting the company's shots, out of almost eight million Americans.[47] Three of those women died, and seven were still in hospitals. The vaccine was put back into circulation with warnings for women deemed most at risk of developing the rare clots. Maine's Dr. Shah believed the review process had shown "the strength of the US vaccine safety system" and directed vaccine administrators to immediately resume use of the shots.[48] He acknowledged signs of "a little bit of softening of demand" for vaccines, among other factors, that resulted in a 20 percent decline in the state's overall vaccination rate during the pause.[49] By the last week of April nearly half a million people had completed their vaccinations, or about 43 percent of those eligible for shots. The daily average of new COVID-19 cases had peaked on the 19th and declined every day since.[50] That metric was also falling nationwide, prompting a sense of relief as the mass vaccination effort continued around the country.[51] That time was also marked by sadness, especially for Americans who completed the vaccinations that might have saved the lives of relatives or friends, or both, who had died in the pandemic.

Governor Mills started that week with a press conference, stepping up to a podium in Maine's statehouse on Monday morning wearing a patterned face mask that matched her sky-blue blazer. There was exasperation in her voice as she launched into an announcement of a bipartisan bill that would create a new state agency to build, own, and manage broadband infrastructure and "close the digital divide" in rural Maine.[52] "Seems like everyone has a story about slow, or no internet access in Maine," she said. "A father of four wrote me from Owl's Head — he has to bring his daughters to a restaurant to connect to Wi-Fi to get their homework done; a doctor in Blue Hill struggles to view his patients' charts during remote telehealth sessions; a high school student in Hope, Maine . . . missed 16 days of school because of dropped connections." This was "unacceptable," she said, adding that high-speed internet access was "the modern equivalent of rural electrification in the 1930s and the Interstate highway system in the 1950s." The governor thanked lawmakers from both parties for "crossing the aisle" to co-sponsor the bill, which would spend $130 million of

Maine's share of federal pandemic aid on the project, "rather than reacting in a piecemeal fashion, as we've done forever, to construct a patchwork of infrastructure."

That night the moon was almost full, so the governor and her niece went outside to look for it after dinner. "Literally every month we'd go out to find the full moon," Julia explained. "Doesn't matter what the weather was, she'd be like, 'Let's go out and see if we can find the full moon.'" She recalled another night when her aunt had read somewhere that the northern lights would be visible in Maine. "So we just got in the car, it was late . . . and we just drove out to some random field. I had no idea where we were. We were just trying to find the northern lights, and we didn't find them but it was so much fun." On that Monday of the last week of April, Julia wrote that she and her aunt did not have to leave the grounds of the Blaine House to find the moon: "It was beautiful behind the magnolia tree."

Tuesday brought the news that Maine would follow the latest federal guidance and lift the mandate that people wear masks outdoors.[53] Face coverings and social distancing were still required indoors, and recommended during outdoor activities in close contact, "so that we can get this pandemic fully behind us," the governor said. Unsurprisingly, the change did little to placate anti-maskers — on Wednesday she mentioned in her journal that there were "four protests" over bills the legislature planned to deal with in its session that day. "So I woke up this morning being blamed for everything from masking mandates . . . to destroying the lobster industry." The former was de rigueur, but the latter was a reference to a rally in Augusta that day, attended by some four hundred fishermen, mostly lobstermen. They had come to protest against the Mills administration's support for two floating offshore wind farms. One of the projects proposed a single turbine in state waters. The other was the first-in-the-nation "research" array of twelve in federal waters that she had announced in November.[54]

At the rally one young boy wearing fisherman's waders carried a large sign with a drawing of a lobster claw gripping a windmill blade. The sign read CRUSH MILLS and SAVE OUR FUTURE.[55] The event was organized in response to a bill the governor planned to introduce in the legislature that day, which she had hoped would allay the industry's objections. The measure proposed a ten-year ban on new offshore wind projects in state waters, where the majority of lobstermen set their traps.[56] It expressly acknowledged fishermen's concerns, including potential environmental harm and loss of key fishing grounds. The bill's language stated that wind projects "may adversely affect resources . . . including commercial fishing."[57] It also made the case that a ban would give Maine time to amend its laws to prevent damage to marine ecosystems, while the relatively new wind energy industry developed further.[58] The lobstermen's rally, in both tenor and attendance, suggested that they either had not read the bill or had other concerns it did not address, if any legislation could. Governor Mills noted in her journal that the event had been promoted by former Governor LePage, "who, people forget, wanted to drill for oil and gas in those same Atlantic waters." Her predecessor had sent a representative but did not attend. Organizers had also claimed that Maine's Democratic congressman Golden would make an appearance; he was later said to have had prior commitments.[59]

Governor Mills knew she faced a fraught, complicated challenge in seeking to balance the interests of fishermen, whose industry had been integral to Maine's character for generations, with her goal for the state to use 80 percent renewable energy by 2030, all while continuing to manage the pandemic. She had also proposed to double the number of clean energy jobs in Maine to thirty thousand in that same period, in the hope of positioning the state to become a major player in the country's growing clean energy industry.[60] Meanwhile its commercial fishermen were facing — or, perhaps, avoiding facing — dire threats to the longevity of their trade, including burdensome regulations to protect endangered whales from entanglement in fishing gear, and climate change; the waters in the Gulf of Maine were warming faster than 99 percent of the world's oceans.[61]

Naturally, many in the industry saw their way of life as a frontier they were losing, and they felt justified in resisting. Some were simply too old to change course. Others, particularly in the next generation, were factoring uncertainty into decisions to pursue alternative careers.[62] Governor Mills had genuine empathy for their plight, despite what many in their industry believed, and she made a point of reiterating her commitment to preserving Maine's lobstering industry. Her broader vision for the state's future also aligned with the Biden administration's commitment to support enough wind projects on the East Coast to power ten million homes with wind energy by 2030.[63] It so happened that on the day the fishermen rallied in Maine, President Biden gave his annual "address to a joint session of Congress." (The speech was customarily known as the State of the Union, except in the first year of a president's term.)[64] Governor Mills called it "dramatic, bold, expansive," noting in her journal that the president had delivered the address "to a gathering of 200 people in the House Chamber designed to hold about 1500." The downsized event was invitation-only due to pandemic protocols.[65] Security in and around the Capitol was still heightened — its grounds fenced off, nearby streets shut down, and the National Guard on duty — as it had been since the riot on January 6.[66]

The president's speech centered on the pandemic but also mentioned issues ranging from child poverty and the country's opioid epidemic to nuclear aggression and competition with China.[67] "There is simply no reason why the blades for wind turbines can't be built in Pittsburgh instead of Beijing, no reason," he said. Another major theme — and one familiar to Mainers, though he never used the word — was the country's resilience. "We all know life can knock us down," he said. "Americans always get up. Today, that's what we're doing: America is rising anew, choosing hope over fear, truth over lies, and light over darkness." After the "rescue and renewal" of President Biden's first hundred days in office, the US was "ready for takeoff" in his view. "We're working again, dreaming again, discovering again, and leading the world again." For Maine's governor that meant "more busy, busy days with a full agenda," as she wrote in her journal that night. "Every day worrying about saving a life, getting people vaccinated and stopping the spread of the coronavirus." However challenging, it was a job she had decided she wanted to keep — her entry ended with the casual aside that she was "not taking anything for granted politically either, and gearing up for the Re-Elect next year."

CHAPTER THIRTEEN

"... in other words, leadership."

By the beginning of May in Temple each year, the sun's gradual return brought mostly welcome changes to the Knapps' daily lives on the homestead. "All the birds are starting to sing, the flowers are blooming, wild greens are popping up and all of the leaves are coming out," Ashirah explained. "Every year it happens, even when I think this year maybe it won't happen." This was also the point each spring when blackflies returned. "So while I'm sitting there enjoying all of the life that's starting to grow around me, I'm also being chewed on," she added. The weather in May 2021 was warm and dry. Although temperatures ranged from the low fifties to upper sixties, they could still drop close to freezing overnight. The risk of a late frost had mostly passed, so the Knapps' garden could now be planted. Ashirah wrote to Governor Mills on the 3rd, with a report that one of the family's goats had miscarried and the other had yet to deliver her kid. "I definitely missed when their heats were," she concluded. "But my daughter's ducks have begun laying, which is fun."

Ashirah's week had been uncommonly stressful; her sister-in-law had gotten a dose of the Pfizer vaccine for COVID-19 and, coincidentally, had also developed a blood clot. "She'll be fine ... and no one thought there was a connection, but it was something to think about — that reminder that you never really know what's coming." Ashirah had also learned that one of the "very sweet patients" at the addiction medicine clinic where she worked was recovering from a near-fatal opioid overdose that needed reversal with medication. She wrote that she did not know specifics, except that the patient "would have been dead without Narcan." She added: "It was hard to think, 'That would have been it.'" That Sunday morning, just as she was "planning and looking forward to (and needing) half a day off," her dog "attempted to eat a porcupine." Ashirah had then spent much of the day at an animal hospital having the quills removed from

Clutch's muzzle. "Also, $500," she noted. "I'm sure he'll do it again so I've been learning about pulling them myself." She then vented for half a page about the hospital's triage policy, or lack thereof — she had called ahead when she was on her way to the clinic with the dog, who was "crying, pacing, drooling and pawing his face" during the drive, only to have to wait an hour to see a veterinarian. "So their manager will be hearing from me," she told Governor Mills. Ashirah closed her letter with a non sequitur in place of her usual joke. "My daughter wants to shave half her head. Sure, why not."

As spring progressed, there were encouraging indicators that the pandemic might be receding in Maine. On May 1 the state dropped all travel restrictions for those who were fully vaccinated, both tourists and residents returning from other states.[1] Dr. Shah explained that the growing number of vaccinated Americans, which had just passed one hundred million, had reduced "the likelihood that any one individual may pose a risk to someone here in Maine."[2] The Mills administration touted that the state was leading the nation for the portion of residents who were fully vaccinated. More than 40 percent of those eligible now had all the shots they needed.[3] In early May an opinion essay published by the *Bangor Daily News* captured the prevailing mood around mass vaccination — the author, a former columnist for the newspaper, had recently volunteered at a large hospital clinic in the post-shot observation area.[4] She described the "overarching atmosphere" there as "a celebratory glow of eye-smiles and relieved inhalations." People were "almost universally patient and cooperative" despite all the logistics. Her own "re-immersion into humanity" after long months of isolation and social distance had made her "giddy with joy." One day she had noticed a technician saying, "Good morning, save some lives," repeatedly to vaccinators as he distributed each batch of syringes, "like a pastor giving communion." For the columnist this was "a quietly profound reminder of what we are doing here, and why we must continue."

While Maine rushed to inoculate younger residents, health officials were still working to close a stubborn gap in vaccination rates between rural areas and cities.[5] There were also inconsistencies among the state's prisons, where some of the largest outbreaks in Maine had developed to date.[6] By the start of May only 17 percent of those incarcerated had been fully vaccinated.[7] Correctional system officials mostly blamed the lengthy vaccine supply shortage. Prison reform advocates criticized Maine's decision not to prioritize inmates — only four states' initial vaccination plans included those incarcerated in the first phase of inoculations; about half later changed course to include prison populations in first or second rounds.[8]

Also by early May more vaccine clinics in Maine had begun accepting people without appointments, and residents of any state could now get vaccinated in Maine, such as college students who lived elsewhere.[9] Dr. Shah was quick to attribute those changes to "the ever-evolving vaccination landscape," as opposed growing vaccine hesitancy or indifference.[10] He also emphasized that all COVID-19 vaccines were free of cost to recipients, noting that this was "something that we've gotten some questions on lately." He warned that variants remained "a concern," along with still-increasing infections among younger residents. Otherwise, Maine's most critical pandemic metrics had continued to stabilize. The seven-day average of new cases was down about a third since mid-April, to 297, mirroring an overall decline nationwide.

On May 4, Governor Mills announced her administration's plan for how to spend the state's latest round of federal aid and "let the world know that Maine is a safe place to live and work."[11] About a quarter of the $4.5 billion American Rescue Plan package was designated for discretionary use. Of that portion, the governor wanted to spend $260 million on helping businesses recover from pandemic losses, among other immediate economic goals. She proposed putting $300 million toward attracting, training, and keeping a diverse workforce, and other longer-term investments. Lastly, she believed the state should spend more than half a billion dollars to revitalize its infrastructure, with the largest portion for expanding broadband access. The funds came on top of better-than-expected state revenue projections at the end of April, which had been boosted in part by earlier rounds of federal pandemic aid.[12] Governor Mills said the influx meant the state was "entering a new era" with "the promise of prosperity." Maine could now "offer the next generation greater goals, aspirations, and opportunities and something even greater than these: we offer them hope." For this round of federal pandemic aid, state lawmakers would be involved in determining how it was allocated, unlike previous packages. The funds "had a much broader reach," and their distribution "really invited, and needed, legislative approval," the governor explained. She kept her tone upbeat heading into that process. "These are truly exciting times!" she said in her radio address that week. "Let's get it done!"

Over the weekend Ashirah wrote with the happy news that the family's pregnant goat had delivered "two big healthy bucklings." The other goat had developed illness after miscarrying. The Knapps decided to "move her out" because of a run of medical issues, as well as "poor milk production and horrible kicking, and having only single babies instead of twins." Whenever the family slaughtered livestock Ashirah considered whether she wanted to continue eating meat. She knew from past experience that she felt healthier with red meat in her diet. Beyond that, animal slaughter was "very much a subsistence kind of skill" that she valued and preferred to do herself. "Then I know how the animal is treated and I know how it was killed and I know that none of it was wasted," she explained. She also appreciated that she could "provide the family with so much good quality meat" even if it was "certainly sad to say goodbye to a friend."

Ashirah's letter also mentioned that this was her final week of work at the addiction medicine clinic. She had been training her replacement and realized in the process that she was "completely burned out" from managing the demands of family, work, teaching her children, and running the homestead. "I'm so ready to be done [but] at the same time I get so much from relating to people." She was also busy helping her husband prepare to reopen their school that summer with programs including a "pack-basket weaving workshop," an eight-day "homestead/backcountry adventure" for a group of girls from a summer camp in midcoast Maine, two "homestead immersion programs" for high school sophomores, and a three-day program with students from the local University of Maine campus. Ashirah wrote that she would have more time to herself in the fall, when her children went back to school. "I need to come up with a plan to spend a little time working with other people again," she told Governor Mills. "Maybe doing ladies' nails in nursing homes or volunteer chaplaincy at the hospital here."

Late that night the state confirmed that more than half of Maine residents who were eligible for vaccines had received their full course. The governor called the milestone "a testament to the willingness of Maine people to do their part," including those giving shots or volunteering in clinics and all the people in state government who were helping coordinate the program. She added that there was "more work to do to get this pandemic behind us," including vaccinating the other half of the state's population. Toward that end the governor launched an incentive program with rewards for those who got vaccinated, including free tickets to minor-league baseball games or car races, free hunting and fishing licenses, gratis day passes for state parks, or a $20 gift card from outdoor retailer L.L.Bean.[13] She announced the program during a livestreamed "virtual meeting" with President Biden and the governors of five other states whose vaccine programs were among the most successful in the country — fellow Democrats Tim Walz of Minnesota and Michelle Lujan Grisham of New Mexico, and Republicans Mike DeWine of Ohio, Spencer Cox of Utah, and Charlie Baker of Massachusetts.[14]

Governor Mills told the president that Maine had dubbed its incentive scheme Your Shot to Get Outdoors. "Oh it's corny, I know," she said, adding that Mainers had "found refuge in mother nature throughout the pandemic so these incentives will encourage that outdoor activity while getting more shots in arms as quickly as possible." She added with a smirk that she knew other states were "doing something different, some are offering shots of booze" — New Jersey had recently partnered with breweries in that state to give vaccine recipients a free beer.[15] Others were doling out cash, such as Maryland's $100 for state employees who got vaccinated.[16] The trend prompted the New York Times to quip that "scoring a dose of the coronavirus vaccine in America, once the equivalent of a winning lottery ticket, has started to resemble something else: a clearance sale."[17] Upon hearing Maine's list of incentives, President Biden told Governor Mills: "My guess is that's probably going to work."

The White House meeting had come in the middle of "another crazy week," as Governor Mills noted in a journal entry. On Monday, May 11, she had finally announced her nominee for chief justice of the state's supreme court, just over a year after the previous justice resigned.[18] If confirmed, her appointee would be the second woman to serve as Maine's chief justice. The governor's entry also noted that she had held a press conference on Thursday "to announce that we are lifting the six-foot distancing requirement and lifting the indoor capacity limit completely" on May 24, just before Memorial Day weekend.[19] During that remote briefing she had also warned Mainers that "we're still living through a pandemic" and urged those who were still unvaccinated to get shots. "Please, I beg you, use common sense," she said. "Please protect yourself, your families, your communities, by getting vaccinated." She added that Maine's indoor mask mandate would remain in place until further notice.

Unbeknownst to the governor, while she was speaking to reporters that afternoon, the US CDC issued what was arguably its most highly anticipated update yet, officially ending the mask-wearing recommendation for vaccinated Americans, except in crowded indoor settings such as planes and hospitals.[20] Those people could "start doing the things that you had stopped doing because of the pandemic," the CDC's director said. She added: "We have all longed for this moment, when we can get back to some sense of normalcy." The news had surprised Governor Mills, who was still in the midst of her press conference. When reporters questioned her about the change she hedged, telling them her administration would "review that guidance when we've actually got it in hand." Otherwise she was "sticking with what we're saying today because we think it's best for Maine's . . . public health needs right now." She was noticeably irked and spoke somewhat tersely during the remainder of the press conference, which went on for another thirty minutes. "I want to be clear," she emphasized, "these changes don't come without some risk, especially for those who remain unvaccinated." Later that night she complained in her journal about the US CDC's unfortunate timing. "Pretty confusing, and not the first time [Washington] has pulled the rug out from under me."

The next day the Mills administration announced that Maine would adopt the new federal guidance on mask-wearing, but not for another ten days — the change would take effect on May 24 along with those the governor had announced the day before.[21] Her official statement added that "in light of the increased role the US CDC has assumed in issuing guidance," the state would "begin retiring" its COVID-19 prevention checklists for businesses and start "transitioning to US CDC guidelines as appropriate." Just over a year earlier, in mid-March 2020, President Trump had told states to find their own sources of medical supplies to prevent and treat COVID-19. "Respirators, ventilators, all of the equipment, try getting it yourselves," he said on a conference call with the nation's governors.[22] "Point of sales, much better, much more direct if you can get it yourself." A month later, in another call regarding plans to lift lockdowns and reopen states' economies, he told the governors: "You're going to call your own shots." The governors had filled the void of presidential leadership, albeit to varying degrees and with dramatically different results, for fourteen all-consuming months. Now, in the unceremonious span of a single line in a one-and-a-half-page press release, the Mills administration had signaled that it would mostly stand down, so to speak. The final sentence noted that "despite having the oldest median age population in the country, Maine, adjusted for population, ranks fourth lowest among states in both the total number of COVID-19 cases and number of deaths . . . according to the US CDC."

Many of those who supported the move to end mask-wearing and social distance requirements, in Maine and the rest of the nation, felt a conflicting sense of disbelief and relief. Some critics worried the change was premature. Others thought further delay was ridiculous, including former Maine governor LePage, who called for his successor to "follow the guidance and IMMEDIATELY remove the mask mandate for those vaccinated."[23] The Retail Association of

Maine's Curtis Picard called the Mills administration's approach a "big step forward towards full reopening" but noted that some stores might continue to require masks in lieu of asking for proof of vaccination.[24] In a Facebook post his group wrote: "We are hopeful additional clarifications are forthcoming. Retailers: if you have specific questions, please let us know."[25] Some concert venues in the state started booking shows for the coming summer season.[26] Elsewhere in New England, the Republican governor of neighboring New Hampshire had lifted that state's mask requirement weeks earlier, but the GOP governor of Massachusetts decided to keep a mask mandate in place there.[27]

Governor Mills had issued the announcement adopting the CDC face-covering guidance on the Friday of her "crazy week." That day she also went to Farmington to tour a career technical education center. She discussed the $20 million in federal pandemic aid that her administration was proposing to put toward more than two dozen other CTEs across the state. That evening she hosted her female cabinet members for cocktails in the backyard of the Blaine House. Nine out of the fifteen commissioners were women, more than in any previous administration. Their occasional gatherings, a solace throughout the pandemic, had morphed into a weekly confab. The next day some protesters gathered outside the Capitol, across the street from the Blaine House, in warm and sunny weather. The governor left Augusta for a break at her camp. "Oh, hello Earth, my old friend," she wrote in a Facebook post with some pictures of the view from her dock as the sun was setting.[28] "I'm breathing unpoisoned air again, listening to your old loons again, waiting for your old sun to sleep again and rise another day in Maine. Still in love with you."

On Sunday, Ashirah took out a single piece of lined notebook paper and started another letter with her usual opening lines of thanks to Governor Mills and her staff. Her next sentence came as a profound surprise: "This will be my last weekly letter — not because I no longer support you and your decisions but because my intent was to continue regular positive feedback through Maine's experience of the Covid pandemic. And I think we're actually really coming through it." The rest of the letter took up only about two-thirds of a page: "Thank you for what you've done during this last year and a few months! It has saved lives. While some people never changed their opinions or practices, and many more just want to see the pandemic behind them and forget the whole of it, there are also those of us who will let the emotions and lessons stay with us. The experience is one that shouldn't be forgotten. There is a lot there for individuals and societies to continue working through. As a part of that, for my family, we will always remember — and retell the story of — a time [when] a government and a leader did what they were meant to do: take care of us. Needless to say (which of course means I'll say it anyways [sic]) we really hope you run for office again."

Ashirah's letter did not reach the Blaine House for six days. In the interim Governor Mills used her weekly radio address to hail the importance of Maine's "7,600 farms of all sizes, scales, and agricultural practices."[29] She reminded listeners that her grandfather "was a potato farmer in Aroostook County" and that she valued "a little dirt under the fingernails." The governor had toured a gristmill in central Maine that week — she was enjoying getting out of Augusta more often now that it was safe to interact with her constituents again. She used the visit to tout farmers and food processors as key to "boosting our economy all around" and outlined her plan to upgrade their infrastructure using another $20 million from Maine's federal pandemic aid. In a nod to Maine lawmakers' role in steering the money, the governor added that she looked forward "to working with the Legislature . . . to continue Maine's economic recovery from the pandemic."

That week the state's daily COVID-19 case counts and hospitalizations continued to fall, and the number of vaccinated residents ticked ever upward, if less sharply. Dr. Shah held a single briefing, having recently scaled back from giving biweekly updates. He told reporters that two more Mainers had died, raising the state's death toll to 807. He then mentioned the new federal guidance on masks, asking people to "be smart, be respectful, be considerate" during "this transitory period" of easing precautions. "Some people may be comfortable chucking their mask . . . Others may not be where you are." He also warned that COVID-19 was "starting to affect younger people far more systematically" — those under age twenty-nine accounted for "almost half" of new cases diagnosed in Maine since April. "That's a stark change from where we were before vaccinations," he said, "which is all the more reason for folks in that age category to start getting vaccinated."

The FDA had recently authorized Pfizer's vaccine for use in children as young as twelve, adding nearly sixty thousand residents to the ranks of those eligible for shots in Maine.[30] Dr. Shah reported that more than half of those approved for vaccines were now "done," but progress had slowed, especially in rural areas. He noted that the state had extended the "mission" of its mobile vaccination unit into July, but after a recent three-day stop in southern Maine, the MVU had administered 552 doses, only about a third of its capacity.[31] In a rural town there called Turner, a reporter from the *Portland Press Herald* asked unvaccinated residents what would change their minds about getting the shots. A thirty-four-year-old woman told him "you can't shame people into doing it. I don't want to be told what to do." A fifty-two-year-old woman said the vaccines seemed "very rushed," and she was "not sure what's behind it all," adding that she did not know anyone who had gotten sick. Turner was also the home of Maine's Senate minority leader, Republican Jeff Timberlake, who had given his party's response to the governor's annual speech in February. "Look, I got the vaccine, I want everyone who wants it to get the vaccine, but I think we need to have a more inclusive message," he told the *Press Herald*. "If people see the benefits and see the state and country opening up as we see more vaccinations, they might say, 'OK, maybe I'll go do it, too.'"

Ashirah's letter was stamped as received by the "Office of the Governor" on May 22, a Saturday, in the midst of the last weekend that Julia was in residence at the Blaine House. She had been accepted to a summer internship program in the patient experience department of a hospital system near Portland and planned to move out on Sunday. "I can tell Janet doesn't want me to leave," she wrote in her diary. "I just told her I'm going down to Portland tomorrow and she said, 'Well your internship doesn't start for a while, you don't have to rush.'" Julia added that she was "pretty sad about it" and would "miss being here all the time." She stayed until the early evening so she could attend a garden party that her aunt hosted on the mansion's grounds. The governor had invited a few dozen people who had been vaccinated. Her guests included some of her siblings, close friends, and a few new acquaintances, as well as the woman who ran the gristmill the governor had toured that week, a well-known chef who owned a famously ecclectic café in midcoast Maine, and several prominent artists, authors, and poets who lived around the state. The day was warm but windy, with gusts over thirty miles per hour that turned over some tables. The governor and company were undeterred and lingered in the garden, mingling without masks, relishing the novelty of company from outside their households. That night Julia left the mansion with her brother and their mother, the governor's sister Dora. "Had a ton of fun at the garden party this evening and am now back in Portland," she wrote in her diary. "Missing Janet . . ."

The next day Mainers woke up to the closest semblance of normal life that they had known for more than a year. The state's indoor mask mandate had expired, along with all capacity limits and physical distancing requirements for indoor and outdoor venues. Exceptions remained for schools, childcare facilities, airports, and public transportation, as well as state and federal buildings. Healthcare facilities also kept mask requirements. That day some Mainers burned their masks while others delighted in running simple errands without them, such as going to the grocery store or signing up for new gym memberships.[32] Some business owners took down long-required signage about the newly lapsed protocols. Others opted to keep mask rules or required employees to keep wearing them. In the midst of it all, Maine had become the first New England state to fully vaccinate half of its population.[33] Masks and social distancing were still recommended for the other half.

At some point that day Governor Mills made time to respond to Ashirah's final letter. "It feels like the end of an era," she wrote. "Vaccines are here. People are back at work. Folks are hugging and shaking hands. Friends and neighbors are visiting again. And lilacs are in bloom. And you have written your last weekly letter of support." She reiterated that Ashirah's letters, "handwritten, heartfelt and real," had helped keep her "grounded throughout this year." They had also helped her staff remember that "families in Maine are dealing with issues every day — training a new dog, homeschooling children, birthing farm animals in the spring, running a business, going to work, putting one foot in front of the other, doing what has to be done to get by." Ashirah's children would "surely remember this time as the year their mother taught them the value of an inquisitive mind, the need for integrity, faith and hard work . . . love for neighbors seen and unseen . . . as well as how to birth a goat kid and how to adore a disruptive dog — in other words, leadership." She thanked Ashirah for her letters and her courage. "I hope when our paths cross . . . on Main Street in Farmington, you will say hello."

The two women had no further contact until Ashirah wrote one more letter of support almost a year and a half later, in late September 2022. By then the country had faced new COVID-19 variants and massive infection surges that dwarfed any it had previously endured. Despite the vaccination of nearly 68 percent of Americans and the development of vaccine boosters, the US death toll had nearly doubled.[34] In Maine, 74 percent of residents had been vaccinated, but the number of deaths in the state had more than tripled.[35] Governor Mills was now running for reelection against former governor Paul LePage in a race that had been defined by their sharply contrasting personalities and political tactics, and opposing views on which issues mattered most to Mainers. In particular she had campaigned on a promise to protect abortion rights in the state after the US Supreme Court overturned the landmark 1973 *Roe v. Wade* ruling in June. "I pledge to the people of Maine that, so long as I am governor, my veto pen will stand in the way of any effort to undermine, roll back, or outright eliminate the right to safe and legal abortion in Maine," she said that day.[36] She had then issued an executive order enhancing legal protections for those who received or provided abortions in Maine.[37]

Governor Mills also highlighted her administration's success in minimizing COVID-19 deaths and protecting the state's economy without raising taxes. Her press releases often ended by noting that Maine had kept its stable, high-quality credit rating from the top firms Moody's and S&P while other states' outlooks were downgraded during the pandemic.[38] Maine had also been one of only ten states that scored an A from the National Bureau of Economic Research on its "Final Report Card on the States' Response to COVID-19."[39] Maine's Independent US senator Angus King called the report "amazing," noting that it was published by "a right wing think tank" — the organization billed itself as independent but the report's three conservative authors included economists who had counseled Donald Trump, one during his presidential campaign and the other as a top adviser in the Trump administration.[40] They had graded states on the variables of mortality, economic performance, and the pandemic's effect on education.[41] Maine ranked eighth overall, using unemployment figures, public school closures, pandemic deaths, and other factors. In particular, Senator King was struck by the mortality ranking: Maine had the country's third lowest rate, of about 145 deaths per 100,000 people. "To me that validates the decisions [Governor Mills] made," he said. (The report's authors noted that they found "no clear pattern in which states had high and low mortality," and it was "therefore unclear" whether "political leaders can be considered responsible for mortality outcomes.") Another study that spring gave Maine the second-best rating in the nation for the performance of its healthcare system during the pandemic, after Hawaii. That report from the Commonwealth Fund, a private health research foundation, considered death rates, vaccination rates, admissions and staffing shortages at hospitals, and other factors.[42]

In former governor LePage's 2022 campaign, he largely avoided the subject of coronavirus, focusing his candidacy instead on his economic record during his two terms, in addition to his worry that inflation was rampant. He sought to portray Governor Mills as out of touch with her constituents' concerns about rising energy, gasoline, and food prices. When he mentioned the pandemic during one of his televised debates with the governor, he quipped that she had "been very, very fortunate that COVID came, because with COVID came nearly $15 billion from Uncle Joe."[43] The comment, referencing pandemic aid from the Biden administration, drew an incredulous look from Governor Mills. "He said that at the end of the debate and I did not have an opportunity to respond or comment on it," she noted. The next day she said privately that there was "nothing lucky about COVID," and she would "give every penny of that federal money back if it would bring back the lives we lost."

While the governor might have understated her disdain for her opponent when in public, she did not hide it. "We can't go back to instability and infighting that stands in the way of solving problems," she said at the outset of one of their debates. As a centrist who abhorred obstructionism, she viewed former governor LePage's approach to leadership and governance as an affront to the people he had been elected to serve, to say nothing of his crass brand of politics. In her view the LePage administration amounted to eight years of "fighting, dysfunction and stalemate," a refrain she used throughout her candidacy.[44]

Enough Mainers disagreed with that assessment to have elected him twice, and some of the governor's closest friends felt that she could have fought a more aggressive campaign, especially during the debates. "She's been careful," said Janice David. "I'd like to see her be less careful, take a few more chances." Janice added that she and the governor had "talked about this a long time ago: there's the first four years, and in order to have a second four years you have to get elected." Charlie Miller remembered wanting "to smash the TV" when he was watching the debates from home. "For every opening LePage has given her, and he's given her a ton — you know, here, he just gave you the jugular, take it out . . . she won't do it," Charlie said. "I think she's had her struggles, had her losses personally. I think she's wounded — I'm saying all this lovingly — and I don't think she likes to engage for that reason. She's not a brawler." Former governor LePage, on the other hand, accused the governor of "using taxpayer money to send people to places where they can get free crack pipes."[45] He also decried the Mills administration's dispersal of a budget surplus back to taxpayers as $850 relief checks as "a gimmick" — the initiative, meant to help Mainers with rising costs, was first proposed by Republican state lawmakers.[46] "This governor spends money like a drunken sailor," her opponent said. "The only difference between Janet Mills and a drunken sailor is a drunken sailor spends his own money."

As the election approached that fall, speculation abounded that the race was closer than polls suggested. One survey released in late September showed Governor Mills with a twelve-point lead.[47] It found that "98% of those who say abortion is their top issue are voting for Mills." About 78 percent of voters who cited threats to democracy as their chief concern planned to vote for her. The poll noted that financial concern "drives LePage's support" — 69 percent of those who named the economy as their primary issue were planning to vote for him. That poll also noted "a significant gender divide," with men favoring former governor LePage by two points while women broke for the incumbent by twenty points. Shortly after those figures were released Ashirah was compelled to weigh in from Temple. "Dear Governor Mills, hi this is Ashirah," her letter began. "I wrote to you through the first year of the COVID pandemic." She explained that with the election "coming up and LePage in the news a lot more," she had wanted "to write another letter of support." Her family was "very much" hoping the governor would win, "but we recognize that a lot of our fellow Mainers feel differently." Ashirah mentioned her teenage son's deduction that Governor Mills had "kept people from getting together and drinking booze and now they're pissed." She added a parenthetical: "In my defense, he came up with that political commentary on his own — I didn't teach it to him! I think he's not wrong though . . ." Ashirah's hope was that the governor would "feel peaceful, whatever happens, knowing that you did the right thing all along the way."

She went on to say that she did not want her letter "to become an exercise in ego," but "it would feel odd" not to give an update on her family "after so long." The past year had been "extremely difficult" for the Knapps. One of their children had "developed a non-dangerous but completely-debilitating neurological condition." The other fractured a vertebra, "which should have healed fine but has instead resulted in 10 months now of chronic pain and severely limited abilities." Both children were "a long way from recovered," but Ashirah was relieved to "have a diagnosis for each of them." She was sad to report that after all her trials with Clutch, the dog had been euthanized — he had developed "rapidly increasing, uncontrollable aggression with inconsistent triggers" and was "becoming dangerous." Since making that decision she had "been able to offer help and support to several other people facing the same thing," which had "felt very worthwhile." The Knapps had since "welcomed a hound-mix into our family" who was "filling the holes in our hearts."

Ashirah wrote that after leaving her job at the addiction medicine clinic, she had decided to apply to college to earn a bachelor's degree in social work and had begun her studies that fall. "It's going to be a many-year project," she told the governor, adding that she looked forward to "one day having the degree that will give me the power to ennact [sic] some of the change I want to see but right now can do nothing about." She closed her letter with the news that one of her children had "shared with us that they identify as bisexual (which I have permission to write)." Her family was now "much more aware of the LGBTQ plus community," which Ashirah had found "to be soothingly welcoming of allies." Then she signed off: "Sending our thoughts and support, Ashirah Knapp." Her letter reached the Blaine House in mid-October, around the time when the latest poll showed the governor's lead had narrowed to ten points, with 10 percent of respondents still undecided.[48] Cost of living was the top concern for more than 70 percent of voters. The COVID-19 pandemic came last, as a main issue of concern for just 9 percent of respondents.

About a week before the election Governor Mills heard from her brother Paul that a mutual friend, who had "been a Republican all his life" and "never voted for a Democrat," announced that he was "voting for Janet." The news had given her hope. "These aren't Trump Republicans," she explained. "They don't like LePage and they don't like Trump. Maybe the Republican party in Maine will have a rebirth and become sane again." Also that week the governor was "doing the gate at Bath Iron Works" — talking to constituents during a shift change at a naval shipyard in the state's midcoast region. She described them as mostly men, who were "very intent, very focused." She added that she had "been there some days when they were just grumpy." This time they "thought it was kind of nice [that] the governor was there," she recalled. "This one guy came up to me, kind of a bulldog fellow with a stern face and a crew cut — I'm looking at my security — and he says, without any expression, 'You better squash that bastard!' I wanted to give him a bear hug, but you don't do that at the BIW gate." This was a working-class crowd that had probably backed former governor LePage before and, she assumed, might do so again. "I thought, they just don't like him anymore."

Three days before the election Governor Mills found some time to write back to Ashirah. "Many thanks for your latest letter of support," she started. "Your ups and downs are different from mine, but yours are a reminder of why I am running again, and your letters have grounded me in a way no Hallmark cards of cheer could ever do." She told Ashirah that the Knapps' struggles "may feel unique" to them, but the family would "look back years from now and remember the comfort, the hope and the love that kept you together — the same things that have kept our state from drowning in despair when things have looked bad, from the Civil War to two World Wars, a depression and a worldwide pandemic." Maine had "a bright and stable future based not on things that divide us but on that which brings us together," she added. There was "a lot more of that in the soul of this state and in the people who make their living in the farms, fisheries and forests here, and who show up at the grange dinners, the county fairs and the town meetings to share in soup, cotton candy and democracy all in major portions." She thanked Ashirah for writing and "for being a good parent," as well as "for going back to school to be able to help others." Then she signed off: "Three days to the election — back to the campaign trail!"

On November 8, 2022, Governor Mills greeted voters at nine polling places in six towns around the state. "The thing I didn't realize, people have not forgotten the pandemic," she said. "I thought they had . . . People kept coming up to me and hugging me, saying thank

you . . . I was in tears. It was heartwarming." One woman told her
the governor had saved her life by expanding the state's Medicaid
eligibility, which had allowed her to have heart surgery. The governor talked to a journalist at one voting site who told her that women
had been saying they were "coming out to vote . . . to protect their
rights." A total of 680,909 Mainers voted in the race that day, more
than 55 percent to reelect Governor Mills.[49] Forty-two percent voted
for Paul LePage. That night he told those who had gathered in the
hope of celebrating a win that he had "failed to make the message"
— that he "should have never got [sic] into politics" if heating oil was
"not as important as abortion." The election was "not over yet," he
added. "Janet Mills, I just hope that your second term, if I lose, is
better than your first term because you are not an honest, sincere
person. You're an elitist."[50] The next day he posted a statement on
his Twitter account to say he accepted the results of the election, but
he never called his opponent to concede.[51]

Governor Mills spoke to her supporters on election night, after
she had been officially declared the winner. She urged the crowd not
to "flaunt our victory to those who would hope for a different result"
but to "embrace them and work to find common ground." She
added: "There are decent people of goodwill who are worried and
who disagree about how to best solve the problems we're facing, and
we should not dismiss these concerns or the people who hold them."
To those who had not voted for her, she promised to do all she could
"to improve your life and your livelihood here in this state that we
both love so much." Nonetheless, the people of Maine had sent "a
pretty clear message," she told the crowd. "We will not go back. We
will continue to fight problems, not one another." The governor also
thanked her administration, including Dr. Shah and Commissioner
Lambrew, who had helped Maine confront the pandemic "better
than nearly every other state in the nation." She also thanked her
staff, family, and friends, and the people of Maine. She was hopeful
about the state's future, she said, "because of the mill workers in
Madawaska, the potato farmers in Ashland, the fishermen in Ston-
ington, the new Maine citizens right here in Portland . . . the ship-
builders in Bath, and the moms and dads all across this great state

who are raising the next generation — the people with backbones of steel and steady hands, compassionate hearts and creative minds — the people showing our children that Maine can become whatever we believe in, whatever we build." In closing, she quoted from the poem that she and her niece had deconstructed in the Blaine House kitchen after Amanda Gorman recited it at President Biden's 2021 inauguration: "There is always light, if only we're brave enough to see it. If only we're brave enough to be it." Then the governor added: "We have a lot of work to do, but tonight let's celebrate . . . all the light in our lives, celebrate hope, celebrate progress."

About four months earlier, in the first few months of her campaign, Governor Mills had reflected on her administration to date and considered the question of whether she had been a good leader, especially in the pandemic. She answered that she had "hired the right people." She was "sure there were mistakes we made," she added. "It's hard to say. I think we made the best decisions we could. If [we] had to do it over, I don't know what we would do differently." In Ashirah's first letter of support she had told the governor that no matter how she responded to the pandemic, people would get sick, lose money, and be angry. There was "no one in the world" who knew how to get through the pandemic, and no path that did not have "death, anger, pain and fear along it." The way that most Mainers had chosen — to take the most effective precautions, follow the best available science, and in the meantime "be kind and take care of one another," as Dr. Shah said at the end of nearly every CDC briefing — had proved to be among the most effective in the country at preventing sickness and death. More than half of voters reelected the woman who had shown them that way. She had also shown that it was possible to win their support decisively and legitimately, without incendiary rhetoric, empty promises, uniform approval, or a perfect record; she had trusted her instincts about what was best for the most Mainers, in the face of inexorable change and forces beyond their control.

In other words, leadership.

Author's Note & Acknowledgments

This book came to be, much like the true story it tells, thanks to a series of thoughtful and extraordinary actions by strangers, acquaintances, and friends. In March 2021, I wrote a little poem for Jamie Wyeth, in appreciation for his help with another project. The poem was silly, and I almost didn't send it to him, but a lot of people had been telling me to be myself for a long time, so off it went. In turn Jamie thought I would enjoy meeting Maine's governor Janet Mills — she wrote poetry too and was "really a character," he told me. "Just fascinating . . . Such a different sort of politician it's hard to believe."

I agreed within seconds of the introduction Jamie had arranged. Governor Mills was offbeat, funny, and at home in herself. She was drawn to all that was good and weird about life, and we recognized each other in a rare and all but wordless way. I was emboldened by her interest in my work and me. The second time we met she mentioned one of her constituents, Ashirah Knapp, who had been sending her handwritten letters of support every week for most of that first pandemic year. The last letter had just arrived, and the governor became emotional as she told me how much their correspondence had meant to her. She allowed me to read the letters, which I found wise and funny, however poignant and sad by turns, but ultimately heartening. Ashirah's voice felt like one that had been missing or muffled, if not drowned out from a long and increasingly cacophonous national conversation dominated by certainty, irrational ideology, and rancor.

The governor allowed me to attempt to publish the letters in some form, along with excerpts from her journal and some of her poems, on the condition that Ashirah agreed, which she graciously did. Ashirah also provided the governor's letters in response to hers. I have not altered their words, apart from exercising editorial judgment in choosing excerpts, and the very few places where I departed from the original chronological order for narrative purposes. The fact that both women allowed publication of their otherwise unedited private thoughts was testament to their extraordinary integrity, the sincerity of their intentions, and their confidence in mine. They gave me their trust from the first, and huge amounts of their time.

Rebecca Hanson did me the honor of telling me that my first draft proposal for this book was a bit tedious, as only a true friend could or would. Anna Wieser lent me her home so I could rewrite the proposal in peace and a beautiful place (augmented by the generosity of my sister and brother-in-law). Meghna Chakrabarti introduced me to the ever-encouraging Bob Neer, who helped me further improve my pitch. Bob also introduced me to my editor and publisher, Chip Fleischer. It was Chip's idea that I write this book as a full-fledged work of literary journalism. Suffice it to say he took a chance on me that was without comparison in my career, and he was preternaturally patient during the writing process. He and his team at Steerforth Press were enthusiastically supportive and delightful to work with at every turn.

Professor Simon Heffer provided vital moral support and consulted on matters of humor, grammar, and adherence to strictures of the common language by which we are separated. Lydia and Chris Bouzaid fed and sheltered me, body and mind, and gave me time and space to work on this book beside my very old dog Mila, who kept me company and in the moment, until she died, a month shy of age fifteen. She is in these pages, as is my late father, Tom, my aunt Jane and my Ont Nancy, all of whom I lost while working on this book.

I am grateful to my subjects and their relatives and friends for the long interviews they gave me, including Chris Knapp, Janice David, Charlie Miller, Paul Mills, Julia Mills Fiori, and Dora Mills, in addition to those generously provided by Senator Angus King, Curtis Picard, Martha Currier, and John Hotchkiss. All of these people shared deeply personal observations and experiences that enriched this book immensely.

Clare Hay lent her philosopher's ear and her wisdom on the

safety of the past. Paul Mills shared his infectious enthusiasm for Maine history, along with his wonderful columns, which deepened my understanding of the place and its people. State historian Earle Shettleworth answered my questions expeditiously and thoughtfully and was always delightful to talk with. Reference librarian Jessica Lundgren at the Maine State Law and Legislative Reference Library provided further support, always comprehensive and non-partisan, which yielded gems I could not have found otherwise. Kaitlyn Megathlin scoured records for digital scans of the few letters that were missing from the governor's hard copy collection and unearthed several that filled crucial gaps in the story. Bob Oakes gave me important advice concerning balance. Ethan Pease eloquently reminded me to forsake perfectionism. Steve Chiasson made the process of recording the audiobook an unexpected mutual delight.

My family and friends (old and new), as well as beloved teachers, insightful editors, inspiring mentors, and other supporters, have encouraged me in countless, crucial ways in this and myriad other endeavors. This book, and the confidence I gained while writing it, are due in great measure to their enduring faith in my ability and the many forms in which they have generously demonstrated that faith. They have my most ardent gratitude.

Notes

Chapter 1

1. *Bangor Daily News*, April 20, 2020, "Hundreds Protest Janet Mills' Restrictions Aimed at Slowing Coronavirus"; *Portland Press Herald*, April 20, 2020, "Hundreds Protest Janet Mills' Restrictions Aimed at Slowing Coronavirus."

2. *Bangor Daily News*, May 4, 2020, "Second Rally in Augusta Protests Virus Rules," A1; Office of Governor Mills, Executive Order No. 28 FY 19/20, March 31, 2020.

3. ABC News, April 19, 2020, "'Trump's Message to 'Liberate' States Dangerous: Washington Gov. Jay Inslee."

4. *Portland Press Herald*, April 20, 2020, "Hundreds Line Capitol Complex in Augusta to Protest Coronavirus Restrictions."

5. Facebook account of Maine representative Chris Johansen, post dated April 20, 2020.

6. *Portland Press Herald*, April 20, 2020, "Hundreds Line Capitol Complex in Augusta to Protest Coronavirus Restrictions."

7. *Portland Press Herald*, April 20, 2020, "Hundreds Line Capitol Complex in Augusta to Protest Coronavirus Restrictions."

8. Maine CDC briefing for April 20, 2020.

9. Office of Governor Mills, media release for March 15, 2020, "Governor Announces Significant Recommendations & Signs Civil Emergency Proclamation to Respond to COVID-19 in Maine."

10. Office of Governor Mills, Executive Order No. 38 FY 19/20, April 10, 2020; Office of Governor Mills, Executive Order No. 38 FY 18/20, March 23, 2020.

11. Associated Press, March 30, 2020, "Trump Administration Rules Gun Shops 'Essential' Amid Virus"; Reuters, March 30, 2020, "Trump Coronavirus Guidance on Keeping Gun Stores Open Draws Criticism."

12. *Maine Monitor*, August 9, 2020, "Maine's Governor Born for Hard Times, and Hard Decisions."

13. *Ellsworth American*, April 17, 2020, "'This Girl Is on Fire': Mills Has Risen to the COVID-19 Challenge."

14. *Maine Monitor*, October 30, 2018, "Janet Mills: The Rebel with a Cause."

15. Office of Governor Mills, July 23, 2020, remarks delivered during Maine's annual Opioid Response Summit.

16. Bates College, Janet Mills oral history, December 20, 1999.

17. *Down East*, March 2019, "How Will a Poet Govern Maine?"; Bates College, Janet Mills oral history, December 20, 1999.

18. Maine Public, January 3, 2019, "Maine Gov. Janet Mills Has a Long History of Firsts."

19. Bates College, Janet Mills oral history, December 20, 1999.

20. Bates College, Janet Mills oral history, December 20, 1999.

21. *Portland Press Herald*, September 23, 2018, "Janet Mills' Mission: Break Yet Another Glass Ceiling."

22. Bates College, Janet Mills oral history, December 20, 1999.

23. Bates College, Janet Mills oral history, December 20, 1999.

24. Bates College, Janet Mills oral history, December 20, 1999.

25. Paul Mills interview, May 26, 2022; *Portland Press Herald*, September 29, 2015, "Maine's Mills Siblings Hailed for Lives of Service."

26. *Bangor Daily News*, July 26, 2013, "Who Are Maine's 'Royal' Families?"

27. US House of Representatives, online biography of Margaret Chase Smith.

28. Maine Public, January 3, 2019, "Maine Gov. Janet Mills Has a Long History of Firsts."

29. US Senate, Classic Senate Speeches, "Margaret Chase Smith: A Declaration of Conscience, June 1, 1950," and speech transcript.

30. Office of Governor Mills, About the Governor.

31. Office of Governor Mills, About the Governor.

32. Associated Press, October 31, 1991, "No Bones About It, Governor Missing"; National Governors Association, biography of Enoch Lincoln; US House of Representatives, biography of Enoch Lincoln.

33. *Down East*, March 2019, "How Will a Poet Govern Maine."

34. *Down East*, March 2019, "How Will a Poet Govern Maine."

35. *Maine Monitor*, October 30, 2018, "Janet Mills: The Rebel with a Cause."

36. "Severe Outcomes Among Patients with Coronavirus Disease 2019 (COVID-19) — United States, February 12–March 16, 2020," US Centers for Disease Control and Prevention, *Morbidity and Mortality Weekly Report*, March 27, 2020.

37. US Census Bureau, Quick Facts page for Maine, persons living in poverty (percent).

38. *Portland Press Herald*, May 22, 2020, "Maine's Biggest Unemployment Jump Ever Put Jobless Rate at Nearly 11% in April."

39. Hospitality Maine, media release for November 29, 2019, "New Report Reveals Hospitality's Lead Role in Maine's Economy."

40. Weather.com, April 11, 2020.

41. Office of Governor Mills, radio address for April 10, 2020, "Governor Mills: Do the Next Right Thing."

42. *Associated Press*, April 15, 2020, "Explosion Caught on Video Damages Paper Mill; No One Hurt."

43. *Sun Journal* (Lewiston, ME), May 15, 2021.

44. National Academy for State Health Policy, 2020 COVID-19 State Restrictions, Re-Openings, and Mask Requirements.

45. *Bangor Daily News*, August 9, 2022, "Some of Janet Mills' Earliest Pandemic Advisers Were Her Family."

46. *Bangor Daily News*, August 9, 2022, "Some of Janet Mills' Earliest Pandemic Advisers Were Her Family."

47. Weather Underground, April 20, 2022.

48. Pence and Whitmer comments reported by ABC News, April 20, 2020, "Governors Dealing with Protests Ask Pence for Help Keeping People Home, Access to Testing Gear."

49. Fox News, *Tucker Carlson Tonight*, April 30, 2020, "Maine Restaurateur Vows to Reopen Friday in Defiance of Lockdown Order: 'It's Time to Go Back to Work.'"

50. Poynter Institute for Media Studies, *Poynter Report* daily media newsletter for July 1, 2020, "Tucker Carlson's Show Not Only Had the Highest-Rated Quarter, It Had the Best Viewership Numbers in the History of Cable News."

51. Twitter account of President Donald Trump, May 3, 2020.

52. Office of Governor Mills, radio address for May 1, 2020, "Governor Mills: We Will Not Give Up on Each Other."

53. *Bangor Daily News*, May 3, 2020, "Hundreds March on Blaine House in Protest of Virus Restrictions."

54. Office of Governor Mills, media release for May 7, 2020, "Mills Administration Secures Major COVID-19 Testing Expansion for Maine."

55. Maine CDC briefing for May 4, 2020.

56. Associated Press, May 7, 2020, "Maine Buying Virus Tests to Triple Capacity; Plant Reopens"; Associated Press, May 7, 2020, "Portland Food Plant Set to Reopen After 51 Workers Tested Positive for Coronavirus, COVID-19."

57. Office of Governor Mills, media release for May 14, 2020, "Mills Administration Allows Lodging Reservations for Future Stays."

58. *Bangor Daily News*, May 1, 2020, "Tourism Industry Rails Against Quarantine Mandate in Janet Mills' Plan to Reopen Economy."

59. *Portland Press Herald*, May 1, 2020, "Maine Restaurant Group Says Industry Will Collapse if Reopening Restrictions Aren't Relaxed."

60. Associated Press, April 30, 2020, "LePage Says Gov. Mills 'Ought to Resign' Over Virus Response."

61. Associated Press, June 16, 2019, "Former Maine Governor Has a New Job, Tending Bar."

62. US Centers for Disease Control and Prevention, Weekly Surveillance Summary for May 15, 2020; *New York Times*, May 15, 2020, "Coronavirus in the US: Latest Map and Case Count."

63. Maine CDC briefing for May 15, 2020.

64. *New York Times*, May 15, 2020, "Coronavirus in the US: Latest Map and Case Count."

65. *Washington Post*, May 4, 2020, "The World Came Together for a Virtual Vaccine Summit. The US Was Conspicuously Absent."

Chapter 2

1. Richard Pierce, "A History of Temple, Maine: Its Rise and Decline" (1946) (provided by the Temple Town Hall, where the dissertation was kept in a locked cabinet).

2. US Census Bureau, 2020 Decennial Census, profile for "Temple Town, Franklin County, Maine."

3. University of Maine at Farmington website, "About UMF."

4. Maine Department of Health and Human Services, COVID-19: Maine Data (a spreadsheet of historical COVID-associated death counts by county, age group, gender, and date) showed that all but four people who died of COVID-19 through April 20, 2020, were aged seventy-plus; Twitter account of *Bangor Daily News* politics editor Michael Shepherd, post dated April 20, 2020.

5. PBS media release for March 23, 2020, "PBS to Make *The Roosevelts* Available as Part of 'American History Night with Ken Burns' on Thursday Nights Beginning March 26."

6. Associated Press, May 27, 2020, "Four Minneapolis Officers Fired After Death of Black Man."

7. *New York Times*, June 13, 2020, "How Black Lives Matter Reached Every Corner of America."

8. Associated Press, June 1, 2020, "Amid Protests, Trump Talks of War — and Reelection."

9. Puritan Medical Products website, company overview; National Public Radio, April 1, 2020, "Swab Manufacturer Works to Meet 'Overwhelming' Demand"; Bloomberg, March 18, 2021, "America's Covid Swab Supply Depends on Two Cousins Who Hate Each Other."

10. *PBS NewsHour* via YouTube, "Trump Calls Some Governors 'Weak' on Protests Across the Country."

11. Transcript of remarks from June 1, 2020, provided by Governor Mills.

12. Facebook account of Ashirah Knapp, post dated May 28, 2020.

13. *Portland Press Herald*, June 5, 2020, "Trump Praises Guilford Workers, Jabs at Mills in Visit That Draws Supporters, Protesters."

14. *Portland Press Herald*, June 5, 2020, "Trump Praises Guilford Workers, Jabs at Mills in Visit That Draws Supporters, Protesters."

15. *Bangor Daily News*, June 5, 2020, "The President Came to a Small Maine Manufacturing Town. Here's What It Looked Like."

16. *Bangor Daily News*, June 5, 2020, "Trump Finds Friendly Crowd in Guilford Address That Veers into Campaign Speech."

17. White House, June 5, 2020, "Remarks by President Trump at Puritan Medical Products."

18. Maine Public Radio, June 5, 2020, "Trump Visits Rural Maine Swab Manufacturer Amid Swarm of Supporters, Protesters"; *Bangor Daily News*, June 5, 2020, "Trump Finds Friendly Crowd in Guilford Address That Veers into Campaign Speech."

19. Maine Public Radio, June 5, 2020 "Trump Visits Rural Maine Swab Manufacturer Amid Swarm of Supporters, Protesters"; *Bangor Daily News*, June 5, 2020, "Trump Finds Friendly Crowd in Guilford Address That Veers into Campaign Speech."

20. Office of Governor Mills, June 5, 2020, "Governor Mills Statement on President's Visit to Maine."

21. Maine Public Radio, June 5, 2020, "Trump Visits Rural Maine Swab Manufacturer Amid Swarm of Supporters, Protesters."

22. *Bangor Daily News*, July 16, 2018, "LePage Has Vetoed More Bills than All Maine Governors Since 1917, Combined."

23. *Portland Press Herald*, January 5, 2011, "LePage's Political Adviser Brent Littlefield Earning Praise."

24. Associated Press, July 11, 2010, "Maine GOP Gov Candidate Had Dickens-Like Childhood."

25. *New York Times*, February 20, 2009, "Rick Santelli: Tea Party Time"; *New York Times*, April 15, 2010, "What the Tea Party Backers Want"; Tea Party official website, "About Us."

26. Associated Press, September 29, 2010, "LePage: I'd Tell Obama to Go to Hell"; Maine Democratic Party, video of LePage forum, September 28, 2010.

27. *Washington Post*, August 29, 2016, "Paul LePage's Most Controversial Comments"; NBC News, January 8, 2016, "Maine Gov. Paul LePage Has History of Controversial Remarks."

28. *Mother Jones*, August 26, 2016, "Maine Governor LePage Threatens State Lawmaker With Profanity-Filled Voicemail"; Reuters, May 1, 2017, "Maine Governor Apologizes for Obscenity-Laced Voicemail."

29. *New York Times*, February 27, 2016, "Inside the Republican Party's Desperate Mission to Stop Donald Trump"; Associated Press, March 5, 2016, "Before There Was Trump There Was Paul LePage."

30. Associated Press, January 7, 2020, "Maine's Former Governor Is Registered to Vote in Florida."

31. *Bangor Daily News*, March 18, 2020, "Maine CDC Plans to Keep Hiring While Stretching to Fight the Coronavirus"; *Down East*, August 2022, "Nirav Shah Is Ambivalent About His Celebrity (and Uncommonly Curious and Deliberate About Everything Else)."

32. *Portland Press Herald*, January 3, 2019, "Mills' 'Executive Order 1' Makes 70,000 More Mainers Eligible for Health Insurance."

33. Maine Department of Health and Human Services, MaineCare (Medicaid) Enrollment Update for June 1, 2020.

34. Maine CDC briefing for June 8, 2020.

35. *Sun Journal* (Lewiston, ME), May 18, 2020, "Some Republican Lawmakers Want to Impeach Janet Mills."

36. *Portland Press Herald*, May 4, 2020, "Mills Rebuffs Republican Criticism Over Administration's Pandemic Response."

37. United States Department of Justice, press release for May 29, 2020, "Department of Justice Files Statement of Interest Challenging the Constitutionality of Maine Governor's COVID-19 Orders That Economically Harm Maine Campgrounds."

38. *Portland Press Herald*, May 4, 2020, "Mills Rebuffs Republican Criticism Over Administration's Pandemic Response"; *Portland Press Herald*, May 1, 2020, "Mills Defends Reopening But Acknowledges Deep Divisions, As Virus Kills Two More Mainers."

39. *Down East*, August 2020, "In Shah We Trust"; Facebook account of "Fans of Dr. Nirav Shah."

40. Maine Center for Disease Control and Prevention, media release for May 23, 2019, "Commissioner Lambrew Announces Director for Maine Center for Disease Control and Prevention"; *Maine Monitor*, June 7, 2019, "Litany of Controversial Decisions Follows New CDC Chief to Maine."

41. *Chicago Tribune*, March 26, 2019, "Ex-State Health Director Dismissed Need to Alert CDC Early in Legionnaires' Outbreak That Eventually Killed a Dozen People: Audit."

42. *Portland Press Herald*, June 11, 2019, "Portland Expo to Serve as Emergency Shelter as Influx of Asylum Seekers Creates 'a Very Critical Situation'"; Associated Press, July 17, 2019, "Portland Helping More than 200 Asylum Seekers Find Homes."

43. *Portland Phoenix*, July 22, 2020, "Maine CDC's Dr. Nirav Shah: 'Public Policy Is Important, but What the Public Does Is Even More Important.'"

44. *Bangor Daily News*, March 21, 2020, "The Most Memorable Quotes from Dr. Nirav Shah."

45. WMTW, March 10, 2021, "One Year with COVID: How Dr. Shah Has Helped Guide Mainers Through Pandemic."

46. WJBK, July 13, 2020, "Dr. Nirav Shah Talks About His Diet Coke Vice on 'The Nite Show.'"

47. *Bangor Daily News*, June 10, 2020, "Maine Saw Fewer New Virus Cases Even with More Tests Over the Past Week."

48. *Bangor Daily News*, June 10, 2020, "Fewer Mainers Turned to the State's Safety Net for Help in May."

49. *Bangor Daily News*, June 13, 2020, "Tourism Groups Ask Janet Mills for $800M in Federal Coronavirus Funds."

50. Office of Governor Mills, radio address for June 12, 2020.

51. Office of Governor Mills, June 8, 2020, "Mills Administration Unveils 'Keep Maine Healthy' Plan to Protect Maine People, Visitors & Support Small Businesses During Tourism Season"; *Bangor Daily News*, June 9, 2020, "Maine Lets Visitors Skip Quarantine with Tests That Aren't Always Widely Available."

52. Office of Governor Mills, radio address for June 19, 2020, "Governor Mills: It Is All Up to Every One of Us."

53. *Portland Press Herald*, June 21, 2020, "Maine Has Nation's Worst COVID-19 Racial Disparity"; Covid Tracking Project at *The Atlantic*, "Maine: All Race & Ethnicity Data."

54. *Portland Press Herald*, June 21, 2020, "Maine Has Nation's Worst COVID-19 Racial Disparity"; Covid Tracking Project at *The Atlantic*, "Maine: All Race & Ethnicity Data."

55. Maine CDC briefing for June 19, 2020.

56. Associated Press, June 23, 2020, "Fauci: Next Few Weeks Critical to Tamping Down Virus Spikes"; BBC News, June 24, 2020, "Top US Health Official Fauci Warns of 'Disturbing' New US Surge."

57. Office of Governor Mills, radio address for June 29, 2020, "Governor Mills: It Is All Up to Every One of Us."

58. Office of Governor Mills, radio address for June 26, 2020, "Governor Mills: Don't Let Down Your Guard Now."

Chapter 3

1. Associated Press, July 3, 2020, "More Fireworks in Americans' Hands for July 4 Raises Risks."

2. Associated Press, July 3, 2020, "Texas Governor Issues Mask Order to Fight Coronavirus."

3. Associated Press, July 3, 2020, "Texas Governor Issues Mask Order to Fight Coronavirus."

4. Associated Press, June 30, 2020, "Fauci: US 'Going in Wrong Direction' in Coronavirus Outbreak"; Associated Press, July 2, 2020, "Confirmed Coronavirus Cases Are Rising in 40 of 50 States."

5. Maine CDC briefing for July 1, 2020.

6. *Bangor Daily News*, August 7, 2020, "More than 75 Percent of Maine Is in Moderate Drought, and It's Severe in The County."

7. National Endowment for the Humanities, Student Activity Plan.

8. *Bangor Daily News*, July 7, 2020, "Why Maine Isn't Treating Mass. Tourists Like Others"; News Center Maine, July 2, 2020, "Mass. Gov. 'Surprised' Over Maine's Travel Exclusion Considering State's Promising Positivity Rate."

9. BallotPedia.org, "Travel Restrictions Issued by States in Response to the Coronavirus (COVID-19) Pandemic, 2020–2022."

10. *Boston Globe*, July 2, 2020, "We Used to Be Friends, Maine."

11. Maine Office of Tourism, 2019 Annual Report, February 2020, 4, 87.

12. *Bangor Daily News*, July 9, 2020, "Maine Virus Cases Back on Decline as Testing Expands."

13. Office of Governor Mills, weekly radio address for July 10, 2020.
14. Office of Governor Mills, press release for July 8, 2020.
15. Maine CDC briefing for July 8, 2020.
16. Office of Governor Mills, press release for April 10, 2020, "Governor Mills Issues Executive Order Moving Primary Election to July 14."
17. National Conference of State Legislatures, State Primary Election Dates, November 3, 2020.
18. Associated Press via *Bangor Daily News*, July 20, 2020, "This November Will Be a Big Test for Absentee Voting in Maine."
19. Twitter account of Governor Janet Mills, July 14, 2020; New England Cable News, July 17, 2020, "Coronavirus Cases Are Decreasing in Just 2 States: Maine and NH."
20. US Coast Guard, October 22, 2019, asset summary and historical information for Tenants Harbor Lighthouse (St. George, ME).
21. Governor's Economic Recovery Committee Report, July 15, 2020, 2, 10.
22. Office of Governor Mills, weekly radio address for July 17, 2020, "Governor Mills: Decisions About Returning to Classrooms Must Be Based on Public Health Data and Not on Politics."
23. Maine CDC briefing for July 17, 2020.
24. *Washington Post*, July 7, 2020, "Trump Administration Sends Letter Withdrawing US From World Health Organization Over Coronavirus Response"; *New York Times*, November 27, 2020, "Trump Gave W.H.O. a List of Demands. Hours Later, He Walked Away."
25. Twitter and Facebook accounts of Governor Janet Mills, July 17, 2020.
26. Associated Press, July 17, 2022, "Maine Keeping Restrictions on Visitors from Mass. and Rhode Island."
27. Maine House Republicans, radio address by Representative Shelley Rudnicki, July 23, 2020.
28. Office of Governor Mills, transcript of governor's remarks as delivered at the Second Annual Opioid Response Summit, "Compassion, Community, Connection," July 23, 2020.
29. Office of Governor Mills, May 23, 2019, "Governor Mills Announces Opioid Response Summit."
30. Office of the Maine Attorney General, press release for October 21, 2020, "Attorney General Releases Drug Death Report for Second Quarter of 2020."
31. US Travel Association, press release for June 17, 2020, "New Study: Travel Spending in US to Plunge 45% This Year."
32. *Bangor Daily News* footage of press conference, July 27, 2020; *Bangor Daily News*, July 27, 2020, "Janet Mills Slams GOP Bid to Relax Maine Limits on Massachusetts, Rhode Island Tourists."
33. WAGM, July 29, 2020, "Maine Legislative Republicans Propose Plan to Salvage Tourism Season"; *Portland Press Herald*, August 5, 2020, "Republican Lawmakers Again Reject Call for Special Session."
34. Office of Governor Mills, press release for July 27, 2020, "Maine Republicans Follow Trump's Lead in Attacking Public Health Measures."
35. *Bangor Daily News*, July 22, 2020, "Maine Spending $2M to Market Itself As Safe Tourism Destination Amid Pandemic"; Maine Office of Tourism website.
36. Hospitality Maine press release June 19, 2020, "Free COVID-19 Hospitality Training Launches."

37. *Bangor Daily News*, May 22, 2020, "Maine Restaurants Can Now Get Certified to Show They Know How to Reopen Safely."

38. Maine Community Colleges, press release, July 29, 2020.

39. Maine Housing Coalition, report on "Evictions in Maine," September 2020.

40. Office of Governor Mills, radio address for July 30, 2020, "Governor Mills: The Last Thing People Need to Worry About in the Middle of a Pandemic Is Losing Their Home."

41. Office of Governor Mills, media release for July 30, 2020, "Mills Administration Announces Further Investment to Address Racial and Ethnic Disparities in COVID-19."

42. Associated Press, February 17, 2016, "Maine Governor: Asylum Seekers Bring Disease Like 'Ziki Fly.'"

43. Associated Press, February 17, 2016, "Maine Governor: Asylum Seekers Bring Disease Like 'Ziki Fly'"; *Bangor Daily News*, July 30, 2020, "Janet Mills Investing $1 Million to Address Racial Disparities in Maine Coronavirus Infections"; *Bangor Daily News*, June 22, 2020, "Maine Has Failed as Racial Disparities in Coronavirus Infections Grow, Immigrant Leaders Say."

44. Associated Press, July 9, 2020, "Former Snowbird Paul LePage Declares Residency in Maine."

45. Associated Press, July 31, 2020, "Record Economic Plunge, Bleak Jobs Numbers Reveal Virus Toll."

46. Associated Press, July 30, 2020, "Trump Floats Idea of Election Delay, a Virtual Impossibility."

47. *New York Times*, July 30, 2020, "Fauci to Testify Before Congress on Coronavirus Response"; *Washington Post*, July 30, 2020, "US Reports More than 1,000 Coronavirus Deaths For Fourth Consecutive Day."

48. *Bangor Daily News*, July 31, 2020, "Maine Continues to Expand Virus Testing," A4; Maine CDC briefing for July 30, 2020.

49. Maine Marine Patrol, Maine Department of Marine Resources, email confirmation July 6, 2022.

50. *Bangor Daily News*, July 30, 2020, "Harpswell Deals with a New Reality . . . ," A1–A2.

51. Associated Press, July 30, 2020, "More Seals Means Learning to Live with Sharks in New England."

52. *Bangor Daily News*, July 30, 2020, "Caution and Compassion, not Fear, After Maine's First Fatal Shark Attack."

53. *Bangor Daily News*, August 3, 2020, "Midcoast Theater Cancels Upcoming 'Jaws' Screenings Following Fatal Shark Attack."

Chapter 4

1. Weather Underground, Farmington, ME, area, August 3, 2020; NOAA National Centers for Environmental Information, August 2020, National Climate Report; *The Old Farmer's Almanac*, June 27, 2022; Maine State Climatologist, University of Maine, Summer 2020 Climate Summary and Drought Update.

2. *Bangor Daily News*, August 3, 2020, B2, "Heavy Rain from Isaias Hits Florida"; National Weather Service, August 1–2, 2020, summary for Tropical Storm Isaias.

3. *Bangor Daily News*, August 1, 2020, "Maine Schools Get Green Light to Reopen," A1.

4. *Portland Press Herald*, September 29, 2014, "Husband of Maine Attorney General Dies from Effects of Stroke"; *Portland Press Herald / Maine Sunday Telegram*, September 28, 2014, obituary for Stanley Kuklinski.

5. *Portland Press Herald*, September 29, 2014, "Husband of Maine Attorney General Dies from Effects of Stroke"; *Portland Press Herald / Maine Sunday Telegram*, September 28, 2014, obituary for Stanley Kuklinski.

6. *New York Times*, September 28, 1994, "Republicans Offer Voters Deal for Takeover of House"; email exchange with Alex Keyssar, Harvard professor of history and social policy, July 11, 2022.

7. Maine State Legislature Law and Legislative Reference Library, Legislative History Collection, 121st legislature (2002–2004), LD 1579.

8. Maine Constitution, Article IX, Section 11; National Association of Attorneys General, "Attorney General Office Characteristics."

9. Quote as told to *Maine Mag*, 2020 (no date specified), "Challenge & Opportunity."

10. Remarks of Attorney General Janet Mills, Joint Democratic Caucus, December 2, 2014, transcript provided by Governor Mills.

11. Remarks of Attorney General Janet Mills, Joint Democratic Caucus, December 2, 2014, transcript provided by Governor Mills.

12. *Portland Press Herald*, December 3, 2014, "Hayes Wins Election as State Treasurer."

13. *Portland Press Herald*, December 3, 2014, "Hayes Wins Election as State Treasurer"; the claim of LePage's refusal to swear in AG Mills is from an interview with Governor Mills, July 3, 2022.

14. Office of the Maine Attorney General, statement of Attorney General Janet Mills, June 8, 2015; remarks of Attorney General Janet T. Mills Joint Democratic Caucus, December 2, 2014; Tribune News Service, November 19, 2014, "Court Blocks Maine Governor's Attempt to Kick Young People Off Medicaid."

15. Associated Press, February 7, 2017, "Maine Joins Opposition to Trump's Travel Ban"; Associated Press, May 1, 2017, "Maine Governor Sues Attorney General for Not Defending Cases."

16. *Portland Press Herald*, May 1, 2017, "LePage Sues Maine's Attorney General, Alleging Abuse of Power."

17. Office of the Maine Attorney General, May 1, 2017, statement of Attorney General Mills; *Portland Press Herald*, May 1, 2017, "LePage Sues Maine's Attorney General, Alleging Abuse of Power."

18. *Portland Press Herald*, July 10, 2017, "Maine Attorney General Janet Mills Enters 2018 Race for Governor."

19. *Portland Press Herald*, July 10, 2017, "Maine Attorney General Janet Mills Enters 2018 Race for Governor."

20. Georgetown Institute of Politics and Public Service, Battleground Civility Poll, August 14, 2020.

21. Facebook account of "Janet Mill's [*sic*] Memes"; Reddit forum r/Maine, September 11, 2020, "To the People with 'F*** MILLS' Stickers on Their Cars."

22. Maine State Climatologist, University of Maine, Summer 2020 Climate Summary and Drought Update; NOAA Centers for Environmental Information, August 2020, National Climate Report.

23. University of Maine Cooperative Extension, May 2021, Maine Wild Blueberry Production Statistics; *Portland Press Herald*, May 9, 2022, "Maine's Wild

Blueberry Crop Rebounded Last Year and Is Poised for Another Bountiful Season"; Maine Department of Agriculture.

24. State of Maine, DOE fact sheet on Maine wild blueberry production; *Portland Press Herald*, April 30, 2020, "Arrival of Maine's Migrant Farm Workers in Limbo."

25. Maine CDC briefing for August 6, 2020; *Bangor Daily News*, August 4, 2020, "Another Maine Blueberry Farm Detects COVID-19 Cases Among Newly Arrived Workers."

26. Maine.gov, portal for links to institutions for higher education in Maine; *Bangor Daily News*, August 7, 2020, "Returning UMaine Students Could Bring the Virus with Them, but Orono Businesses Need Them to Survive."

27. News Center Maine, August 9, 2020, "To-Go Cocktails a 'Lifeboat' for Small Businesses in Maine."

28. News Center Maine, August 9, 2020, "To-Go Cocktails a 'Lifeboat' for Small Businesses in Maine."

29. *Savage et al. v. Mills*, August 7, 2020, Order on the Defendant's Motion to Dismiss, Lance Walker, US district judge; Associated Press, April 12, 2018, "'Trump Judicial Nomination Praised by Maine Senators."

30. *Savage et al. v. Mills*, August 7, 2020, Order on the Defendant's Motion to Dismiss, Lance Walker, US district judge; News Center Maine, "Sunday River Brewing, Others Lose Lawsuit Against Gov. Mills."

31. *Portland Press Herald*, August 21, 2020, "Business Owners Who Sued Mills Over Pandemic Restrictions to Appeal Dismissal."

32. Office of Governor Mills, media release for August 11, 2020, "Mills Administration Approves Second Round of COVID-19 Prevention and Protection Awards Under Keep Maine Healthy Plan."

33. Office of Governor Mills, radio address for August 21, 2020, "Governor Mills: Small Businesses Can Begin Applying Now to the Maine Economic Recovery Grant Program."

34. Office of Governor Mills, radio address for August 7, 2020, "Governor Mills: Step Up and Be Counted in the 2020 Census to Make Sure That You, and All of Our State, Gets Our Fair Share."

35. Joint State-Federal National Mortgage Servicing Settlements website, "State Attorneys General Who Signed the Joint State-Federal Mortgage Settlement by State"; *State of Colorado v. Wyeth Pharmaceuticals*, 2014; letter from state attorneys general to the US Department of Education, March 18, 2016; National Association of Attorneys General, Multistate Litigation Database, numerous actions against the EPA during both AGs' tenures.

36. WMTW, August 12, 2020, "Maine Democrats Express Support for Joe Biden's Pick of Kamala Harris as Running Mate"; News Center Maine, August 12, 2020, "Republicans Call Her 'Extreme,' Dems Call Her a 'Tough Trailblazer': Maine Politicians React to Kamala Harris' VP Nod"; White House, biography for Vice President Harris.

37. Associated Press, August 14, 2020, "Democrats Tested in First Party Convention of Pandemic Era."

38. *Down East*, August 1999, "The Lost Village of Flagstaff"; Salt Institute for Documentary Studies, Salt Story Archive, 2015, "15 Feet Below" (multimedia reporting project).

39. Office of Governor Mills, radio address for August 25, 2020, "Governor Mills: One Little Match Can Spark a Big Fire That We Might Be Unable to Put Out."
40. *Bangor Daily News*, August 28, 2020, "Guests Had Temps Taken at Millinocket Lake Wedding Reception, but COVID-19 Still Took Root."
41. Office of Governor Mills, radio address for August 25, 2020, "Governor Mills: One Little Match Can Spark a Big Fire That We Might Be Unable to Put Out."
42. Maine CDC briefing for September 15, 2020; *Washington Post*, September 16, 2020; *Portland Press Herald*, August 21, 2020; *Bangor Daily News*, August 28, 2020, "Guests Had Temps Taken at Millinocket Lake Wedding Reception, but COVID-19 Still Took Root."
43. National Weather Service, climate almanac for August 29, 2020; Timeanddate .com, August 29, 2020, past weather in Temple, ME.
44. *Bangor Daily News*, August 29, 2020, "How a Single Wedding Changed the Contours of Maine's Coronavirus Outbreak."

Chapter 5

1. *Maine Monitor*, September 27, 2020, "Playing God with Public Health."
2. Twitter account of Pastor Todd Bell, @preachertbell," post dated September 1, 2020.
3. Maine Department of Education, 2020–2021 Framework for Reopening Schools and Returning to In-Person Instruction, Part I: Physical Health and Safety.
4. Maine CDC briefing for September 3, 2020.
5. *Maine Monitor*, August 31, 2020, "The Preacher and the Outbreak"; NBC News, September 30, 2020, "Pastor Linked to Superspreader Wedding in Maine Told to Wear Mask at Son's Marriage."
6. *Bangor Daily News*, September 5, 2020, "York County Schools Face Limits After Five Virus Outbreaks," A1.
7. Maine CDC briefing for September 3, 2020.
8. Pastor Bell biographical details in this paragraph obtained from Calvary Baptist Church website, "Our Pastor."
9. FlightAware.com, registration for N91EH, photo of Cessna 310 on Pastor Bell's Twitter account header photo and tagged as #C310 in his August 6, 2020, tweet; *Maine Monitor*, September 27, 2020, "Playing God with Public Health"; Rhode Island Department of Public Health, August 2–August 8, 2020, 60 cases per 100K people.
10. *Maine Monitor / Bangor Daily News*, September 27, 2020, "Sanford Pastor Continues to Defy State and Local Orders Aimed to Control Virus Spread"; *Elle*, March 15, 2021, "The Maine Event."
11. P. Mahale, C. Rothfuss, S. Bly, et al., "Multiple COVID-19 Outbreaks Linked to a Wedding Reception in Rural Maine — August 7–September 14, 2020," US Centers for Disease Control and Prevention, *Morbidity and Mortality Weekly Report*.
12. Anchor Baptist Missions International; *Maine Monitor*, August 31, 2020.
13. *Elle*, March 15, 2021, "The Maine Event."
14. P. Mahale, C. Rothfuss, S. Bly, et al., "Multiple COVID-19 Outbreaks Linked to a Wedding Reception in Rural Maine — August 7–September 14, 2020," US Centers for Disease Control and Prevention, *Morbidity and Mortality Weekly Report*.

15. Gallup Poll, August 7, 2020, "US Face Mask Usage Relatively Uncommon in Outdoor Settings."

16. Gallup Poll, August 7, 2020, "US Face Mask Usage Relatively Uncommon in Outdoor Settings."

17. Maine CDC briefings for September 25, 2020, and September 27, 2020; WMTW, September 7, 2020.

18. Fox News, August 26, 2020, "Coronavirus Cases Linked to Maine Wedding Reach Jail, Nursing Home"; NPR, August 28, 2020, "Coronavirus Outbreak from Maine Wedding Spreads to Jail, Rehabilitation Center"; CNN, August 25, 2020, "Coronavirus Cases Connected to Maine Wedding Include Outbreaks at Nursing Home, County Jail"; *Newsweek*, August 25, 2020, "Coronavirus Cases Connected to Maine Wedding Include Outbreaks at Nursing Home, County Jail"; *Washington Post*, September 15, 2020, "Maine Wedding 'Superspreader' Event Is Now Linked to Seven Deaths. None of Those People Attended."

19. Smith College Archives, June 3, 1956, Commencement Address by Archibald MacLeish, 17.

20. *Bangor Daily News*, September 2, 2020, "Sanford Preacher Linked to Virus Outbreak Tells Followers to Put Faith in God Not Government"; sermon excerpts obtained from Calvary Baptist video posted on YouTube that was subsequently removed from public access.

21. *Portland Press Herald*, September 1, 2020, "Pastor Defiant About Outbreak as Anxiety Increases in Sanford."

22. *Bangor Daily News*, September 2, 2020; *National Geographic*, November 19, 2021; US Centers for Disease Control and Prevention, July 20, 2022, Myths & Facts About COVID-19 Vaccines; National Institutes of Health, July 13, 2021, "Helping Patients with Ethical Concerns About COVID-19 Vaccines in Light of Fetal Cell Lines Used in Some COVID-19 Vaccines" (study by Dr. Richard Zimmerman, University of Pittsburgh, School of Medicine, Department of Family Medicine).

23. Associated Press, September 15, 2020; *Portland Press Herald*, August 31, 2020.

24. *Maine Monitor*, August 31, 2020, and September 27, 2020.

25. *Bangor Daily News*, September 5, 2020; *Portland Press Herald*, September 6, 2020; News Center Maine, September 7, 2020.

26. P. Mahale, C. Rothfuss, S. Bly, et al., "Multiple COVID-19 Outbreaks Linked to a Wedding Reception in Rural Maine — August 7–September 14, 2020," US Centers for Disease Control and Prevention, *Morbidity and Mortality Weekly Report*; *Bangor Daily News*, November 12, 2020, "Without Guest List, Maine CDC Likely Undercounted Cases Linked to Aug. 7 Wedding."

27. P. Mahale, C. Rothfuss, S. Bly, et al., "Multiple COVID-19 Outbreaks Linked to a Wedding Reception in Rural Maine — August 7–September 14, 2020," US Centers for Disease Control and Prevention, *Morbidity and Mortality Weekly Report*; *Bangor Daily News*, November 12, 2020, "Without Guest List, Maine CDC Likely Undercounted Cases Linked to Aug. 7 Wedding."

28. *Bangor Daily News*, September 19, 2020, "Madison Nursing Home Let Worker Put in 10 Hours Despite Aches, Chills, Sore Throat. Then She Tested Positive."

29. *Bangor Daily News*, September 19, 2020, "Madison Nursing Home Let Worker Put in 10 Hours Despite Aches, Chills, Sore Throat. Then She Tested Positive."

30. *Bangor Daily News*, September 19, 2020, "Madison Nursing Home Let Worker Put in 10 Hours Despite Aches, Chills, Sore Throat. Then She Tested Positive."

31. National Public Radio, November 19, 2020, "Some Faith Leaders Defiant, Others Transparent Over COVID-19 Outbreaks."

32. Lea Hamner, Polly Dubbel, Ian Capron, et al., "High SARS-CoV-2 Attack Rate Following Exposure at a Choir Practice — Skagit County, Washington, March 2020," US Centers for Disease Control and Prevention, *Morbidity and Mortality Weekly Report*, May 15, 2020.

33. US District Court of Maine, *Calvary Chapel v. Janet Mills*, Judge's Denial of Plaintiff's Motion, May 9, 2020.

34. News Center Maine, May 7, 2020, "Orrington Church Sues Governor Mills Over COVID-19 Executive Order"; *Down East*, November 2020, "Maine Helped Rescue Him from Addiction. Now He's Helping Others"; *Bangor Daily News*, September 10, 2020, "Orrington Church Fights Maine's Coronavirus Restrictions in Federal Appeals Court."

35. *Bangor Daily News*, September 5, 2020, "Most Churches Are Following Maine's COVID-19 Restrictions, Even as Loud Minority Fights Them"; Associated Press, August 13, 2020, "More US Churches Sue to Challenge COVID-19 Restrictions"; *New York Times*, July 24, 2020, "Split 5 to 4, Supreme Court Rejects Nevada Church's Challenge to Shutdown Restrictions."

36. Pew Research Center, August 7, 2020, "Americans Oppose Religious Exemptions from Coronavirus-Related Restrictions."

37. *Portland Press Herald*, May 29, 2020; Maine Public, April 7, 2020, "Faith Communities Adapt to COVID-19: How Different Religious Groups Are Reacting to the Crisis"; *Bangor Daily News*, September 5, 2020.

38. Maine Public, April 7, 2020, "Faith Communities Adapt to COVID-19: How Different Religious Groups Are Reacting to the Crisis."

39. WGME, September 4, 2020; WPFO Fox23 Maine, September 3, 2020; CNN, September 3, 2020.

40. *Bangor Daily News*, September 2, 2020, "UNE Investigating Safety Violations," B2.

41. University of Maine Graduate and Professional Center, September 3, 2020, "Introduction to the Series and the Pandemic."

42. Dr. Mills was referring to four camps that were featured in a study published in late August by the US Centers for Disease Control and Prevention. The review examined precautions taken before and after 642 children and 380 staff members, ages seven to seventy, traveled to the camps from forty-one states and six countries. One positive case was detected at three of the four locations, but staff and campers had prevented any further transmission through strict compliance with the state's restrictions.

43. Office of Governor Mills, executive order 8 FY 20/21, August 26, 2020, "An Order to Facilitate the November 2020 General Election, to Ensure the Integrity of the Ballot, and to Protect the Public Health During the COVID-19 Emergency."

44. Pew Charitable Trusts, *Stateline*, October 16, 2020, "Rise in Use of Ballot Drop Boxes Sparks Partisan Battles"; ABC News, October 16, 2020, "As Popularity Skyrockets, Ballot Drop Boxes Face Unexpected Obstacles."

45. Twitter account of "@realdonaldtrump," post dated August 23, 2020, and suspended account notice; Reuters.com, August 23, 2020, "Twitter Attaches Disclaimer on Trump's 'Mail Drop Boxes' Tweet."

46. ABC News, October 16, 2020, "As Popularity Skyrockets, Ballot Drop Boxes Face Unexpected Obstacles"; FoxNews.com, October 14, 2020, "Trump Directs California GOP to 'Fight Hard in Court' Over Ballot Boxes Despite Prosecution Threat."

47. Pew Charitable Trusts, *Stateline*, October 16, 2020, "Rise in Use of Ballot Drop Boxes Sparks Partisan Battles"; ABC News, October 16, 2020, "As Popularity Skyrockets, Ballot Drop Boxes Face Unexpected Obstacles."

48. Southern Maine Community College, December 14, 2020; *Sun Journal* (Lewiston, ME), March 26, 2020, "SMCC Professor Creates Device to Help with Shortage of Ventilators."

49. State of Maine, Master Agreement for the manufacture of Exterior Election Ballot Boxes, September 29, 2020.

50. WGME, local CBS affiliate, October 23, 2020, "Ballot Drop Boxes Designed, Manufactured in Maine to Meet Needs of Voters."

51. *Bangor Daily News*, July 30, 2020, "Maine Faces Budget Shortfall from COVID-19," A1, A8.

52. National Public Radio, interview with Dr. Shah, September 16, 2020.

53. Maine CDC briefing for September 15, 2020; News Center Maine, NBC local affiliate, September 15, 2020, "Maine CDC, Mills 'Concerned About Where We Are' with Containing Coronavirus."

54. *Bangor Daily News*, September 15, 2020, "Mainers Still Trust Janet Mills More than Trump on Virus, but Her Approval Lowest in Region"; *Bangor Daily News*, June 16, 2020, "Poll: Most Mainers Support Continued Shutdown with 1 in 5 Affected by Layoffs."

55. *Bangor Daily News*, September 15, 2020, "Mainers Still Trust Janet Mills More than Trump on Virus, but Her Approval Lowest in Region"; *Bangor Daily News*, June 16, 2020, "Poll: Most Mainers Support Continued Shutdown with 1 in 5 Affected by Layoffs."; Moody's Analytics, Back-to-Normal Index Methodology, August 20, 2020; CNN Business, September 16, 2020, "Here's Why Some State Economies Are Recovering Faster than Others."

56. Twitter account of Governor Janet Mills," post dated September 16, 2020.

57. NPR, September 18, 2020, "Justice Ruth Bader Ginsburg, Champion of Gender Equality, Dies At 87."

58. Official Twitter account of C-SPAN, footage and post dated September 18, 2020; NPR, September 18, 2020, "'Titan of the Law': Trump Reacts to Ginsburg's Death."

59. White House, September 18, 2020, "Statement on the Passing of Supreme Court Associate Justice Ruth Bader Ginsburg."

60. Office of Senate Leader Mitch McConnell, "McConnell Statement on the Passing of Justice Ruth Bader Ginsburg," September 18, 2020; CBS News, September 19, 2020, "McConnell Says Trump's Nominee to Replace Ruth Bader Ginsburg 'Will Receive a Vote on the Floor' of Senate."

61. *Politico*, February 13, 2016, "McConnell Throws Down the Gauntlet: No Scalia Replacement Under Obama"; PBS, September 19, 2020, "What Every Republican Senator Has Said About Filling a Supreme Court Vacancy in An Election Year.

62. *Bangor Daily News*, September 21, 2020, "Collins: Fill Vacant Seat After Election," A1, A5.

63. Office of Governor Mills, September 18, 2020, "Governor Janet Mills Mourns Passing of Justice Ruth Bader Ginsburg."

64. Associated Press, September 20, 2020, "8th Coronavirus Death Tied to Wedding in Maine."

65. News Center Maine, September 20, 2020, "12 Cases of COVID-19 at Sanford High School and Regional Technical Center."

66. Associated Press, September 22, 2020, "'Unfathomable': US Death Toll from Coronavirus Hits 200,000."

67. Office of the Maine Attorney General, January 6, 2009, "Remarks of Janet T. Mills upon Being Sworn in as Maine's 55th Attorney General."

68. Facebook, personal account of Janet T. Mills, October 11, 2014.

69. Baxter State Park Authority, meeting minutes, October 14, 2016; *Bangor Daily News*, column by George Smith, July 6, 2018; CentralMaine.com, September 19, 2018.

70. Maine Department of Health and Human Services, press release for September 23, 2020, "Mills Administration Exempts Massachusetts from Quarantine Requirement or Testing Requirement."

71. Maine Department of Health and Human Services, press release for September 23, 2020, "Mills Administration Exempts Massachusetts from Quarantine Requirement or Testing Requirement."

72. State of Maine, foliage report for September 23, 2020.

73. *Bangor Daily News*, September 28, 2020, A2; and September 25, 2020, B3.

74. Aroostook County Tourism Office, fact page on "The Maine Potato"; USDA, Aroostook County profile, 2017.

75. *Bangor Daily News*, September 29, 2020, "Warm Day Doesn't Slow Early Hunters as Moose Season Opens," A1.

76. *Bangor Daily News*, September 25, 2020, "Dusty Roads Present Hazard for Moose Hunters as Season Starts," B3.

77. World Health Organization, Coronavirus "Global Epidemiological Situation," September 27, 2020; *New York Times*, September 28, 2020, "Coronavirus Deaths Pass One Million Worldwide"; BBC News, September 29, 2020, "Coronavirus: Global Covid-19 Death Toll Passes One Million."

78. Office of Governor Mills, May 7, 2020, "Mills Administration Secures Major COVID-19 Testing Expansion for Maine"; idexx.com.

79. *Maine Monitor*, September 27, 2020, "Sanford Pastor Continues to Defy State and Local Orders Aimed to Control Virus Spread."

Chapter 6

1. Maine Center for Disease Control and Prevention, October 16, 2020, "Interim Draft COVID-19 Vaccination Plan."

2. Associated Press, October 3, 2020, "Trump, Stricken by COVID-19, Flown to Military Hospital"; *New York Times*, October 2, 2020, "Trump Hospitalized with Coronavirus."

3. Associated Press, October 5, 2020, "Trump, Still Infectious, Back at White House — Without Mask."

4. Associated Press, October 5, 2020, "Trump, Still Infectious, Back at White House — Without Mask."

5. *New York Times*, October 5, 2020, "Coronavirus in the US, Latest Map and Case Count."

6. Maine CDC briefing for October 1, 2020.

7. Maine CDC briefing for October 6, 2020.

8. Maine CDC briefing for October 6, 2020.

9. Maine CDC briefing for October 6, 2020.

10. Office of Governor Mills, radio address for October 9, 2020, "Governor Mills: Wearing a Face Covering, Staying Six Feet Apart, Avoiding Large Gatherings, and Washing Our Hands — All of That Is Key to Keeping Maine Open and Keeping Maine Safe and Healthy"; Maine CDC briefing for October 6, 2020.

11. *Bangor Daily News*, October 3, 2020, "In a Maine County with Surging Virus Cases, No Surprise Over Trump's Infection."

12. *Bangor Daily News*, October 3, 2020, "In a Maine County with Surging Virus Cases, No Surprise Over Trump's Infection."

13. *Bangor Daily News*, October 3, 2020, "In a Maine County with Surging Virus Cases, No Surprise Over Trump's Infection."

14 Associated Press, October 3, 2020, "Some of Maine's Farm Fairs Try to Salvage Season Online."

15. Facebook account of the Fryeburg Fair, June 1, 2020; New England Cable News, October 4, 2020, "Some of Maine's Farm Fairs Try to Salvage Season Online."

16. US Supreme Court docket, October 2, 2020, *David A. Jones, et al., Applicants, v. Matthew Dunlap, Maine Secretary of State, et al.*; Associated Press, October 6, 2020, "Supreme Court Turns Away Republican Appeal on Ranked Voting."

17. State of Maine website, foliage report for October 7, 2020, "Maine Fall Foliage Seaason Nears Its End."

18. National Archives, transcript of the Emancipation Proclamation.

19. Office of Governor Mills, April 8, 2020, statement in response to the resignation of Chief Justice Leigh Saufley.

20. State of Maine Judicial Branch, May 6, 2021, COVID-19 Phased Management Plan (version 8), 11; *Kennebec Journal*, September 18, 2020, "Pandemic, Shortage of Judges, and Social Distancing Slow Wheels of Justice."

21. Office of Governor Mills, August 14, 2020, "Governor Mills Thanks Chief Legal Counsel Derek Langhauser for Service to Maine."

22. CNN, October 12, 2020, "These States Are Ditching Columbus Day to Observe Indigenous Peoples' Day Instead"; *USA Today*, October 12, 2020, "Indigenous Peoples Day or Columbus Day? 14 States Celebrate, Honor Native American Histories and Cultures" (notes fourteen states but fails to account for Virginia, which made the change in 2020).

23. Facebook account of the band Ghost of Paul Revere, post dated October 12, 2020.

24. *Portland Press Herald*, October 13, 2020, "Coronavirus Task Force Coordinator Birx Urges Vigilance in Visit to SMCC."

25. Maine CDC briefing for October 15, 2020.

26. *Bangor Daily News*, October 19, 2020, "Parts of Maine Hit with First Snowfall of Season," B1.

27. Associated Press, October 16, 2020, "Record Avalanche of Early Votes Transforms the 2020 Election."

28. *Bangor Daily News*, October 20, 2020, "Maine Sets Absentee Voting Record with 2 Weeks Until Election Day."

29. *Bangor Daily News*, October 26, 2020, "Emhoff Stumps in Aroostook"; *Vox*, October 20, 2020, "How Biden — or Trump — Could Win 270 Electoral Votes."

30. Smithsonian.com, November 5, 2020, "Why Do Maine and Nebraska Split Their Electoral Votes?"; CNBC, October 26, 2020, "These House Districts in Maine and Nebraska Could Hold the Key to Who Wins the White House"; Central Maine.com, column by Paul Mills, October 9, 2016, "Paul Mills: The History of Maine's Distinctive Electoral College Voting System."

31. CentralMaine.com, column by Paul Mills, October 9, 2016, "Paul Mills: The History of Maine's Distinctive Electoral College Voting System."; Associated Press, November 4, 2020, "Democrat Joe Biden Garners Rare Nebraska Vote."

32. *New York Times*, November 9, 2016, "42 States Shifted to the Right in 2016"; *Bangor Daily News, October 29, 2020, "Donald Trump Jr. Says Maine's Second District Could Decide Election, at Orrington Rally."

33. Dysart's Service Center website.

34. *Portland Press Herald*, October 19, 2020, "Pence Rallies Northern Maine Voters as Presidential Campaign Enters Final Weeks"; *Bangor Daily News*, October 22, 2022, "Mills Criticizes Pence for Size of Hermon Rally," B1.

35. *Portland Press Herald*, October 19, 2020, "Pence Rallies Northern Maine Voters As Presidential Campaign Enters Final Weeks"; *Bangor Daily News*, October 22, 2022, "Mills Criticizes Pence For Size of Hermon Rally," B1.

36. Associated Press, October 15, 2020, "Biden Campaign Flips COVID-19 Threat into New Trump Contrast."

37. Associated Press, October 15, 2020, "Biden Campaign Flips COVID-19 Threat into New Trump Contrast."

38. Maine CDC briefing for October 20, 2020.

39. *Portland Press Herald*, October 26, 2020, "Maine Official Was Alerted to Potential COVID Exposure After Pence Visit"; *Bangor Daily News*, October 28, 2020, "Orchard Regrets Trump Event Drew Unmasked Crowd," A2.

40. NPR, October 25, 2020, "Pence Aide Tests Positive as Coronavirus Consumes Final Days of Campaign"; *Washington Post*, October 25, 2020, "Pence's Chief of Staff, Mark Short, Tests Positive for the Coronavirus."

41. CNN, October 25, 2020, "White House Chief of Staff: 'We're Not Going to Control the Pandemic.'"

42. Press conference footage provided by News Center Maine, October 25, 2020 (the governor referenced Meadows's remarks).

43. *Bangor Daily News*, October 17, 2020, "York County Schools Can Now Open Full Time," B1.

44. Maine CDC briefing for October 20, 2020.

45. Maine CDC briefing for October 20, 2020; *Bangor Daily News*, October 20, 2020, "Pastor of Brooks Church with Outbreak Works at Waldo County Hospital," A1.

46. *Bangor Daily News*, October 20, 2020, "Pastor of Brooks Church with Outbreak Works at Waldo County Hospital," A1.

47. Maine CDC briefing for October 22, 2020; *Bangor Daily News* October 24, 2020, "Waldo County Church Outbreak Drives School Safety Downgrade," B1.

48. Office of the Maine Attorney General, press release for October 21, 2020, "Attorney General Releases Drug Death Report for Second Quarter of 2020."

49. *Portland Press Herald*, October 21, 2020, "Overdose Deaths Surged in Maine in First Half of 2020"; *Bangor Daily News*, October 22, 2020, "Maine Drug Deaths Climb 27% in First Half of the Year," B1.

50. Office of Governor Mills, press release for October 21, 2020, "Mills Administration Announces OPTIONS Initiative to Support Maine People with Substance Use Disorder."

51. Associated Press, October 21, 2020, "Oxycontin Maker Purdue Pharma to Plead to 3 Criminal Charges."

52. Associated Press, October 23, 2020, "Analysis: Debate is Brief Interlude of Normalcy in 2020 Race."

53. Office of Governor Mills, radio address for October 23, 2020.

54. *Bangor Daily News* via *Star-Herald*, October 26, 2020, "Emhoff Stumps in Aroostook," B1; website for the County Bluegrass campground and concert venue.

55. Treworgy Family Orchard website, October 25, 2020, "Regarding Hosting the President."

56. *Bangor Daily News*, October 26, 2020, "Trump Pays Last Minute Visit to Maine"; *Portland Press Herald*, October 25, 2020, "Trump Courts Maine Voters in 2nd District Campaign Stop."

57. *Bangor Daily News*, October 26, 2020, "Trump Pays Last Minute Visit to Maine"; *Portland Press Herald*, October 25, 2020, "Trump Courts Maine Voters in 2nd District Campaign Stop."

58. *Bangor Daily News*, October 26, 2020, "Trump Doesn't Care About Maine Working People, Mills Says," A1; *Portland Press Herald*, October 25, 2020, "Trump Courts Maine Voters in 2nd District Campaign Stop"; footage of press conference provided by News Center Maine, October 25, 2020.

59. *Portland Press Herald*, November 8, 2020, "Collins -Gideon Contest Second Most Expensive Senate Race in US."

60. *Bangor Daily News*, October 26, 2020, "Trump Doesn't Care About Working Maine People, Mills Says," A1; *Portland Press Herald*, October 25, 2020, "Trump Courts Maine Voters in 2nd District Campaign Stop."

61. *Bangor Daily News*, October 25, 2020, "61 New Coronavirus Cases Have Been Reported in Maine."

62. *Portland Press Herald*, October 25, 2020, "Trump Courts Maine Voters in 2nd District Campaign Stop"; *Bangor Daily News*, October 28, 2020, "Orchard Regrets Trump Event Drew Unmasked Crowd."

63. *New York Times*, October 23, 2020, "Susan Collins Hasn't Changed Much, but Maine Has."

64. *Bangor Daily News*, October 24, 2020, "Collins, Gideon Clash on Money, Party Leadership," A6.

65. *Portland Press Herald*, October 29, 2020, "Our View: Maine Needs No Advice About COVID from South Dakota."

66. *Portland Press Herald*, October 29, 2020, "Our View: Maine Needs No Advice About COVID from South Dakota."

67. *Bangor Daily News*, October 27, 2020, "Jill Biden Makes Character Argument for Her Husband in Tuesday Visit to Bangor."

68. *Bangor Daily News*, October 29, 2020, "Donald Trump Jr. Says Maine's 2nd District Could Decide Election at Orrington Rally."

69. News Center Maine, October 26, 2020, "Donald Trump Jr. Holds 'MAGA' Rally in Orrington."

70. *Bangor Daily News*, October 29, 2020, "Early Voters Keep Maine Clerks Busy as Coronavirus Reshapes Election Day."

71. Associated Press, October 26, 2020, "Maine Virus Count Tops 50 on Consecutive Days After Lull."

72. Maine CDC briefing for October 28, 2020.

73. Twitter account of Dr. Nirav Shah, post dated October 30, 2020.

74. Statement provided on October 30, 2020, to multiple media outlets, including *Bangor Daily News*, News Center Maine, Maine Public Radio.

75. Facebook, personal account of Janet T. Mills, October 27, 2020.

Chapter 7

1. Weather Underground, historical weather for Temple, Maine, on November 1, 2020.

2. Office of Governor Mills, announcement of new COVID-19 restrictions, November 1, 2020.

3. Office of Governor Mills, announcement of new COVID-19 restrictions, November 1, 2020.

4. Office of Governor Mills, official documents, Executive Order 57, June 9, 2020.

5. Office of Governor Mills, radio address for November 7, 2020.

6. *Bangor Daily News*, November 2, 2020, "Pittsfield Church Becomes Third Within a Month to Have COVID-19 Outbreak."

7. National Public Radio, November 19, 2020, "Some Faith Leaders Defiant, Others Transparent Over COVID-19 Outbreaks."

8. *New York Times*, November 3, 2020, "In Midnight Vote, Biden Sweeps Dixville Notch. Trump Takes Another New Hampshire Town"; Associated Press, February 11, 2020, "Small New Hampshire Town Votes for Bloomberg in Primary."

9. *New York Times*, November 3, 2020, "In Midnight Vote, Biden Sweeps Dixville Notch. Trump Takes Another New Hampshire Town"; Associated Press, February 11, 2020, "Small New Hampshire Town Votes for Bloomberg in Primary."

10. *Bangor Daily News*, November 3, 2020, "Maine's Election Day Snowstorm Wasn't Much. Warmer Weather Follows."

11. *Bangor Daily News*, November 26, 2020, "Maine's 2020 Election Turnout Among Highest in the Nation," A7.

12. *Bangor Daily News*, November 26, 2020, "Maine's 2020 Election Turnout Among Highest in the Nation," A7.

13. American Civil Liberties Union, press release, September 1, 2020; Brief of American Civil Liberties Union of Maine Foundation and Maine Conservation Voters as Amici Curiae, submitted September 1, 2020, Superior Court Civil Action Docket No. CV-20-95.

14. News Center Maine, September 30, 2020, "Court Rules in Favor of Maine Sec. of State Over Extending Absentee Ballot Deadline"; Maine Supreme Judicial Court (via Justia), decision in docket Ken-20-262, October 23, 2020, *Alliance of Retired Americans et al v. Secretary of State et al.*

15. Associated Press, November 4, 2020, "Biden Wins Maine's Popular Vote, At Least Three Electoral Votes."

16. *Portland Press Herald*, November 4, 2020, "Biden Wins Maine but Trump Picks Up Electoral Vote in the 2nd Congressional District"; News Center Maine, November 4, 2020, "Biden Wins Maine Popular Vote, CD-1, While Trump Claims CD-2."

17. News Center Maine, November 4, 2020, "Rep Jared Golden Wins Re-election in Maine's CD-2 Race."

18. *Bangor Daily News*, November 5, 2020, "Maine Dems Oust Top GOP Legislator as Republicans Erode House Majority," A1, A4 (for all statewide results in this paragraph).

19. *Bangor Daily News*, November 16, 2020, "A Black Doctor Will Be 1st Democrat in 30 Years to Serve a Conservative Piece of Maine."

20. Associated Press, November 5, 2020, "Trump Hits Election Integrity with Unsupported Complaints."

21. Trump White House (archived) via YouTube, November 5, 2020.

22. National Public Radio, November 6, 2020, "Twitter Permanently Suspends Steve Bannon Account After Beheading Comments."

23. *New York Times*, November 5, 2020, "COVID in the US: Maps, Case and Death Count."

24. Office of Governor Mills, press release for November 5, 2020, "Following Record COVID-19, Governor Mills Announces New Face Covering Executive Order"; Office of Governor Mills, Executive Order 16 FY 20/21, November 4, 2020.

25. *The West Wing*, NBC/John Wells Productions, season 6, episode 22, "2162 Votes."

26. Office of the Maine Attorney General, September 16, 2014, AG Janet Mills Remarks to the Maine State Bar Assoc. Glassman Award Luncheon; *Portland Press Herald*, September 23, 2018, "Janet Mills' mission: Break yet another glass ceiling."

27. Bates College, Janet Mills oral history, December 20, 1999.

28. *New York Times*, November 10, 2016, "Women Actually Do Govern Differently"

29. Nichole M. Bauer, Jeong Hyun Kim, and Yesola Kweon, "Women Leaders and Policy Compliance During a Public Health Crisis," *Politics & Gender*, August 17, 2020.

30. Maine Republican Party website; StopMills.com (paid for by the Maine Republican Party).

31. Office of Governor Mills, radio address for June 12, 2020.

32. Office of Governor Mills, radio address for June 12, 2020.

33. Office of Governor Mills, radio address for November 7, 2020; Associated Press, November 7, 2020, "Biden Defeats Trump for White House, says 'Time to Heal.'"

34. Associated Press via *Bangor Daily News*, November 6, 2020, "Biden Urges Patience, Trump Takes Legal Steps as Vote Count Continues," A1.

35. Maine CDC briefing for November 6, 2020.

36. Associated Press, November 7, 2020, "Biden Defeats Trump for White House, says 'Time to Heal.'"

37. Associated Press, November 7, 2020, "Biden Defeats Trump for White House, says 'Time to Heal.'"

38. Associated Press, November 7, 2020, "Trump Hits Election Integrity with Unsupported Integrity Complaints"; Associated Press, data for the 2020 election as of 12:00 P.M. EST, November 19, 2020.

39. Pew Research Center, January 28, 2021, "Turnout Surged in 2020 As Nearly Two-Thirds of Eligible US Voters Cast Ballots for President"; WMTW, April 21, 2021, "Maine Legislators Consider Bills to Make Absentee Ballot Tracking, Drop Boxes Permanent."

40. WMTW, April 21, 2021, "Maine Legislators Consider Bills to Make Absentee Ballot Tracking, Drop Boxes Permanent."

41. Associated Press, November 9, 2020, "Biden Targets Virus as His White House Transition Begins."

42. Associated Press, November 9, 2020, "Biden Targets Virus as His White House Transition Begins."

43. Maine CDC briefing for November 9, 2020; Bangor Daily News, November 10, 2020, "Surge Drives Outbreaks at Churches, Schools."

44. Maine CDC briefing for November 9, 2020; Bangor Daily News, November 10, 2020, "Surge Drives Outbreaks at Churches, Schools."

45. Bangor Daily News, November 10, 2020, "Outbreak at Windham Prison Grows to 131 Cases."

46. Bangor Daily News (October 14, 20, 29, and November 10) and Portland Press Herald (October 4, 23, 29) ongoing 2020 coverage of prison outbreaks; Maine Beacon, September 23, 2020, "Mainers in Jail 'Paying the Price' for Lack of Action to Prevent Outbreaks."

47. Maine legislature, report to the Government Oversight Committee from the Office of Program Evaluation and Government Accountability, November 2020, key findings on page 10.

48. ProPublica via Maine Monitor, November 11, 2020, "Maine Governor Won't Fund Reforms for Public Defense Agency Without Accountability"; Bangor Daily News, November 10, 2020, "Watchdog Finds Flaws in Maine's Indigent Legal Defense System," A1.

49. Maine CDC briefing for November 12, 2020.

50. CNBC, November 4, 2020, "France, Germany and England Impose New Lockdowns as Pandemic Fatigue Seeps in Across Europe and Covid Cases Soar"; The Economist, November 7, 2020, "The Second Wave of Covid-19 Has Sent Much of Europe Back into Lockdown"; Reuters, November 3, 2020, "Netherlands Tightens Lockdown to Slow Second COVID-19 Wave"; Reuters, November 4, 2020, "Belgian COVID-19 Hospitalisations Rise Back to Pre-Lockdown Level"; Lonely Planet, November 2, 2020, "Strict lockdowns are being imposed in Europe — here's what you need to know."

51. Gallup, November 11, 2020, "Americans Less Amenable to Another COVID-19 Lockdown."

52. Associated Press, November 16, 2020, "Governors Ratchet Up Restrictions Ahead of Thanksgiving."

53. Office of Governor Mills, radio address for November 13, 2020; NPR, November 16, 2020, "Moderna's COVID-19 Vaccine Shines in Clinical Trial."

54. Office of Governor Mills, November 5, 2020, announcement of a new executive order regarding face coverings.

55. Bangor Daily News, November 20, 2020, "Maine Will Stop Probing Suspected Virus Cases Until Tests Confirm Them," A7.

56. *Bangor Daily News*, November 20 and 21, 2020; Maine CDC briefing for November 18, 2020.

57. *Bangor Daily News*, November 18, 2020, "Attorney: Millinocket Inn Responsible for COVID-19 Death Linked to Wedding."

58. Twitter account of Pastor Todd Bell, post dated November 28, 2020.

59. Twitter account of Pastor Todd Bell, posts dated November 25, 2020, and November 23, 2020.

60. WMTW, November 24, 2020, "Sunday River Brewing Company Owners to Comply with Judge's Order to Close."

61. Maine CDC briefing for November 18, 2020.

62. Office of Governor Mills, advisory for November 19, 2020.

63. Associated Press, November 15, 2020, "Trump Seems to Acknowledge Biden Win, but He Won't Concede."

64. TikTok profile of Jacob Knowles, late October 2020.

65. News Center Maine, November 15, 2020, "Maine Fisherman Goes Viral on TikTok"; *Bangor Daily News*, November 17, 2020, "Lobsterman Goes Viral on TikTok," B1.

66. *Bangor Daily News*, November 18, 2020, "'We'll Take Care of Ya': Lobsterman Making Waves on the Internet," A8.

67. Office of Governor Mills, November 20, 2020, "Governor Mills Announces Intent to Expand Research and Development of Floating Offshore Wind in Maine."

68. National Conference of State Legislatures, September 2, 2022, "How States Are Spending Their Stimulus Funds."

69. Office of Governor Mills, November 20, 2020, "Governor Mills Dedicates $6.2 Million More to Rent Relief to Support Maine Families."

70. Office of Governor Mills, November 20, 2020, "Mills Administration Awards $5.6 Million to Build High Speed Internet Infrastructure for Students in Underserved Maine Communities"; Office of Governor Mills, November 20, 2020, "Governor Mills Announces Second Round of Economic Recovery Grants to Maine Small Businesses & Non-Profit."

71. Facebook, personal account of Janet T. Mills, November 22, 2020; Mainebyfoot .com, October 5, 2021.

72. The Sierra Club via William Frederic Badè, *The Life and Letters of John Muir* (Boston and New York: Houghton Mifflin, 1924).

73. Henry Wadsworth Longfellow, *Flower-de-Luce* (Boston: Ticknor and Fields, 1867).

74. Enoch Lincoln, *The Village: A Poem, with an Appendix* (Portland: Edward Little, 1816); Samuel Kettell (ed.), *Specimens of American Poetry* (Boston: S. G. Goodrich, 1829).

75. Twitter account of Dr. Nirav Shah, post dated November 24, 2020.

76. Associated Press, November 23, 2020, "Biden Transition Gets Govt OK After Trump Out of Options."

77. Associated Press, November 23, 2020, "Biden Transition Gets Govt OK After Trump Out of Options."

78. *Bangor Daily News*, December 2, 2020, "With 67 Deaths Last Month Was Maine's Deadliest of the Pandemic," A1.

79. Maine CDC briefing for November 30, 2020.

Chapter 8

1. C-SPAN, December 2, 2020, President Trump statement on 2020 election results.

2. Associated Press, December 2, 2020, "In Video, Trump Recycles Unsubstantiated Voter Fraud Claims"; *New York Times*, December 2, 2020, "Trump, in Video from White House, Delivers a 46-Minute Diatribe on the 'Rigged' Election"; The American Presidency Project, transcript of "Remarks on the Presidential Election" by Donald J. Trump, December 2, 2020.

3. *Washington Post*, December 2, 2020, "CDC Director Issues Stark Warning as New US Coronavirus Cases Top 200,000"; NBC News, December 2, 2020; *New York Times*, December 2, 2020, "Coronavirus in the US: Latest Map and Case Count."

4. Maine CDC briefing for December 2, 2020.

5. Brookings Institution, December 2, 2020, "The Health Care Workforce Needs Higher Wages and Better Opportunities"; Maine Public, January 19, 2021, "'I Just Cannot Get the Help I Need' — Direct Care Worker Shortage Leaves Older Mainers Unsupported."

6. Margaret Heffernan, *Willful Blindness* (New York, London, New Delhi, Sydney: Bloomsbury, 2011), 1, 3.

7. Heffernan, *Willful Blindness*, 1; Judge Sim Lake's instruction is also referenced in Skilling's appeal (via Findlaw.com), January 6, 2009, *UNITED STATES of America, Plaintiff-Appellee, v. Jeffrey K. SKILLING, Defendant-Appellant*. No. 06-20885.

8. Heffernan, *Willful Blindness*, 2, 4, 6.

9. Heffernan, *Willful Blindness*, 247.

10. Associated Press, December 3, 2020, "States Plan for Vaccines as Daily US Virus Deaths Top 3,100."

11. Maine Department of Health and Human Services, announcement of formal COVID-19 vaccination request, December 4, 2020; MaineHealth media release for December 10, 2020, "MaineHealth Establishes Plan for Inoculating Front-Line Care Givers Following State Plan for Distribution of COVID-19 Vaccines."

12. *Portland Press Herald*, December 4, 2020, "'Ferocious Levels' of Virus Transmission Will Spur Changes to Maine CDC Investigations."

13. John F. Kennedy Library archives, speech delivered at the Jefferson-Jackson Day dinner, Pawtuxet, Rhode Island, April 26, 1953, 9–10.

14. Office of Governor Mills, December 5, 2020, "Governor Mills Announces Negative COVID-19 Test."

15. *Washington Post*, December 6, 2020, "Powerful Winter Storm Slams New England with Heavy Snow, Howling Winds"; NPR, December 6, 2020, "Nor'easter Leaves Thousands Without Power Across New England."

16. *Bangor Daily News*, December 8, 2020, "Death of Cows in Weekend Storm Just the Latest Struggle for Dairy Farmers"; WABI (Bangor, ME CBS affiliate), December 8, 2020, "Troy Dairy Farm Struck by Tragedy; Community Steps In."

17. Maine CDC briefing for December 7, 2020.

18. Associated Press, December 8, 2020, "UK Starts Virus Campaign with a Shot Watched Round the World."

19. Associated Press, December 10, 2020, "US Panel Endorses Widespread Use of Pfizer COVID-19 Vaccine."

20. Associated Press, December 11, 2020, "White House Threatens FDA Chief's Job Over Vaccine Approval."

21. Associated Press, December 10, 2020, "US Panel Endorses Widespread Use of Pfizer COVID-19 Vaccine."

22. Office of Governor Mills, radio address for December 11, 2020, "Governor Mills: No Matter How or What You Celebrate This Year, I Wish You a Season Filled with Peace and Joy, and a New Year Filled with Love and Light."

23. Office of Governor Mills, media release for December 9, 2020, "Mills Administration Announces One-Time Relief Payment for Mainers Unemployed Due to COVID-19."

24. Office of Governor Mills, media release for December 11, 2020, "Mills Administration Commits Full $1.25 Billion of Federal Coronavirus Relief Funding."

25. Office of Governor Mills, December 11, 2020, "Governor Mills Issues Executive Order Strengthening Enforcement of Face Covering Requirement in All Indoor Public Spaces"; Office of Governor Mills, Executive Order 19, December 11, 2020.

26. Office of Governor Mills, list of official documents.

27. Office of Governor Mills, cabinet officials, biography of Jeanne Lambrew.

28. *Amherst* (Amherst College alumni magazine), profile, January 14, 2020.

29. *Amherst* (Amherst College alumni magazine), profile, January 14, 2020.

30. *Portland Press Herald*, December 14, 2018, "Mills Names Mainer with White House Experience to Lead State's 'Most Important Department"; *Bangor Daily News*, December 14, 2018, "Mills Picks Former Obama Healthcare Reform Leader to Run DHHS."

31. Direct interview with Governor Mills, May 22, 2022.

32. Associated Press, December 14, 2020, "First COVID-19 Vaccines in Maine Given to Healthcare Workers"; Maine CDC briefing for December 14, 2020.

33. Twitter account of Governor Janet T. Mills, December 14, 2020.

34. *Bangor Daily News*, December 4, 2020, "'Secret Santa' Program Aims to Boost Small Businesses."

35. Coastal Maine Botanical Gardens.

36. *Bangor Daily News*, December 2, 2020, "With Parades Canceled, Towns Are Trying Something Different This Year to Spread Holiday Cheer."

37. Facebook account of Calvary Baptist Church, December 14, 2020.

38. Office of Governor Mills, Executive Order 19A, December 15, 2020.

39. Office of Governor Mills, "Guidance on Enforcing Face-Covering Rules in Public Settings," November 23, 2020; *Bangor Daily News*, December 17, 2020, "Businesses Could Face $10,000 Fine for Not Enforcing Janet Mills' Mask Mandate."

40. Cumberland Club website.

41. Maine Legislative Record, May 6, 1969, pages 1800–1801.

42. Associated Press, May 23, 1969, "Legality of Bill Is Questioned."

43. *Portland Press Herald*, June 11, 1969, "To What Degree May Government Control Private Organizations."

44. *Bangor Daily News* / Associated Press, August 15, 1979, "Cumberland Club to Admit Women."

45. Associated Press, December 20, 2020, "Congress Seals Agreement on $900 Billion COVID Relief Bill."

46. Reuters, December 22, 2020, "Trump Threatens to Not Sign COVID-19 Bill, Wants Bigger Stimulus Checks."

47. NBC News, November 23, 2020 (updated December 10, 2020), "Trump's Election Fight Includes Over 50 Lawsuits."

48. *Bangor Daily News*, December 23, 2020, "Maine Sees Most New Jobless Claims Since July as Trump Puts Stimulus in Limbo."

49. Maine CDC briefing for December 23, 2020.

50. Maine Department of Transportation via YouTube, New England governors' happy holidays message, December 23, 2020.

51. Retail Association of Maine via YouTube, December 23, 2020, "Let's Be Kind" video campaign.

52. *Bangor Daily News*, December 30, 2020, "Sunday River Loses Bid to Get Restaurant License Back," B1, B2; *Portland Press Herald*, December 22, 2020, "Rick Savage Out During Sunday River Brewing Appeal Hearing."

53. National Weather Service, historical weather data for Caribou Station, December 25, 2020.

54. US Centers for Disease Control and Prevention, brief by the National Center for Immunization and Respiratory Diseases Division of Viral Diseases, December 22, 2020; *New York Times*, December 21, 2020, "The UK Coronavirus Variant: What We Know."

55. Associated Press, December 27, 2020, "Trump Signs Massive Measure Funding Government, COVID Relief"; *New York Times*, December 27, 2020, "Trump Signs Pandemic Relief Bill After Unemployment Aid Lapses."

56. *Bangor Daily News*, December 28, 2020, "Bangor Toilet Paper Factory That Opened as Pandemic Began Has 'Banner' Year," A1, A5.

57. *Bangor Daily News*, "Good Birding" column for December 30, 2020, "A Rare Wren and Gull Made It into This Maine Birder's 2020 Year in Review."

58. Government of Canada, news release on updated travel restrictions, October 30, 2020.

59. Maine CDC briefing for December 30, 2020.

60. Office of Governor Mills, media release for December 30, 2020, "Mills Administration Continues Early Business Closing Time Amid Increase in COVID-19 Positivity Rate and Hospitalizations."

61. Facebook account of @crossingsfk, December 30, 2020.

62. Northern Maine Medical Center, media release (undated), "NMMC Physician Recognized by Board of Radiology."

63. LinkedIn account of Dr. John Hotchkiss.

64. The 2020 Decennial Census lists the total population of Fort Kent at 4,067 people. US Census Bureau; University of Maine at Fort Kent, 2020 presidential search prospectus, 2.

65. *New York Times*, December 9, 2020, "'There's No Place for Them to Go': ICU Beds Near Capacity Across US."

66. NPR, December 24, 2020, "California Is 1st State to Hit 2 Million Cases, and Hospitals Are Out of ICU Beds"; *New York Times*, December 25, 2020, "Southern California's Hospitals Are Overwhelmed, and It May Get Worse."

67. *New York Times*, December 25, 2020, "Southern California's Hospitals Are Overwhelmed, and It May Get Worse"; Associated Press, December 17, 2020, "Hot Spot: California Hospitals Buckle as Virus Cases Surge."

68. Office of Governor Mills, radio address for December 31, 2020.

69. Facebook, official account of Governor Janet Mills, post dated December 31, 2020.

70. *New York Times*, December 30, 2020, "US Officials Say Covid-19 Vaccination Effort Has Lagged"; *Los Angeles Times*, December 31, 2020, "Some Healthcare Workers Refuse to Take COVID-19 Vaccine, Even with Priority Access"; *New York Times*, December 29, 2020, "First US Case of Highly Contagious Coronavirus Variant Is Found in Colorado."

71. *Bangor Daily News*, December 17, 2020, "Janet Mills May Get Coronavirus Vaccine in Public but Is Waiting to Find Her Place in Line."

Chapter 9

1. Office of Governor Mills, May 28, 2019, "Governor Mills Signs Groundbreaking Paid Leave Bill into Law."

2. Reuters, January 1, 2021, "US COVID-19 Cases Surpass 20 Million as Deaths Mount"; NPR, January 1, 2021, "US Surpasses 20 Million Confirmed Coronavirus Cases."

3. Associated Press, January 28, 2021, "US Economy Shrank 3.5% in 2020 After Growing 4% Last Quarter."

4. National Conference of State Legislatures, September 9, 2022; Kaiser Family Foundation, December 14, 2020, "Coronavirus Puts a Spotlight on Paid Leave Policies," fig. 1.

5. US Department of Labor, Families First Coronavirus Response Act: Employee Paid Leave Rights; Pew Charitable Trusts, *Stateline*, September 16, 2022; "Pandemic Prompts More States to Mandate Paid Sick Leave"; Stefan Pichler, Katherine Wen, and Nicolas R. Ziebarth, "COVID-19 Emergency Sick Leave Has Helped Flatten the Curve in the United States," *Health Affairs* 39, no. 12 (October 15, 2020); *Time*, September 28, 2022, "The Pandemic Changed Paid Sick Leave Policies, but Not for Everyone."

6. *Bangor Daily News*, January 4, 2021, "COVID-19 Could Be the Center of Maine Lawmakers' Political Fights this Session."

7. Maine Public, December 2, 2020, "In Historic Day, Maine Legislature Kicks Off Session at Augusta Civic Center"; Maine legislature, session schedule for the 130th legislature.

8. *Bangor Daily News*, January 19, 2021, "In Email Thread, Maine Lawmakers Air Frustration That They Still Aren't Meeting in Person."

9. *Bangor Daily News*, January 4, 2021, "A Look Inside the Bills for the Next Maine Legislative Session," LR 1599 and LR 217.

10. *Bangor Daily News*, January 4, 2021, "A Look Inside the Bills for the Next Maine Legislative Session," LR 544 and LR 1026.

11. *Bangor Daily News*, January 4, 2021, "A Look Inside the Bills for the Next Maine Legislative Session," bills that mention "identification" in the context of voting are found on 10, 138, 142; bills that mention "absentee" in the context of ballots or voting are found on 137–38.

12. Brennan Center for Justice, January 26, 2021, "Voting Laws Roundup: January 2021."

13. *Bangor Daily News*, January 4, 2021, "COVID-19 Could Be the Center of Maine Lawmakers' Political Fights This Session."

14. Associated Press, January 3, 2021, "Trump, on Tape, Presses Ga. Official to 'Find' Him Votes."
15. Office of US Senator Susan Collins, media release, January 3, 2021.
16. Associated Press, January 6, 2021, "Warnock, Ossoff Win in Georgia, Handing Dems Senate Control."
17. Maine Public, January 6, 2022, "Maine's Members of Congress Had Different Perspectives of the Jan. 6 Riot. They Still Do."
18. *Bangor Daily News*, January 11, 2021, "Susan Collins Recounts the Moment Rioters Stormed the Capitol."
19. National Public Radio, January 5, 2022, "A Timeline of How the Jan. 6 Attack Unfolded — Including Who Said What and When"; CNN, July 29, 2022, "The January 6 Insurrection: Minute-by-Minute."
20. *New York Times*, January 5, 2022, "These Are the People Who Died in Connection with the Capitol Riot."
21. *Smithsonian*, January 8, 2021, "The History of Violent Attacks on the US Capitol"; Associated Press, January 6, 2021, "Capitol Has Seen Violence Over 220 Years, but Not Like This."
22. Facebook account of Ashirah Knapp, post dated January 2, 2021.
23. Associated Press, January 7, 2021, "After Excusing Violence, Trump Acknowledges Biden Transition"; Associated Press, January 8, 2021, "Twitter Bans Trump, Citing Risk of Violent Incitement"; NBC News, January 8, 2021, "Twitter Permanently Suspends President Donald Trump."
24. Associated Press, January 7, 2021, "After Excusing Violence, Trump Acknowledges Biden Transition."
25. Library of Congress, The Constitution Annotated (CONAN), Twenty-Fifth Amendment, Historical Background, section 3, 4, published 2020.
26. *Portland Press Herald*, January 7, 2021, "King Says 25th Amendment Should Be Considered; Pingree Backs Trump's Removal"; News Center Maine, January 7, 2021, "Sen. King, Rep. Pingree Suggest President Trump's Removal from Office."
27. Associated Press, January 8, 2021, "State Capitols Reassess Safety After Violence at US Capitol"; News Center Maine, January 7, 2021, "Police and Lawmakers Talk Security at State House."
28. Office of Governor Mills, January 8, 2021, Governor Mills budget letter to legislature.
29. Maine Policy Institute, January 14, 2021, "The Real Story Behind Governor Mills' Second Budget Proposal."
30. Associated Press, January 13, 2021, "Trump Impeached After Capitol Riot in Historic Second Charge"; Associated Press, January 13, 2021, "Trump's Wall of GOP Support Breaks During Impeachment Vote."
31. Associated Press, January 12, 2021, "US Shifts to Speed COVID Shots as Cases and Deaths Rise."
32. Office of Governor Mills, radio address for January 15, 2021.
33. Maine CDC briefing for January 13, 2021; Office of Governor Mills, media release for January 13, 2021, "Governor Mills Updates Maine's Vaccine Strategy to Focus on Protecting Those Most Vulnerable to COVID-19."
34. Office of Governor Mills, media release for January 13, 2021, "Governor Mills Updates Maine's Vaccine Strategy to Focus on Protecting Those Most Vulnerable to COVID-19."

35. Office of Governor Mills, radio address for January 15, 2021; Reuters, January 15, 2021, "Trump Administration Accused of Deception in Pledging Release of Vaccine Stockpile."

36. Maine CDC briefing for January 13, 2021.

37. Office of Governor Mills, radio address for January 15, 2021.

38. Office of Governor Mills, media release for January 15, 2021, "Governor Mills Receives First Dose of COVID-19 Vaccine."

39. Maine CDC briefing for January 15, 2021.

40. ABC News, January 11, 2021, "Armed Protests Being Planned at All 50 State Capitols, FBI Bulletin Says"; Associated Press, January 11, 2021, "FBI Warns of Plans for Nationwide Armed Protests Next Week."

41. Office of Governor Mills, media release for January 15, 2021, "Out of Abundance of Caution, Governor Mills Activates Maine National Guard."

42. *Mainer*, January 15, 2021, "Chief of Maine's Capitol Police Radicalized by Far-Right Conspiracies."

43. BBC News, January 11, 2021, "Parler Social Network Sues Amazon for Pulling Support"; Associated Press, January 11, 2021, "Right-Wing App Parler Booted Off Internet Over Ties to Siege."

44. *Mainer*, January 15, 2021, "Chief of Maine's Capitol Police Radicalized by Far-Right Conspiracies."

45. Associated Press, January 16, 2020, "Maine Capitol Police Chief Apologizes for Social Media Posts."

46. Associated Press, January 16, 2020, "Maine Capitol Police Chief Apologizes for Social Media Posts."

47. *New York Times*, October 8, 2020, "FBI Says Michigan Anti-Government Group Plotted to Kidnap Gov. Gretchen Whitmer."

48. Maine Capitol Police, Capitol Area Activity Permit obtained by Jennifer Crowley, November 17–20, 2020.

49. *Bangor Daily News*, January 19, 2021, "Owls Head Graffiti Threatens Janet Mills' Life."

50. MaineHealth, media release for January 18, 2021, "MaineHealth Rolling Out COVID-19 Vaccine for Mainers Over 70 on a Limited Basis at Its Local Health Systems."

51. Maine CDC briefing for January 19, 2021.

52. Maine CDC briefing for January 19, 2021.

53. Associated Press, January 19, 2021, "Lawmakers Want Capitol Police Chief to Be Placed on Leave"; Associated Press, January 20, 2021, "New Leader Takes Over Capitol Police After Social Media Flap."

54. Maine Public, January 25, 2021, "Maine Lawmakers Fight Over What's a Proper Face Covering."

55. Governor Mills mentioned both the response to fishermen and the judge's decision in her journal entry for January 20, 2021; Office of Governor Mills, media release for February 5, 2021, "Mills Administration Announces Landmark Agreement That Charts Path Toward Ending Three-Decades Long AMHI Consent Decree."

56. All details on Augusta protesters were reported by the *Kennebec Journal* via CentralMaine.com, January 20, 2021, "Few Turn Out to Protest in Augusta . . ."

57. *Bangor Daily News*, January 15, 2021, "Piscataquis Commissioners Pass Anti-Mills Resolution Based on COVID-19 Misinformation"; *Sun Journal* (Lewiston, ME), January 20, 2021, "Divided Androscoggin Commissioners Bristle Over Masks, COVID Protocols."

58. Maine Department of Labor, Center for Workforce Research and Information, county profiles; Piscataquis County website, January 13, 2021, "Resolution of Protest for Piscataquis County."

59. Piscataquis County website, January 13, 2021, "Resolution of Protest for Piscataquis County"; WGME, January 20, 2021, "Piscataquis County Commissioners Sign Controversial COVID-19 Resolution."

60. *Sun Journal*, January 20, 2021, "Divided Androscoggin Commissioners Bristle Over Masks, COVID Protocols."

61. *Portland Press Herald*, January 22, 2021, "Face Shields Worn by 2 Lawmakers Not Effective Against Transmission of COVID-19, Says Maine CDC."

62. Associated Press, January 4, 2021, "Statehouses Could Prove to Be Hothouses for Virus Infection."

63. Maine Public, January 25, 2021, "Maine Lawmakers Fight Over What's a Proper Face Covering."

64. Maine CDC briefing for January 28, 2021, referencing Maine's seven-day average PCR positivity rate of 6.06 percent reached on January 8, 2021.

65. *Bangor Daily News* / Associated Press, January 27, 2021, "Mills 'Encouraged' by Plan to Bump Up COVID-19 Vaccine Deliveries to States," A1, A5.

66. New England Patriots, media release for February 2, 2021.

67. *Bangor Daily News*, January 31, 2021, "Maine Sees Fewest New Coronavirus Cases in Months and No Deaths."

Chapter 10

1. *New York Times*, February 2, 2021, "The Storm Was Among the Biggest in New York City's Recent History."

2. Maine CDC briefing for February 2, 2021.

3. *Bangor Daily News*, February 1, 2021, "Snowstorm to Disrupt COVID-19 Vaccination Effort in Much of Maine"; Associated Press, February 1, 2021, "'A Long Two Days': Major Storm Pummels Northeast with Snow."

4. Maine CDC briefing for February 2, 2021.

5. Northern Light Health media release for January 27, 2021, "Cross Insurance Center Named COVID-19 Community Vaccination Center for Bangor Region"; Associated Press, February 3, 2021, "Mass COVID-19 Immunization Site Is Opening in Southern Maine"; Cross Insurance Center website, "Fun Facts."

6. *Bangor Daily News*, February 1, 2021, "Northern Light to Vaccinate 1,800 People This Week at Cross Center"; Maine CDC briefing for February 2, 2021.

7. *Los Angeles Times*, February 1, 2021, "Rapid Spread of UK Coronavirus Variant in Southern California Sparks Alarm"; Associated Press, February 11, 2021, "UK Variant Likely in Vermont After City Wastewater Testing."

8. *Bangor Daily News*, February 4, 2021, "Belfast Officials Call for Civility on 'Protest Corner' After Anti-Mask Tensions Escalate"; Maine Public, February 9, 2021, "As Anti-Mask Protesters Occupy Prominent Belfast Corner, Officials Encourage Nonengagement."

9. *Bangor Daily News*, February 8, 2021, "Belfast Police Cite 2 for Disorderly Conduct After Anti-Mask Protest Escalates."

10. *Bangor Daily News*, February 4, 2021, "Belfast Officials Call for Civility on 'Protest Corner' After Anti-Mask Tensions Escalate."

11. Remarks exchanged here were transcribed from footage provided by the *Bangor Daily News*, February 8, 2021, "Belfast Police Cite 2 for Disorderly Conduct After Anti-Mask Protest Escalates."

12. *Bangor Daily News*, February 6, 2021, "Maine AG Sends Letters to Piscataquis, Androscoggin Commissioners Telling Them to Mask Up."

13. *Portland Press Herald*, February 18, 2021, "Group Drops Recall Effort Against Two Androscoggin County Commissioners."

14. Official website of Androscoggin County, commissioners' meeting minutes for December 15, 2021.

15. Maine Public, February 5, 2021, "Janet Mills Says Plan Puts to Rest Three-Decade Mental Health Consent Decree."

16. White House, biography of Julie Chavez Rodriguez; Associated Press, June 28, 2021, "Cesar Chavez's Legacy Lives on in Biden's Staff, Oval Office."

17. Associated Press, February 4, 2021, "FBI: 2 New Englanders Arrested for Roles in Capitol Riot."

18. *Bangor Daily News*, February 1, 2021, "Sara Gideon Gives Chunk of Leftover Campaign Cash to Democratic Groups."

19. Office of Governor Mills, media release for February 17, 2021, "Governor Mills to Deliver Virtual State of the Budget Address."

20. World Health Organization statement for January 23, 2020, "Statement on the First Meeting of the International Health Regulations (2005) Emergency Committee Regarding the Outbreak of Novel Coronavirus (2019-nCoV)."

21. Archives of the Maine Attorney General's Office, September 25, 2009, "Day of Remembrance Address: Parents of Murdered Children."

22. Archives of the Maine Attorney General's Office, October 20, 2009, "Remarks of Attorney General Mills at the Maine Prosecutors Association Annual Meeting."

23. Office of Governor Mills, September 23, 2019, "Speaking Before the United Nations, Governor Mills Announces Maine Will Be Carbon Neutral by 2045."

24. Maine State Library, digital repository, inaugural address of Governor Janet T. Mills, January 2, 2019; News Center Maine, recorded broadcast of Janet Mills inaugural address, January 2, 2019.

25. *New York Times*, May 8, 2006, "Sister Rose Thering, Nun Dedicated to Bridging Gap with Judaism, Dies at 85"; Seton Hall University, death notice for Sister Rose Thering.

26. *The Howie Carr Show*, April 29, 2020, "Former Governor LePage: 'I'm Coming Back'"; *Bangor Daily News*, April 29, 2020, "Paul LePage Says 'I Am Going to Challenge Janet Mills' in 2022."

27. *Bangor Daily News*, December 22, 2020, "Janet Mills 'Likely' to Run for 2022 Reelection as Showdown with Paul LePage Looms."

28. Maine CDC press release, February 10, 2021, "Case of B.1.1.7 COVID-19 Variant Confirmed in Maine."

29. Maine CDC briefing for February 11, 2021.

30. Maine CDC briefing for February 11, 2021; White House, media release and fact sheet for February 2, 2021, "President Biden Announces Increased Vaccine Supply, Initial Launch of the Federal Retail Pharmacy Program, and Expansion of FEMA Reimbursement to States."

31. National Governors Association, February 15, 2021, "Executive Committee Letter to President Regarding Vaccine Distribution Process."

32. *Portland Press Herald*, February 21, 2021, "Maine Eligibility Guidelines for COVID-19 Vaccine Confuse, Frustrate"; *Bangor Daily News*, February 10, 2021, "Maine Criticized for Lack of Clarity on Janet Mills' Vaccine Priority Decisions"; National Public Radio, February 16, 2021, "Biden Administration Says It Has Increased Vaccine Supply."

33. *Portland Press Herald*, February 21, 2021, "Maine Eligibility Guidelines for COVID-19 Vaccine Confuse, Frustrate"; *Bangor Daily News*, February 10, 2021, "Maine Criticized for Lack of Clarity on Janet Mills' Vaccine Priority Decisions."

34. *Portland Press Herald*, February 21, 2021, "Maine Eligibility Guidelines for COVID-19 Vaccine Confuse, Frustrate."

35. *Boston Globe*, February 11, 2021, "'Willing to Pay': People on Craigslist Are Offering to Drive Seniors to Get a COVID-19 Vaccine in Exchange for a Shot Themselves"; *New York Times*, February 12, 2021, "Massachusetts' Vaccine Buddy System Sets Off 'Old Rush.'"

36. *Boston Globe*, February 11, 2021, "'Willing to Pay': People on Craigslist Are Offering to Drive Seniors to Get a COVID-19 Vaccine in Exchange for a Shot Themselves."

37. Office of Governor Mills, February 12, 2021, "Governor Mills: Everyone in This State Is Essential."

38. WMTW, February 12, 2021, "Governor Mills Makes First Visit to Cross Insurance Center's Vaccine Clinic."

39. Northern Light Health, media release for February 13, 2021, "Governor Mills Visits Cross Insurance Center Vaccination Site."

40. Facebook, personal account of Janet T. Mills, February 13, 2021.

41. *Washington Post*, December 16, 2015, "This May Be the Only Police Department in America with a Funny Facebook Page."

42. *Bangor Daily News*, July 14, 2014, "Police Department Duck of Justice Gaining Fame in Bangor."

43. Facebook account of the Bangor Police Department, September 22, 2018.

44. Associated Press, July 18, 2022, "'Duck of Justice' Creator Retires to Pursue Writing Career."

45. Facebook account of Ashirah Knapp, post dated February 13, 2021.

46. National Public Radio, January 15, 2021, "Biden Administration Will Rename 'Operation Warp Speed,' Citing Trump 'Failures'"; Associated Press, February 11, 2021, "'Overwhelm the Problem': Inside Biden's War on COVID-19."

47. National Public Radio, February 16, 2021, "Biden Administration Says It Has Increased Vaccine Supply"; Associated Press, February 10, 2021, "AP-NORC Poll: A Third of US Adults Skeptical of COVID Shots"; Associated Press, February 17, 2021, "Thousands of Service Members Saying No to COVID-19 Vaccine"; *The New Yorker*, February 2, 2021, "Why Are So Many Health-Care Workers Resisting the COVID Vaccine?"; Associated Press, February 12, 2021, "Vaccination of Black People Lagging Behind Whites in Alabama"; *New York Times*,

February 2, 2021, "The Wealthy Are Getting More Vaccinations, Even in Poorer Neighborhoods."

48. Maine CDC briefing for February 16, 2021.

49. Maine Department of Health and Human Services, February 16, 2021, "COVID-19 Vaccine Update for Sites."

50. Maine Department of Health and Human Services, February 16, 2021, "State of Maine COVID-19 Vaccine Efficient and Full Use Policy."

51. *Portland Press Herald*, February 7, 2021, "Flouting CDC Rules, MaineHealth Offered Vaccines to All Employees, Even Remote Workers."

52. *Portland Press Herald*, February 7, 2021, "Flouting CDC Rules, MaineHealth Offered Vaccines to All Employees, Even Remote Workers."

53. *Bangor Daily News*, February 9, 2021, "Maine Had 'Strong Concerns' About Hospital Vaccine Plans. Staff Seeing No Patients Got Shots Anyway."

54. Office of the Maine Attorney General, February 16, 2021, "AG Frey Warns Vaccine Providers Against Giving COVID-19 Vaccine to Ineligible Individuals."

55. Associated Press, January 26, 2021, "Baseball Gathers Behind Home Plate to Honor Hammerin' Hank"; *New York Times*, January 31, 2021, "Never Mind the Skeptics, Officials Say: Hank Aaron's Death Had Nothing to Do with the Covid-19 Vaccine."

56. Office of Governor Mills, July 1, 2021, "Promise Kept: Governor Mills Signs Strong, Bipartisan Budget Achieving 55 Percent of Education Costs for First Time in Maine History"; WMTW, August 5, 2022, "Which Maine Governor Spent More on Public Education, Janet Mills or Paul LePage?"

57. All rebuttal remarks by Senator Timberlake were transcribed from a live-streamed video recorded and posted online by Maine Public on February 23, 2021, "Maine State of the Budget Address by Governor Janet Mills," which was followed by the senator's Republican response; *Bangor Daily News*, November 11, 2020, "GOP Picks Longtime Lawmakers to Lead Maine Senate Minority."

58. *Portland Press Herald*, May 3, 2020, "Republican Leaders Demand Removal of Mills' Emergency Powers"; News Center Maine, May 3, 2020, "Republican Leaders Ask for Legislative Session to End Maine Governor Janet Mills' Coronavirus Emergency Authority."

59. Maine Senate Republicans, May 2, 2020, "Letter from Legislative Republicans to the Presiding Officers."

60. *Portland Press Herald*, May 4, 2020, "Mills Rebuffs Republican Criticism Over Administration's Pandemic Response."

61. *Sun Journal*, November 5, 2021, Leader of Maine Senate Republicans Jeff Timberlake Seeks a Third Term in the State Senate"; *Maine Senate Republicans*, undated biography for Jeff Timberlake.

62. *Portland Press Herald*, May 4, 2020, "Mills Rebuffs Republican Criticism Over Administration's Pandemic Response."

63. *Portland Press Herald*, May 3, 2020, "Republican Leaders Demand Removal of Mills' Emergency Powers."

64. *Portland Press Herald*, April 16, 2020, "Mills Administration Held Secret Meetings on Pandemic with State Lawmakers."

65. *New York Times*, January 25, 2021, "Biden Is Vowing to Reopen Schools Quickly. It Won't Be Easy"; *Washington Post*, February 12, 2021, "CDC Offers Road Map for Safely Reopening Schools."

66. Maine Department of Health and Human Services, media release for February 16, 2021, "Maine Expands School-Based COVID-19 Testing to Support In-Person Learning."

67. *New York Times*, January 25, 2021, "Biden Is Vowing to Reopen Schools Quickly. It Won't Be Easy."

68. Associated Press, February 3, 2021, "San Francisco Sues its Own School District to Reopen Classes"; *New York Times*, February 10, 2021, "Rhode Island Kept Its Schools Open. This Is What Happened"; Associated Press, July 10, 2021, "'Tears, Politics and Money: School Boards Become Battle Zones."

69. Facebook account of the Maine Republican Party, February 24, 2021 (the day after the speech was broadcast).

70. Office of Governor Mills, January 8, 2021, Governor Mills budget letter to legislature.

71. News Center Maine, February 23, 2021, post-speech commentary by political analyst Ethan Strimling.

72. *Bangor Daily News*, February 14, 2021, "Who Is Lobbying Janet Mills for Early COVID-19 Vaccine Access."

73. Maine CDC vaccination briefing, February 26, 2021; *Portland Press Herald*, February 26, 2021, "Mainers 60 and Older Eligible for COVID-19 Vaccine Next Week as State Shifts to Age-Based Rollout."

74. Maine CDC vaccination briefing, February 26, 2021; *Bangor Daily News*, February 26, 2021, "Mainers 60 and Older Will Qualify for COVID-19 Vaccines in Switch to Age-Based System."

75. NBC News, February 27, 2021, "Some States Offering Covid Vaccines by Age. It's Simpler, but Is It Fair?"

76. Gallup COVID-19 probability-based web panel survey (February 14–21, 2021), results published March 11, 2021, "Amid Pandemic, 79% of K-12 Parents Support In-Person School."

77. Maine Department of Health and Human Services, Vaccination Consortia Proposal for February 21, 2021, "Maine Adopts Age-Based Approach to COVID-19 Eligibility," section on "Clinics for Age-Eligible School Teachers and Staff."

78. Office of Governor Mills, press release for February 26, 2021, "Maine Adopts Age-Based Approach to Expanding Vaccine Eligibility."

79. *Bangor Daily News*, February 11, 2021, "Maine Allowed Ski Patrol to Get Vaccinated, Then Janet Mills Reversed Course."

80. Twitter account of Janet Mills, post dated October 17, 2018.

81. CEI Capital Management, media release, April 13, 2021, "$1.49 Million Maine New Markets Capital Investment from CEI Capital Management Supports Rangeley Community in Reviving Saddleback Mountain Ski Resort, Creating Jobs and Expanding Economic Activity."

82. *Portland Press Herald*, April 4, 2021, "Skiers Rave About Upgrades, Atmosphere in Saddleback's First Year Back."

83. *The Irregular* (a weekly newspaper serving "the western mountains of Maine where the kids grow straight and tall and the women are all good looking"), March 3, 2021, "Governor Mills Visits Saddleback."

84. Facebook, personal account of Janet Mills, post dated March 4, 2021.

85. WMTW, June 5, 2018, Maine gubernatorial debate.

Chapter 11

1. Henry Wadsworth Longfellow, *Complete Poetical Works*, IV. *A Chronological List of Mr. Longfellow's Poems* (appendix) (1893); Henry Wadsworth Longfellow, *Ballads and Other Poems* (1841).

2. Maine Historical Society, "The Longfellow House & the Emergence of Portland"; Maine Historical Society, "The Life of Henry Wadsworth Longfellow"; The Poetry Foundation, "Henry Wadsworth Longfellow"; Maine Historical Society, "The Rainy Day."

3. Associated Press, March 2, 2021, "High Winds Leave Tens of Thousands Without Power"; News Center Maine, March 2, 2021, "Mainers Without Power Tuesday Due to High Winds"; News Center Maine, February 28, 2021, "Arctic Front Passes Monday, Bitter Cold for Tuesday."

4. Associated Press, March 2, 2021, "High Winds Leave Tens of Thousands Without Power"; News Center Maine, March 2, 2021, "Mainers Without Power Tuesday Due to High Winds"; News Center Maine, February 28, 2021, "Arctic Front Passes Monday, Bitter Cold for Tuesday."

5. Associated Press, March 2, 2021, "Biden Vows Enough Vaccine for All US Adults by End of May."

6. Associated Press, March 2, 2021, "Biden Vows Enough Vaccine for All US Adults by End of May."; Associated Press, February 27, 2021, "J&J's 1-Dose Shot Cleared, Giving US 3rd COVID-19 Vaccine."

7. Office of Governor Mills, March 5, 2021, "Maine Schedules COVID-19 Vaccine Clinics for Teachers and School Staff Age 60 and Older."

8. Associated Press, March 2, 2021, "Biden Vows Enough Vaccine for All US Adults by End of May."

9. Maine CDC briefing for March 2, 2021.

10. Maine CDC briefing for March 2, 2021.

11. Office of Governor Mills, media release for March 5, 2021, "Governor Mills Unveils Plan to Protect Public Health, Support Maine's Economy During Upcoming Tourism Season."

12. Associated Press, January 21, 2021, "Federal Court Upholds Maine's Out-of-State Quarantine Rule."

13. Facebook account of the Retail Association of Maine, post dated March 5, 2021.

14. Facebook account of Ashirah Knapp, post dated March 7, 2021.

15. US Centers for Disease Control, media release for March 8, 2021, "CDC Issues First Set of Guidelines on How Fully Vaccinated People Can Visit Safely with Others."

16. Associated Press, March 10, 2021, "Congress OKs $1.9T Virus Relief Bill in Win for Biden, Dems."

17. Associated Press, March 10, 2021, "What's Inside the $1.9T COVID-19 Bill Passed by Congress."

18. Maine Center for Economic Policy, April 2, 2021, "Transformative 'American Rescue Plan' Will Deliver $6 Billion to Maine's Economy"; *Bangor Daily News*, March 13, 2021, "A Guide to the $6B Coming to Maine in the Massive Stimulus Bill"; *Portland Press Herald*, March 9, 2021, "Maine Stands to Get Billions in Relief from Biden's American Rescue Plan."

19. Office of Senator Collins, media release for March 6, 2021, "Senator Collins Opposes Partisan $1.9 Trillion Spending Bill."

20. Office of Congressman Golden, media release for March 10, 2021, "Golden Statement on Vote Against Nearly $1.9 Trillion Legislative Package."

21. Office of Senator King, March 6, 2021, "King Votes to Deliver Desperately-Needed COVID Relief to the American People."

22. *Bangor Daily News*, March 10, 2021, "Democrats Vote Down GOP Bid to Strip Janet Mills of Pandemic Emergency Powers"; *Portland Press Herald*, March 12, 2021, "State Senate Rejects Bid to End State of Emergency."

23. Maine legislature, 130th session, HP 596, sponsored by Rep. Peter Lyford (R-Eddington), "Joint Resolution Terminating the State of Emergency Proclaimed by the Governor."

24. A review of the database of "States' COVID-19 Public Health Emergency Declarations and Mask Requirements" kept by the National Academy for State Health Policy showed that Michigan was the only state that did not have an emergency declaration in place as of March 2021; Associated Press, October 2, 2020, "Michigan Governor's Virus Powers Upended with Court Ruling."

25. All details related to the bill's vote in this paragraph were reported by *Bangor Daily News*, March 10, 2021, "Democrats Vote Down GOP Bid to Strip Janet Mills of Pandemic Emergency Powers."

26. National Conference of State Legislatures, "Oversight of Executive Powers: 2021 Bills and Resolutions."

27. Kaiser Family Foundation, *Kaiser Health News*, September 15, 2021, "Over Half of States Have Rolled Back Public Health Powers in Pandemic."

28. Associated Press, April 10, 2021, "Lawmakers Seek Long-Term Limit on Governors' Emergency Power"; Pew Charitable Trusts, *Stateline*, November 17, 2020, "GOP Lawsuits Restrain Governors' COVID-19 Actions"; *New York Times*, February 2, 2021, "State Lawmakers Defy Governors in a Covid-Era Battle for Power."

29. Pew Charitable Trusts, *Stateline*, January 22, 2021, "Lawmakers Move to Strip Governors' Emergency Powers"; Washington State Legislature, bill information for HB1020, "Concerning the emergency powers of the governor"; Washington State Legislature, bill information for HB1067, "Designating the Suciasaurus Rex as the Official Dinosaur of the State of Washington"; Washington Policy Center, January 26, 2021, "Emergency Powers Reform Takes Backseat to State Dinosaur."

30. Maine CDC briefing for March 11, 2021.

31. Associated Press, March 11, 2021, "AP-NORC Poll: 1 in 5 in US Lost Someone Close in Pandemic."

32. YouTube, official account of Governor Janet Mills, March 12, 2021, "Governor Mills Statement on One Year Anniversary of First COVID-19 Case in Maine."

33. White House website, biographies of First Families, Anna Eleanor Roosevelt.

34. White House website, briefing room, March 11, 2021, "Remarks by President Biden on the Anniversary of the COVID-19 Shutdown."

35. Office of Governor Mills, March 12, 2021, "Governor Mills Accelerates Maine's Vaccination Timeline to Make All Adults Eligible for COVID-19 Vaccine by May 1."

36. *New York Times*, "Coronavirus in the US: Latest Map and Case Count." Daily average case numbers on March 12, 2021, were 54,964; on January 12, 2021, they were 250,506.

37. White House website, fact sheet on the American Rescue Plan Child Tax Credit.

38. French & Webb shipyard website, video presentation on the USS *Sequoia* restoration.

39. White House Historical Association, May 21, 2015, "The Floating White House."

40. Sources for the "remarkable historic events" mentioned in this paragraph include Associated Press, August 12, 2022, "Former Presidential Yacht to Be Restored at Maine Shipyard"; *New York Times*, May 28, 1982, "The *Sequoia* Returns to Service in Style"; C-SPAN, October 19, 2010, "American Artifacts: Tour of the Presidential Yacht USS *Sequoia*"; *Daily Mail*, December 5, 2016, "The Sad Decline of the 'Floating White House'"; *Politico*, March 25, 2009, feature story on the anniversary of the day in 1933 when the USS *Sequoia* became the presidential yacht; National Museum of the US Navy, photography exhibit on the USS *Sequoia*; World Book Encyclopedia online, November 17, 2016, "*Sequoia*, the Presidential Yacht."

41. *Daily Mail*, December 5, 2016, "The Sad Decline of the 'Floating White House'"; French & Webb shipyard website, video presentation on the USS *Sequoia* restoration.

42. Belfast City Council, action minutes for March 16, 2021; Belfast City Council website, video recording of meeting on March 16, 2021.

43. Belfast City Council, action minutes for March 16, 2021; Belfast City Council website, video recording of meeting on March 16, 2021; *Bangor Daily News*, March 17, 2021, "Belfast Limits Megaphone Use After Complaints About Anti-Mask Protesters."

44. Office of Governor Mills, March 18, 2021, "Governor Mills Signs Bipartisan Supplemental Budget Supporting Maine Businesses & Workers into Law."

45. Associated Press, March 18, 2021, "Mills Signs Supplemental Budget; Extends Tax Filing Deadline."

46. Office of Governor Mills, March 18, 2021, "Governor Mills Signs Bipartisan Supplemental Budget Supporting Maine Businesses & Workers into Law."

47. *Bangor Daily News*, March 11, 2021, "Maine Legislature Inks Budget Deal as House GOP Softens Line on Business Tax Cuts."

48. Maine CDC briefing for March 2021.

49. White House, March 18, 2021, "Remarks by President Biden on the 100 Million Shot Goal."

50. Office of Governor Mills, March 19, 2021, "Governor Mills Announces Acceleration of Maine's COVID-19 Vaccination Timeline."

51. Office of Governor Mills, March 19, 2021, "Governor Mills Announces Acceleration of Maine's COVID-19 Vaccination Timeline"; National Public Radio, March 16, 2021, "What COVID-19 Vaccine Rollout Is Looking Like in Maine, Missouri and Pennsylvania"; *Fortune*, March 17, 2021, "28.5% of American Adults Have Gotten a COVID Vaccine: How Each US State Is Doing."

52. Associated Press, March 21, 2021, "A Rapid COVID-19 Vaccine Rollout Backfired in Some US States."

53. Associated Press, March 21, 2021, "A Rapid COVID-19 Vaccine Rollout Backfired in Some US States."

54. Associated Press, March 24, 2021, "Brighter Outlook for US as Vaccinations Rise and Deaths Fall."

55. Office of Governor Mills, March 19, 2021, "Governor Mills Announces
    Acceleration of Maine's COVID-19 Vaccination Timeline."
56. Maine CDC briefing for March 25, 2021; *New York Times*, "Coronavirus in the
    US: Latest Map and Case Count," readings for the US showed increases in the
    daily average every day from March 20 through April 14, 2021.
57. Facebook account of the Piscataquis Regional Organization for Action,
    February 26, 2021, "Goals Statement."
58. *Bangor Daily News*, February 15, 2021, "Maine County Commissioners Have
    'Huge Incentive' to Pass Extreme Resolutions."
59. *Bangor Daily News*, March 28, 2021, "In Piscataquis County, Commissioners'
    Anti-Mask Vote Has Created a Fraught Political Climate."
60. Associated Press, March 30, 2021, "Biden, CDC Director Warn of Virus Rebound
    If Nation Lets Up."
61. Maine CDC briefing for March 30, 2021.

Chapter 12

1. Maine Department of Inland Fisheries & Wildlife website, "Species Spotlight:
   Spring Peeper."
2. Maine Department of Inland Fisheries & Wildlife blog, post dated June 16, 2021,
   "Be Bear Wise."
3. Associated Press, March 22, 2021, "2 Hikers Who Died in Acadia National Park
   Are Identified."
4. Maine Department of Fisheries & Wildlife press release, April 4, 2021, "Maine
   Warden Service Rescues Stranded Family, Hypothermic Hiker in Two Separate
   Rescues."
5. Maine CDC briefing for April 1, 2021; Office of Governor Mills, April 1, 2021,
   "Governor Mills Announces All Maine Residents Age 16 and Older Are Eligible
   for a COVID-19 Vaccine Beginning Next Wednesday, April 7, 2021."
6. US Centers for Disease Control and Prevention, April 2, 2021, "Covid Data
   Tracker Weekly Review: The Race to Vaccinate."
7. US Centers for Disease Control and Prevention, April 2, 2021, "Covid Data
   Tracker Weekly Review: The Race to Vaccinate."
8. US Centers for Disease Control and Prevention, media release for April 2, 2021,
   "CDC Issues Updated Guidance on Travel for Fully Vaccinated People."
9. Maine CDC briefing for April 1, 2021, calculation based on 435,700 first doses
   given and 277,097 second doses among a population of 1.372 million.
10. M. G. Thompson, J. L. Burgess, A. L. Naleway, et al., *Morbidity and Mortality
    Weekly Report*, "Interim Estimates of Vaccine Effectiveness of BNT162b2 and
    mRNA-1273 COVID-19 Vaccines in Preventing SARS-CoV-2 Infection Among
    Health Care Personnel, First Responders, and Other Essential and Frontline
    Workers — Eight US Locations, December 2020–March 2021," US Centers for
    Disease Control and Prevention, April 2, 2021.
11. Office of Governor Mills, weekly radio address for April 2, 2021, "Governor
    Mills: Starting April 7th, All Maine Residents Age 16 and Older Will Be Eligible
    for a COVID-19 Vaccine."
12. Maine Republican Party website; Facebook account of the Maine Republican
    Party, post dated April 8, 2021.

13. WGME, April 20, 2021, "Maine GOP Takes Initial Step to Clear Path for Paul LePage Return Bid."

14. Facebook, personal account of Janet T. Mills, post dated April 5, 2021.

15. Facebook, personal account of Janet T. Mills, post dated April 5, 2021; Maine State Law and Legislative Reference Library, Legislative Record for the House of Representatives, 122nd Legislature, Vol. II First Special Session, June 15, 2005, H-1013.

16. Maine Public, February 5, 2021, "Janet Mills Says Plan Puts to Rest Three-Decade Mental Health Consent Decree"; National Public Radio, November 30, 2017, "How the Loss of US Psychiatric Hospitals Led to a Mental Health Crisis"; *The Atlantic*, May 25, 2021, "The Truth About Deinstitutionalization."

17. Office of Governor Mills, February 5, 2021, "Mills Administration Announces Landmark Agreement That Charts Path Toward Ending Three-Decades Long AMHI Consent Decree"; Associated Press, February 6, 2021, "Agreement Could End Court Oversight of Mental Health Service."

18. *Kennebec Journal / Portland Press Herald*, September 12, 2015, "Memorial to Deceased AMHI Patients to Be Dedicated Friday."

19. National Park Service, National Register Database; National Park Service, Digital Asset Management System, National Register of Historic Places Registration Form filed by the Maine Historic Preservation Commission, June 27, 2001.

20. Maine State Law and Legislative Reference Library, Augusta State Facilities Master Plan, August 2001, 1.9.

21. Office of Governor Mills, media release for April 6, 2021, "Mills Administration, FEMA Partner on Mobile Vaccination Unit to Provide COVID-19 Vaccines to Rural, Under-Served Communities Across Maine."

22. WGME, April 12, 2021, consultation of photos and footage from "Maine Deploys Its First Mobile Covid-19 Vaccine Unit."

23. DataCommons.org, profiles for the Maine localities of Biddeford and Madawaska.

24. US Centers for Disease Control, April 9, 2021, Covid Data Tracker Weekly Review, "Vigilance Matters When Viruses Vary."

25. Associated Press, March 29, 2021, "Jurors Shown Video at Ex-Officer's Trial in Floyd's Death."

26. National Public Radio, April 7, 2021, "Derek Chauvin Trial Breaks 'Blue Wall of Silence,' but Will It Transform Policing?"

27. Associated Press, April 13, 2021, "US Recommends 'Pause' for J&J Shots in Blow to Vaccine Drive."

28. Maine CDC briefing for April 15, 2021.

29. *New York Times*, "Coronavirus in the US: Latest Map and Case Count." Data for Maine showed a daily average of 454 cases on December 23, 2020, and 446 on April 15, 2021.

30. *Star Trek II: The Wrath of Khan*, Paramount Pictures (1982); *New York Times*, June 4, 1982, "New Star Trek Full of Gadgets and Fun."

31. Maine CDC, "Rural Health in Maine" (fact sheet).

32. Maine CDC, "Rural Health in Maine" (fact sheet).

33. Office of Governor Mills, February 23, 2021, "Governor Mills in Budget Address: Maine's Budget Focuses on Health Care, Education & Economy; Maintains Needed Stability."

34. State of Maine Broadband Action Plan, January 2020, 6.

35. *Bangor Daily News*, April 19, 2021, "Vaccine Hesitancy Remains Low in Maine," B1.

36. Office of Governor Mills, April 18, 2021, "Governor Mills Announces Half of Maine People 16 and Older Have Received at Least One Dose of COVID-19 Vaccine."

37. Office of Governor Mills, radio address for April 16, 2021, "Governor Mills: Stay Safe During This Spring Break."

38. Associated Press, April 9, 2021, "Unemployment Claims Rise in Maine Despite Growth in Hiring."

39. CSX media release for July 29, 2021, "Maine Governor Adds Name to Growing List of Supporters of the CSX/Pan Am Merger."

40. Facebook account of Ashirah Knapp, post dated April 20, 2021.

41. Maine CDC briefing for April 22, 2021.

42. US Centers for Disease Control & Prevention, April 23, 2021, "Covid Data Tracker Weekly Review: Have You Heard? We're at One-Third!"

43. *Portland Press Herald*, April 11, 2021, "Better Act Fast: Campground Reservations at Maine State Parks Are on a Record Pace."

44. Associated Press, April 26, 2021, "Help Wanted: In Pandemic, Worry About Finding Summer Workers."

45. NECN, April 16, 2021, "April Snow Is 'Extra Bonus' for Maine Ski Resorts"; SnoCountry, April 17, 2021, "Spring Nor'Easter Delivers Up to 20 Inches for New England Resorts."

46. Maine Emergency Management Agency, State of Maine Drought Task Force (DTF), April 22, 2021, Report on Current Hydrologic Conditions, Statement on DTF Preliminary Activation; *Piscataquis Observer*, April 22, 2021, "Maine Activates State Drought Task Force as Abnormally Dry Conditions Evident in 15 Counties."

47. Associated Press, April 23, 2021, "US to Resume J&J COVID Vaccinations Despite Rare Clot Risk."

48. Maine Department of Health & Human Services, media release for April 23, 2023, "Maine Resumes Use of Johnson & Johnson COVID-19 Vaccine."

49. *Bangor Daily News*, April 25, 2021, "Maine Sees Large Dip in COVID-19 Vaccinations Linked to 11-Day J&J Pause."

50. Maine CDC briefing for April 27, 2021; *New York Times*, "Coronavirus in the US: Latest Map and Case Count." Data for Maine showed that showed the daily average of new cases peaked at 470 on April 19, 2020, then declined daily through April 28, 2021.

51. *New York Times*, "Coronavirus in the US: Latest Map and Case Count," April 2021.

52. Office of Governor Mills, April 26, 2021, "Governor Mills, Lawmakers Unveil Bipartisan Legislation to Achieve Universal Availability of Affordable Broadband in Maine"; News Center Maine via YouTube, April 26, 2021, video of press conference, "Gov. Janet Mills Unveils Legislation to Achieve Universal Affordable Broadband in Maine."

53. Office of Governor Mills, April 27, 2021, "Maine Updates Public Health Guidance on Use of Face Coverings in Outdoor Public Settings."

54. *Bangor Daily News*, April 28, 2021, "Fishermen's Protest Previews Offshore Wind as Potent Political Issue for Janet Mills"; *Portland Press Herald*, April 28, 2021, "Mills Pushes for 10-Year Ban on Offshore Wind Development in State Waters."

55. Maine Public, April 28, 2021, "Hundreds of Lobstermen Gather in Augusta to Protest Wind Energy Projects."

56. Office of Governor Mills, April 28, 2021, "Mills Administration Introduces Bill to Prohibit Offshore Wind in Maine's Heavily Fished Waters for 10 Years."

57. Office of Governor Mills, April 28, 2021, S.P.512, An Act to Establish a Moratorium on Offshore Wind Power Projects in Maine's Territorial Waters.

58. Office of Governor Mills, April 28, 2021, S.P.512, An Act to Establish a Moratorium on Offshore Wind Power Projects in Maine's Territorial Waters.

59. *Bangor Daily News*, April 28, 2021, "Fishermen's Protest Previews Offshore Wind as Potent Political Issue for Janet Mills."

60. Office of Governor Mills, "Energy, Environment, and Climate Change" (summary).

61. Associated Press, March 29, 2022, "Fast-Warming Gulf of Maine Set New Record in 2021."

62. National Public Radio, September 19, 2021, "Maine's Next Generation of Lobstermen Brace for Unprecedented Change."

63. Office of Governor Mills, April 28, 2021, "Mills Administration Introduces Bill to Prohibit Offshore Wind in Maine's Heavily Fished Waters for 10 Years."

64. White House, April 29, 2021, "Remarks by President Biden in Address to a Joint Session of Congress"; Associated Press, April 27, 2021, "Cooling the Temperature: Biden Faces Fractious Congress."

65. Associated Press, April 27, 2021, "President Biden's First Address to Congress Is Invite-Only."

66. Associated Press, April 27, 2021, "President Biden's First Address to Congress Is Invite-Only."

67. White House, April 29, 2021, "Remarks by President Biden in Address to a Joint Session of Congress."

Chapter 13

1. Maine CDC briefing for April 27, 2020; Office of Governor Mills, media release for March 5, 2021, "Governor Mills Unveils Plan to Protect Public Health, Support Maine's Economy During Upcoming Tourism Season."

2. Maine CDC briefing for April 27, 2020; Office of Governor Mills, media release for March 5, 2021, "Governor Mills Unveils Plan to Protect Public Health, Support Maine's Economy During Upcoming Tourism Season"; Associated Press, April 30, 2020, "Number of Americans Fully Vaccinated Tops 100 Million."

3. Office of Governor Mills, media release for May 7, 2021, "Governor Mills Announces More than Half of Maine People 16 and Older Have Now Received Final Dose of a COVID-19 Vaccine."

4. *Bangor Daily News*, May 4, 2021, "Good Morning. Save Some Lives."

5. Maine CDC briefing for May 4, 2020; MaineHealth media release for May 6, 2021, "MaineHealth Shifts COVID-19 Vaccination Strategy, Placing Emphasis on Reaching Adolescents and Younger Adults"; Northern Light Health, media release for May 14, 2021, "Northern Light Walk-In Care in Waterville to Offer Walk-In COVID-19 Vaccinations"; Maine Public Radio, May 5, 2021, "Mercy Hospital Opening Walk-In COVID-19 Clinic in Portland."

6. *Portland Press Herald*, March 26, 2021, "Jails Struggle to Get Vaccines for People in Custody"; *Bangor Daily News*, May 6, 2021, "State Jails Make Uneven Progress on Vaccinating Their Inmates," A1.

7. *Bangor Daily News*, May 6, 2021, "State Jails Make Uneven Progress on Vaccinating Their Inmates," A1.

8. *Guardian*, February 9, 2021, "'A Death Sentence': US Prisons Could Receive Covid Vaccines Last Despite Being Hotspots"; R. Strodel, L. Dayton, H. Garrison-Desany, G. Eber, C. Beyrer, J. Arscott, L. Rubenstein, and C. Sufrin, "COVID-19 vaccine prioritization of incarcerated people relative to other vulnerable groups: An analysis of state plans," published June 15, 2021, National Institutes of Health, National Library of Medicine.

9. Associated Press, May 5, 2021, "Maine's Tourism Industry Took a 27% Hit Last Summer"; *New York Times*, May 2021, "Coronavirus in the US: Latest Map and Case Count."

10. Maine CDC briefing for May 4, 2020.

11. Office of Governor Mills, media release for May 4, 2021, "Governor Mills Unveils Transformative Plan to Spur Economic Recovery & Achieve Long-Term Economic Growth"; Office of Governor Mills, radio address for May 7, 2021, "Governor Mills: We Are Entering a New Era."

12. Office of Governor Mills, April 27, 2021, "Revenue Forecasting Committee Projects State Revenues to Exceed Pre-Pandemic Levels."

13. Office of Governor Mills, media release for May 11, 2021, "During Discussion with President Biden, Governor Mills Announces 'Your Shot to Get Outdoors' Public-Private Initiative to Encourage COVID-19 Vaccinations"; White House, May 11, 2021, "President Biden Meets Virtually with a Bipartisan Group of Governors."

14. White House, May 11, 2021, "Remarks by President Biden at a Virtual Meeting with a Bipartisan Group of Governors."

15. Twitter account of New Jersey governor Phil Murphy, post dated May 3, 2021.

16. Office of Maryland Governor Larry Hogan, media release for May 3, 2021, "Governor Hogan Announces Financial Incentive Program for State Employees to Encourage COVID-19 Vaccinations."

17. *New York Times*, May 3, 2021, "Beer? Money? States and Cities Offer Incentives to Get Vaccinated."

18. Office of Governor Mills, media release for May 10, 2021, "Governor Mills Nominates Justice Valerie Stanfill as Chief Justice of Maine Supreme Judicial Court."

19. Mills administration press conference, May 13, 2021; Office of Governor Mills, media release for March 13, 2021, "Governor Mills Updates Moving Maine Forward Plan, Lifts Restrictions."

20. Associated Press, May 14, 2021, "Fully Vaccinated Can Drop the Masks, Skip Social Distancing."

21. Office of Governor Mills, May 14, 2021, "Maine to Adopt US CDC's New COVID-19 Guidance."

22. *New York Times*, March 16, 2020, "Trump to Governors on Ventilators: 'Try Getting It Yourselves.'"

23. Facebook account of Governor Paul LePage, post dated May 14, 2021.

24. *Bangor Daily News*, May 15, 2021, "Maine's Private Sector Won't Drop Mask Requirements All at Once."
25. Facebook account of the Retail Association of Maine, post dated May 18, 2021.
26. *Portland Press Herald*, May 13, 2021, "Summer Concerts Planned, Sea Dogs Increase Capacity as State Drops Distance Requirement."
27. State of Vermont, Office of Governor Phil Scott, media release for May 14, 2021, "Governor Phil Scott Lifts Mask Mandate for Vaccinated Individuals, Accelerates Vermont Forward Plan"; Associated Press, May 29, 2021, "Massachusetts Lifts Mask Rule; Maine Reports 108 New Cases"; State of New Hampshire, Office of Governor Chris Sununu, media release for April 15, 2021, "Governor Chris Sununu Announces Statewide Mask Mandate to Expire."
28. Facebook, personal account of Janet Mills, post dated May 15, 2021.
29. Office of Governor Mills, radio address for May 20, 2021, "Governor Mills: Our Farming Industry Is at the Heart of Not Only My History — It's at the Heart of Our State."
30. Office of Governor Mills, media release for May 10, 2021, "Mills Administration Statement on FDA's Authorization of Pfizer's COVID-19 Vaccine for 12- to 15-Year-Olds."
31. *Portland Press Herald*, May 16, 2021, "Even When the Vaccine Travels to Them, Many Mainers Won't Take It."
32. *Bangor Daily News*, May 25, 2021, "Masks Come Off in Maine After 'a Long Fifteen Months'"; *Portland Press Herald*, May 24, 2021, "Businesses Celebrate Unmasking, but Some Customers Hesitate."
33. *Bangor Daily News*, May 24, 2021, "Maine Is the 1st New England State to Give More than Half of Its Population a Final COVID-19 Vaccine Dose."
34. US Centers for Disease Control and Prevention, COVID Data Tracker Weekly Review for May 28, 2021, and September 30, 2022.
35. Maine CDC, figures as reported by *Bangor Daily News* on May 24, 2021, and September 29, 2021.
36. Office of Governor Mills, June 24, 2022, "Governor Mills on Supreme Court Decision."
37. Office of Governor Mills, July 5, 2022, "Governor Mills Signs Executive Order to Safeguard Reproductive Health Care, Protect Maine Health Care Providers and Patients in Wake of Supreme Court Decision Overturning *Roe v. Wade*."
38. Office of Governor Mills, July 1, 2022, "Governor Mills, Treasurer Beck Announce Moody's and S&P Affirm Maine's Strong Credit Rating."
39. P. Kerpen, S. Moore, and C. Mulligan, "A Final Report Card on the States' Response to COVID-19," National Bureau of Economic Research, April 2022.
40. University of Chicago, media release for September 6, 2018, "Casey Mulligan Named Chief Economist for the Council of Economic Advisers"; American Commitment website, "About," names Phil Kerpen as the organization's leader.
41. National Bureau of Economic Research website, "About the NBER"; P. Kerpen, S. Moore, and C. Mulligan, "A Final Report Card on the States' Response to COVID-19," National Bureau of Economic Research, April 2022.
42. Pew Charitable Trusts, *Stateline*, June 16, 2022, "Hawaii and Maine Have Scored Highest on Health Care During Pandemic"; Commonwealth Fund, 2022 Scorecard on State Health System Performance: Appendices, 8.

43. Associated Press, October 6, 2022, "LePage: Gov. Mills 'Very Fortunate' That COVID Came to Maine."

44. Associated Press, November 3, 2022, "Mills, LePage Debate for a Final Time in Race for Governor."

45. *Portland Press Herald*, October 13, 2022, "Our View: LePage's Repeated Use of 'Crack Pipe' Irresponsible at Best"; News Center Maine, September 28, 2022, "LePage Accuses Mills, Harm Reduction Strategies for Maine's Opioid Epidemic."

46. Maine Public Radio, October 25, 2022, "Behind in the Polls, LePage Ratchets Up Attacks on Mills During Second TV Debate"; Office of Governor Mills, "Amid High Costs, $850 Relief Checks Are Being Sent to an Estimated 858,000 Maine People" (relief checks fact page).

47. Emerson College Polling, September 23, 2022, "Maine Poll: Mills Leads LePage by 12."

48. Pan Atlantic Research, October 2022, "59th Omnibus Poll: The Benchmark of Maine Public Opinion," 18.

49. Maine Secretary of State, November 8, 2022, general election results.

50. CBS 13 news via YouTube, November 8, 2022, "Former Governor LePage Frustrated After Losing Election."

51. Twitter account of Governor Paul LePage, post dated November 9, 2022.

Dear Governor Mills,

Governor

We are homesteading family in the f
area who business that teac
resilienc writi
express when who they're being is n
Our bu kick-in-the-metaphorical-butt
for as afraid of doing it because th
draini duality. So my own question th
to be able to decide which i
I think part of it is groun
like carrying wood, growing
just needs to happen when av
any of that, then there
liness and bound

EAST MAINE 04
08 JUL 2020 PM 1

Governor Mills
210 State St.
Augusta, ME
04333